SOUP OF THE DAY

KATE McMILLAN

PHOTOGRAPHY BY ERIN KUNKEL

weldonowen

CONTENTS

A SOUP FOR EVERY DAY

Consider the myriad collection of fresh ingredients that combine in a single bowl of soup and recognize the subtle star of seasonal cooking. Soups and stews offer the ultimate canvas for blending the best of each month's choice ingredients with the traditions, techniques, and cultural trends that influence their creation. Considered by many to be the ultimate comfort food, they are welcome additions to the dining table throughout the months, marking seasons and occasions with flavorful flair.

This updated collection of sumptuous recipes will encourage you to make soups on any day of the year. Using what's fresh as your guide, draw on seasonal ingredients—asparagus and peas in spring; corn, peppers, and tomatoes in summer; cruciferous vegetables and hearty greens during the fall; and root vegetables in winter—to inspire your creations.

Versatile, flexible, and easy to stretch, soups are a smart way to cook. Some are perfect for casual weeknight meals, while others offer an elegant way to begin a dinner party. Soups are easy to dress up by adding texture, flavor, or a festive touch with simple garnishes—a topping of crisp garlic croutons; a swirl of pesto, olive oil, or crème fraîche; or a sprinkle of chopped fresh herbs. You can also personalize them to your own taste by swapping in alternative ingredients or changing the texture by puréeing them or leaving them chunky. Many soups can be made ahead and reheated just before serving, while others can be prepared in large batches and frozen for quick meal options on busy nights. You'll learn these approaches and many more on the pages that follow.

The recipes in this new compilation of seasonal soups and stews, 365 in all, are organized by calendar month and are designed to stimulate ideas for cooking any day of the year. You can use the calendar pages in the front of each chapter as a road map for your soup-making adventures, or feel free to meander through the recipes at your leisure, knowing that there will always be a dish to inspire you, no matter what the season. There are also dozens of full-color photographs to guide and entice you along the way.

The delicious recipes, colorful photographs, and daily culinary wisdom inside these pages are sure to satisfy a yearning for soup, no matter what the day brings.

During the cold and dark start of the year, warming soups provide nourishment and comfort—and fill the house with delicious scents. Savory broths and spicy stews are the backdrop for January's sturdy vegetables, including cabbage, broccoli, and cauliflower, which are ideal partners for beans, sausage, and noodles of all types. Fresh herbs, aromatic spices, and winter citrus offer hits of bright flavor to seafood and vegetarian dishes.

january

1

*This vegetarian
version of the
popular tortilla
soup (see page 191
for a meat version)
comes together
quickly and hits
all the high notes.
You can trade out
the cool-weather
pumpkin used here
for fresh corn in
the summer and for
mushrooms in the
spring. Serve with
cheese quesadillas
and with a salad of
sliced oranges and
sweet onions dressed
with a toasted cumin
vinaigrette.*

PUMPKIN TORTILLA SOUP

serves 4–6

3 corn tortillas

3 Tbsp canola or vegetable oil

Salt and freshly ground pepper

½ white onion, chopped

2 cloves garlic, chopped

1 small jalapeño chile, seeded, deribbed,
and chopped

2 tsp ground cumin

½ tsp dried Mexican oregano

1 can (14½ oz/455 g) fire-roasted diced
tomatoes with juices

1 can (15 oz/470 g) black beans, drained

3 cups (24 fl oz/750 ml) vegetable
or chicken broth

3 cups (20 oz/625 g) cubed peeled pumpkin
(1-inch/2.5-cm cubes)

1 avocado, pitted, peeled, and cubed

½ cup (2 oz/60 g) shredded
Monterey jack cheese, optional

3 green onions, white and tender
green parts, chopped

2 radishes, stemmed, halved,
and thinly sliced

Preheat the oven to 450°F (230°C). Stack
the tortillas and cut them in half, then
into ½-inch (12-mm) strips. In a bowl, toss
together the tortilla strips and 1 Tbsp of the
oil. Place in a single layer on a baking sheet
and season generously with salt. Bake until
golden brown and crispy, about 5 minutes.
Set aside.

In a large, heavy pot, warm the remaining
2 Tbsp oil over medium-high heat. Add the
white onion and cook, stirring occasionally,
until soft, about 6 minutes. Add the garlic
and jalapeño and cook, stirring occasionally,
until soft, about 2 minutes. Stir in the cumin
and oregano, and season with salt and
pepper. Cook, stirring, to toast the spices,
about 1 minute. Add the tomatoes with their
juices, the beans, and broth and bring to
a boil. Add the pumpkin, reduce the heat
to low, and simmer until the pumpkin is
fork-tender, 15–18 minutes. Season with salt
and pepper.

Serve, topped with the tortilla strips,
avocado, cheese (if using), green onions,
and radishes.

2

*Traditional French
onion soup relies
on rich beef broth
for its deep, full
flavor. You can find
high-quality broth
at meat markets or
specialty-food stores.*

FRENCH ONION SOUP

serves 6

3 Tbsp unsalted butter

1 Tbsp canola oil

2½ lb (1.25 kg) yellow onions, thinly sliced

Pinch of sugar

Salt and freshly ground pepper

2 cups (16 fl oz/500 ml) dry white wine

8 cups (64 fl oz/2 l) beef broth

1 bay leaf

6 thick slices country-style bread

3 cups (12 oz/375 g) shredded
Comté or Gruyère cheese

In a large, heavy pot, melt the butter with the
oil over medium-low heat. Add the onions
and sugar, and season with salt and pepper.
Cover and cook, stirring occasionally, until
the onions are meltingly soft, golden, and
lightly caramelized, 25–30 minutes.

Add the wine, raise the heat to high, and
cook until the liquid is reduced by about
half, 8–10 minutes. Add the broth and bay
leaf, reduce the heat to medium-low, and
simmer, uncovered, until the soup is dark
and fully flavored, about 45 minutes. If the
liquid is evaporating too quickly and the
soup tastes too strong, add a little water,
then cover the pot and continue cooking.

Preheat the oven to 400°F (200°C). Arrange
the bread slices on a baking sheet and toast,
turning once, until golden, 3–5 minutes
per side. Set the toasts aside.

Remove and discard the bay leaf. Ladle the
soup into ovenproof bowls arranged on the
baking sheet. Place a piece of toast on top of
the soup in each bowl and sprinkle with the
cheese. Bake until the cheese is melted and
the toasts are lightly browned around the
edges, about 15 minutes. Serve.

3

Make this creamy, snowy white soup on a cold winter weeknight, when time is short and a hot supper in a bowl sounds good to everyone at the table. Serve as is or garnish with a scattering of crumbled crisply fried bacon, and accompany with a tossed green salad and crusty bread.

CHEDDAR-CAULIFLOWER SOUP

serves 6–8

2 Tbsp olive oil

1 yellow onion, diced

1 head cauliflower (about 2½ lb/1.25 kg), trimmed and cut into florets

5 cups (40 fl oz/1.25 l) chicken broth

2 cups (16 fl oz/500 ml) heavy cream

Salt and freshly ground pepper

½ lb (250 g) white Cheddar cheese, shredded

Toasted country-style bread for serving

In a large, heavy pot, warm the oil over medium-high heat. Add the onion and cook, stirring occasionally, until tender, 5–7 minutes. Add the cauliflower and cook, stirring occasionally, until light golden brown, about 5 minutes. Add the broth, cream, 2 tsp salt, and pepper to taste, and bring to a boil. Reduce the heat to low and simmer until the cauliflower is fork-tender, about 10 minutes. Let cool slightly.

Working in batches, purée the soup in a food processor or blender. Return to the pot, add the cheese, and stir until melted and well combined with the soup. Taste and adjust the seasoning. Serve with toasted bread.

4

Butcher shops or the butcher's counter at most grocery stores carry ham hocks, or better yet, you can use the ham bone left over from your holiday ham. Look for soppressata, a cured Italian salami full of flavor and spice, at a delicatessen that stocks good-quality cured meats. If you cannot find it, prosciutto can be substituted. Use caution when seasoning with salt, as both the ham hock and the soppressata are naturally a bit salty.

HAM HOCK & POTATO CHOWDER WITH CRISPY SOPPRESSATA

serves 4–6

5 thin slices soppressata

1 Tbsp olive oil

2 Tbsp unsalted butter

½ yellow onion, chopped

2 celery ribs, chopped

Salt and freshly ground pepper

½ lb (250 g) small Yukon Gold potatoes, cut into ¼-inch (6-mm) pieces

1 smoked ham hock (about 1½ lb/750 g), cut in half by the butcher, meat removed from the bone and reserved

4 cups (32 fl oz/1 l) chicken broth

1 cup (6 oz/185 g) frozen corn kernels, thawed

1 cup (8 fl oz/250 ml) half-and-half

In a large, heavy nonstick pot, fry the soppressata over medium-high heat, flipping a few times, until crispy, about 7 minutes total. Transfer to a plate. When cool enough to handle, tear into bite-sized pieces.

In the same pot (do not clean it), melt the butter with the oil over medium-high heat. Add the onion and celery, season with salt and pepper, and cook, stirring occasionally, until soft, about 6 minutes. Add the potatoes, ham meat pieces, ham bones, and broth and bring to a boil. Reduce the heat to low and simmer until the potatoes are fork-tender, about 15 minutes. Remove and discard the ham bones.

Stir in the corn and half-and-half, raise the heat to medium, and simmer until the soup thickens, about 3 minutes. Season with salt and pepper. Serve, topped with the soppressata.

5

POSOLE

serves 12

1 lb (500 g) dried posole or
2 lb (1 kg) presoaked dried posole

3 Tbsp olive oil

2 yellow onions, finely chopped

8 cloves garlic, finely chopped

1 Tbsp dried Mexican or regular oregano

1 tsp red pepper flakes

5 cups (40 fl oz/1.25 l) chicken broth

½–1 lb (250–500 g) boneless pork shoulder, trimmed and cut into ½-inch (12-mm) cubes

Salt and freshly ground pepper

Posole is a special comfort food of the Southwest. You can easily use canned hominy, but the authentic dried corn, soaked and simmered with a few simple seasonings, is far tastier. Look for dried posole in a well-stocked grocery or Hispanic market.

If using dried posole, in a large bowl, combine the posole with water to cover and let stand overnight, stirring occasionally. Drain and set aside.

In a large, heavy pot, warm the oil over medium heat. Add the onions, garlic, oregano, and pepper flakes. Cover and cook, stirring occasionally, until the onions and garlic are almost tender, about 10 minutes. Add 8 cups (64 fl oz/2 l) water, the broth, and the posole and bring to a simmer.

Meanwhile, place a large frying pan over medium-low heat. Scatter the pork in the pan and sauté until it has lost its pink color and has released a generous amount of liquid, about 10 minutes. Raise the heat to medium-high and cook, stirring, until the liquid evaporates and the meat is well browned, 10–12 minutes. Transfer the meat to the pot with the posole. Add 2 cups (16 fl oz/500 ml) of the posole cooking liquid to the frying pan off the heat and stir to scrape up any browned bits on the pan bottom. Return the liquid to the pot.

Bring to a simmer, cover partially, and cook, stirring occasionally, for 1 hour. Add 2 tsp salt and 1 tsp pepper and continue to simmer, partially covered, stirring occasionally, until the meat is tender and most of the posole kernels have burst, 1–1½ hours longer, adding more water as necessary to keep the consistency soupy. Season with salt and pepper and serve.

6

VEGETARIAN CHILI

serves 6–8

2 cups (14 oz/440 g) dried pinto beans, picked over and rinsed

3 Tbsp canola oil

2 yellow onions, finely chopped

5 cloves garlic, minced

1 Tbsp plus 1 tsp dried oregano

1 Tbsp plus 1 tsp ground cumin

1 tsp ground coriander

1 Tbsp paprika

¼ tsp cayenne pepper

¼ cup (1 oz/30 g) chili powder

1 can (15 oz/470 g) diced tomatoes

1 canned chipotle chile in adobo, minced

5 cups (40 fl oz/1.25 l) vegetable broth

1 Tbsp balsamic vinegar

3 Tbsp finely chopped cilantro

Salt

In some parts, traditional chili may require beef, but more liberal interpretations call for just beans and vegetables, for a lean but filling dinner-in-a-bowl. Cumin, cayenne, chipotle, and cilantro pack a nice Latin kick in this version.

Place the dried beans in a bowl with cold water to cover and soak for at least 4 hours or up to overnight. Drain and set aside.

In a large, heavy pot, warm the oil over medium heat. Add the onions and garlic and sauté until softened, about 7 minutes. Add the oregano, cumin, coriander, paprika, cayenne, and chili powder and stir to combine. Cook, stirring, for about 3 minutes.

Add the tomatoes, chipotle, broth, and beans and bring to a boil. Reduce the heat to low and cook, partially covered, until the beans are tender yet firm, 1–1½ hours. If the chili seems too thick, add a little water.

Add the vinegar and cook for 1 minute. Stir in the chopped cilantro and season with salt, then serve.

7

AVGOLEMONO

serves 4

6 cups (48 fl oz/1.5 l) chicken broth

½ cup (3½ oz/105 g) long-grain white rice

4 egg yolks, lightly beaten

¼ cup (2 fl oz/60 ml) fresh lemon juice

1 tsp finely chopped lemon zest

Salt and ground white pepper

2 Tbsp finely chopped flat-leaf parsley

This rich, lemony chicken-and-rice soup is a signature dish of Greece. To help prevent the eggs from curdling, they must be tempered by whisking a small amount of hot liquid into the yolks to heat them slightly before adding them to the hot mixture.

In a large, heavy pot, bring the broth to a boil over medium-high heat. Add the rice and cook, uncovered, until tender, about 15 minutes.

In a bowl, whisk together the egg yolks, lemon juice, and lemon zest. Whisking constantly, slowly pour 1 cup (8 fl oz/250 ml) of the hot broth into the egg mixture. Reduce the heat under the broth to medium-low and slowly stir the egg mixture into the pot. Cook, stirring, until the soup is slightly thickened, 3–4 minutes. Do not let it boil.

Season with salt and pepper and serve, garnished with the parsley.

8

POTATO & BROCCOLI SOUP WITH BLUE CHEESE

serves 4

3 Tbsp unsalted butter

½ cup (2½ oz/75 g) chopped shallots

1 lb (500 g) Yukon Gold potatoes, cubed

1½ lb (750 g) broccoli, tough stems peeled, florets and stems coarsely chopped

Salt and freshly ground pepper

3 Tbsp all-purpose flour

4 cups (32 fl oz/1 l) chicken broth

¼ lb (125 g) blue cheese, crumbled

Broccoli is often combined with potatoes to make a thick, flavorful soup, and cheese, especially Cheddar, is a favorite addition. Using blue cheese instead of Cheddar shifts the flavor slightly toward the tangy side but keeps the creamy texture. This is a good soup for serving with crackers, including breaking a few into the pot to make it even richer.

In a large, heavy pot, melt the butter over medium-high heat. When it foams, add the shallots and cook, stirring occasionally, until limp, about 1 minute. Stir in the potatoes and broccoli. Sprinkle with ½ tsp salt, ¼ tsp pepper, and the flour and stir until the flour is incorporated, about 1 minute. Add about ½ cup (4 fl oz/125 ml) of the broth, stirring to make a paste, then gradually add the remaining broth and bring to a boil. Reduce the heat to medium-low and simmer until the potatoes and broccoli stems are fork-tender, about 15 minutes. Let cool slightly.

Working in batches, purée the soup in a food processor or blender. Return the soup to the pot, place over medium-high heat, and bring to a simmer. Sprinkle in half of the cheese and stir until it melts, about 1 minute. Serve with the remaining cheese on the side.

9

This traditional Russian beet soup, ideally a vibrant ruby red, is a heart-warming favorite of the winter months—espeically when made heartier with shredded beef and a rich broth.

BEEF BORSCHT

serves 4

3 beets (about 1½ lb/750 g)

2 Tbsp canola oil

1 leek, white and pale green parts, sliced

1 parsnip, peeled and chopped

1 large carrot, peeled and chopped

1 celery rib, chopped

2 cloves garlic, minced

6 cups (48 fl oz/1.5 l) beef broth

2 cups (12 oz/375 g) shredded cooked beef

⅛ tsp ground allspice

Salt and freshly ground pepper

2 cups (4 oz/125 g) chopped green cabbage

1 cup (6 oz/185 g) canned diced tomatoes

2 Yukon gold potatoes, peeled, each cut lengthwise into 4 wedges

2 Tbsp red wine vinegar, plus more as needed

½ cup (4 oz/125 g) sour cream

1 Tbsp small dill sprigs

Preheat the oven to 350°F (180°C). Wrap each beet in foil and roast until tender when pierced with a knife, about 1 hour. Let cool, still wrapped, for 15 minutes. Using a paring knife, peel and discard the skins. Shred the beets into a bowl. Set aside.

In a large, heavy pot, warm the oil over medium-low heat. Add the leek, parsnip, carrot, celery, and garlic and cook, stirring often, until tender, about 10 minutes. Add the broth, beef, allspice, 2 tsp salt, and ¼ tsp pepper. Bring to a boil, reduce the heat to low, cover, and cook until the vegetables are tender, 25–30 minutes. Stir in the beets, cabbage, and tomatoes. Raise the heat to medium-low and cook, uncovered, until the cabbage is tender, about 10 minutes.

Meanwhile, put the potatoes in a saucepan and add water to cover and ½ tsp salt. Cover and bring to a boil. Reduce the heat to medium-low and simmer until the potatoes are tender, 15 minutes. Drain and keep warm.

Reduce the heat under the soup to low and stir in the 2 Tbsp vinegar. If the soup tastes a little dull, add a bit more vinegar, salt, or pepper. Divide the potato wedges among bowls and ladle soup over them. Garnish with the sour cream and dill, then serve.

10

Instead of pasta, try adding ¼ cup (2 oz/60 g) rice to the soup 15 minutes before it is done. Or try small pastas, like orzo, stelline, or ditalini. A squeeze of lemon brightens the chicken flavor.

CLASSIC CHICKEN NOODLE SOUP

serves 4

1 Tbsp canola oil

2 celery ribs, finely chopped

1 leek, white part only, halved and thinly sliced

1 carrot, peeled and finely chopped

5 cups (40 fl oz/1.25 l) chicken broth

1 bay leaf

¼ tsp dried thyme

2 cups (12 oz/375 g) cooked shredded chicken

½ lb (250 g) dried egg noodles

Salt and freshly ground pepper

¼ cup (⅓ oz/10 g) minced flat-leaf parsley

In a large saucepan, warm the oil over medium heat. When it is hot, add the celery, leek, and carrot and sauté until softened, about 5 minutes. Add the broth, bay leaf, thyme, and shredded chicken. Bring to a boil over medium-high heat. Add the noodles, stir well, and cook just until the noodles are tender, about 10 minutes.

Remove and discard the bay leaf from the soup. Season to taste with salt and pepper and serve, garnished with the parsley.

11

Fresh dates, with their thin skins and intense sweetness, are occasionally mistaken for a dried fruit. They're not— these characteristics merely come from growing in the desert. Here they add a depth of flavor to the stew and marry well with the pungent spices.

MOROCCAN LAMB STEW

serves 6

4 Tbsp (2 fl oz/60 ml) olive oil

2 yellow onions, finely chopped

3 carrots, peeled and chopped

½ cup (2½ oz/75 g) all-purpose flour

Salt and freshly ground pepper

3 lb (1.5 kg) cubed lamb for stewing

3 cloves garlic, minced

1 tsp ground cumin

¼ tsp saffron threads

1 Tbsp peeled and minced fresh ginger

2½ cups (20 fl oz/625 ml) beef broth

1 cup (8 oz/250 g) canned crushed tomatoes

1 cup (6 oz/185 g) chopped pitted dates

Grated zest and juice of 1 orange

2 Tbsp finely chopped flat-leaf parsley

Preheat the oven to 350°F (180°C). In a large, heavy pot, warm 1 Tbsp of the oil over medium heat. Add the onions and sauté until softened, about 7 minutes. Add the carrots and sauté until slightly softened, about 3 minutes. Transfer to a bowl.

In a resealable plastic bag, combine the flour, ½ tsp salt, and ½ tsp pepper. Add the lamb, seal the bag, and shake to coat. Add the remaining 3 Tbsp oil to the pot and warm over medium-high heat. Working in batches, remove the lamb from the bag, shaking off excess flour, and add to the pot in a single layer. Brown on all sides, 4–5 minutes per batch. Transfer to a bowl.

Return the onion mixture and browned lamb to the pot. Add the garlic, cumin, saffron, and ginger and stir to coat the meat and vegetables. Add the broth and bring to a boil, stirring to scrape up any browned bits on the bottom of the pot. Add the tomatoes, dates, and orange zest and juice and bring to a boil over high heat. Cover and bake until the meat is tender, 1½–2 hours.

Season with salt and pepper and serve, garnished with parsley.

12

Portuguese linguiça or chorizo is often the choice for soups with greens and beans, but using low-fat turkey kielbasa imparts the same smoky, spicy flavor.

KALE & WHITE BEAN SOUP

serves 4

1 bunch kale (about ¾ lb/375 g)

1 Yukon Gold potato (about ½ lb/250 g)

2 oz (60 g) pork or turkey kielbasa sausage

2 tsp olive oil

1 large yellow onion, chopped

4 cloves garlic, chopped

⅛ tsp red pepper flakes

Salt and freshly ground pepper

1 can (15 oz/470 g) white beans, drained

Remove the tough stems from the kale and cut the leaves crosswise into strips ½ inch (12 mm) wide. You will have about 5 cups (10 oz/315 g). Cut the potato into 1-inch (2.5-cm) pieces. Slice the kielbasa. Set aside.

In a large, heavy pot, warm the oil over medium-high heat. Add the onion and garlic and sauté until translucent, about 5 minutes. Stir in the kale, potato, kielbasa, and red pepper flakes. Season generously with salt. Pour in 8 cups (64 fl oz/2 l) water. Bring to a boil, reduce the heat to medium-low, and simmer, uncovered, until the kale is almost tender, about 20 minutes.

Add the beans and cook until heated through, about 5 minutes. Season with salt and pepper and serve.

13

In the winter when tomatoes are not in season, canned tomatoes are the best choice for adding to soups. San Marzano tomatoes, a plum variety from Italy, are widely acknowledged as the gold standard of canned tomatoes.

CREAM OF TOMATO SOUP

serves 4–6

¼ cup (2 oz/60 g) unsalted butter

1 celery rib with leaves, finely chopped

½ cup (2½ oz/75 g) chopped shallots

1 clove garlic, minced

⅓ cup (2 oz/60 g) all-purpose flour

1 can (28 oz/875 g) diced tomatoes

2 cups (16 fl oz/500 ml) chicken broth

2 cups (16 fl oz/500 ml) half-and-half

1 tsp chopped marjoram or oregano, plus sprigs for garnish

Salt and freshly ground pepper

In a large, heavy pot, melt the butter over medium heat. Add the celery and cook, stirring occasionally, until it begins to soften, about 2 minutes. Add the shallots and garlic and cook, stirring often, until the shallots soften, about 2 minutes.

Sprinkle the flour over the vegetables and stir well. Stir in the tomatoes with their juices, the broth, the half-and-half, and the chopped marjoram and stir well. Bring to a boil over high heat, stirring often. Reduce the heat to medium-low and simmer, uncovered, until the soup is slightly thickened, about 30 minutes.

Season with salt and pepper and serve, garnished with the herb sprigs.

14

The are many stories about the origins of this San Francisco specialty. Most locals believe it is related to the Italian cacciucco, a fish stew of Livorno, and to the fish stews of the Friuli region, which are made with red wine. Serve with grilled coarse country bread rubbed with garlic.

CIOPPINO

serves 6

½ cup (4 fl oz/125 ml) olive oil

3 large yellow onions, chopped

5 celery ribs, chopped

6 cloves garlic, minced

2 small bay leaves

2 thyme sprigs

2 tsp ground fennel seeds

1–2 tsp red pepper flakes

5 cups (40 fl oz/1.25 l) fish broth

3 cups (18 fl oz/560 ml) canned diced tomatoes

1½ cups (12 fl oz/375 ml) dry red wine

½ cup (4 fl oz/125 ml) thick tomato purée

Salt and freshly ground pepper

18 clams, scrubbed

1 crab or lobster, cooked, cracked, and cut into 2–3-inch (5–7.5-cm) pieces

18 shrimp, peeled and deveined

18 sea scallops, tough muscles removed

18 mussels, scrubbed and debearded

¼ cup (⅓ oz/10 g) chopped flat-leaf parsley

In a large, heavy pot, warm the oil over medium heat. Add the onions and sauté until translucent, about 7 minutes. Add the celery, garlic, bay leaves, thyme, fennel seeds, and red pepper flakes and sauté until the celery is soft, about 5 minutes. Add the broth, tomatoes, wine, and tomato purée and simmer for about 10 minutes to blend the flavors. Season with salt and pepper.

Add the clams, discarding any that do not close to the touch. Add the crab, cover, and simmer briskly until the clams start to open, about 5 minutes. Add the shrimp, scallops, and mussels, discarding any mussels that do not close to the touch, and continue to cook until the shrimp turn pink, the scallops are opaque throughout, and the mussels open, 3–5 minutes. Discard any unopened clams or mussels.

Season with salt and pepper and serve, sprinkled with the parsley.

BARLEY-LEEK SOUP WITH MINI CHICKEN MEATBALLS

serves 8–10

1 Tbsp unsalted butter

2 Tbsp olive oil

3 leeks, white and pale green parts, chopped

3 cloves garlic, minced

½ lb (250 g) cremini mushrooms, sliced

2 Tbsp tomato paste

¼ cup (2 fl oz/60 ml) dry white wine

2 cups (12 oz/375 g) pearl barley

8 cups (64 fl oz/2 l) chicken broth, plus more as needed

FOR THE MEATBALLS

1 lb (500 g) ground chicken

½ cup (2 oz/60 g) grated Parmesan cheese

¼ cup (1 oz/30 g) plain dried bread crumbs

2 Tbsp minced flat-leaf parsley, plus ½ cup (¾ oz/20 g) chopped parsley for garnish

1 Tbsp tomato paste

Salt and freshly ground pepper

This is a great soup to make with kids, who will have fun forming the meatballs and love eating the end result. The meatballs are also delicious served with pasta or couscous. The meatballs can be made ahead and frozen.

In a large, heavy pot, melt the butter with the oil over medium-high heat. Add the leeks and garlic and sauté until very soft, about 5 minutes. Add the mushrooms and cook, stirring often, until they begin to soften, about 5 minutes. Add the tomato paste and wine, stir to combine, and cook for 4 minutes. Add the barley and 8 cups (64 fl oz/2 l) broth and bring to a boil. Reduce the heat to low, cover, and simmer until the barley is tender, about 45 minutes.

Meanwhile, to make the meatballs, preheat the oven to 375°F (190°C). Oil a baking sheet. In a bowl, combine the chicken, Parmesan, bread crumbs, 2 Tbsp parsley, and tomato paste. Add 1 tsp salt and ½ tsp pepper and stir to combine. The mixture will be very sticky. To form the meatballs, use two small spoons to scoop up the mixture and transfer it to the prepared sheet. Bake until the meatballs are cooked through and no longer pink in the center, 10–12 minutes.

Add the meatballs to the soup and stir in gently. If the soup is too thick, add more broth and heat through. Season with salt and pepper and serve, garnished with the ½ cup (¾ oz/20 g) parsley.

MUSSELS IN TOMATO & CREAM BROTH

serves 4–6

2 Tbsp olive oil

1 shallot, minced

3 cloves garlic, minced

1 tsp ground cumin

½ tsp paprika

½ tsp ground ginger

¼ tsp ground cinnamon

1 cup (8 fl oz/250 ml) bottled clam juice

2 cups (16 fl oz/500 ml) chicken broth

3 lb (1.5 kg) mussels, scrubbed and debearded

3 plum tomatoes, seeded and diced

½ cup (4 fl oz/125 ml) heavy cream

Salt and freshly ground pepper

2 Tbsp minced flat-leaf parsley

For a hit of spice, add a few drops of hot-pepper sauce to this creamy mussel soup. Mussels often have "beards," fibrous tufts with which they cling to rocks (farm-raised mussels may not have these). If present, scrape away the fibers with a paring knife or scissors before cooking.

In a heavy-bottomed saucepan, warm the oil over medium heat. Add the shallot and garlic and sauté until soft, about 4 minutes. Add the cumin, paprika, ginger, and cinnamon and allow the spices to toast, stirring constantly, for 2 minutes. Add the clam juice and the chicken broth and bring to a boil. Add the mussels, discarding any that don't close to the touch. Cover the pan tightly and steam the mussels until they open, 5–7 minutes. Discard any unopened mussels.

Stir in the tomatoes and cream and return to a gentle boil. Season with salt and pepper, stir in the parsley, and serve.

17

SAVOY CABBAGE, FONTINA & RYE BREAD SOUP

serves 4–6

High up in the Alps between France and Switzerland sits Italy's smallest region, the Valle d'Aosta. The cows that graze on the mountain slopes produce the milk for its famed Fontina. Here, it is used in a rustic soup traditionally made with the local dark rye bread, pane nero.

Salt and freshly ground pepper

1 head savoy cabbage (about 1 lb/500 g), cut lengthwise into quarters and cored

1 lb (375 g) Fontina cheese

6 cups (48 fl oz/1.5 l) chicken broth

Pinch of grated nutmeg

Pinch of ground cinnamon

12 slices crusty rye bread, toasted

2 tsp unsalted butter, cut into bits

Bring a pot of water to a boil. Add a pinch of salt and the cabbage. Reduce the heat to low and cook, uncovered, until the cabbage is tender, about 30 minutes. Drain and let cool, then cut crosswise into thin slices.

Preheat the oven to 350°F (180°C). Coarsely shred enough cheese to measure ½ cup (2 oz/60 g). Thinly slice the remainder. In a large saucepan, combine the broth, nutmeg, and cinnamon and season with salt and pepper. Bring to a simmer.

Arrange 4 of the bread slices in the bottom of a deep 3-qt (3-l) baking dish. Cover with half each of the cabbage and the cheese slices. Repeat the layers, then cover with the remaining bread. Pour the hot broth over the top. Sprinkle with the shredded cheese and dot with the butter.

Bake until the soup is bubbling and browned, about 45 minutes. Let stand for 5 minutes, then serve.

18

GINGERY BEEF BROTH WITH SOBA NOODLES & BOK CHOY

serves 4–6

Just 20 minutes and a handful of ingredients yields this ultraflavorful broth, to which you can add any combination of noodles and greens. The soup can be made ahead and frozen. When serving, tongs make easy work of dividing the noodles and bok choy among bowls; ladle the broth on top.

2 green onions

3 cups (24 fl oz/750 ml) beef broth

2-inch (5-cm) piece fresh ginger, peeled and thinly sliced

1 large clove garlic, crushed

Salt

1 Tbsp canola oil

2 baby bok choy, quartered

¼ lb (125 g) cremini mushrooms, thinly sliced

5 oz (155 g) soba noodles

1 tsp soy sauce

Hot sauce, such as Sriracha, for serving (optional)

Thinly slice the green onions, reserving the white and pale green parts in one bowl and the dark green parts in a separate bowl.

In a large, heavy pot, combine the broth, 3 cups (24 fl oz/750 ml) water, the ginger, garlic, and the white and light green parts of the green onion and bring to a boil over medium-high heat. Reduce the heat to low and simmer for 20 minutes. Strain the liquid, discarding the solids, and return the broth to the pot. Season with salt and keep warm over low heat.

In a frying pan over medium-high heat, warm the oil. Add the bok choy and mushrooms and sauté, stirring frequently, until the vegetables begin to caramelize and soften, about 6 minutes. Set aside.

Return the broth to a boil and add the soba noodles. Cook, stirring occasionally, for 4 minutes. Add the bok choy, mushrooms, and soy sauce and stir to combine.

Serve, garnished with the dark green onion slices. Pass the hot sauce at the table, if using.

19

SAFFRON WINTER STEW WITH SALT COD

serves 4

½ lb (250 g) salt cod

1 Tbsp olive oil

1 yellow onion, coarsely chopped

2 cloves garlic, minced

2 tsp ground cumin

1 tsp saffron threads

Salt and freshly ground black pepper

4 cups (32 fl oz/1 l) chicken broth

½ lb (250 g) rutabagas, peeled and cubed

1 lb (500 g) potatoes, peeled and cubed

½ cup (3 oz/90 g) chopped, canned plum tomatoes with juices

12 Kalamata olives, pitted

½ cup (5 oz/155 g) fresh or frozen peas

1 tsp red pepper flakes

1 cup (1 oz/30 g) chopped kale

1 Tbsp chopped oregano

1 Tbsp chopped thyme

Saffron is cultivated in Spain and salt cod is a traditional Spanish food, which makes their marriage here no surprise. The cod must be refreshed in several changes of cold water and left to soak overnight before cooking, so plan on two days for making this stew: the first to prepare the cod and the second for simmering the stew.

Place the salt cod in a bowl, add cold water to cover, and refrigerate for 1 hour. Drain and repeat three more times. Drain again, add fresh water, and refrigerate overnight. Drain the cod and remove and discard any bones. Cut into ½-inch (12-mm) pieces, cover, and refrigerate.

In a large, heavy pot, warm the oil over medium heat. Add the onion and garlic and cook, stirring occasionally, until the onion is translucent, about 2 minutes. Sprinkle in the cumin, saffron, and 1 tsp black pepper and stir for 1 minute. Add a little of the broth and 1 cup (8 fl oz/250 ml) water and stir to mix well. Add the remaining broth and bring to a boil. Reduce the heat to low and simmer for about 30 minutes.

Add the rutabagas, potatoes, tomatoes, and olives. Cover and simmer until the vegetables are almost tender (they should offer some resistance when pierced with a fork), about 30 minutes. ⤖

Add the peas and red pepper flakes and simmer for 2–3 minutes. Add the cod, kale, oregano, and thyme. Cover and simmer until the cod is just cooked and flakes when pulled apart with a fork, 4–5 minutes.

Taste and season with salt, if needed, and serve.

20

BROCCOLI & CHEDDAR SOUP

serves 6–8

2 Tbsp unsalted butter

1 yellow onion, finely chopped

¼ cup (1½ oz/45 g) all-purpose flour

5 cups (40 fl oz/1.25 l) chicken broth

1½ lb (750 g) broccoli, tough stems peeled, florets and stems coarsely chopped

1½ Tbsp fresh thyme leaves or ½ tsp dried

1 Tbsp fresh lemon juice

2 cups (16 fl oz/500 ml) milk

½ lb (250 g) sharp Cheddar cheese, shredded

Salt and ground white pepper

If you prefer, instead of puréeing you can finely chop the broccoli into small florets and peel and finely dice the stem for a chunkier consistency.

In a large, heavy pot, melt the butter over medium heat. Add the onion and sauté until very tender, about 8 minutes. Stir in the flour and sauté for 1 minute. Add the broth, broccoli, thyme, and lemon juice and bring to a boil. Reduce the heat to low, cover, and simmer until the broccoli is tender, about 20 minutes. Remove from the heat and let cool slightly.

Working in batches, purée the soup in a blender. Return to the pot, stir in the milk, and bring to a simmer over low heat. Stir in half of the cheese and continue stirring until melted. Season with salt and pepper. Serve, garnished with the remaining cheese.

21

*This soup is a
great way to use
leftovers, as you
can make it with
any meat or seafood
and substitute just
about any type of
vegetable. Serve
the soup with both
a spoon and a fork
or chopsticks.*

ROAST PORK & UDON NOODLE SOUP

serves 4

½ lb (250 g) pork tenderloin

1 Tbsp olive oil

Salt and freshly ground pepper

1 Tbsp canola oil

3 oz (90 g) shiitake mushrooms, thinly sliced

2 baby bok choy, quartered lengthwise

5 cups (40 fl oz/1.25 l) chicken broth

5 Tbsp soy sauce

3 Tbsp mirin

6 oz (185 g) udon noodles

Preheat the oven to 400°F (200°C). Put the pork on a baking sheet, brush with the olive oil, and season with salt and pepper. Roast until an instant-read thermometer inserted into the thickest part registers 135°–140°F (57°–60°C), 20–25 minutes. Let the pork rest for at least 10 minutes and then chop into bite-sized pieces.

While the pork is resting, in a small frying pan, warm the canola oil over medium heat. Add the mushrooms and bok choy and sauté until they begin to caramelize, 5–7 minutes. Remove from the heat and set aside.

In a large, heavy pot, combine the broth, soy sauce, and mirin and bring to a boil over medium-high heat. Add the udon and cook, stirring occasionally, for 4 minutes. Add the pork, mushrooms, and bok choy and reduce the heat to a simmer for 5 minutes. Serve.

22

*Kumquats are
tiny citrus fruits
that are packed
with flavor. Do
not peel them
when you make
this soup. The
peel is the sweet
part of the fruit
and balances the
tartness of the flesh.*

KUMQUAT-CARROT PURÉE WITH TOASTED FENNEL SEEDS

serves 4

2 tsp fennel seeds

4 Tbsp (2 oz/60 g) unsalted butter

1 small yellow onion, chopped

2 cloves garlic, minced

1 cup kumquats, unpeeled, chopped, plus kumquat slices for garnish

2 lb (1 kg) carrots, peeled and thinly sliced

5 cups (40 fl oz/1.25 l) chicken broth

Salt and freshly ground pepper

In a small frying pan, toast the fennel seeds over medium heat just until fragrant, about 3 minutes. Transfer to a spice grinder and grind finely.

In a large, heavy pot, melt the butter over medium-high heat. Add the onion and garlic and sauté until translucent, about 5 minutes. Add the kumquats and carrots and sauté for 10 minutes. Add the broth and bring to a boil. Reduce the heat to low and simmer, uncovered, until the carrots and kumquats are very soft, 35–40 minutes. Remove from the heat and let cool slightly.

Working in batches, purée the soup in a blender. Return to the pot and stir in the ground fennel. Season with salt and pepper and serve, garnished with kumquat slices.

23

SPICY SAUSAGE & BROCCOLI RABE SOUP

serves 4–6

1 lb (500 g) spicy Italian sausages

2 Tbsp olive oil

1 large yellow onion, chopped

5 cloves garlic, thinly sliced

6 cups (48 fl oz/1.5 l) chicken broth

½ bunch broccoli rabe, tough stems peeled, cut into ¾-inch (2-cm) pieces

2 Tbsp tomato paste

Salt and freshly ground pepper

Grated pecorino cheese for serving

Tone down the spice in this soup by using half spicy and half sweet or all sweet Italian sausage. Serve with warm garlic bread.

In a frying pan, cook the sausages over medium heat, turning occasionally, until golden brown and cooked all the way through, about 15 minutes. Let cool, then cut into slices ¼ inch (6 mm) thick. Set aside.

In a large, heavy pot, warm the oil over medium-high heat. Add the onion and garlic and sauté until translucent, about 5 minutes. Add the broth and bring to a boil. Add the broccoli rabe, tomato paste, and sliced sausage, adjust the heat to maintain a simmer, and cook, uncovered, until the broccoli rabe is tender, 7–8 minutes. Season with salt and pepper and serve, topped with grated cheese.

24

CREAMY CELERY ROOT & BARLEY SOUP

serves 4–5

¼ cup (2 oz/60 g) pearl barley

Salt

2 Tbsp unsalted butter

1 leek, white and pale green parts, minced

1 celery root (about 1 lb/500 g), peeled and diced

4 cups (32 fl oz/1 l) chicken or vegetable broth

½ cup (4 fl oz/125 ml) half-and-half

½ cup (4 fl oz/125 ml) milk

1 cup (1 oz/30 g) baby spinach, julienned

Barley is one of the ancient grains making a contemporary comeback in salads, in risotto-style dishes, and in soups beyond the well-known beef and barley. Celery root, used here instead of beef, has a slightly tangy celery-like flavor that provides a strong vegetable background for the hearty grain.

In a saucepan, combine the barley, 3 cups (24 fl oz/750 ml) water, and ½ tsp salt. Place over medium-high heat and bring to a boil. Reduce the heat to low, cover, and cook until the barley is tender, 1 hour. Drain and set aside.

In a large, heavy pot, melt the butter over medium heat. Add the leek and celery root and cook, stirring occasionally, until the leek begins to change color, 3–4 minutes. Add the broth, 2 cups (16 fl oz/500 ml) water, and ½ tsp salt. Raise the heat to high and bring to a boil. Reduce the heat to low and simmer until the celery root is tender, about 10 minutes. Let cool slightly.

Purée half of the soup in a food processor or blender. Return to the pot and stir to combine. Place over medium heat and add the barley, the half-and-half, milk, and spinach. Bring to a simmer and cook just until the spinach wilts and the soup is hot, about 5 minutes, then serve.

25

JANUARY

This classic French stew makes a great thick, brothy soup. The beef cooks for a long time, so you need to use a cut with some fat, which will keep the meat moist as it braises, resulting in a melt-in-your-mouth-tender finish. The addition of rich, silky egg noodles will make grown-ups and kids alike happy.

BEEF BOURGUIGNON & EGG NOODLE STEW

serves 6

4 slices thick-cut applewood smoked bacon

2 lb (1 kg) beef chuck, cut into ¾-inch (2-cm) pieces

Salt and freshly ground pepper

3 Tbsp olive oil

1 small yellow onion, chopped

3 carrots, peeled and cut into ½-inch (12-mm) pieces

2 parsnips, peeled and cut into ½-inch (12-mm) pieces

2 cloves garlic, chopped

3 Tbsp tomato paste

6 cups (48 fl oz/1.5 l) beef broth

1 cup (8 fl oz/250 ml) dry red wine

2 Tbsp unsalted butter

½ lb (250 g) cremini mushrooms, quartered

3 cups (8 oz/250 g) egg noodles

¼ cup (¼ oz/7 g) flat-leaf parsley leaves, chopped

In a large, heavy pot, fry the bacon over medium-high heat, flipping once, until crispy, about 8 minutes total. Transfer to a paper towel–lined plate. When cool enough to handle, tear into bite-sized pieces. Set aside.

Return the pot (do not clean it) to medium-high heat. Season the beef generously with salt and pepper. Working in 2 batches, add the beef to the pot and cook, flipping with tongs, until browned on all sides, about 5 minutes per batch. Using a slotted spoon, transfer the beef to a bowl and set aside.

In the same pot, warm 2 Tbsp of the oil over medium-high heat. Add the onion, carrots, and parsnips, and season with salt and pepper. Cook, stirring occasionally, until the vegetables begin to soften, about 8 minutes. Add the garlic and cook, stirring occasionally, until soft, about 2 minutes. Stir in the tomato paste, broth, wine, and the beef along with the accumulated juices and bring to a boil. Reduce the heat to low, cover partially, and simmer until the beef is tender, about 1½ hours. »→

Meanwhile, in a frying pan, melt the butter with the remaining 1 Tbsp oil over medium-high heat. Add the mushrooms, season with salt and pepper, and cook, stirring frequently, until the mushrooms deepen in color and soften, but still hold their shape, about 5 minutes. Set aside.

Bring a large pot of salted water to a boil. Add the egg noodles and cook according to the package directions. Drain, rinse under cold water, and drain again. Set aside.

When the stew is done, stir in the mushrooms, noodles, and parsley, and season with salt and pepper. Serve, topped with the bacon.

26

JANUARY

Quick and simple to prepare, this soup also freezes well. Freshly cracked black pepper or small crackers make an elegant topping.

FENNEL-CELERY BISQUE

serves 4

4 Tbsp (2 oz/60 g) unsalted butter

2 shallots, minced

2 fennel bulbs, stalks and fronds removed, chopped

5 celery ribs, chopped

¼ cup (2 fl oz/60 ml) dry white wine

2 cups (16 fl oz/500 ml) vegetable broth

½ cup (4 fl oz/125 ml) heavy cream

Salt and ground white pepper

In a large, heavy pot, melt the butter over medium-high heat. Add the shallots, fennel, and celery and sauté until the vegetables soften, about 10 minutes. Add the wine and cook for 5 minutes. Add the broth, bring to a boil, reduce the heat to low, and simmer until the vegetables are very tender, about 20 minutes. Remove from the heat and let cool slightly.

Working in batches, purée the soup in a blender. Return to the pot and add the cream. Bring the soup just to a boil over low heat. Season with salt and pepper and serve.

TURKEY SOUP WITH CHIPOTLE & LIME

serves 4

Serve this classic Southwestern soup with thick wedges of corn bread and cold Mexican beer.

1 small can chipotle chiles in adobo

1 Tbsp olive oil

1 red onion, minced

2 cloves garlic, minced

4 cups (32 fl oz/1 l) chicken broth

1 can (15 oz/470 g) crushed tomatoes

½ tsp ground cumin

2 cups (12 oz/375 g) shredded cooked turkey

3 Tbsp fresh lime juice

Corn tortilla chips, crumbled queso fresco, diced avocado, and cilantro leaves for serving

Purée the chipotles in a blender. Measure out ½–1 tsp of the purée. Refrigerate the remainder for another use (it will keep for 1 month).

In a large, heavy pot, warm the oil over medium heat. Add the onion and garlic and sauté until the onion is soft, about 6 minutes. Add the broth, tomatoes, and cumin and bring to a boil. Reduce the heat to low, cover, and simmer for 10 minutes. Stir in the turkey, lime juice, and chipotle purée to taste. Serve, garnished with tortilla chips, cheese, avocado, and cilantro.

MAC & CHEESE CHILI

serves 4–6

Here's a dish to feed a crowd, and it can be prepared a couple of days in advance and stored, tightly covered, in the refrigerator. You can experiment with the flavors by using crumbled spicy sausage or ground turkey in place of the beef or by trading out the Monterey jack for pepper jack. Pasta-based soups tend to absorb a lot of broth when they sit, so be sure to have extra broth on hand to adjust the consistency as needed. To add vegetables to this meal, serve the chili in shallow bowls, spooning it atop a bed of sautéed kale.

2 Tbsp olive oil

½ yellow onion, chopped

2 cloves garlic, chopped

¾ lb (375 g) lean ground beef

1 Tbsp chili powder

1½ tsp ground cumin

Salt and freshly ground pepper

1 can (14½ oz/455 g) fire-roasted diced tomatoes with juices

1 can (16 oz/500 g) pinto beans, drained

4 cups (32 fl oz/1 l) chicken broth

2 cups (7 oz/220 g) elbow macaroni

½ cup (2 oz/60 g) shredded sharp Cheddar cheese

½ cup (2 oz/60 g) shredded Monterey jack cheese

3 green onions, white and tender green parts, chopped

In a large, heavy pot, warm the oil over medium-high heat. Add the yellow onion and cook, stirring occasionally, until translucent, about 6 minutes. Add the garlic and cook, stirring occasionally, until soft, about 2 minutes. Add the ground beef and cook, breaking it up with a wooden spoon, until browned, about 5 minutes. Stir in the chili powder, cumin, and ¼ tsp salt. Add the tomatoes with their juices, the beans, and broth and bring to a boil. Add the macaroni, cover, and reduce the heat to medium. Cook until the pasta is al dente, about 10 minutes.

Stir in half of the Cheddar and Monterey jack cheeses and all of the green onions. Season with salt and pepper. Serve, topped with the remaining cheese.

29

VEGETABLE-LENTIL SOUP WITH SHERRY

serves 6

2 Tbsp olive oil

1 yellow onion, chopped

1 clove garlic, minced

1 carrot, peeled and chopped

1 red bell pepper, seeded and chopped

6 cups (48 fl oz/1.5 l) chicken broth

2 cups (14 oz/440 g) lentils, picked over and rinsed

1 can (28 oz/875 g) diced tomatoes

1 tsp smoked paprika

1 tsp ground cumin

Salt and freshly ground pepper

4 oz (125 g) baby spinach leaves, coarsely chopped

2 Tbsp dry sherry

2-oz (60-g) piece Parmesan cheese

There's nothing more satisfying than a hearty bowl of soup like this one, chock-full of bright vegetables and tender lentils. Unlike other dried legumes, lentils need no presoaking, and they cook relatively quickly. For a vegetarian version of this soup, use vegetable broth instead of chicken.

In a large, heavy pot, warm the oil over medium-high heat. Add the onion and sauté until soft, about 5 minutes. Add the garlic, carrot, and bell pepper and sauté for 3 minutes. Stir in the broth, lentils, tomatoes with their juices, paprika, and cumin. Season with ½ tsp salt and ¼ tsp pepper. Bring to a boil. Reduce the heat to maintain a simmer, cover, and cook until the lentils are very tender, about 20 minutes.

Stir in the spinach and cook, uncovered, just until it is wilted, about 2 minutes. Stir in the sherry. Season with salt and pepper and serve, using a vegetable peeler to garnish the soup with shavings of Parmesan.

30

SMOKED TROUT CHOWDER

serves 4–6

3 Tbsp unsalted butter

1 yellow onion, chopped

1 fennel bulb (¾ lb/375 g), stalks and fronds removed, quartered, cored, and thinly sliced

2 cups (16 fl oz/500 ml) chicken broth

1 cup (8 fl oz/250 ml) bottled clam juice

3 small red potatoes, cut into small dice

1 cup (8 fl oz/250 ml) heavy cream

8 oz (250 g) smoked trout, crumbled

2 tsp fresh lemon juice

1 Tbsp minced dill

Salt and freshly ground pepper

Here's a fresh take on a classic chowder, made with flavorful smoked fish. For a lighter version, use whole milk in place of the cream.

In a large, heavy pot, melt the butter over medium-high heat. Add the onion and fennel and sauté until soft, about 7 minutes. Add the broth and clam juice and bring to a boil. Add the potatoes, reduce the heat to medium-low, and simmer until the potatoes are tender, about 8 minutes. Add the cream, smoked trout, lemon juice, and dill and cook for 4 minutes. Season with salt and pepper and serve.

31

OLD-FASHIONED TOMATO & RICE SOUP

serves 6

3 Tbsp unsalted butter

1 small yellow onion, chopped

2 cloves garlic, minced

2 cans (28 oz/875 g each) diced tomatoes

¼ cup (2 fl oz/60 ml) heavy cream

1 cup (5 oz/155 g) steamed white rice

Salt and freshly ground pepper

This classic soup, loved by both kids and adults, is a great way to use leftover steamed white rice.

In a large saucepan, melt the butter over medium-high heat. Add the onion and garlic and sauté until translucent, about 5 minutes. Add the tomatoes with their juices and bring to a boil. Reduce the heat to low and simmer for 20 minutes. Remove from the heat and let cool slightly.

Working in batches, purée the soup in a blender. Return to the saucepan. Stir in the cream and rice and return to a gentle boil. Season with salt and pepper and serve.

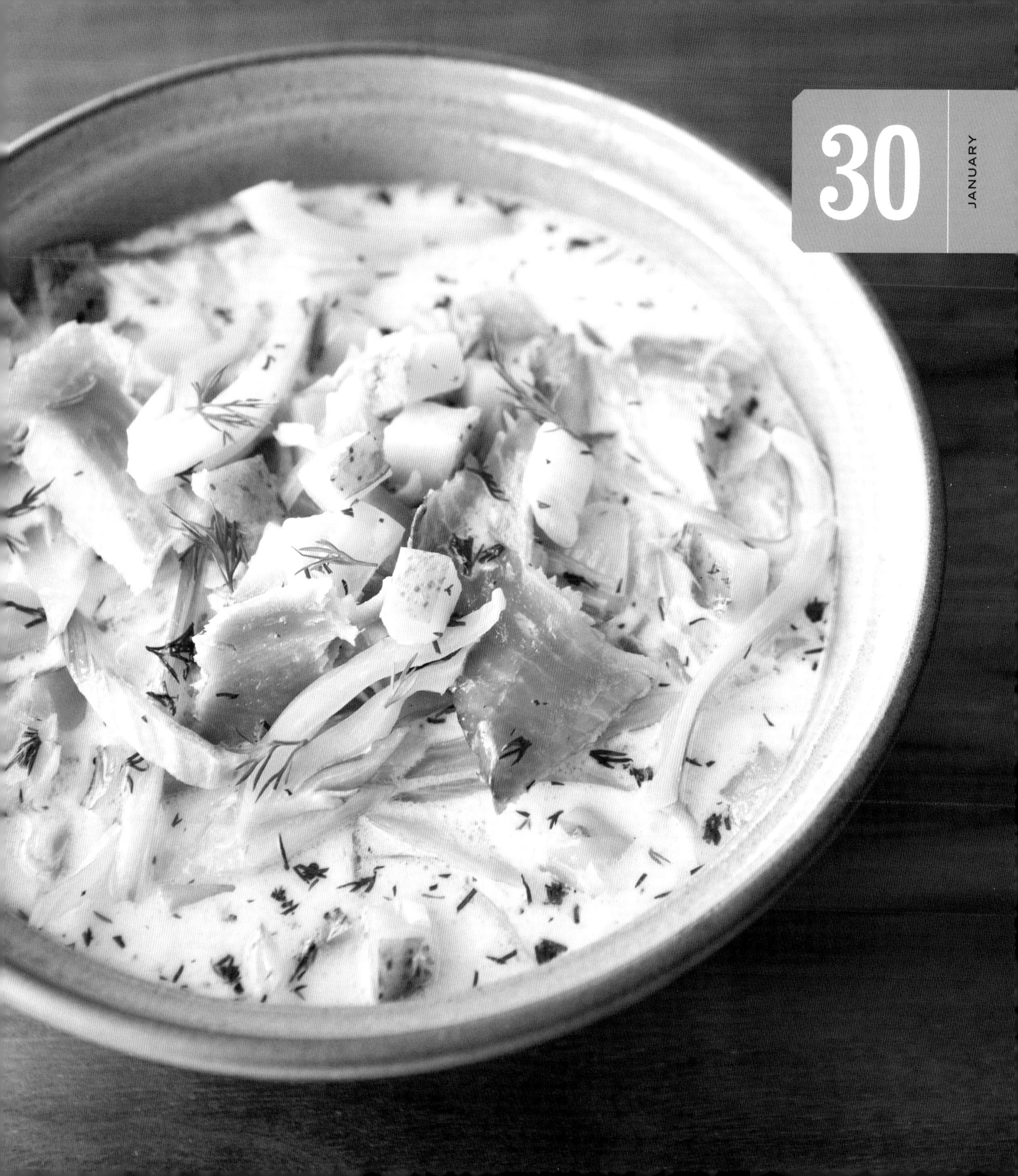

30

JANUARY

*Stews, chilis, and
creamy bisques—
satisfying, flavorful,
and rich—are the
cherished soups of
winter. These long-
simmered concoctions
can be made with
virtually any type
of meat, fish, or
vegetable, making
them easy to vary
according to palate
and occasion. Draw
on fresh, seasonal
ingredients like
winter greens, dried
beans, root vegetables,
shellfish, and cured
meats, each offering
its own distinctive
flavor to the hearty
brews in this month's
steaming pots.*

february

1

WINTER GREENS & SHIITAKE SOUP WITH POACHED EGGS

serves 6

Rustic and homey in feel—yet polished in presentation with the addition of a poached egg—this becomes a complete meal with a side of crusty bread. Substitute any sturdy green for the chard.

3 Tbsp olive oil

1 small yellow onion, chopped

4 cloves garlic, minced

1 lb (500 g) shiitake mushrooms, stemmed and sliced

2 bunches chard, chopped

5 cups (40 fl oz/1.25 l) chicken broth, plus more as needed

Salt and freshly ground pepper

½ tsp white vinegar

6 eggs

In a large, heavy pot, warm the oil over medium-high heat. Add the onion, garlic, and mushrooms and sauté until the mushrooms begin to turn golden, 5–7 minutes. Add the chard, stir well, and cook for 3 minutes. Add the broth and bring to a boil. Reduce the heat to low and simmer until the chard is tender but not mushy, about 12 minutes, adding more broth if needed. Season with salt and pepper.

In a frying pan, heat 1 inch (2.5 cm) of water over medium heat. Add the vinegar and reduce the heat to bring the water to a gentle simmer. Break an egg into a small bowl and, using a large spoon, place it gently in the water. Using a tablespoon, occasionally spoon the hot water over the top of the exposed egg. Cook until the egg is set but the yolk is still runny, about 5 minutes. Remove the egg with a slotted spoon. Repeat to poach the remaining eggs.

Ladle the soup into bowls, top with the poached eggs, and serve.

2

CREAMY BRUSSELS SPROUT SOUP WITH MAPLE BACON

serves 4–6

Here's a great way to introduce Brussels sprouts to a young and discerning eater. This is a creamy and healthful soup topped with a familiar crowd-pleaser: bacon! And it's hard to think of a dish that isn't better with the addition of candied bacon. Be sure to look for pure maple syrup, passing up any bottle that lists artificial sweeteners.

8 slices thick-cut applewood smoked bacon

3 Tbsp pure maple syrup

1 small yellow onion, chopped

1 lb (500 g) Brussels sprouts, halved

1 russet potato (about ¾ lb/375 g), peeled and cut into ½-inch (12-mm) pieces

Salt and freshly ground pepper

2 cloves garlic, chopped

2 thyme sprigs

4 cups (32 fl oz/1 l) chicken broth

Preheat the oven to 400°F (200°C).

Working in batches if necessary, in a large, heavy pot, fry the bacon over medium-high heat, flipping once, about 6 minutes total (the bacon will not be fully cooked). Using tongs, transfer the bacon to a baking sheet and let cool slightly. Brush the bacon slices on one side with the maple syrup and bake until cooked through, 8–10 minutes. Let cool, then cut into bite-sized pieces. Set aside.

Pour off all but 2 Tbsp of the fat from the pot and return to medium-high heat. Add the onion, Brussels sprouts, and potato, and season with salt and pepper. Cook, stirring frequently, until the vegetables begin to soften, about 8 minutes. Add the garlic and thyme sprigs and cook, stirring frequently, until the garlic is soft, about 2 minutes. Add the broth, raise the heat to high, and bring to a boil. Reduce the heat to low and simmer until the Brussels sprouts are tender, 8–10 minutes. Remove and discard the thyme sprigs. Let cool slightly.

Working in batches, purée the soup in a food processor or blender. Return to the pot and season with salt and pepper. Serve, topped with the maple bacon.

LAMB STEW WITH SWEET POTATOES & POBLANO CHILES

serves 4–6

Lamb is popular in many kitchens around the globe, and this recipe draws on the culinary traditions of two regions in which it is enjoyed. Poblano chiles and sweet potatoes from Latin America are combined with the pomegranates used in the cooking of the Middle East and the Mediterranean to create this substantial and colorful stew.

1½ lb (750 g) yellow- or orange-fleshed sweet potatoes, cut into slices 1½ inches (4 cm) thick

3 poblano chiles

1 lb (500 g) boneless lamb shoulder, cut into 1-inch (2.5-cm) pieces

Salt and freshly ground black pepper

1 Tbsp olive oil

2 cloves garlic, minced

1 Tbsp all-purpose flour

1 tsp ground turmeric

½ tsp ground cumin

¼ tsp cayenne pepper

Juice of 1 lemon

1 cup (8 fl oz/250 ml) chicken broth

¼ cup (1 oz/30 g) pomegranate seeds

Place the sweet potatoes on a steamer rack set over boiling water. Cover and steam until fork-tender, about 30 minutes. Remove from the steamer and, when cool enough to handle, peel the sweet potatoes and set aside.

Heat a stove-top grill pan over medium-high heat until hot. Place the poblano chiles on the pan and roast, turning often, until the skin is charred, about 5 minutes. Transfer to a plastic bag and let steam for 10 minutes. When cool enough to handle, peel or scrape away the charred skins, cut the chiles in half lengthwise, and remove the stems and seeds. Cut the flesh lengthwise into thin strips. Set aside.

Season the lamb with ½ tsp salt and ¼ tsp black pepper.

In a large, heavy pot, warm the oil over medium heat. Add the garlic and cook, stirring occasionally, until soft, about 1 minute. Add the lamb and sear on all sides, turning as needed, 5–6 minutes.

Sprinkle the lamb with the flour, turmeric, cumin, and cayenne. Turn the meat, browning the flour and spices, for 3–4 minutes. Add the lemon juice and a little of the broth, stirring to scrape up the browned bits from the bottom of the pot. Add the remaining broth and 1 cup (8 fl oz/250 ml) water ⟫→

and bring to a boil. Reduce the heat to low and simmer until the lamb is fork-tender, about 1 hour.

Add the sweet potatoes and chiles and simmer for 5 minutes. Transfer to a serving bowl, garnish with the pomegranate seeds, and serve.

ORECCHIETTE IN AROMATIC BROTH

serves 6–8

Orecchiette (or "little ears") are perfectly shaped to trap the fragrant broth in their indentations, but you can substitute any small pasta shape you like. Use a good-quality aged balsamic vinegar for the best flavor.

1 Tbsp olive oil

4 oz (125 g) sliced pancetta, finely chopped

6 large yellow onions, thinly sliced

2 leeks, white and pale green parts, thinly sliced

7 cups (56 fl oz/1.75 l) chicken broth

6 oz (185 g) orecchiette pasta

6 slices country-style bread

2 cloves garlic

3 Tbsp balsamic vinegar

Salt and freshly ground pepper

In a large, heavy pot, warm the oil over medium heat. Add the pancetta, onions, and leeks and sauté until the onions and leeks are soft, about 15 minutes. Add the broth and simmer, covered, for 15 minutes. Add the orecchiette and continue to simmer, covered, until al dente, 12–15 minutes.

Meanwhile, in a toaster or under a broiler, toast the bread slices until golden. Rub one side of each slice with garlic.

Add the vinegar to the soup and season with salt and pepper. Stir to mix well and serve with the garlic toasts.

5

*Root vegetables
maintain their
shape when cooked,
making them a
good choice for a
chunky, hearty
ragout. Saffron,
which adds rich
color and a hint of
the exotic, provides
a lush background
of yellow-orange to
the white swirl of
crème fraîche. Fresh
herbs, sprinkled on
just before serving,
echo the herbs used
during cooking.*

SAFFRON ROOT VEGETABLE RAGOUT WITH KALE

serves 8

1½ tsp saffron threads

1 cup (8 fl oz/250 ml) hot water

2 Tbsp olive oil

2 yellow onions, coarsely chopped

4 cloves garlic, minced

3 tsp ground cumin

Salt and freshly ground black pepper

8 cups (64 fl oz/2 l) vegetable broth

½ lb (250 g) rutabagas, peeled and cut into 1-inch (2.5-cm) pieces

1 lb (500 g) carrots, peeled and cut into ½-inch (12-mm) pieces

1 lb (500 g) parsnips, peeled and cut into 1-inch (2.5-cm) pieces

1 lb (500 g) potatoes, peeled and cut into 1-inch (2.5-cm) pieces

1 cup (6 oz/185 g) chopped canned plum tomatoes with juices

12 Kalamata olives, pitted

1 tsp red pepper flakes

2 cups (2 oz/60 g) chopped kale

2 Tbsp minced oregano

2 Tbsp minced thyme

3 Tbsp crème fraîche

In a small bowl, combine the saffron threads and hot water and let stand for 10–15 minutes.

In a large, heavy pot, warm the oil over medium-high heat. Add the onions and cook, stirring occasionally, until translucent, 2–3 minutes. Add the garlic and cook, stirring occasionally, for 1 minute. Sprinkle in the cumin and 1 tsp black pepper and stir for 1 minute.

Stir in a little of the broth, then add the remaining broth and the saffron water and bring to a boil. Reduce the heat to low and simmer for 30 minutes. Add the rutabagas, carrots, parsnips, potatoes, tomatoes with their juices, olives, and ½ tsp salt. Cover and simmer until the vegetables are almost tender, offering just a little resistance when pierced with a fork, 20–30 minutes. ⇥

Add the red pepper flakes, kale, oregano, and thyme and simmer until the kale wilts and is tender, about 5 minutes. Taste and adjust the seasoning. Serve, topped with a swirl of the crème fraîche.

Add the cooked vegetables to the pot and stir well. Season with salt and pepper and serve.

6

*Be sure you have
ovenproof bowls
on hand for this
filling soup, which
is topped with
slices of toasted
bread covered in
melted cheese. You
can use any small
tubular pasta, such
as ditalini or even
macaroni, in place
of the pennette.*

PASTA & BEAN SOUP WITH FONTINA

serves 6

3 Tbsp olive oil

2 yellow onions, chopped

2 Tbsp minced garlic

4 oz (125 g) sliced pancetta, finely chopped

1 can (15 oz/470 g) white beans, drained

1 cup (6 oz/185 g) canned diced tomatoes, with juices

6 cups (48 fl oz/1.5 l) beef broth

¼ cup (⅓ oz/10 g) minced flat-leaf parsley

2 Tbsp minced oregano

Salt and freshly ground pepper

8 oz (250 g) pennette pasta

6 slices country-style bread, toasted

3 cups (12 oz/375 g) shredded Fontina cheese

Preheat the oven to 350°F (180°C). In a large, heavy pot, warm the oil over low heat. Add the onions and sauté until very tender, 10–15 minutes. Add the garlic and sauté for about 2 minutes. Add the pancetta and sauté for about 5 minutes. Add the beans, tomatoes, broth, parsley, and oregano and simmer, stirring occasionally, for about 10 minutes.

Meanwhile, bring a large pot of water to a boil. Add 2 tsp salt and the pennette and cook until almost al dente, about 9 minutes or according to the package directions. Drain and add to the soup. Season with salt and pepper.

Ladle the soup into ovenproof bowls. Top each with a piece of toasted bread and sprinkle with cheese. Place on a baking sheet and bake until the cheese is completely melted, about 10 minutes. Serve.

FEBRUARY 7

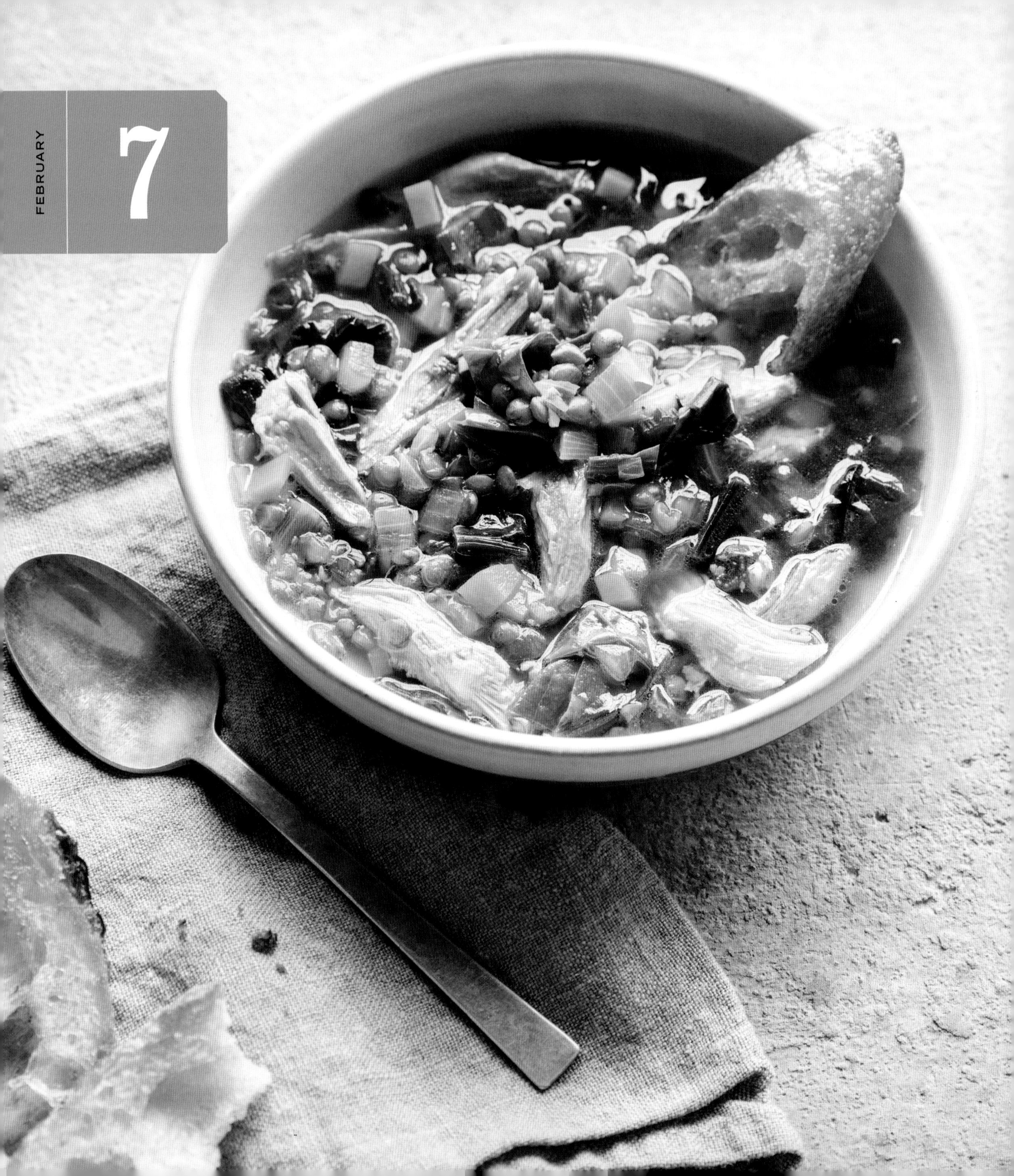

7

LENTIL & CHARD SOUP WITH DUCK CONFIT

serves 8

2 tsp olive oil, plus 2 Tbsp

1 yellow onion, minced

1 clove garlic, minced

1 carrot, peeled and minced

2 cups (14 oz/440 g) lentils, picked over and rinsed

1 bay leaf

4 thyme sprigs

Salt and freshly ground pepper

6 large chard leaves, chopped, including ribs

2 duck legs confit

8 baguette slices, cut on the diagonal

Lentils combine successfully with any number of different ingredients, but in southwestern France, duck confit is one of the most common foods used to flavor lentils as well as soups and stews. Duck leg confit can be purchased at many supermarkets, ready to use. Crusty baguette croutons finish the dish.

In a large, heavy pot, warm the 2 tsp oil over medium heat. Add the onion and cook, stirring occasionally, until translucent, about 2 minutes. Add the garlic and carrot and cook, stirring occasionally, for 2 minutes. Stir in the lentils and 10 cups (80 fl oz/2.5 l) water and bring to a boil, then reduce the heat to low. Add the bay leaf, thyme, 1 tsp salt, and ½ tsp pepper and simmer for 15 minutes. Add the chard and duck legs and cook until the lentils are almost tender, 20–25 minutes.

Transfer the duck legs to a cutting board and, when cool enough to handle, remove and discard the skin. Cut off the meat, discarding the bones. Coarsely chop the meat and stir all but about ¼ cup (1½ oz/45 g) into the soup. Cook until the lentils are tender but not mushy, about 10 minutes longer. Remove and discard the bay leaf and thyme sprigs. Stir in ½ tsp salt.

Meanwhile, in a large frying pan, warm the 2 Tbsp oil over medium-high heat. Add half of the baguette slices and fry until golden, about 3 minutes. Turn and fry until golden on the other side, about 2 minutes. Transfer to a paper towel–lined plate. Repeat with the remaining baguette slices.

Ladle the soup into bowls. Garnish each with a fried crouton topped with a bit of the reserved duck meat.

8

LEMONGRASS SOUP WITH SHRIMP & CHILE

serves 4

2 tsp canola oil

5 lemongrass stalks, center white parts only, thinly sliced

1 Tbsp peeled and minced fresh ginger

4 cups (32 fl oz/1 l) chicken broth

1 small red chile, seeded and thinly sliced

½ lb (250 g) medium shrimp, peeled and deveined

2 green onions, dark and light green parts, chopped

1 Tbsp minced cilantro

Add cubed chicken breast, tofu, or sliced vegetables in place of, or along with, the shrimp. If using chicken, add it to the broth before simmering it for 15 minutes. A squeeze of fresh lime juice just before serving will brighten the flavors.

In a large, heavy pot, warm the oil over medium-high heat. Add the lemongrass and the ginger and sauté for 3 minutes. Add the broth and 1 cup (8 fl oz/240 ml) water and bring to a boil. Reduce the heat to low and simmer, uncovered, for 15 minutes. Add the chile and shrimp and cook until the shrimp are bright pink, 2–3 minutes. Remove from the heat, stir in the green onions and cilantro, and serve.

9

SEARED DUCK & BEET GREENS SOUP

serves 4

2 small duck breasts (¾ lb/375 g total weight), skin on

3 Tbsp olive oil

Salt and freshly ground pepper

1 small yellow onion, chopped

3 cloves garlic, minced

1 bunch beet greens, tough stems discarded, leaves chopped

4 cups (32 fl oz/1 l) chicken broth

10 drops Asian sesame oil

2 green onions, white and tender green parts, chopped

Grocery stores will often cut the beet greens off of the bunches of beets, so if you don't see them at the market, ask the produce manager. Once cut from the stems, the greens wilt quickly, so use them the day you purchase them.

Brush the duck breasts with 1 Tbsp of the olive oil and season with salt and pepper. Heat a grill pan over high heat until it is very hot. Put the duck breasts in the pan, skin side down, and cook for 7 minutes. Turn the duck breasts over and cook to medium rare, 5–7 minutes more. Transfer to a cutting board and let rest for at least 10 minutes. Remove and discard the skin. Shred the meat into bite-sized pieces. Set aside.

In a large, heavy pot, warm the remaining 2 Tbsp olive oil over medium-high heat. Add the onion and garlic and cook the onions until translucent, about 5 minutes. Add the beet greens, stir, and sauté for 3 minutes. Add the broth, shredded duck, and sesame oil. Stir to combine and simmer for 5 minutes to blend the flavors. Stir in the green onions, season with salt and pepper, and serve.

10

CREAM OF CHICKEN SOUP WITH SUNCHOKES & SHALLOTS

serves 4–6

¾ lb (375 g) skinless, boneless chicken breast halves

1 lemon, halved

Salt and freshly ground pepper

4 Tbsp (2 oz/60 g) unsalted butter

2 shallots, chopped

2 celery ribs, chopped

¾ lb (375 g) sunchokes, peeled and cut into ½-inch (12-mm) pieces

2 cloves garlic, chopped

¼ cup (1½ oz/45 g) all-purpose flour

3½ cups (28 fl oz/875 ml) chicken broth

1 cup (8 fl oz/250 ml) half-and-half

2 green onions, white and tender green parts, chopped

The addition of meaty sunchokes (aka Jerusalem artichokes) gives this classic soup a modern twist. Sunchokes have a relatively short season, so when they are no longer in the market, you can use mushrooms, squash, potatoes, or even asparagus in their place here. Stirring in lemon juice just before serving brightens the overall flavor of the soup and complements the faint artichoke taste of the sunchokes.

Place the chicken in a heavy saucepan and cover by 2 inches (5 cm) with cold water. Add a lemon half and season with salt and pepper. Place over high heat and bring to a boil. Reduce the heat to medium-low and simmer until the chicken is opaque throughout, 15–18 minutes. Using tongs, transfer the chicken to a cutting board and, when cool enough to handle, cut into ¼-inch (6-mm) pieces. Set aside.

In a large, heavy pot, melt the butter over medium-high heat. Add the shallots and celery and cook, stirring occasionally, until soft, about 6 minutes. Add the sunchokes and garlic, season with salt and pepper, and cook, stirring occasionally, until the vegetables begin to soften, about 4 minutes. Stir in the flour and cook, stirring frequently, for about 2 minutes. Add the broth and the chicken and bring to a boil. Reduce the heat to medium-low and simmer until the sunchokes are very tender, about 20 minutes. Stir in the half-and-half and cook, stirring frequently, until the soup thickens, about 3 minutes. Stir in the juice from the remaining lemon half and season with salt and pepper.

Garnish with the green onions and serve.

11

Inspired by Spain's beloved paella, this saffron-scented dish features an enticing combination of briny mussels, sweet shrimp, and salty Spanish ham. If you can't find Spanish serrano ham, prosciutto can be substituted. Clams can be substituted for the mussels.

SEAFOOD STEW WITH SAFFRON, SERRANO HAM & ALMONDS

serves 6

1 cup (5½ oz/170 g) blanched almonds

6 cups (48 fl oz/1.5 l) chicken broth

¼ cup (2 fl oz/60 ml) olive oil

2 yellow onions, chopped

1 red bell pepper, chopped

½ tsp ground cumin

3 cloves garlic, minced

1 cup (6 oz/185 g) chopped serrano ham

1 can (15 oz/470 g) diced tomatoes

½ cup (3½ oz/105 g) long-grain white rice

¼ tsp saffron threads

Salt and freshly ground pepper

1 lb (500 g) medium shrimp, peeled and deveined

12 mussels, scrubbed and debearded

1 cup (5 oz/155 g) frozen peas, thawed

¼ cup (⅓ oz/10 g) minced flat-leaf parsley

Process the almonds in a food processor until very finely ground. Add 1 cup (8 fl oz/250 ml) of the broth and process until the mixture looks milky. Strain through a fine-mesh sieve into a bowl, pressing hard on the solids. Discard the solids.

In a large, heavy pot, warm the oil over medium-high heat. Add the onions and sauté until just beginning to look translucent, about 2 minutes. Add the bell pepper, cumin, garlic, and ham and cook until the vegetables are tender, about 5 minutes. Add the tomatoes and remaining 5 cups (40 fl oz/1.25 l) broth and bring to a simmer. Reduce the heat and simmer for 10 minutes to blend the flavors.

Meanwhile, in a saucepan, bring 1 cup (8 fl oz/250 ml) water to a boil over medium heat. Rinse the rice under cold running water until the water runs clear. Add the rice, saffron, and ¼ tsp salt to the boiling water. Cover, reduce the heat to low, and cook the rice for 15 minutes. Remove from the heat and let stand undisturbed for 5 minutes. Fluff the rice. ⤚→

Raise the heat under the soup to medium-high and add the reserved almond liquid, the shrimp, the mussels (discarding any that do not close to the touch), and the peas. Cook, stirring occasionally, until the shrimp are pink and the mussels have opened, about 5 minutes. Discard any unopened mussels. Season with salt and pepper.

Place a scoop of the rice in each bowl and top with the stew. Garnish with the parsley and serve.

12

CHICKEN STEW WITH BUTTERMILK-CHIVE DUMPLINGS

serves 4

This is a great way to use up leftover cooked chicken; just skip the first step, and substitute chicken broth for the poaching liquid. Feel free to change up the vegetables: add spinach, sweet potatoes, or peas.

2 skinless, boneless chicken breast halves

2 skinless, boneless chicken thighs

1 bay leaf

3 peppercorns

Salt and freshly ground pepper

4 Tbsp (2 oz/60 g) unsalted butter

2 leeks, white parts only, chopped

2 carrots, peeled and sliced

3 celery ribs, sliced

2 Tbsp all-purpose flour

4 cups (32 fl oz/1 l) chicken broth

1 russet potato, peeled and cut into ½-inch (12-mm) dice

2 Tbsp heavy cream

FOR THE DUMPLINGS

1¼ cups (6½ oz/200 g) all-purpose flour

1 tsp baking soda

½ tsp salt

1 Tbsp chopped chives

Large pinch of cayenne

3 Tbsp cold unsalted butter, cut into bits

½ cup (4 fl oz/125 ml) buttermilk

Put the chicken breasts and thighs, bay leaf, peppercorns, and ¼ tsp salt in a saucepan and add cold water to cover by 1 inch (2.5 cm). Bring to a boil, then reduce the heat to medium-low. Simmer until the chicken is cooked through, 15–20 minutes, skimming off any foam on the surface. Remove the chicken, shred the meat, and set aside. Reserve 2 cups (16 fl oz/500 ml) of the poaching liquid.

In a large saucepan, melt the butter over medium-high heat. Add the leeks, carrots, and celery and sauté until they begin to soften, about 5 minutes. Add the flour and cook for 2 minutes, stirring. Add the broth and the reserved poaching liquid and bring to a boil. Add the potato and reduce the heat to medium-low. Cook until the potato begins to soften, about 10 minutes. ⤳

Add the chicken and cream and continue to cook until the soup thickens and the potatoes are very tender, 5 minutes. Season with salt and pepper.

To make the dumplings, sift together the flour, baking soda, and salt into a bowl. Stir in the chives and cayenne. With a pastry blender, cut in the cold butter until it resembles coarse cornmeal. Add the buttermilk and stir just to combine. Use your hands to form small dumplings and add them to the soup, cover, and let steam for 20 minutes. Serve.

13

SUN-DRIED TOMATO SOUP WITH CRAB

serves 4

Sun-dried tomatoes give this soup a stunning, deep red color and complex flavor. The crab garnish gives it a luxurious and indulgent feel, but you could easily substitute cooked shrimp or even herbed croutons.

2 Tbsp unsalted butter

2 shallots, minced

1 cup (5 oz/150 g) drained oil-packed sun-dried tomatoes, julienned

1 can (15 oz/470 g) diced tomatoes

1½ cups (12 fl oz/375 ml) chicken broth

3 Tbsp heavy cream

Salt and freshly ground pepper

¼ lb (125 g) fresh lump crabmeat, picked over for shell fragments

2 Tbsp chopped chives

In a large saucepan, melt the butter over medium-high heat. Add the shallots and sauté until soft, about 5 minutes. Add the sun-dried tomatoes, diced tomatoes, and broth and bring to a boil. Reduce the heat to low and simmer for 20 minutes. Remove from the heat and let cool slightly.

Working in batches, purée the soup in a blender or food processor. Return to the saucepan over low heat and add the cream. Stir to combine, season with salt and pepper, and serve, topped with the crabmeat and sprinkled with the chives.

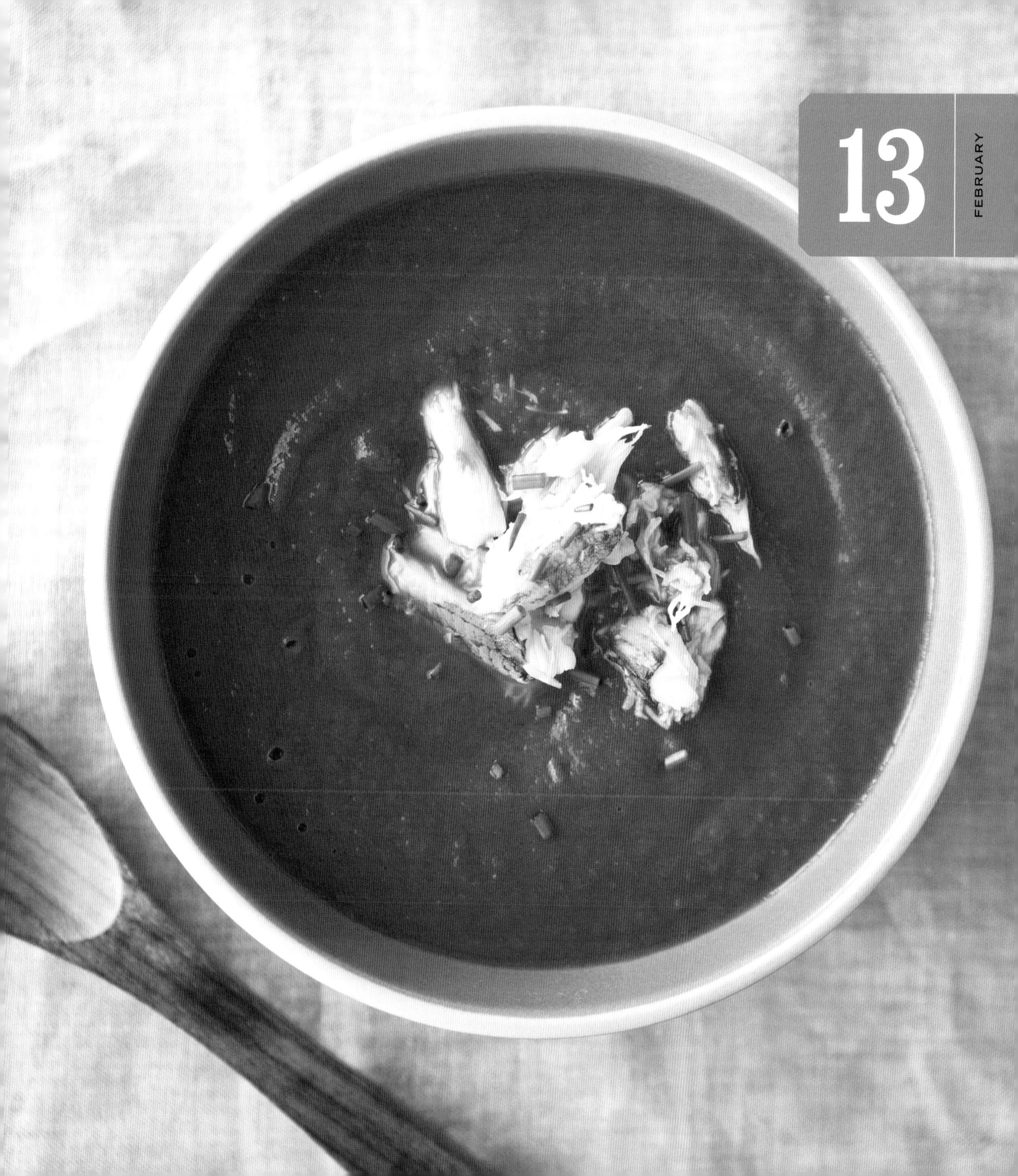

14

*Oysters have long
been thought to have
aphrodisiac qualities,
so what better soup
than this to serve
on Valentine's Day?
Spring for fresh
oysters if you can,
and do not overcook
them, or they will
become rubbery.*

CELERY, LEEK & OYSTER BISQUE

serves 6

18 small oysters in the shell
or bottled shucked oysters

2 Tbsp unsalted butter

1 yellow onion, coarsely chopped

5 large leeks, white and pale green parts,
coarsely chopped

5 celery ribs, coarsely chopped

3 bottles (8 fl oz/250 ml each) clam juice

½ cup (4 fl oz/125 ml) heavy cream

1–2 tsp fresh lemon juice

Salt and freshly ground pepper

If using oysters in the shell, shuck them,
reserving their liquor. If using bottled
oysters, drain them, reserving the liquor.
Refrigerate the oysters, then strain the liquor.

In a large, heavy pot, melt the butter over
medium-low heat. Add the onion, leeks, and
celery and sauté until soft, about 20 minutes.
Add the clam juice, 3 cups (24 fl oz/750 ml)
water, and the reserved oyster liquor. Bring
to a boil over high heat. Reduce the heat to
medium and simmer, uncovered, until the
vegetables are very soft, about 30 minutes.
Remove from the heat and let cool slightly.

Working in batches, purée the soup in a
blender until very smooth, 3–4 minutes per
batch. Strain the purée through a fine-mesh
sieve into a large saucepan. Add the reserved
oysters, cream, and lemon juice and bring to
a gentle simmer over medium heat. Simmer,
uncovered, until the oysters are slightly
firm to the touch and opaque and their
edges curl slightly, 1–2 minutes. Season
with salt and pepper and serve.

15

*Be careful not to
over-salt the soup,
as the prosciutto
garnish will add
a good amount
of salt. To make
it vegetarian, use
vegetable broth in
place of the chicken
broth and crispy
fried shallots for the
prosciutto.*

CREAMY CAULIFLOWER SOUP WITH CRISPY PROSCIUTTO

serves 4–6

2 oz (60 g) thinly sliced prosciutto

2 Tbsp unsalted butter

1 yellow onion, chopped

2 celery ribs, chopped

2 cloves garlic, minced

1 head cauliflower (about 1¾ lb/875 g),
coarsely chopped (about 4 cups)

¼ tsp freshly grated nutmeg

4 cups (36 fl oz/1 l) chicken broth,
plus more as needed

¼ cup (2 fl oz/60 ml) heavy cream

Salt and ground white pepper

Preheat the oven to 375°F (190°C). Place the
prosciutto slices in a single layer on a baking
sheet. Bake until crispy, 15–18 minutes. Let
cool, then crumble.

In a large, heavy pot, melt the butter over
medium-high heat. Add the onion, celery,
and garlic and sauté until soft, 5–7 minutes.
Add the cauliflower and nutmeg, stir well
to coat, and cook for 5 minutes. Add the
4 cups (32 fl oz/1 l) broth and bring to a boil.
Reduce the heat to low and simmer until the
cauliflower is very tender, 20–25 minutes.
Remove from the heat and let cool slightly.

Working in batches, purée the soup in a
blender. Return to the pot and add more
broth if the soup is too thick. Stir in the
cream. Return the soup just to a boil,
season with salt and pepper, and serve,
garnished with the prosciutto.

16

BLACK-EYED PEA SOUP WITH HERBS & GARLIC

serves 8–10

1 lb (500 g) black-eyed peas, picked over and rinsed

¼ cup (2 fl oz/60 ml) olive oil

1 large yellow onion, chopped

6 cloves garlic, thinly sliced

½ cup (4 fl oz/125 ml) dry white wine

4 cups (32 fl oz/1 l) chicken broth, plus more as needed

2 Tbsp tomato paste

Bouquet Garni (see left)

½ cup (¾ oz/20 g) chopped flat-leaf parsley

Salt and freshly ground pepper

A bouquet garni refers to a bundle of fresh herbs tied together with kitchen string. For this recipe, use 3 flat-leaf parsley sprigs, 2 thyme sprigs, and a bay leaf. Remember to remove and discard the bouquet garni prior to serving.

Put the black-eyed peas in a bowl with water to cover and soak for at least 4 hours or up to overnight. Drain.

In a large, heavy pot, warm the oil over medium-high heat. Add the onion and garlic and sauté until translucent, about 5 minutes. Add the wine and cook for 3 minutes. Add the black-eyed peas, 4 cups (32 fl oz/1 l) broth, and tomato paste and stir to combine. Bring the soup to a boil. Reduce the heat to low, add the bouquet garni, and simmer, uncovered, until the peas are tender, 45–55 minutes.

Remove the bouquet garni and add more broth if necessary. Stir in the chopped parsley, season with salt and pepper, and serve.

17

STONE SOUP

serves 6

3 Tbsp olive oil

2 yellow onions, chopped

2 cloves garlic, minced

¼ lb (125 g) bacon, in one piece

¼ lb (125 g) Mexican chorizo or fresh garlic sausage

4 boiling potatoes, peeled and chopped

4 carrots, peeled and chopped

2 turnips, peeled and chopped

1 small head savoy cabbage or 1 bunch kale, trimmed and shredded

2 cups (12 oz/375 g) canned diced plum tomatoes

1 bay leaf

8 cups (64 fl oz/2 l) chicken broth

1 can (15 oz/470 g) kidney beans, drained

½ cup (¾ oz/20 g) chopped cilantro

Salt and freshly ground pepper

This is the proverbial "stone" soup, created from the various ingredients given by curious villagers. In that vein, feel free to vary the ingredients depending on what you have available.

In a large, heavy pot, warm the oil over medium heat. Add the onions and garlic and sauté until tender, 7–10 minutes. Add the bacon, chorizo, potatoes, carrots, turnips, cabbage, tomatoes, bay leaf, and broth. Bring to a boil over high heat, reduce the heat to very low, and simmer until the vegetables are tender, about 30 minutes.

Skim off any foam from the surface and discard the bay leaf. Remove the meats and cut into bite-sized pieces. Return the meats to the pot and add the beans and cilantro. Simmer over medium heat for 5 minutes to warm through. Season with salt and pepper and serve.

18

Moles, sauces thickened with nuts, seeds, and, most famously, chocolate, are also made with a focus on vegetables, like this one, which derives its green color and some of its flavor from romaine lettuce. The stew, which also includes green chiles and cilantro, can be served on its own or over rice. Warm corn tortillas make a good accompaniment.

CHICKEN STEW IN GREEN MOLE SAUCE

serves 8

FOR THE CHICKEN & BROTH

1 chicken (about 4 lb/2 kg), cut into 8 serving pieces

1½ yellow onions, quartered

2-inch (5-cm) piece fresh ginger, peeled

2 carrots, halved crosswise

2 serrano chiles, halved and seeded

Salt and freshly ground pepper

FOR THE MOLE SAUCE

4 green Anaheim chiles

2 serrano chiles

4 tomatillos, papery husks removed

3–3½ cups (24–28 fl oz/750–875 ml) broth reserved from cooking chicken

2 Tbsp canola or sunflower oil

1 Tbsp hulled pumpkin seeds

2 tsp sesame seeds

8 blanched almonds

2 cloves garlic, chopped

½ yellow onion, coarsely chopped

1 green bell pepper, seeded and coarsely chopped

1 Tbsp unsalted peanut butter

2 allspice berries

1 tomato, seeded and chopped

1 cup (1½ oz/45 g) chopped flat-leaf parsley

1 large head romaine lettuce, leaves separated

1 corn tortilla, torn or chopped into coarse pieces, plus more as needed

Salt

To make the chicken and broth, put the chicken pieces in a large, heavy pot and add water to cover, about 10 cups (80 fl oz/2.5 l). Add the onions, ginger, carrots, serrano chiles, 2 tsp salt, and 2 tsp pepper. Place over high heat and bring to a boil. Reduce the heat to medium and simmer until the chicken is opaque throughout, about 1 hour and 15 minutes. Using tongs, transfer the chicken to a large bowl, cover, and set aside. Strain the broth through a fine-mesh sieve lined with cheesecloth, discarding the solids. This can be done a day ahead of time; refrigerate the chicken and broth until ready to use. »→

To make the mole sauce, place the Anaheim and serrano chiles under a broiler or on a preheated griddle. Roast, turning often, until the skin is charred, 3–5 minutes. Transfer to a plastic bag and let steam for 10 minutes.

Put the tomatillos on the griddle or in a dry frying pan and toast over medium heat until they just start to soften, about 2 minutes. Transfer to a small bowl. When the chiles are cool enough to handle, peel or scrape away the charred skins, cut the chiles in half lengthwise, and remove the stems, seeds, and ribs. In a food processor or blender, combine the chiles, tomatillos, and 1 cup (8 fl oz/250 ml) of the broth and process until smooth. Let stand for 15 minutes to allow the flavors to develop.

In a frying pan, warm the oil over medium-high heat. Add the pumpkin seeds, sesame seeds, and almonds and cook, stirring, until fragrant and just turning pale gold, 2–3 minutes. Transfer to the food processor or blender with the chile mixture, and add the garlic, onion, bell pepper, peanut butter, allspice, and tomato.

Add ½ cup (4 fl oz/125 ml) of the broth and purée until smooth. Add the parsley, lettuce, and tortilla pieces and purée again. The mixture will be bright green and somewhat thick. The consistency will vary depending on how much moisture was in the vegetables. If the sauce is too thick, add a little more broth. If it is too thin, add more tortilla pieces, a few at a time. Ideally, you will use 2–2½ cups (16–20 fl oz/500–625 ml) broth, and the sauce will have the consistency of thick cream.

Transfer the sauce to a saucepan, place over medium heat, and heat until the sauce turns a darker green, 10–15 minutes. Taste and season with salt to taste.

To assemble and serve, preheat the oven to 350°F (180°C). Arrange the chicken pieces in a baking dish, cover with aluminum foil, and bake until warmed throughout, about 30 minutes. Transfer the chicken to a deep serving platter or bowl, pour the sauce over it, and serve.

19

NEW ENGLAND CLAM CHOWDER

serves 6–8

3 strips bacon, chopped

1 Tbsp unsalted butter

2 celery ribs, chopped

1 yellow onion, finely chopped

3 fresh thyme sprigs or ¼ tsp dried thyme

2 large russet potatoes, peeled and cut into ½-inch (12-mm) cubes

2 cans (6½ oz/200 g each) clam meat, drained and chopped, clam juice reserved

1½ cups (12 fl oz/375 ml) milk

1 cup (8 fl oz/250 ml) heavy cream

Salt and freshly ground pepper

Chopped flat-leaf parsley for garnish

You can use the meat of 2 lb (1 kg) freshly steamed clams if you prefer. Littleneck or cherrystones are good varieties for chowder. Discard any clams that fail to close to the touch, then steam them in a wide, covered saucepan with 1 cup (8 fl oz/ 250 ml) water until they open, about 5 minutes. Discard any clams that do not open. Let cool, then remove the meat from the shells.

In a large saucepan over medium heat, cook the bacon, stirring often, until it starts to brown and has rendered some of its fat, about 3 minutes. Using a slotted spoon, transfer to paper towels to drain. Add the butter to the bacon drippings. When it melts, add the celery, onion, and thyme and sauté until the onion is translucent, about 3 minutes. Add the potatoes and stir well. Add the reserved clam liquor and 2 cups (16 fl oz/500 ml) water and bring to a boil. Reduce the heat to low, cover, and simmer until the potatoes are tender, about 20 minutes.

Add the milk and cream, stirring well to combine. Add the clam meat, heat through, and season to taste with salt and pepper. Discard the thyme sprigs and serve, sprinkled with the reserved bacon and parsley.

20

PARMESAN STRACIATELLA WITH KALE

serves 6–8

8 cups (64 fl oz/2 l) chicken broth

1 bunch kale, thick stems and ribs removed, roughly torn

1 tsp cornstarch

5 eggs

Salt and freshly ground pepper

1 cup (4 oz/125 g) grated good-quality Parmesan cheese

2 Tbsp extra-virgin olive oil

Just a few elements make up this simple soup, so use only the finest-quality ingredients you can find, like rich chicken broth, farm-fresh eggs, and freshly grated Parmigiano-Reggiano cheese. Spinach can be substituted for the kale.

In a large saucepan, bring the broth to a simmer over medium-high heat. Divide the kale among bowls.

In a bowl, mix together the cornstarch and 2 tsp water. Add the eggs, season with salt and pepper, and whisk to blend.

Stir two-thirds of the cheese and the oil into the broth. Stir the egg mixture and drizzle into the broth in a circular motion. Stir gently so that the egg forms thin ribbons. Remove from the heat and let stand until the eggs are cooked through, about 1½ minutes. Ladle the broth over the kale and serve, passing the remaining cheese at the table.

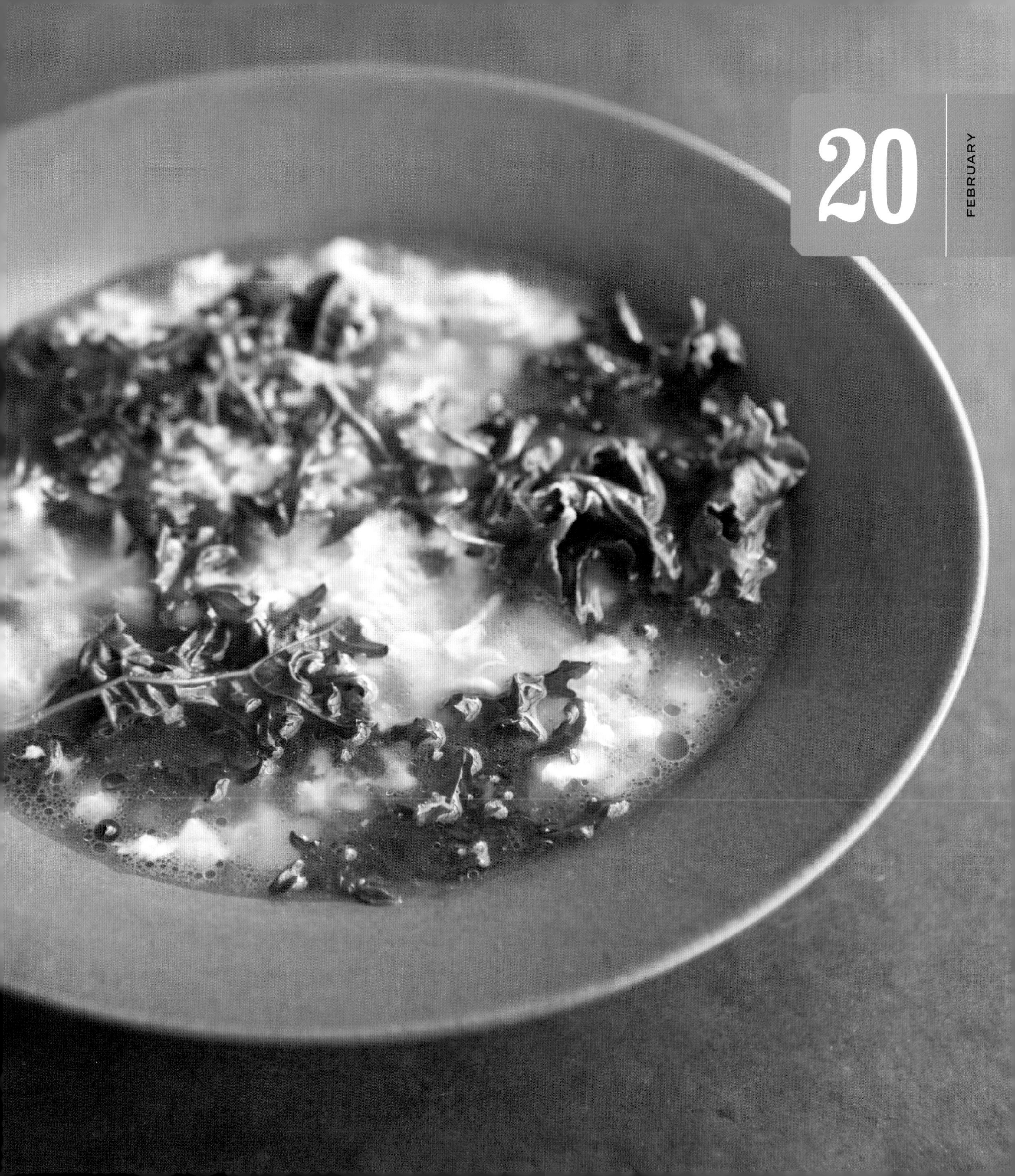

FEBRUARY

21

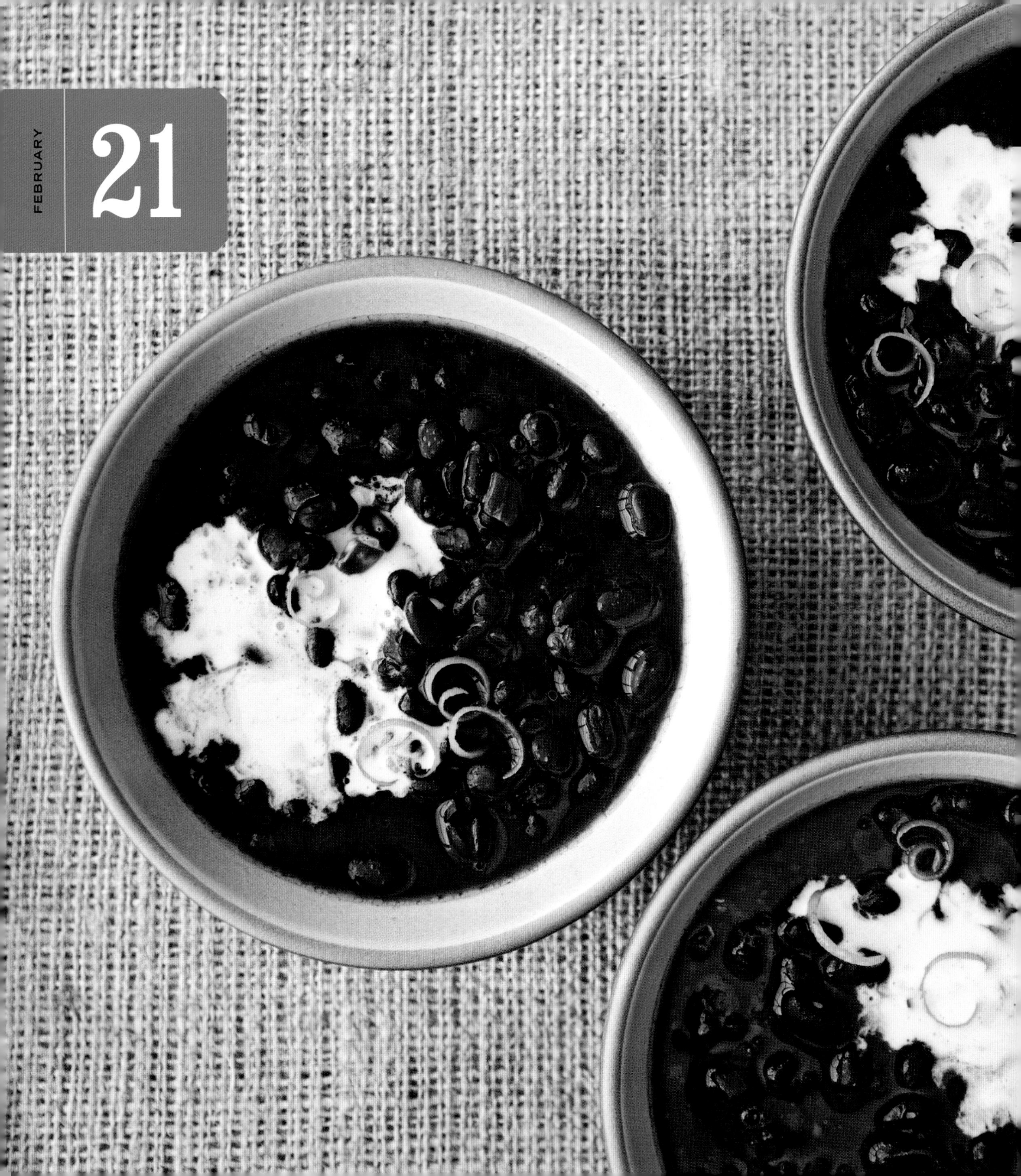

21

BLACK BEAN SOUP WITH MEYER LEMON CRÈME FRAÎCHE

serves 4–6

½ lb (250 g) dried black beans, picked over and rinsed

1 Tbsp olive oil

1 small white onion, chopped

2 cloves garlic, minced

1 small jalapeño chile, seeded and minced

1 tsp ground cumin

¼ cup (2 fl oz/60 ml) dry sherry

4 cups (32 fl oz/1 l) chicken or vegetable broth

Salt and freshly ground pepper

Meyer Lemon Crème Fraîche (left)

2 green onions, dark and light green parts only, sliced (optional)

To make the Meyer lemon crème fraîche, in a small bowl, combine ½ cup (4 oz/125 g) room-temperature crème fraîche or sour cream, the grated zest of 1 Meyer lemon, 1 Tbsp fresh Meyer lemon juice, and a pinch of salt.

Place the dried beans in a bowl with cold water to cover and soak for at least 4 hours or up to overnight. Drain.

In a large, heavy pot, warm the oil over medium-high heat. Add the onion and garlic and sauté until softened, about 5 minutes. Add the jalapeño and cumin and cook, stirring constantly, for 2 minutes. Add the beans, sherry, and broth and bring to a boil. Reduce the heat to low and simmer, covered, until the beans are tender, about 1¼ hours.

For a smooth soup, remove the pot from the heat and let cool slightly. Working in batches, purée the soup in a blender. Return to the pot and warm over low heat. Season with salt and pepper.

Top the soup with the crème fraîche and green onions, if using, and serve.

22

THAI SQUASH & COCONUT MILK SOUP

serves 6

4 shallots, quartered

2 red or green serrano or jalapeño chiles, seeded

1 lemongrass stalk, center white part only, smashed and chopped

1 can (14 fl oz/430 ml) coconut milk

2 cups (16 fl oz/500 ml) chicken broth or water

6 kaffir lime leaves, spines removed

1 kabocha, acorn, or butternut squash (about 1 lb/500 g), peeled, seeded, and cut into ¾-inch (2-cm) pieces

1½ Tbsp Asian fish sauce

1 Tbsp fresh lime juice

½ tsp sugar

½ cup (½ oz/15 g) basil leaves, preferably Thai

Fresh Thai basil, which has a more assertive flavor than Italian sweet basil, is worth seeking out to garnish this soup. For a heartier meal, serve the soup over a bed of steamed jasmine rice.

In a blender, combine the shallots, chiles, lemongrass, and ¼ cup (2 fl oz/60 ml) water. Process to form a smooth paste.

Open the can of coconut milk without shaking it. Scrape the thick cream from the top into a large, heavy pot. Stir in the spice paste and bring to a boil over medium-high heat. Reduce the heat to medium and cook uncovered, stirring occasionally, until fragrant, about 5 minutes. Add the remaining coconut milk, broth, lime leaves, and squash. Stir to combine, raise the heat to medium-high, and bring to a boil. Reduce the heat to low and simmer uncovered, stirring once or twice, until the squash is tender, about 15 minutes.

Stir in the fish sauce, lime juice, sugar, and basil, and serve.

23

Kalamata olives lend a strong briny flavor to this rich stew, although pitted green olives would be delicious as well. Buy an organic orange, if you can, or else be sure to wash the orange thoroughly before removing the zest.

BEEF STEW WITH ORANGE ZEST & RED WINE

serves 6–8

2 Tbsp all-purpose flour

Salt and freshly ground pepper

3 lb (1.5 kg) beef chuck roast, trimmed and cut into 1½-inch (4-cm) chunks

3 Tbsp olive oil

1 orange

2 yellow onions, chopped

3 cloves garlic, minced

2 tsp minced thyme

1½ Tbsp fennel seeds, crushed

¾ cup (6 fl oz/180 ml) dry red wine

¾ cup (6 fl oz/180 ml) chicken broth

1 cup (6 oz/185 g) canned diced tomatoes

4 carrots, peeled and sliced

1½ cups (7 oz/220 g) Kalamata olives, pitted and halved

¼ cup (⅓ oz/10 g) finely chopped flat-leaf parsley

In a resealable plastic bag, combine the flour, 2 tsp salt, and 1 tsp pepper. Add the beef, seal the bag, and shake to coat. In a large, heavy pot, warm 1 Tbsp of the oil over medium-high heat. Remove half the beef pieces from the bag, shaking off excess flour, and add to the pot in a single layer. Cook without stirring until deeply browned, about 4 minutes. Turn and cook without stirring until deeply browned on the second side, about 4 minutes. Transfer to a bowl. Repeat with 1 Tbsp of the oil and the remaining beef. Wipe the pot clean.

Using a vegetable peeler, remove the zest from half of the orange in wide strips. Finely grate the zest from the remaining orange half. Set aside.

Add the remaining 1 Tbsp oil to the pot and warm over medium heat. Add the onions and sauté until just starting to soften, about 2 minutes. Stir in the garlic, orange zest strips, thyme, and fennel seeds and sauté until fragrant, about 45 seconds. Add the wine, raise the heat to high, and bring to a boil, stirring to scrape up any browned ⤞

bits on the bottom of the pot. Cook until reduced by half, about 4 minutes. Stir in the broth and tomatoes with their juices, then add the browned beef and any accumulated juices. Bring to a boil, reduce the heat to low, cover, and simmer until the beef is tender, about 2½ hours.

Add the carrots and olives, pushing them down into the liquid. Raise the heat to medium, cover, and cook until the carrots are tender, about 8 minutes. Stir in the grated orange zest and the parsley, season with salt and pepper, and serve.

- -

24

This recipe departs just a bit from the traditional split pea soup: instead of adding the ham during the cooking process, it is sautéed and served crispy as a garnish, adding flavor and texture at the same time.

YELLOW SPLIT PEA SOUP WITH HAM

serves 4

3 oz (90 g) thinly sliced ham

1 Tbsp unsalted butter

1 Tbsp olive oil

1 yellow onion, chopped

1 celery rib, chopped

4 cups (32 fl oz/1 l) chicken broth

½ lb (250 g) yellow split peas, picked over and rinsed

Salt and freshly ground pepper

Heat a large, heavy pot over medium-high heat. Add the ham and cook, turning once, until crisp, 7–8 minutes. Let cool, then crumble into bite-sized pieces.

Add the butter and oil to the pot and heat over medium-high heat until the butter is melted. Add the onion and celery and sauté until soft, about 5 minutes. Add the broth and bring to a boil. Add the peas, reduce the heat to low, and cook, partially covered and stirring occasionally, until the peas are tender, 45–50 minutes. Season with salt and pepper and serve, garnished with ham.

PASTA & CHICKPEA SOUP

serves 4–6

1¼ cups (7½ oz/235 g) dried chickpeas, picked over and rinsed

3 Tbsp olive oil, plus ½ cup (4 fl oz/125 ml)

2 carrots, peeled and finely diced

1 large yellow onion, finely diced

1½ tsp minced garlic

⅓ cup (2 oz/60 g) diced tomato

2 thyme sprigs

Salt and freshly ground pepper

½ lb (250 g) tubetti pasta

¼ cup (2 fl oz/60 ml) vegetable oil

3 rosemary sprigs, cut into 1½-inch (4-cm) lengths

Shaved Parmesan cheese for serving

The marriage of pasta and legumes is a favorite in Italian cuisine. In this rustic Roman soup, known as pasta e ceci, chickpeas are paired with tubetti in a hearty broth—delicious proof that the simple can be sublime. If you cannot find tubetti, another short pasta, such as ditalini or garganelli, can be substituted.

Put the chickpeas in a bowl with cold water to cover and soak for at least 4 hours or up to overnight. Drain and set aside.

In a large, heavy pot, warm the 3 Tbsp olive oil over medium heat. Add the carrots and onion and cook, stirring occasionally, until softened, about 8 minutes. Add the garlic and tomato and cook, stirring frequently, for 1 minute. Add the chickpeas, thyme sprigs, and 6 cups (48 fl oz/1.5 l) water, raise the heat to medium-high, and bring to a boil. Reduce the heat to medium-low and simmer until the chickpeas are tender, about 1 hour. Remove and discard the thyme sprigs.

Meanwhile, bring a pot of salted water to a boil. Add the pasta and cook until al dente according to the package directions. Drain and set aside.

In a small sauté pan, warm the vegetable oil over medium-high heat. Add the rosemary sprigs and fry, stirring occasionally, until crisp, 1–1½ minutes. Transfer to a paper towel–lined plate and season lightly with salt.

Drain the chickpeas, reserving the cooking liquid. Place 2 cups (14 oz/440 g) of the chickpeas in a wide, shallow bowl and mash until almost smooth. ↠

Transfer to a large, heavy pot. Add the remaining chickpeas and 1 cup (8 fl oz/250 ml) of the cooking liquid and bring to a simmer over medium-high heat. Add the pasta and the ½ cup (4 fl oz/125 ml) olive oil and stir until emulsified. Season with salt and pepper.

Serve, garnished with the fried rosemary sprigs and cheese.

SAUSAGE & KALE SOUP

serves 4–6

¼ cup (2 fl oz/60 ml) olive oil

2 yellow onions, finely chopped

4 cloves garlic, minced

3 large russet potatoes (about 2½ lb/1.25 kg), peeled and thinly sliced

6 cups (48 fl oz/1.5 l) chicken or vegetable broth

¾ lb (375 g) kielbasa or other cooked sausage, sliced

1 bunch kale, thick stems and ribs removed, thinly sliced

Salt and freshly ground pepper

Extra-virgin olive oil for drizzling

In Portugal, where this dish is known as caldo verde (or "green broth"), kale is a staple ingredient. Linguiça or chorizo are the commonly used sausages, but any garlicky pork sausage, such as kielbasa, will do. Serve with warm corn bread.

In a large, heavy pot, warm the olive oil over medium heat. Add the onions and garlic and sauté until golden, 5–7 minutes. Add the potatoes and sauté for about 2 minutes. Add the broth, cover, and bring to a boil. Reduce the heat to a simmer and cook until the potatoes are tender, about 20 minutes. Remove from the heat and let cool slightly.

Working in batches, coarsely purée the soup in a blender, leaving some potato slices intact. Return to the pot, add the sausage, cover, and simmer over medium heat until the sausage is heated through, about 5 minutes. Add the kale and cook, uncovered, until wilted but still bright green, 3–5 minutes. Season with salt and pepper and serve, drizzled with extra-virgin olive oil.

27

The French are known for their frugality in the kitchen, and potage, a generic term for a thick soup, is an excellent example of how they accomplish food with character while making the most of simple ingredients. Carrots are used here, but nearly any vegetable can be prepared this same way, cooked in broth with a little potato for thickening.

CLASSIC FRENCH POTAGE
serves 4–6

3 cups (24 fl oz/750 ml) each chicken or vegetable broth and water

1 lb (500 g) potatoes, peeled and chopped

½ yellow onion, chopped

2 large carrots, peeled and chopped

2 celery ribs, chopped

2 cups (4 oz/125 g) chopped spinach or chard

¼ cup (¼ oz/7 g) flat-leaf parsley leaves

Salt and freshly ground pepper

In a large, heavy pot, bring the broth to a simmer over medium-high heat. Add the potatoes, onion, carrots, celery, spinach, parsley, ½ tsp salt, and ½ tsp pepper and bring to a boil. Reduce the heat to medium-low, cover, and simmer until the vegetables are fork-tender, 30–40 minutes. Let cool slightly.

Working in batches, purée the soup in a food processor or blender. Return to the pot, taste and adjust the seasoning, and serve.

28

Long, slow simmering gives this Texas-style chili time to develop a complex, robust flavor and hearty texture. You can garnish the chili with just about anything you like, from sour cream to chopped onions to shredded cheese.

CHILI CON CARNE
serves 4–6

2 lb (1 kg) boneless beef chuck, trimmed and cut into ½-inch (12-mm) cubes

Salt and freshly ground pepper

2 Tbsp canola oil

½ cup (2 oz/60 g) finely chopped mixed chiles, such as jalapeño, serrano, and poblano, seeded if desired

1 small red bell pepper, seeded and finely chopped

8 cloves garlic, minced

4 tsp chili powder

1 tsp ground cumin

½ tsp ground coriander

1 can (28 oz/875 g) diced tomatoes

1 tsp dried oregano

2 cups (16 fl oz/500 ml) beef broth or water

1 cup (8 oz/250 g) sour cream (optional)

Leaves from 12 cilantro sprigs

Sprinkle the meat evenly with salt and pepper. In a large, heavy frying pan, warm 1 Tbsp of the oil over medium heat. Working in batches, brown the beef cubes on all sides, about 5 minutes per batch. Transfer to a large, heavy pot.

Warm the remaining 1 Tbsp oil in the pan over medium heat. Add the chiles, bell pepper, and garlic and sauté until the vegetables are softened and beginning to turn golden, about 5 minutes. Stir in the chili powder, cumin, and coriander and cook for about 1 minute. Add the tomatoes with their juices and the oregano, season with salt and pepper, and stir well to scrape up any browned bits on the pan bottom.

Add the vegetable mixture to the pot with the beef. Place over medium heat, add the broth, and bring to a gentle boil, stirring occasionally. Reduce the heat to maintain a gentle simmer, cover, and cook until the meat is very tender and the liquid is slightly thickened, about 2½ hours. If the chili seems too soupy, uncover the pot for the last 30 minutes to evaporate some of the liquid.

Season the chili with salt and pepper and serve, garnished with sour cream, if desired, and cilantro leaves.

5
BROCCOLI-LEEK SOUP
page 61

6
WILD RICE SOUP WITH BACON
page 61

7
SWEET POTATO–PUMPKIN SOUP WITH BRUSSELS SPROUT HASH
page 63

12
LEMONY ASPARAGUS & RICE SOUP WITH PARMESAN
page 65

13
BABY BOK CHOY & BEEF NOODLE SOUP
page 66

14
CREAM OF ASPARAGUS SOUP
page 66

19
EAM OF PORTOBELLO MUSHROOM SOUP WITH CHERVIL CREAM
page 71

20
PASTA IN BROTH WITH CHIVES
page 71

21
MISO SOUP WITH SLIVERED ROOT VEGETABLES & WATERCRESS
page 72

26
FIVE-SPICE BROTH WITH SALMON & ONION DUMPLINGS
page 76

27
FENNEL BROTH WITH CHARD & CHORIZO
page 77

28
BLACK-EYED PEA STEW
page 77

As frost wanes and temperatures warm, tender, green vegetables begin to break ground. Celadon-hued stalks, such as asparagus, lemongrass, and early artichokes appear, along with delicate greens like sorrel, watercress, and pea shoots. In soups, these young vegetables pair nicely with fresh herbs, mellow spices, and citrus. Rainy days mixed with breaks of sun make for prime mushroom season, adding meaty flavor and texture to the soup pot.

march

1

GREEN GARLIC & NEW POTATO SOUP

serves 6

1 Tbsp unsalted butter

20 heads green garlic (about 6 oz/185 g), ½–1 inch (12 mm–2.5 cm) in diameter at root end

8 cups (64 fl oz/2 l) chicken broth

1¼ lb (625 g) red new potatoes, peeled and quartered

FOR THE GARNISH

1½ Tbsp extra-virgin olive oil

3 heads green garlic, ½–1 inch (12 mm–2.5 cm) in diameter at root end, bulbs minced

2 Tbsp chopped flat-leaf parsley

Salt and freshly ground pepper

¼ cup (2 fl oz/60 ml) heavy cream

2 Tbsp white wine vinegar

Just as new potatoes are potatoes that haven't reached maturity, green garlic is simply immature garlic. Mild in flavor, it resembles a baby leek or green onion. Look for it at farmers' markets in early spring, or substitute 1 clove of mature garlic for every head of green garlic.

In a large, heavy pot, melt the butter over low heat. Coarsely chop the green garlic bulbs. Add to the pot along with ½ cup (4 fl oz/125 ml) of the broth. Cover and cook until the garlic is soft, about 20 minutes. Add the potatoes and the remaining 7½ cups (60 fl oz/1.75 l) broth and raise the heat to medium-high. Simmer, covered, until the potatoes are soft, about 20 minutes.

Meanwhile, to make the garnish, in a small saucepan over low heat, warm the oil. Add the minced green garlic bulbs and sauté until soft, about 2 minutes. Do not let the garlic turn golden. Let cool for 10 minutes. Stir in the parsley and season with salt and pepper. Set aside.

Remove the soup from the heat and let cool slightly. Working in batches, purée the soup well in a blender. Strain through a fine-mesh sieve into a clean pot. Stir in the cream and vinegar. Season with salt and pepper and serve, topped with the garnish.

2

THAI CHICKEN & BASIL SOUP

serves 6

8 cups (64 fl oz/2 l) chicken broth

4 skinless, boneless chicken breast halves (about 1½ lb/750 g total weight)

½ cup (¾ oz/20 g) chopped Thai or Italian basil, plus sprigs for garnish

1 Tbsp minced garlic

2 Tbsp peeled and minced fresh ginger

2 serrano chiles, seeded and minced

4 green onions, sliced

Salt and freshly ground pepper

Thai basil has green leaves veined with purple stems, and a sweet, slightly anise taste that is an important part of the Thai flavor profile. It's used here to infuse the broth and as a garnish. If you cannot find Thai basil, holy basil, which comes in two types, light green and red-stemmed with a reddish tint on the leaves, can be substituted. It is a popular Thai ingredient as well and has a spicier flavor. More easily found green or purple basil can also be used.

In a large, heavy pot, bring the broth to a simmer over medium-high heat. Add the chicken, reduce the heat to medium-low, and simmer until the chicken is opaque throughout, about 20 minutes. Using tongs, transfer the chicken to a cutting board and, when cool enough to handle, shred or dice the meat and return it to the broth.

Add ¼ cup (⅓ oz/10 g) of the basil, the garlic, ginger, chiles, green onions, ½ tsp salt, and ¼ tsp pepper and simmer over medium-high heat for 5 minutes. Taste and adjust the seasoning. Stir in the remaining ¼ cup (⅓ oz/10 g) basil and serve, garnished with basil sprigs.

3

Dried morel mushrooms create a sumptuous butter topping for this soup, which showcases a favorite spring vegetable. Trimming artichokes takes some technique, but it's worth learning how to do it for the tender hearts. This soup is excellent served with a roast chicken.

ARTICHOKE SOUP WITH MOREL BUTTER

serves 4–6

FOR THE MOREL BUTTER

1 Tbsp small pieces dried morel mushrooms

Boiling water as needed

1 small clove garlic

Salt

¼ cup (2 oz/60 g) unsalted butter, at room temperature

1 Tbsp white wine vinegar, or juice of ½ lemon

4 large or 5–6 medium artichokes (about 2½ lb/1.25 kg)

1 Tbsp unsalted butter

3 Tbsp olive oil

4 shallots, chopped

2 cloves garlic, chopped

½ cup (4 fl oz/125 ml) dry white wine

2 cups (16 fl oz/500 ml) chicken broth

1 bay leaf, 3 thyme sprigs, and 4 large flat-leaf parsley sprigs tied together to make a bouquet garni

Salt and freshly ground pepper

To make the morel butter, in a small bowl, combine the mushrooms with boiling water to cover. Cover and soak for 30 minutes. Drain, rinsing if they are gritty, then squeeze out the excess moisture. In a small food processor, process the garlic with a pinch of salt until minced. Add the mushrooms and process until finely chopped. Add the butter and process until mixed. Transfer to a bowl and refrigerate.

Fill a large bowl with water and add the vinegar. Peel, then cut off the stem of each artichoke flush with the bottom. Slice the stems and add to the vinegar water. Snap off the outer leaves until you reach the tender inner leaves, placing the outer leaves in a saucepan. Cut off the top one-third of each artichoke and quarter the rest lengthwise. Cut out the choke from each quarter. As you work, add the quarters to the vinegar water.

Add 5 cups (40 fl oz/1.25 l) water to the saucepan holding the outer leaves. Bring to a boil over medium-high heat. Cook, uncovered, until the water takes on the mineral flavor of artichokes, 15 minutes. ⇥

Strain through a fine-mesh sieve into a large measuring cup. Discard the leaves. You should have about 4 cups (32 fl oz/1 l) liquid.

Drain the artichokes and chop. In a large, heavy pot, melt the butter with the oil over medium-high heat. Add the shallots and garlic and sauté until softened, about 5 minutes. Add the chopped artichokes and sauté until half cooked, about 5 minutes. Add the wine and cook until reduced to 1–2 Tbsp. Add the artichoke liquid, the broth, and the bouquet garni. Bring to a boil, reduce the heat to medium, and cook, uncovered, until the artichokes are just tender, 10–15 minutes.

Remove from the heat and discard the bouquet. Using a slotted spoon, transfer the artichoke pieces to a food processor. Add a small amount of the cooking liquid, and purée. Return to the pot and stir to combine. Reheat over medium-high heat and season with salt and pepper. Serve, topped with some of the morel butter.

4

Sorrel has a slightly sharp flavor and is a wonderful addition to light soups such as this one. If you can't find sorrel, add a Latin twist with a squeeze of fresh lime juice and a sprinkle of minced cilantro and jalapeño chile just before serving.

SHRIMP, MUSHROOM & SORREL SOUP

serves 4–6

3 oz (90 g) sorrel or baby spinach

3 Tbsp olive oil

2 shallots, minced

4 cloves garlic, minced

½ lb (250 g) white mushrooms, sliced

5 cups (40 fl oz/1.25 l) chicken broth

1 lb (500 g) shrimp, peeled and deveined

Salt and freshly ground pepper

Remove any tough stems from the sorrel and cut the leaves crosswise into ribbons.

In a saucepan, warm the olive oil over medium-high heat. Add the shallots and garlic and sauté until soft, about 5 minutes. Add the mushrooms and sauté, stirring often, until they are soft and brown, 7–10 minutes. Add the broth and bring to a boil. Add the shrimp and cook until they are bright pink, 2–3 minutes. Remove the pan from the heat and stir in the sorrel. Season with salt and pepper and serve.

5

MARCH

BROCCOLI-LEEK SOUP

serves 4

2 Tbsp olive oil

2 leeks, white and pale green parts, finely chopped

1½ lb (750 g) broccoli, tough stems peeled, florets and stems cut into 1-inch (2.5-cm) pieces

4 cups (32 fl oz/1 l) chicken broth

Salt and ground white pepper

¼ cup (2 oz/60 g) sour cream or plain yogurt

Garlic Croutons (left)

2 Tbsp finely chopped chives

To make the garlic croutons, cut 3 slices coarse country bread into bite-sized cubes. In a frying pan over medium-high heat, combine 3 Tbsp olive oil and 2 cloves garlic, thinly sliced. Fry until the garlic turns brown; do not let it burn. Scoop out and discard the garlic. Add the bread to the pan and fry, stirring often, until golden brown, about 5 minutes.

In a large, heavy pot, warm the oil over medium heat. Add the leeks and sauté until softened, 3–5 minutes. Add the broccoli and sauté until slightly softened, about 2 minutes. Add the broth and bring to a simmer over medium heat. Cover partially and cook until the vegetables are tender, 15–20 minutes. Remove from the heat and let cool.

Working in batches, purée the soup in a blender or food processor. Return to the pot and reheat over medium heat. Season with salt and pepper and serve, garnished with the sour cream, croutons, and chives.

6

MARCH

WILD RICE SOUP WITH BACON

serves 4

8 slices thick-cut bacon

1 Tbsp unsalted butter

1 carrot, peeled and chopped

1 yellow onion, chopped

2 cloves garlic, minced

½ tsp dried thyme

¼ cup (2 fl oz/60 ml) dry white wine

4 cups (32 fl oz/1 l) chicken broth

1 cup (6 oz/185 g) wild rice

2 Tbsp heavy cream

Salt and freshly ground pepper

Wild rice brings chewy texture and a nutty, earthy flavor to soup. Here, a touch of cream and smoky bacon transform a simple soup into a luxurious treat. Serve with a green salad dressed with a citrus vinaigrette.

Lay the bacon slices on the bottom of a large, heavy pot. Place over medium-high heat and cook, turning once, until crisp, about 8 minutes. Transfer to paper towels to drain. Let cool, then cut into 1-inch (2.5-cm) pieces. Set aside.

Add the butter, carrot, onion, and garlic to the pot and cook over medium-high heat, stirring occasionally, until the carrot begins to soften, 5–7 minutes. Stir in the thyme and cook for 1 minute. Add the wine and cook for about 3 minutes, stirring to scrape up any browned bits on the bottom of the pot. Add the broth and rice and bring to a boil. Reduce the heat to low, cover, and simmer until the rice is tender, about 1 hour.

Add the cream and bacon to the soup, return to a simmer, and cook, uncovered, until the soup thickens, about 5 minutes. Season with salt and pepper and serve.

MARCH

7

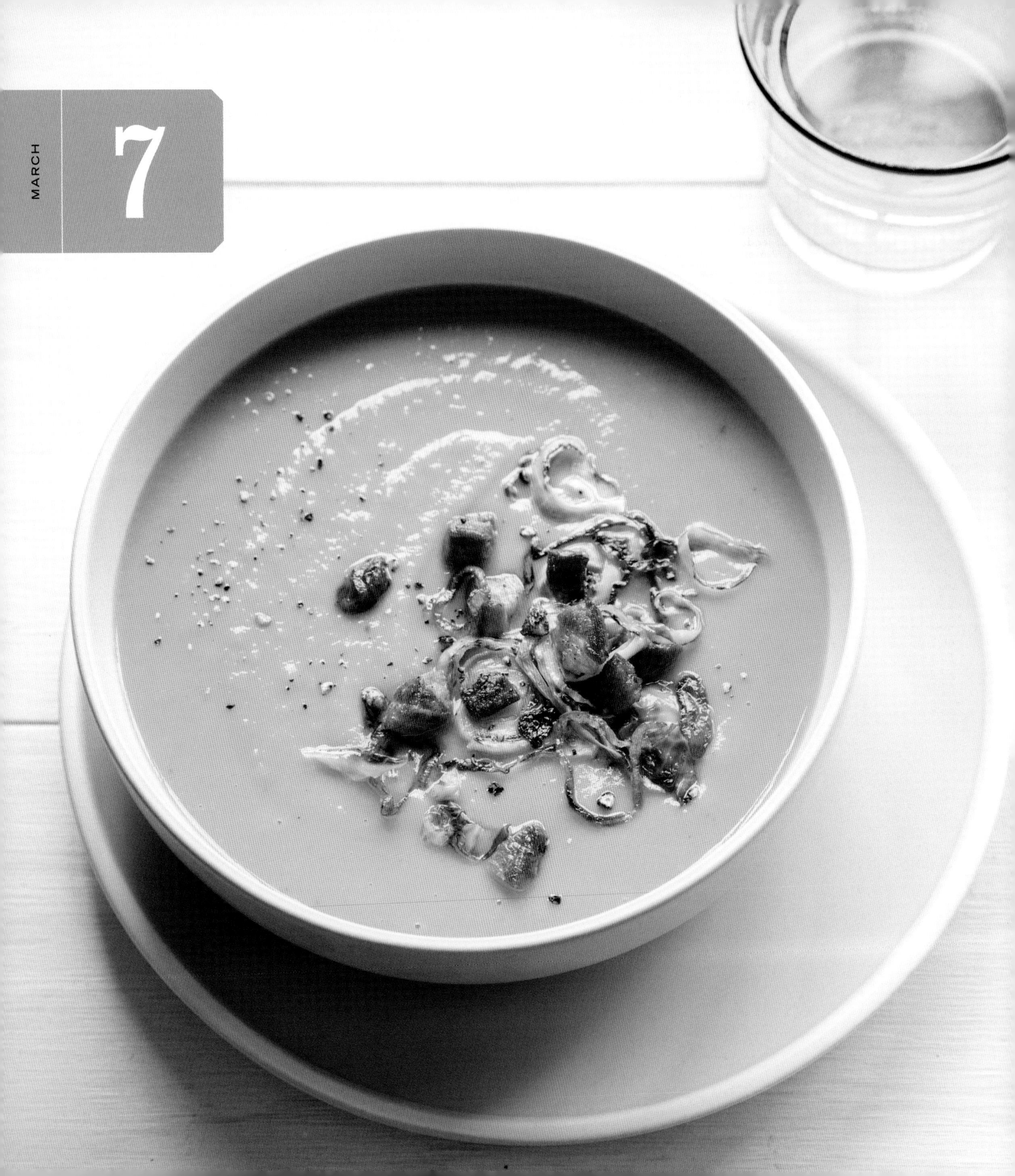

7

This soup is like Thanksgiving in a bowl. The slightly chunky texture of the hash garnish contrasts delightfully with the creamy soup, and the mix of colors makes for a beautiful presentation. It's okay to substitute canned pumpkin, but be certain you buy one that lists only one ingredient: pumpkin. If you have hash left over, serve it with a poached egg for breakfast or over roast pork for another weeknight dinner.

SWEET POTATO–PUMPKIN SOUP WITH BRUSSELS SPROUT HASH

serves 4–6

2 sweet potatoes (about 1¼ lb/625 g total weight), peeled and cut into 1-inch (2.5-cm) pieces

1 small pumpkin (about 2½ lb/1.25 kg), peeled, seeded, and cut into 1-inch (2.5-cm) pieces

6 Tbsp (3 fl oz/90 ml) olive oil

Salt and freshly ground pepper

1 yellow onion, chopped

½ tsp ground nutmeg

4 cups (32 fl oz/1 l) chicken broth

FOR THE BRUSSELS SPROUT–PANCETTA HASH

¼ lb (125 g) pancetta, diced

1 large shallot, halved and thinly sliced

⅓ lb (170 g) Brussels sprouts, cut into ¼-inch (6-mm) pieces

1 Tbsp olive oil

Salt and freshly ground pepper

Preheat the oven to 400°F (200°C). Line a baking sheet with parchment paper. Pile the sweet potatoes and pumpkin on the prepared baking sheet and toss with 4 Tbsp (2 fl oz/60 ml) of the oil. Spread in a single layer and season generously with salt and pepper. Roast, stirring once, until the vegetables are golden, about 30 minutes. Set aside.

In a large, heavy pot, warm the remaining 2 Tbsp oil over medium-high heat. Add the onion, season with salt and pepper, and cook, stirring occasionally, until translucent, about 6 minutes. Stir in the nutmeg and toast for 1 minute. Add the sweet potatoes, pumpkin, and broth and stir to combine. Let cool slightly.

Working in batches, purée the soup in a food processor or blender. Return to the pot and place over high heat. Bring to a boil, reduce the heat to low, and simmer for 15 minutes. Season with salt and pepper and keep warm over low heat.

To make the Brussels sprout–pancetta hash, in a frying pan, cook the pancetta over medium heat, stirring frequently, until most of the fat is rendered, about 4 minutes (it will not be fully cooked). ↠

Stir in the shallot and raise the heat to medium-high. Cook, stirring occasionally, until the shallot is soft and beginning to turn golden, about 4 minutes. Add the Brussels sprouts and oil, season with salt and pepper, and cook, stirring frequently, until the sprouts are fork-tender, about 6 minutes.

Serve the soup, topped with the hash.

8

A creamy vegetable soup is a hallmark of home cooking. Here, cauliflower is simmered with potato and milk and then puréed to a smooth, velvety texture. To make the soup even creamier, use a mixture of cream and milk.

CAULIFLOWER SOUP WITH CHERVIL

serves 6

1 small head cauliflower (about ¾ lb/375 g), coarsely chopped (including core)

1 boiling potato (about ½ lb/250 g), peeled and diced

3¼–3½ cups (26–28 fl oz/810–875 ml) milk

Salt and ground white pepper

2 Tbsp unsalted butter

⅛ tsp grated nutmeg

¼ cup (⅓ oz/10 g) chervil or flat-leaf parsley leaves

Bring a large saucepan of water to a boil over medium-high heat. Add the cauliflower and potato, reduce the heat to medium, and cook until the vegetables soften slightly, about 5 minutes. Drain well and return to the pan. Add 2½ cups (20 fl oz/625 ml) of the milk and ½ tsp salt and bring to a boil over medium-high heat. Reduce the heat to medium, cover, and cook until the cauliflower and potato are tender, 15–20 minutes. Remove from the heat and let cool slightly.

Working in batches, purée the soup in a blender or food processor, adding the remaining milk as needed to reach the desired creamy consistency. Transfer to a clean saucepan and bring to a simmer over medium heat. Stir in the butter, the nutmeg, and ¼ tsp pepper. Serve, garnished with the chervil.

9

TURKEY CHILI WITH TWO BEANS

serves 10–12

Here, traditional chili has been lightened up by swapping out the usual beef for ground turkey. Increase the amount of chili powder and red pepper flakes if you are favor highly spiced chili. In addition to the garnishes suggested, you might also offer chopped green or red onions, chopped tomatoes, and a selection of cheeses, and instead of dressing the bowls in the kitchen, set out all of the garnishes on the table and let guests top their own bowls. You can store leftovers in the freezer for up to 2 months.

¾ lb (375 g) dried Snow Cap beans, picked over and rinsed

¾ lb (375 g) dried Good Mother Stallard beans, picked over and rinsed

2 Tbsp canola oil

2 lb (1 kg) ground turkey

Salt and freshly ground black pepper

3 jalapeño chiles, seeded and diced

2 yellow onions, diced

1 large red bell pepper, seeded and diced

3 cloves garlic, minced

2 Tbsp tomato paste

¼ cup (1 oz/30 g) chili powder

1 tsp ground cumin

1 tsp dried oregano

½ tsp red pepper flakes

2 cans (14½ oz/455 g each) diced tomatoes with juices

2 sweet potatoes (about 1 lb/500 g each), peeled and cut into ½-inch (12-mm) dice

2 cups (16 fl oz/500 ml) chicken broth

½ head green cabbage, quartered, cored, and shredded

Juice of 1 lime

¼ cup (⅓ oz/10 g) chopped cilantro

Grated Monterey jack cheese for serving

Diced avocado for serving

Put the beans in a large bowl with cold water to cover and soak for at least 4 hours or up to overnight. Drain and set aside.

In a large sauté pan, warm 1 Tbsp of the oil over medium-high heat. Add the ground turkey and cook, breaking it up with a wooden spoon, until browned, about 10 minutes. Season with salt and black pepper. Transfer to a bowl.

In the same pan, warm the remaining 1 Tbsp oil. Add the jalapeños, onions, and bell pepper and cook, stirring occasionally, until softened, 4–6 minutes. Add the garlic, tomato paste, chili powder, cumin, oregano, and red pepper flakes and cook, stirring occasionally, until fragrant, 1–2 minutes. Add the tomatoes with their juices, the beans, sweet potatoes, broth, 2 cups (16 fl oz/500 ml) water, and the turkey and bring to a simmer.

↠

Transfer the contents of the pan to a large, heavy pot, place over medium-high heat, and bring to a boil. Reduce the heat to medium-low, cover partially, and simmer, stirring occasionally, until the beans are tender, about 1 hour. If the chili becomes too dry, add a little more water. Skim the excess fat off the chili. Taste and adjust the seasoning.

In a bowl, toss together the cabbage, lime juice, and cilantro and season with salt. Serve the chili, garnished with the cabbage slaw, cheese, and avocado.

10

CREAMY PEA SOUP WITH CITRUS OIL & CHIVES

serves 4–6

To make the citrus oil, in a small saucepan combine ½ cup (4 fl oz/ 125 ml) extra-virgin olive oil; ½ cup (4 fl oz/125 ml) grapeseed oil; and the grated zest of 1 Meyer lemon. Bring to a simmer over medium-low heat and cook for 10 minutes. Let cool to room temperature. Strain into a small bowl.

1 Tbsp unsalted butter

1 Tbsp olive oil

1 small yellow onion, chopped

4 cups (32 fl oz/1 l) chicken or vegetable broth

5 cups (25 oz/780 g) fresh or frozen peas

⅓ cup (3 fl oz/80 ml) heavy cream

Salt and freshly ground pepper

Citrus Oil for topping (left)

Thinly sliced chives for garnish

In a large, heavy pot, melt the butter with the oil over medium-high heat. Add the onion and sauté until translucent, about 5 minutes. Add the broth and bring to a boil. Add the peas and cook for 5 minutes. Remove from the heat and let cool slightly.

Working in batches, purée the soup in a blender. Pass the soup through a fine-mesh sieve set over a bowl, pressing with a spoon to extract all the liquid. Return the soup to the pot and add the cream. Bring to a boil over medium-high heat and remove from the heat. Season with salt and pepper.

Serve the soup, drizzled with the citrus oil and garnished with the chives.

11

THREE-ONION SOUP WITH CAMBOZOLA GRILLED CHEESE

serves 6

Onion soup is particularly tasty with cheese, whether grated or crusted atop. Here, a lighter version of the classic French onion soup finds the perfect match in a creamy, buttery grilled cheese sandwich.

2 Tbsp unsalted butter

¼ cup (2 fl oz/60 ml) olive oil

3 large yellow onions, sliced

6 shallots, sliced

3 leeks, white and pale green parts, sliced

1 Tbsp light brown sugar

¼ cup (2 fl oz/60 ml) dry white wine

4 cups (32 fl oz/1 l) chicken broth

Salt and freshly ground pepper

FOR THE GRILLED CHEESE

12 thin slices cranberry-walnut or other fruit-and-nut bread

2 Tbsp unsalted butter, at room temperature

6 oz (185 g) Cambozola or Camembert cheese, at room temperature

In a large, heavy pot, melt the butter with the oil over high heat. Add the onions, shallots, and leeks and sauté until the onions soften, 8–10 minutes. Reduce the heat to low and continue to cook, stirring occasionally, for 30 minutes. Sprinkle the brown sugar over the onions, stir, and cook for 10 minutes. Add the white wine and bring to a simmer, stirring to scrape up any browned bits on the bottom of the pan. Cook until the wine is absorbed, 3–4 minutes. Add the broth and bring to a boil over medium-high heat. Reduce the heat to medium and simmer, uncovered, for 10 minutes. Remove from the heat and let cool slightly.

Purée half of the soup in a blender and return to the pot. Season with salt and pepper.

To make the grilled cheese, spread one side of each slice of bread with the butter. Spread 1 oz (30 g) of the Cambozola on the unbuttered side of each of 6 bread slices and top with another slice of bread, with the buttered sides on the outside of the sandwich. In a frying pan, cook the sandwiches over medium-low heat until the bread is toasted and the cheese is melted, about 4 minutes per side. Cut each sandwich in half.

Ladle the soup into bowls and serve with the grilled cheese on the side.

12

LEMONY ASPARAGUS & RICE SOUP WITH PARMESAN

serves 4

This is a great way to use up leftover cooked white rice. The tough ends of the asparagus don't go to waste here: they infuse the flavor of the vegetable into the broth. Do not add the asparagus spears until you are ready to serve the soup, as they lose their beautiful green coloring quickly.

2 bunches asparagus

4 cups (32 fl oz/1 l) chicken broth

3 Tbsp unsalted butter

1 small yellow onion, finely chopped

3 cloves garlic, minced

1½ cups (7½ oz/235 g) cooked white rice

Grated zest of 1 lemon

3 Tbsp fresh lemon juice

Salt and freshly ground pepper

Grated Parmesan cheese for serving

Snap the tough ends from the asparagus spears and reserve them. Cut the spears into 1-inch (2.5-cm) pieces. In a saucepan, combine the broth and tough asparagus ends. Bring to a boil over medium-high heat, reduce the heat to low, and simmer for 10 minutes. Strain the broth into a bowl. Discard the solids.

In large, heavy pot, melt the butter over medium-high heat. Add the onion and garlic and sauté until translucent, about 5 minutes. Add the broth and bring to a boil. Reduce the heat to low, add the rice, asparagus pieces, lemon zest, and lemon juice, and simmer just until the asparagus is crisp-tender, about 3 minutes.

Season with salt and pepper and serve, topped with grated cheese.

13

Peppery and piquant, fresh ginger invigorates any dish. Here, cinnamon and star anise add flavor complexity, while chewy noodles and tender slices of beef add heartiness. Nearly any Asian-style noodles, including rice vermicelli, can be used; consult the package for cooking instructions.

BABY BOK CHOY & BEEF NOODLE SOUP

serves 6–8

4-inch (10-cm) piece fresh ginger

2 Tbsp canola oil

1 yellow onion, thinly sliced

4 cinnamon sticks

1 star anise

5 cloves garlic, crushed and thinly sliced

2 tsp Asian chile garlic paste

4 cups (32 fl oz/1 l) chicken broth

½ cup (4 fl oz/125 ml) soy sauce

2 lb (1 kg) beef blade steak, trimmed and cut into slices ¼-inch (6-mm) thick

Salt

1½ lb (750 g) fresh Chinese egg noodles

5 heads baby bok choy (about 1½ lb/750 g), trimmed, each cut lengthwise into quarters

4 green onions, thinly sliced

Peel the ginger, cut into thin slices, and crush each slice with the flat side of a chef's knife.

In a large, heavy pot, warm the oil over medium-high heat. Add the onion and sauté until softened, about 3 minutes. Add the cinnamon sticks and star anise and cook, stirring, until the spices are fragrant and the cinnamon sticks begin to uncurl, about 2 minutes. Add the crushed ginger, the garlic, and the chile garlic paste and cook, stirring, until fragrant, about 45 seconds. Add the broth and soy sauce. Pour in 4½ cups (36 fl oz/1.1 l) water, raise the heat to high, cover, and bring to a boil. Stir in the beef and return to a boil. Reduce the heat to low, cover partially, and simmer until the beef is very tender, about 1½ hours.

In a large saucepan, bring 4 qt (4 l) water to a boil over high heat. Stir in 1 Tbsp salt and the noodles, return to a boil, and cook until the noodles are tender, about 3 minutes. Drain the noodles, rinse well under warm running water, and drain again. Divide the noodles among bowls. ↠

Using a slotted spoon, remove and discard the cinnamon sticks, star anise, and ginger from the soup. Add the bok choy and cook just until crisp-tender, about 5 minutes. Stir in half of the green onions. Ladle the soup over the noodles, distributing the beef and bok choy evenly. Garnish with the remaining green onions and serve.

14

To trim a stalk of asparagus, gently bend it about 2 inches (5 cm) from the bottom and the stalk should snap naturally, right at the point where the tender and tough parts meet. Peel any thicker stems.

CREAM OF ASPARAGUS SOUP

serves 4–6

1 Tbsp unsalted butter

2 Tbsp olive oil

2 leeks, white and light green parts, finely chopped

1 lb (500 g) thick asparagus, trimmed, peeled, and cut into 2-inch (5-cm) pieces, tips reserved

1 russet potato, peeled and cut into 2-inch (5-cm) chunks

4 cups (32 fl oz/1 l) chicken broth

Salt and ground white pepper

Juice of ½ lemon

3 Tbsp crème fraîche or sour cream

1 Tbsp finely chopped chives

In a large, heavy pot, melt the butter with the oil over medium heat. Add the leeks and sauté until softened, about 5 minutes. Add the asparagus stalks and potato and sauté until beginning to soften, about 3 minutes. Add the broth and season with salt and pepper. Bring to a boil over medium-high heat. Reduce the heat to low, cover partially, and cook until the vegetables are very tender, about 15 minutes.

Meanwhile, bring a small saucepan of water to a boil. Add the lemon juice and reserved asparagus tips and cook until crisp-tender, about 3 minutes. Drain and let cool slightly.

Working in batches, purée the soup in a blender. Return to the pot and reheat over low heat. Serve, garnished with the crème fraîche, asparagus tips, and chives.

MARCH 15

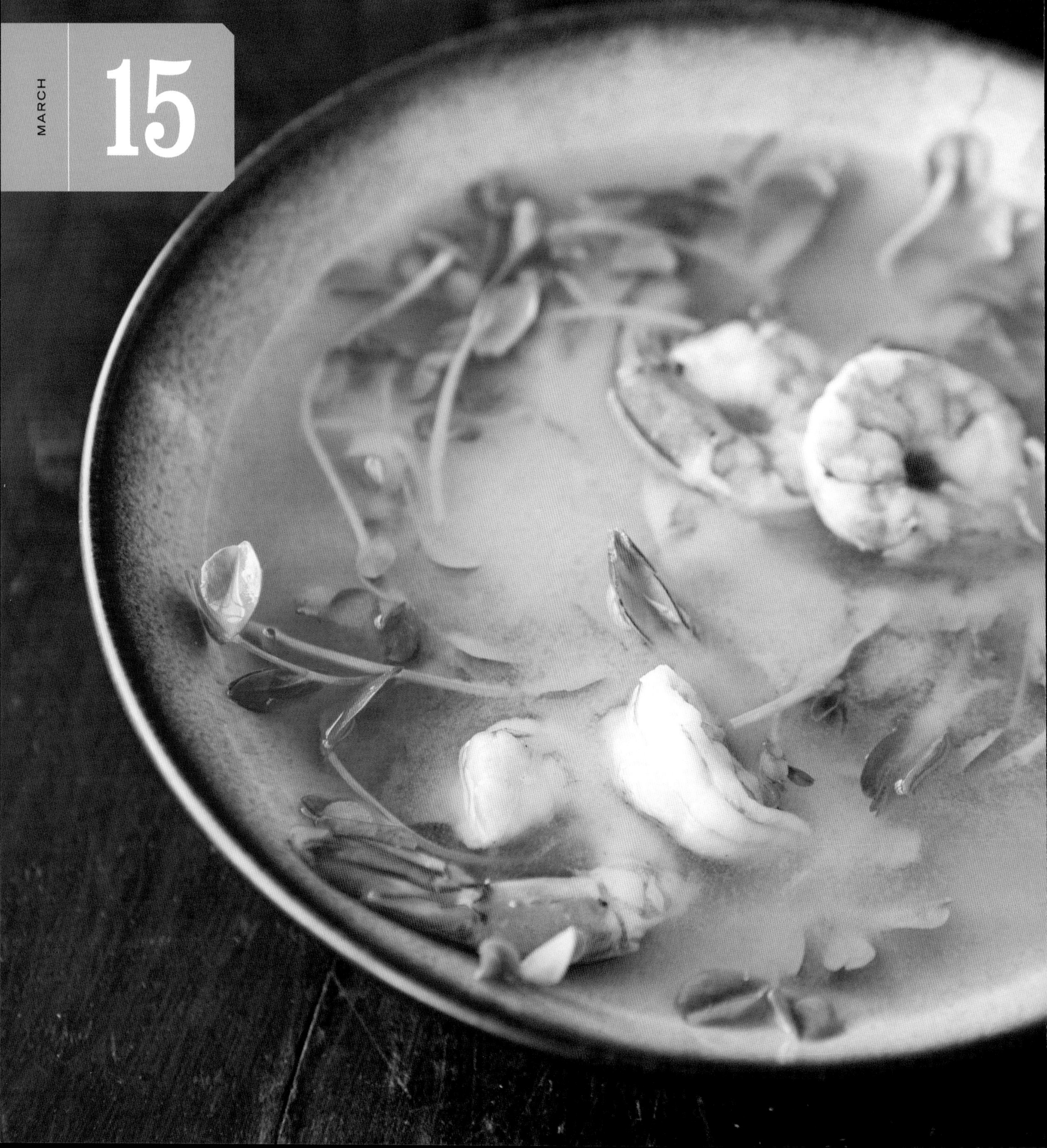

15

MISO SOUP WITH SHRIMP & PEA SHOOTS

serves 2

3-inch (7.5-cm) piece kombu

½ cup (½ oz/15 g) bonito flakes

2 Tbsp light miso paste

¼ lb (125 g) shrimp, peeled and deveined

⅓ cup (⅓ oz/10 g) pea shoots

Traditional miso soup is served with dried shiitake mushrooms, sliced scallions, and tiny cubes of tofu; here it gets a springtime profile with shrimp and pea shoots.

In a large saucepan, combine the kombu and 3 cups (24 fl oz/750 ml) cold water. Bring to a boil over medium heat. Remove and discard the kombu. Remove from the heat, add the bonito flakes, and stir gently once. Let stand for 5 minutes. Strain the broth through a fine-mesh sieve, discarding the bonito flakes. Return the broth to the saucepan.

In a small bowl, combine the miso paste with ¼ cup (2 fl oz/60 ml) of the warm broth. Stir until the paste is softened and very smooth. Stir into the broth and warm gently over medium heat, taking care not to boil the soup.

Add the shrimp and simmer just until bright pink, about 3 minutes. Stir in the pea shoots and serve.

16

BEEF & MUSHROOM SOUP WITH FARRO

serves 6–8

¾ oz (20 g) dried porcini mushrooms

1½ Tbsp olive oil

¾ lb (375 g) fresh cremini mushrooms, thinly sliced

1 yellow onion, finely chopped

3 carrots, peeled and cut into slices ¼ inch (6 mm) thick

3 cloves garlic, minced

1½ tsp minced thyme

¾ cup (4 oz/125 g) canned diced tomatoes

1½ cups (9 oz/280 g) farro, rinsed and drained

8 cups (64 fl oz/2 l) beef broth

2 cups (12 oz/375 g) shredded cooked beef

4 Tbsp (⅓ oz/10 g) chopped flat-leaf parsley

Salt and freshly ground pepper

Dried porcini mushrooms have a woodsy flavor and an intense earthy aroma that easily matches the richness of beef. Farro, with its nutty taste and chewy texture, adds yet another hearty element to this soup.

In a heatproof bowl, combine the porcini with hot water to cover. Soak for 30 minutes. Lift out the mushrooms, reserving the soaking liquid. Rinse if they are gritty, then squeeze out the excess moisture. Slice thinly. Pour the soaking liquid through a coffee filter into another bowl. Set aside.

In a large, heavy pot, warm 1 Tbsp of the oil over medium heat. Add the cremini mushrooms and sauté until they release their liquid and the liquid evaporates, about 7 minutes. Add the remaining ½ Tbsp oil and then the onion, carrots, garlic, and thyme. Sauté until the vegetables are softened and beginning to brown, about 7 minutes. Add the porcini and their soaking liquid, the tomatoes with their juices, the farro, and the beef broth. Bring to a boil over high heat. Reduce the heat to low and simmer, stirring occasionally, until the farro is almost tender, about 20 minutes.

Add the shredded beef, half of the parsley, and 1½ tsp salt. Season with pepper and stir to mix well. Simmer until the meat is heated through and the farro is completely tender, about 10 minutes. Serve, garnished with the remaining parsley.

17

Nothing against corned beef and cabbage, but St. Patty's day might be even more delicious with this country-style lamb and vegetable stew. Simmering for 2 hours yields especially tender results. Serve thick slices of Irish soda bread alongside.

IRISH LAMB STEW

serves 4–6

2 lb (1 kg) boneless lamb shoulder, trimmed and cut into 1-inch (2.5-cm) cubes

4 white boiling potatoes, peeled and cut into slices ½ inch (12 mm) thick

2 yellow onions, cut in half lengthwise and then crosswise into slices ½ inch (12 mm) thick

1 large turnip, peeled and cut into slices ¼ inch (6 mm) thick

2 thyme sprigs, or 4 tsp dried thyme

3 flat-leaf parsley sprigs, plus more for garnish

Salt and freshly ground pepper

In a large, heavy pot, combine the lamb cubes with water to cover. Drain and add fresh water to cover by 1 inch (2.5 cm). Bring to a boil over high heat and boil for 5 minutes. Using a slotted spoon, transfer the lamb to a dish. Pour the broth into a bowl.

Layer half of the potato slices in the bottom of the same pot. Cover with half of the onion slices and then top with all of the turnip slices. Distribute the lamb evenly over the turnips and top with the thyme and the 3 parsley sprigs. Season with 1 tsp salt and 4 tsp pepper. Top with the remaining onions and then the remaining potatoes. Strain the lamb broth through a fine-mesh sieve over the potatoes. Bring to a low boil over high heat. Reduce the heat to medium-low, cover, and simmer until the lamb is tender, about 2 hours. Discard the thyme and parsley sprigs from the pot. Serve, garnished with parsley sprigs.

18

Two kinds of rice give texture and flavor to this fragrant soup. Full of aromatic cold-fighters like ginger, garlic, and cilantro, this soup makes a comforting dish to bring to a friend who is under the weather.

CHICKEN & WILD RICE SOUP WITH GINGER

serves 6

½ cup (3 oz/90 g) wild rice, rinsed

1 Tbsp Asian sesame oil

1 Tbsp canola oil

1 yellow onion, chopped

1 Tbsp peeled and grated fresh ginger

2 cloves garlic, minced

4 cups (32 fl oz/1 l) chicken broth

1 carrot, peeled and diced

3 skinless, bone-in chicken breast halves

2 skinless, bone-in chicken thighs

½ cup (3½ oz/105 g) long-grain white rice

¼ cup (¾ oz/20 g) thinly sliced green onions

¼ cup (⅓ oz/10 g) chopped cilantro

Salt and freshly ground pepper

In a small saucepan, bring 2 cups (16 fl oz/ 500 ml) water to a boil. Add the wild rice, reduce the heat to a simmer, cover, and cook until tender, 45–50 minutes. Drain.

Meanwhile, in a large, heavy pot, warm the sesame and canola oils over medium-high heat. Add the yellow onion and sauté until softened, 3–5 minutes. Add the ginger and garlic and sauté for 2 minutes. Add the broth, carrot, chicken pieces, and white rice. Pour in 2 cups (16 fl oz/500 ml) water and bring to a simmer. Reduce the heat to medium-low, cover, and cook until the chicken is opaque throughout, about 15 minutes.

Transfer the chicken to a plate to cool. Remove the meat from the bones and tear into bite-sized pieces. Stir the chicken back into the soup along with the green onions, cilantro, and wild rice. Season with salt and pepper and serve.

19

For many, just the mention of cream of mushroom soup brings back childhood memories. This updated version of the classic calls for portobello mushrooms, which are incredibly flavorful, especially when they are sautéed. The soup and chervil cream can be made a couple of days ahead and stored in the refrigerator, but the croutons will be best served hot and toasty right out of the pan.

CREAM OF PORTOBELLO MUSHROOM SOUP WITH CHERVIL CREAM

serves 4–6

3 Tbsp olive oil

2 shallots, chopped

2 cloves garlic, chopped

1½ lb (750 g) portobello mushroom caps, cut into 1-inch (2.5-cm) pieces

Salt and freshly ground pepper

3 cups (24 fl oz/750 ml) vegetable or chicken broth

¾ cup (6 fl oz/180 ml) heavy cream

FOR THE CHERVIL CREAM

½ cup (4 oz/125 g) crème fraîche or sour cream, at room temperature

2 Tbsp heavy cream

2 Tbsp minced chervil

1 Tbsp grated lemon zest

Salt and freshly ground pepper

FOR THE CROUTONS

1 Tbsp unsalted butter

1 Tbsp olive oil

2 slices crusty sourdough bread, cut into ¼-inch (6-mm) cubes

Salt and freshly ground pepper

In a large, heavy pot, warm 1 Tbsp of the oil over medium-high heat. Add the shallots and garlic and cook, stirring occasionally, until soft, about 3 minutes. Add the mushrooms and the remaining 2 Tbsp oil, and season with salt and pepper. Cook, stirring frequently, until the mushrooms deepen in color and soften, about 4 minutes. Add the broth and bring to a boil. Reduce the heat to low and simmer until the mushrooms are very soft, about 10 minutes. Let cool slightly.

Working in batches, purée the soup in a food processor or blender. Return to the pot, place over medium heat, and stir in the cream. Simmer until the soup thickens, about 3 minutes. Season with salt and pepper and keep warm over low heat.

To make the chervil cream, in a small bowl, stir together the crème fraîche, cream, chervil, and lemon zest, and season with salt and pepper. Set aside at room temperature.

↠

To make the croutons, in a small frying pan, melt the butter with the oil over medium-high heat. Add the bread cubes and stir to coat with the butter and oil. Season generously with salt and pepper and toast the croutons, stirring only a couple of times, about 6 minutes.

Serve the soup, topped with a dollop of the chervil cream and several warm croutons.

20

In Italy, this soup is called pasta en brodo. *It makes a wonderful first course, or lends itself well to embellishments and improvisations. For extra color and flavor, try adding green beans, fresh herbs, peas, Swiss chard, or spinach.*

PASTA IN BROTH WITH CHIVES

serves 6

2 lb (1 kg) chicken necks and backs, fat removed

1 small yellow onion, quartered

1 small carrot, peeled and coarsely chopped

⅛ tsp dried thyme

5 oz (155 g) stelline, ditalini, farfalline, or other small soup pasta

1 Tbsp minced chives

Salt and freshly ground pepper

½ cup (2 oz/60 g) grated Parmesan cheese

In a large, heavy pot, combine the chicken, onion, carrot, and thyme. Pour in 8 cups (64 fl oz/2 l) water and bring to a boil. Reduce the heat to low and simmer, uncovered, for 3 hours, skimming off any foam on the surface. Periodically add water to the pot to maintain the original level. Strain the broth into a clean pot. Discard the bones. Skim the fat and discard. You should have 8 cups (64 fl oz/2 l); add more water if necessary.

Heat the broth over medium-high heat. Add the pasta and cook until al dente, 2–3 minutes or according to the package directions. Stir in the chives and season with salt and pepper. Serve sprinkled with the cheese.

21

MISO SOUP WITH SLIVERED ROOT VEGETABLES & WATERCRESS

serves 4

In this soup, miso, the thick fermented soybean paste that Japanese cooks use with everything from tofu and fish to meats and vegetables, imparts a deep, rich, almost-mysterious flavor to the broth. Be careful not to allow the soup to boil once the miso has been added, as high heat will damage its unique flavor and aroma.

2 Tbsp white miso

2 oz (60 g) small white mushrooms, halved

1 small carrot, peeled and julienned

1 piece daikon radish, 3 inches (7.5 cm) long, julienned

2 oz (60 g) firm tofu, cut into ½-inch (12-mm) cubes

1 cup (1 oz/30 g) watercress leaves

In a heavy pot, bring 6 cups (48 fl oz/1.5 l) water to a boil over medium-high heat. Stir in the miso and reduce the heat to medium. Stir in the mushrooms, carrot, daikon radish, and tofu and cook until the vegetables are tender, about 5 minutes. Serve, garnished with the watercress.

22

MOROCCAN LAMB MEATBALL & COUSCOUS SOUP

serves 4–6

Israeli couscous has much bigger pearls than Moroccan couscous, but it is still very quick-cooking. The meatballs also make a delicious dinner on their own over a bed of couscous.

FOR THE MEATBALLS

1 tsp ground coriander

1 tsp ground cumin

¼ tsp curry powder

¼ teaspoon dried oregano

¼ tsp dried thyme

⅛ tsp dry mustard

⅛ tsp chili powder

Pinch of ground cinnamon

Salt and freshly ground pepper

1 lb (500 g) ground lamb

2 Tbsp tomato paste

1 cup (6 oz/185 g) Israeli couscous

3 Tbsp olive oil

2 shallots, minced

5 cloves garlic, minced

3 cups (24 fl oz/750 ml) chicken broth

1 Tbsp chopped mint

Salt and freshly ground pepper

To make the meatballs, preheat the oven to 375°F (190°C). Oil a baking sheet. In a small bowl, combine the coriander, cumin, curry powder, oregano, thyme, mustard, chili powder, and cinnamon. Stir in ½ tsp salt. Add the lamb and tomato paste and mix to combine with your hands. For each meatball, scoop up 1 tsp of the lamb mixture, form into a meatball, and place on the prepared pan. Bake until the meatballs are cooked through, about 10 minutes.

In a small saucepan, bring 1¼ cups (10 fl oz/310 ml) water to a boil over high heat. Add the couscous, reduce the heat to low, cover, and cook until all the liquid is absorbed, 8–10 minutes.

Meanwhile, in a large, heavy pot, warm the oil over medium-high heat. Add the shallots and garlic and sauté for 1 minute. Add the broth and bring to a boil. Reduce the heat to low and add the meatballs and couscous and simmer for 10 minutes. Remove from the heat. Stir in the mint, season with salt and pepper, and serve.

MARCH

23

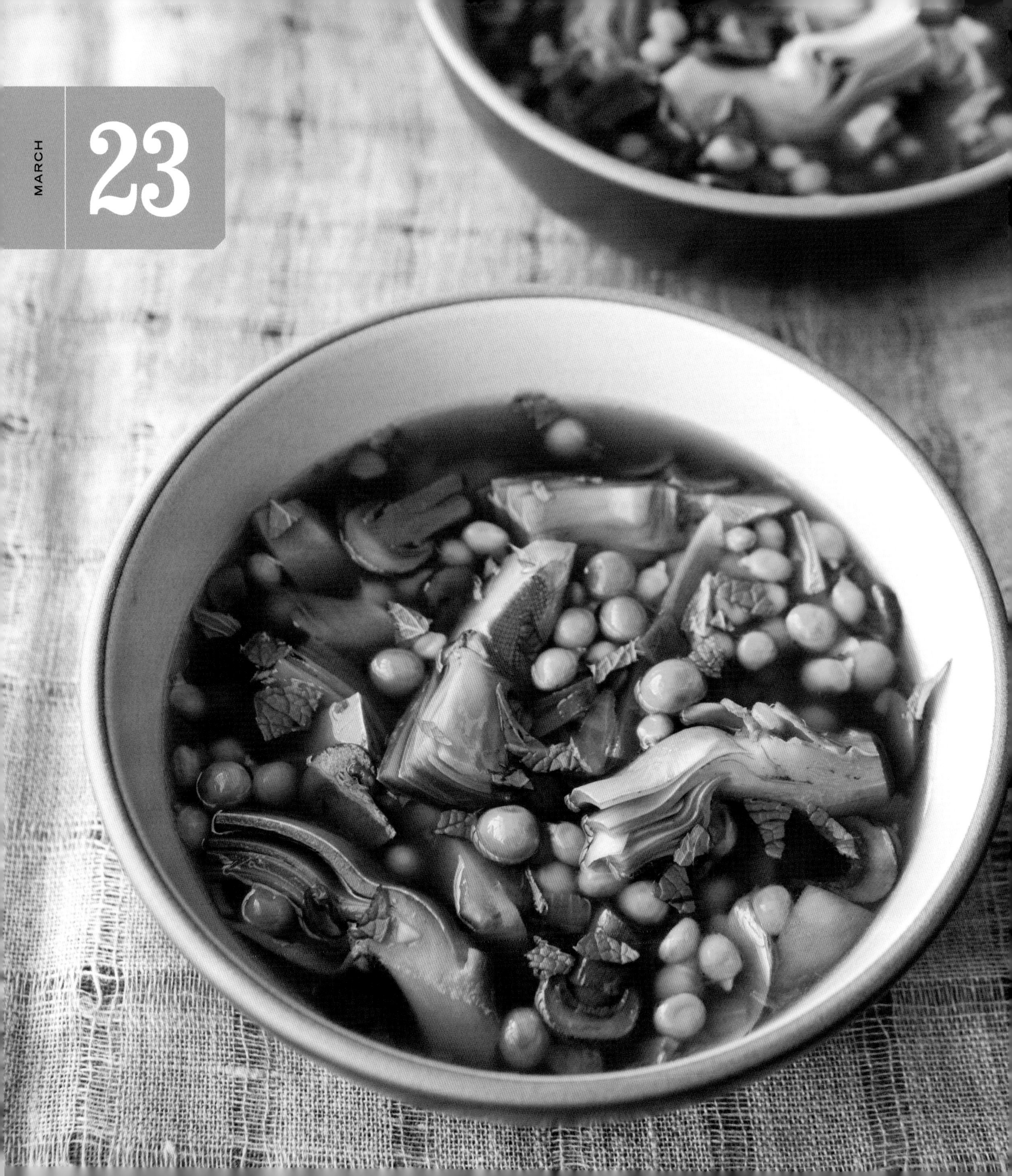

23

ARTICHOKE, SPRING PEA & MINT SOUP

serves 4–6

Juice of ½ lemon

12 small artichokes

2 Tbsp unsalted butter

1 yellow onion, finely chopped

2 cloves garlic, minced

½ lb (250 g) cremini mushrooms, thinly sliced

5 cups (40 fl oz/1.25 l) chicken broth

1 cup (5 oz/155 g) fresh peas

2 Tbsp chopped mint

Salt and freshly ground pepper

The clear broth of this soup allows the green hues of the artichokes and peas to really shine. Use a shallow bowl to present the soup so that you can see all the elements.

Fill a bowl with water and add the lemon juice. Cut off the stem of each artichoke flush with the bottom. Snap off the outer leaves until you reach the tender inner leaves. Cut off the top one-third of each artichoke to remove the pointed tips. Quarter the artichoke lengthwise. Cut out the choke from each quarter. As you work, add the quarters to the lemon water.

In a large, heavy pot, melt the butter over medium heat. Add the onion and garlic and cook until translucent, about 5 minutes. Drain the artichoke quarters and add to the pan with the mushrooms. Stir to coat, and cook for 4 minutes. Add the broth and bring to a boil. Reduce the heat to low and simmer, uncovered, until the artichokes are tender but not mushy, about 10 minutes. Add the peas and cook for 3 minutes. Stir in the mint, season with salt and pepper, and serve.

24

PORK TENDERLOIN SOUP WITH FARRO & SWEET POTATO

serves 4–6

1 lb (500 g) pork tenderloin

3 Tbsp olive oil

1 Tbsp chopped rosemary

Salt and freshly ground pepper

1 small yellow onion, chopped

2 small sweet potatoes (about ¾ lb/375 g total weight), peeled and cut into 1-inch (2.5-cm) pieces

1 clove garlic, chopped

6 cups (48 fl oz/1.5 l) chicken broth

1 cup (6 oz/185 g) farro, rinsed and drained

Juice of ½ lemon

2 cups (2 oz/60 g) packed spinach

This hearty soup contains a protein, a vegetable, and a healthful grain, making it the perfect one-pot meal. Think of this recipe as a template for using up leftovers, too. For example, you can trade out the sweet potatoes, pork, and farro for leftover broccoli rabe, grilled chicken, and wild rice, respectively. Or skip the soup and serve the rosemary-seasoned pork tenderloin as a delicious main course with roasted apples and red onions on the side.

Preheat the oven to 400°F (200°C). Place the pork tenderloin in a baking dish. Brush with 1 Tbsp of the oil, sprinkle with the rosemary, and season generously with salt and pepper. Roast until an instant-read thermometer inserted into the thickest part of the tenderloin registers 145°F (63°C), 25–30 minutes. Transfer to a cutting board and let rest for at least 10 minutes, then cut into ½-inch (12-mm) pieces. Set aside.

In a large, heavy pot, warm the remaining 2 Tbsp oil over medium-high heat. Add the onion and sweet potatoes and cook, stirring occasionally, until the sweet potatoes begin to soften, about 6 minutes. Add the garlic, season with salt and pepper, and cook, stirring occasionally, until the garlic is soft, about 2 minutes. Add the broth and bring to a boil. Stir in the farro, reduce the heat to medium-low, and cook until the farro is al dente, about 20 minutes. Stir in the pork, lemon juice, and spinach and cook just until the spinach wilts, about 3 minutes. Season with salt and pepper and serve.

LAMB & CHICKPEA CHILI WITH CUMIN CREMA

serves 4–6

This lamb chili is a delicious way to welcome a favorite springtime meat. You can double the recipe and freeze half of it for another meal. Divide the half you are freezing into two-serving portions to cut down on thawing and reheating time. Serve this chili with broccoli rabe sautéed in olive oil with garlic and finished with a big squeeze of fresh lemon juice.

2 Tbsp olive oil

1 small yellow onion, chopped

1 red bell pepper, seeded and cut into ½-inch (12-mm) pieces

2 cloves garlic, chopped

1 lb (500 g) ground lamb

1 Tbsp plus 1 tsp chili powder

2 tsp ground cumin

1 tsp smoked paprika

Salt and freshly ground pepper

1 can (15 oz/470 g) chickpeas, drained

1 can (14½ oz/455 g) diced tomatoes with juices

1 cup (8 fl oz/250 ml) chicken broth

2 cups (2 oz/60 g) baby kale leaves, or ½ bunch kale, ribs removed, leaves chopped

FOR THE CUMIN CREMA

½ cup (4 oz/125 g) sour cream

1 Tbsp ground cumin

Juice of ½ lemon

Salt

In a large, heavy pot, warm the oil over medium-high heat. Add the onion and bell pepper and cook, stirring occasionally, until soft, about 6 minutes. Add the garlic and cook, stirring occasionally, until soft, about 2 minutes. Add the ground lamb and cook, breaking it up with a wooden spoon, until browned, about 5 minutes. Stir in the chili powder, cumin, paprika, and 2 tsp salt and toast the spices for 1 minute, stirring. Add the chickpeas, tomatoes with their juices, and broth and bring to a boil. Reduce the heat to low and simmer for 15 minutes. Season with salt and pepper, stir in the kale, and cook just until it wilts, about 3 minutes. Keep warm over low heat.

To make the cumin crema, in a small bowl, stir together the sour cream, cumin, and lemon juice and season with salt.

Serve the chili, topped with a generous dollop of the cumin crema.

FIVE-SPICE BROTH WITH SALMON & ONION DUMPLINGS

serves 4

This aromatic soup is best served right away, as the dumplings do not reheat well. You can make the broth and assemble the dumplings ahead of time, but don't cook the dumplings until just before you are ready to serve.

2 Tbsp canola oil

1 large shallot, minced

1½ tsp peeled and minced fresh ginger

¼ tsp Chinese five-spice powder

4 cups (32 fl oz/1 l) chicken broth

Salt

FOR THE DUMPLINGS

¼ lb (125 g) salmon fillet, skin and pin bones removed, finely chopped

2 green onions, white and pale green parts, finely chopped

½ tsp canola oil

Salt and freshly ground pepper

20 wonton wrappers

2 green onions, dark green parts only, sliced

In a large saucepan, warm the 2 Tbsp oil over medium-high heat. Add the shallot and ginger and sauté for 3 minutes. Add the five-spice powder, the broth, 2 cups (16 fl oz/500 ml) water, and 2 tsp salt. Bring to a boil. Reduce the heat to low and simmer, uncovered, for about 15 minutes to blend the flavors. Remove from the heat and season with salt.

To make the dumplings, in a bowl, stir together the salmon, chopped green onions, and ½ tsp oil. Stir in ¼ tsp salt and ⅛ tsp pepper. Place 1 tsp of the salmon mixture in the middle of each wonton wrapper. Using your fingers, apply a small amount of water on all edges of the wrapper. Fold the wrapper diagonally, forcing out any air bubbles as you press to seal. Take the 2 points on the longest side of the triangle and fold so that the tips meet. Apply a small amount of water on the tips and firmly press to stick them together.

Return the soup to a simmer. Carefully add the dumplings and cook until just tender, about 3 minutes. Ladle the soup into bowls, garnish with the sliced green onions, and serve.

27

FENNEL BROTH WITH CHARD & CHORIZO

serves 4

¾ lb (375 g) smoked Spanish chorizo, halved lengthwise then cut into ¼-inch (6-mm) slices

1 Tbsp olive oil

2 shallots, minced

3 cloves garlic, minced

1 fennel bulb, stalks and fronds removed, quartered and thinly sliced

⅓ cup (3 fl oz/80 ml) dry white wine

4 cups (32 fl oz/1 l) chicken broth

1 bunch chard, ribs removed, leaves coarsely chopped

Salt and freshly ground pepper

Grated pecorino romano cheese for serving

In a large, heavy pot, sauté the chorizo over medium-high heat until browned on both sides, about 7 minutes. Transfer to a bowl and set aside.

In the same pot, combine the olive oil, shallots, garlic, and fennel. Sauté until the fennel softens and begins to caramelize, about 10 minutes. Add the white wine and bring to a simmer, stirring to scrape up any browned bits on the bottom of the pot. Add the broth, stir to combine, bring to a simmer, and cook for 5 minutes. Add the chard and chorizo, stir to combine, and simmer for 5 minutes. Season with salt and pepper and serve, topped with the cheese.

This fennel broth tastes light, but it is packed with flavor. The chard gives texture, and the spicy chorizo adds a taste explosion. You can substitute Parmesan cheese for the pecorino romano.

28

BLACK-EYED PEA STEW

serves 4–6

2 Tbsp olive oil

1 large yellow onion, chopped

4 cloves garlic, minced

1 bunch collard greens, chopped

5 oz (155 g) cooked ham steak, cubed

3 cups (24 fl oz/750 ml) chicken broth, plus more as needed

2 cans (15 oz/470 g each) black-eyed peas, drained

2 Tbsp tomato paste

Salt and freshly ground pepper

In a large, heavy pot, warm the oil over medium-high heat. Add the onion and garlic and sauté until soft, 5–7 minutes. Add the collard greens and ham and cook, stirring often, for 5 minutes. Add the broth and bring to a boil. Reduce the heat to low, add the black-eyed peas and tomato paste, stir well, and simmer for 30 minutes. Add more chicken broth if necessary. Season with salt and pepper and serve.

Here is a shortened and slightly healthier version of the traditional Southern stew. Garnish with chopped onion and serve with warm jalapeño corn bread.

29

PEA & ARBORIO RICE PURÉE

serves 4

1 Tbsp canola oil

1 leek, white part only, chopped

1 white onion, chopped

1 small zucchini, trimmed and chopped

1 Tbsp Arborio rice

2 cups (10 oz/315 g) fresh or frozen peas

Salt

In a large saucepan, warm the oil over medium-high heat. Add the leek, onion, and zucchini and stir to coat with the oil. Reduce the heat to low, cover tightly, and cook until the vegetables are soft, about 10 minutes. Add the rice and 3 cups (24 fl oz/750 ml) water, raise the heat to medium, and bring to a boil, then reduce to a simmer, cover, and cook for 10 minutes. Add the peas, cover, and cook until tender, 5–10 minutes. Remove from the heat and let cool slightly. Working in batches, purée the soup in a blender. Season with salt and serve.

Fresh peas have a short season, but when available, they are well worth the added step of shucking. For the sweetest results, try to use them the day of purchase. Arborio rice adds body and creaminess to the soup without dulling the flavor of the peas. Garnish with minced fresh mint.

30

This is a lighter version of the classic vichyssoise. It delivers the buttery flavor of the original by using yellow-fleshed potatoes and just a modest amount of butter.

CHILLED POTATO & LEEK SOUP

serves 4

4 leeks, white part only, chopped

4 large green onions, white part only, chopped

3 cups (24 fl oz/750 ml) chicken broth

1 lb (500 g) Yukon Gold potatoes, peeled and chopped

1½ Tbsp unsalted butter

Salt and ground white pepper

2 Tbsp minced chives

In a large, heavy pot over medium-high heat, combine the leeks, the green onions, and ½ cup (4 fl oz/125 ml) of the broth. Bring to a boil, reduce the heat to low, cover, and cook until the vegetables have wilted and begin to soften, about 8 minutes. Add the potatoes and remaining 2½ cups (20 fl oz/625 ml) broth, cover, and cook until the vegetables are very soft, 25–30 minutes. Let cool for 15 minutes. Stir in the butter.

Working in batches, purée the soup in a blender. Return to the pot. Stir in ¼ tsp salt and season with pepper. Cover and refrigerate until well chilled, 3–4 hours or up to overnight. The soup will thicken and become very creamy. Serve, garnished with the chives.

31

To make the fried rosemary, in a small frying pan, warm 2 Tbsp olive oil over high heat. Add 4 sprigs rosemary, 2 at a time, and fry for 1 minute on each side. Transfer to paper towels to drain. Once they are cool enough to handle, remove the leaves and chop, if desired.

CHICKPEA & ROASTED TOMATO SOUP WITH FRIED ROSEMARY

serves 4–6

1 lb (500 g) Roma (plum) tomatoes

4 Tbsp olive oil

Salt and freshly ground pepper

1 large yellow onion, chopped

4 cloves garlic, minced

1 tsp ground cumin

½ tsp paprika

1 cinnamon stick

3 cans (15 oz/470 g each) chickpeas, drained

4 cups (32 fl oz/1 l) chicken broth

1 Tbsp sour cream

Fried Rosemary for garnish (see note)

Preheat the oven to 450°F (230°C). Slice the tomatoes in half and place in a single layer on a baking sheet. Drizzle with 2 Tbsp of the oil and season with salt and pepper. Roast the tomatoes until they are soft and caramelized, 25–30 minutes. Set aside.

In a large, heavy pot, warm the remaining 2 Tbsp oil over medium-high heat. Add the onion and the garlic and sauté until soft, about 5 minutes. Add the cumin, paprika, and cinnamon stick and toast the spices, stirring often, for 2 minutes. Add the chickpeas, roasted tomatoes, and broth, stir to combine, and bring to a boil. Reduce the heat to low and simmer until the chickpeas are very tender, about 45 minutes. Remove from the heat and let cool slightly.

Transfer about two-thirds of the chickpeas and broth to a blender and purée. Return to the pot and stir in the sour cream.

Season the soup with salt and pepper and serve, garnished with fried rosemary.

Lengthening daylight hours nurture an expanding array of fresh ingredients to enhance spring soups. Tender roots such as parsnips, baby carrots and lotus root meet young alliums like onions and leeks at farmers' market stands. Add the freshness of fava beans and snow peas from the season's slender vines, and the full, grassy flavor of this month's harvest is amply realized.

april

1

SPRING VEGETABLE SOUP

serves 6–8

Juice of ½ lemon

8 baby artichokes

4 thyme sprigs

Salt and freshly ground pepper

3 lb (1.5 kg) fava beans in the pods, shelled

2 Tbsp olive oil

8 small leeks, white and pale green parts, cut into 1-inch (2.5-cm) slices

1 bunch green onions, chopped

6 slices prosciutto, torn into strips ½ inch (12 mm) wide

6 cups (48 fl oz/1.5 l) chicken broth

1 cup (2 oz/60 g) shredded chard

1 cup (2 oz/60 g) shredded sorrel

1 cup (1 oz/30 g) baby spinach leaves

1 cup (5 oz/155 g) fresh or frozen peas

½ cup (½ oz/15 g) packed mint leaves

In Italy, this soup is known as vignole, *which loosely means "a celebration of spring," so feel free to throw in any spring vegetable you can find. Swirl a spoonful of pesto on top, and serve with rustic bread and a bright Italian white wine such as Vermentino.*

Fill a bowl with water and add the lemon juice. Cut off the stem of each artichoke flush with the bottom. Snap off the outer leaves until you reach the tender inner leaves. Cut off the top one-third of each artichoke to remove the pointed tips. As you work, add the artichokes to the lemon water. Fill a saucepan with water and add the thyme and a large pinch of salt. Drain the artichokes and add to the pan. Bring to a boil over medium-high heat and cook until the artichokes are tender, about 10 minutes. Let cool in the water. Drain the artichokes and halve lengthwise. Cut out the chokes.

Bring a saucepan of water to a boil over high heat. Add the fava beans and cook for 1 minute. Drain, rinse under cold running water, and drain again. Split open the skin of each bean along its edge and slip the bean from the skin. Discard the skins.

In a large, heavy pot, warm the oil over medium heat. Add the leeks, green onions, and prosciutto and sauté until the prosciutto is lightly browned, about 3 minutes. Add the broth and bring to a boil. Add the chard, sorrel, spinach, peas, artichokes, and fava beans. Simmer until the vegetables are bright green and the peas float to the top, 3–4 minutes. Season with salt and pepper, stir in the mint, and serve.

2

TORTELLINI IN HERBACEOUS BROTH WITH SNOW PEAS

serves 4–6

2 Tbsp olive oil

2 small leeks, white and pale green parts, halved and thinly sliced

3 cloves garlic, chopped

Salt and freshly ground pepper

6 cups (48 fl oz/1.5 l) chicken broth

1 package (9 oz/280 g) fresh cheese tortellini

½ lb (250 g) snow peas, halved diagonally, trimmed

¼ cup (¼ oz/7 g) loosely packed tarragon leaves, chopped

¼ cup (¼ oz/7 g) loosely packed basil leaves, chopped

2 oz (60 g) Parmesan cheese, grated

Every household should have a few superfast weeknight recipes like this one. Packed with antioxidants, essential oils, and vitamins, fresh herbs are not only nutritional powerhouses but also contribute an incredible amount of flavor to this and other soups. Look for flat, crisp, evenly green snow peas, and be careful not to overcook them.

In a large, heavy pot, warm the oil over medium-high heat. Add the leeks and cook, stirring occasionally, until soft, about 6 minutes. Add the garlic, season with salt and pepper, and cook, stirring occasionally, until soft, about 2 minutes. Add the broth and bring to a boil. Add the tortellini and cook for 5 minutes. Add the snow peas, tarragon, and basil and cook until the tortellini is al dente, about 2 minutes.

Serve, garnished with a generous helping of the cheese.

3

This soup, sweet with caramelized onions and savory with beef broth and blue cheese, gets a touch of acidity and brightness from the addition of dry vermouth.

CARAMELIZED ONION SOUP WITH GORGONZOLA CROUTONS

serves 6

7 Tbsp (3½ oz/105 g) unsalted butter, at room temperature

2 lb (1 kg) yellow onions, thinly sliced

2 lb (1 kg) sweet onions, such as Vidalia, thinly sliced

Salt and freshly ground pepper

¾ cup (6 fl oz/180 ml) dry vermouth

4 cups (32 fl oz/1 l) chicken broth

2 cups (16 fl oz/500 ml) beef broth

3 flat-leaf parsley sprigs, 2 thyme sprigs, and 2 small bay leaves, tied together to make a bouquet garni

1 baguette, cut on the diagonal into slices 1 inch (2.5 cm) thick

6 oz (185 g) tangy blue cheese, such as Gorgonzola or Roquefort

In a large, heavy pot, melt 3 Tbsp of the butter over medium heat. Add all the onions and 1 tsp salt. Cook, stirring often, until the onions release their moisture, the moisture evaporates, and browned bits form on the bottom of the pot, about 45 minutes. Raise the heat to medium-high, add ⅓ cup (3 fl oz/80 ml) water, bring to a simmer, and stir to scrape up the browned bits from the bottom of the pot. Cook until the water evaporates and browned bits form again, about 5 minutes. Repeat four times, adding ⅓ cup water at a time.

Add the vermouth, stir to scrape up the browned bits, and cook until the liquid has almost evaporated, about 4 minutes. Add the chicken and beef broths, the bouquet garni, and 1½ tsp salt. Bring to a boil over high heat. Reduce the heat to low, cover, and simmer for about 30 minutes to blend the flavors.

Meanwhile, preheat the oven to 425°F (220°C). Arrange the baguette slices on a baking sheet and toast until lightly browned, about 5 minutes. Remove from the oven and preheat the broiler. Crumble the blue cheese into a bowl. Add 2 Tbsp of the butter and, using a fork, mash to form a fairly smooth paste. ⇥

Spread each baguette slice with a scant tablespoon of the blue cheese mixture and return to the baking sheet. Broil until the cheese is golden brown in spots, about 1½ minutes.

Add the remaining 2 Tbsp butter to the soup and stir vigorously to blend. Remove and discard the bouquet. Season with salt and pepper and serve, topping each bowl with 2 baguette slices.

4

Risotto rice lends its creamy consistency to this surprisingly quick and easy soup, punctuated with a handful of verdant green peas. Finish with a sprinkle of grated lemon zest.

VENETIAN RICE & PEA SOUP

serves 4

2 Tbsp unsalted butter

1 shallot, minced

1 celery rib, chopped

½ cup (3½ oz/105 g) medium-grain white rice, such as Arborio

3 cups (24 fl oz/750 ml) chicken broth

2 cups (10 oz/315 g) fresh or frozen peas

½ cup (2 oz/60 g) grated Parmesan cheese

1 Tbsp minced flat-leaf parsley

Salt and freshly ground pepper

In a large, heavy pot, melt the butter over medium heat. Add the shallot and celery and sauté until the shallot is translucent, about 2 minutes. Add the rice and cook, stirring, until the grains are translucent with a white dot in the center, about 1 minute.

Raise the heat to medium-high, add the broth and 2 cups (16 fl oz/500 ml) water, and bring to a boil. Reduce the heat to low, cover, and simmer until the rice is tender, about 15 minutes. Add the peas and cook, stirring occasionally, for 5 minutes. Stir in the Parmesan and parsley, season with salt and pepper, and serve.

5

SORREL PURÉE WITH TORN CROUTONS

serves 6

FOR THE TORN CROUTONS

¼ lb (125 g) day-old country-style sourdough bread, crusts removed

3 Tbsp unsalted butter, melted

Salt and freshly ground pepper

2 Tbsp unsalted butter

2 yellow onions, chopped

9 oz (280 g) sorrel leaves, stemmed, or baby spinach

1¼ lb (625 g) small red or new potatoes, peeled and thinly sliced

2 cups (16 fl oz/500 ml) chicken or vegetable broth

½ cup (4 fl oz/125 ml) heavy cream

Salt and freshly ground pepper

Sorrel leaves resemble those of spinach and arugula and, like the latter, are often classified as herbs. The plant thrives in the coolness of early spring, when its young leaves have their most delicate taste and texture.

To make the croutons, preheat the oven to 400°F (200°C). Tear the bread into ½-inch (12-mm) pieces and place on a baking sheet. Drizzle the 3 Tbsp butter over the bread, sprinkle with salt and pepper, and toss to coat evenly. Bake until golden and crisp, 10–15 minutes. Let cool.

In a large, heavy pot, melt the 2 Tbsp butter over medium heat. Add the onions and sauté until softened, about 2 minutes. Raise the heat to high and add the sorrel, potatoes, and broth. Pour in 4 cups (32 fl oz/1 l) water and bring to a boil. Reduce the heat to medium-low, cover, and simmer until the potatoes are soft, 15–20 minutes. Remove from the heat and let cool slightly.

Working in batches, purée the soup well in a blender. Strain through a fine-mesh sieve into a clean pot. Stir in the cream and season with salt and pepper. Reheat over medium heat. Serve, garnished with the croutons.

6

LEEK & CELERY ROOT SOUP WITH CHEESE CROUTONS

serves 4

2 Tbsp unsalted butter

3 leeks, white and pale green parts, minced

1 large celery root (about 1 lb/500 kg), peeled and cut into 1-inch (2.5-cm) cubes

2 Yukon Gold potatoes, peeled and cut into 1-inch (2.5-cm) cubes

2–3 cups (16–24 fl oz/500–750 ml) chicken broth

Salt and freshly ground pepper

8 slices baguette, cut on the diagonal

1 Tbsp olive oil

1 cup (4 oz/125 g) grated white Cheddar cheese

Leeks are components in many soups and stocks because of the sweet onion flavor they bring. In this simple recipe, celery root adds its own unique flavor to the pot, resulting in a distinctive soup that calls for just a few ingredients. The cheese croutons can be dipped into the soup, where they will add extra flavor and texture, or they can be eaten as an accompaniment.

In a large, heavy pot, melt the butter over medium heat. Add the leeks, celery root, and potatoes and cook, stirring occasionally, for 2–3 minutes. Add the broth and bring to a simmer, then reduce the heat to medium-low and simmer until the celery root and potatoes are fork-tender, about 20 minutes. Taste and adjust the seasoning with salt and pepper.

For a chunky soup, mash the vegetables with the back of a fork. For a smooth soup, let cool slightly, then working in batches, purée the soup in a food processor or blender. Return to the pot and keep warm over low heat.

Preheat the oven to 400°F (200°C).

Place the baguette slices on a baking sheet and brush on both sides with the oil. Bake until the slices are golden on top, about 10 minutes. Turn and bake until the other side is dry, about 5 minutes. Remove from the oven, sprinkle with the cheese, and bake until melted, about 5 minutes.

Ladle the soup into bowls, lay the croutons on the rim or edge of the bowls, and serve.

7

Feathery bonito flakes, a staple in the Japanese pantry, infuse their savory, smoky flavor into a broth called dashi. Mild-tasting kombu, or dried sea kelp, is also a key ingredient in dashi. You can find both at well-stocked markets and Asian groceries.

DASHI WITH SCALLOPS, WATERCRESS & SOBA NOODLES

serves 6–8

1 lb (500 g) large sea scallops, tough muscles removed

2 pieces kombu, about 4 inches (10 cm) each

1½ cups (1½ oz/45 g) lightly packed bonito flakes

½ lb (250 g) buckwheat soba noodles

5 Tbsp (3 fl oz/80 ml) soy sauce

3 Tbsp mirin

Salt

1 bunch watercress, tough stems removed

Cut each scallop crosswise into thirds. Cover and refrigerate until needed.

In a large saucepan, combine the kombu and 8 cups (64 fl oz/2 l) water and bring to a simmer over medium heat; do not let it boil. As soon as the liquid reaches a simmer, remove and discard the kombu. Stir in the bonito flakes. Remove from the heat and let stand, covered, until the flakes sink to the bottom of the pot and the dashi, or stock, is fragrant, about 5 minutes.

Meanwhile, in another large saucepan, bring another 8 cups water to a boil over high heat. Add the noodles, reduce the heat to medium, and simmer until tender, about 3 minutes. Drain the noodles, rinse well with warm water, drain again, and divide among bowls.

Strain the dashi through a fine-mesh sieve into a large bowl and discard the bonito flakes. Return the dashi to the pan. Add the soy sauce and mirin and bring to a simmer over medium heat. Add the scallops, reduce the heat to low, and simmer gently until the scallops are opaque throughout, about 3 minutes.

Taste the dashi and adjust the seasoning with salt. Add the watercress to the bowls with the noodles. Ladle the dashi and scallops into the bowls and serve.

8

There are countless family recipes for this classic comfort food, often served during the Passover festivities in spring. Here, herb-flecked matzoh balls are simmered in a flavorful chicken broth infused with leek and ginger.

MATZOH BALL SOUP

serves 6

4 eggs

3 Tbsp canola oil

1 cup (5 oz/155 g) matzoh meal

2 Tbsp chopped flat-leaf parsley

¼ cup (⅓ oz/10 g) chopped cilantro

Salt and freshly ground pepper

2–4 Tbsp seltzer water

6 cups (48 fl oz/1.5 l) chicken broth

8 slices peeled ginger

1 leek, white and pale green parts, chopped

2 Tbsp minced chives

In a bowl, whisk together the eggs and oil. Stir in the matzoh meal, parsley, cilantro, ½ tsp salt, and ⅛ tsp pepper. Add 2 Tbsp seltzer and stir to form a slightly sticky mixture. If it is too dry, add 1–2 additional Tbsp seltzer. Cover the bowl with plastic wrap and refrigerate until cold, about 2 hours.

Fill a large, heavy pot three-fourths full with water and add 1 Tbsp salt. Bring to a boil over high heat, then reduce to a simmer. Form the matzoh mixture into balls 1 inch (2.5 cm) in diameter. You should have 12 balls in all. Drop the balls into the simmering water and cook, uncovered, until they rise to the top and are cooked all the way through, 30–40 minutes. Using a slotted spoon, transfer the matzoh balls to a baking sheet. Set aside.

Add the chicken broth and ginger to a saucepan and bring to a simmer over medium-high heat. Reduce the heat to medium-low, add the leek, and simmer, uncovered, until tender, about 10 minutes. Discard the ginger.

Add the matzoh balls to the simmering broth and reheat for 3 minutes. Ladle the broth into bowls and place 2 matzoh balls in each bowl. Serve, garnished with the chives.

9

When cooking with chiles, both fresh and dried, you never know how hot they are until you taste them. Most of the heat is in the membrane that attaches the seeds to the pepper, and the chiles get hotter as they cook, so start by adding just one ancho chile to the broth, as you can always add more.

BEEF BRISKET STEW IN TOMATO–ANCHO CHILE BROTH

serves 4–6

1 can (28 oz/875 g) diced tomatoes with juices

2½ lb (1.25 kg) beef brisket

Salt and freshly ground pepper

2 dried ancho chiles

2 Tbsp canola oil

½ white onion, chopped

2 cloves garlic, chopped

3 cups (24 fl oz/750 ml) chicken broth

¼ cup (¼ oz/7 g) packed cilantro leaves, chopped

FOR THE PICO DE GALLO

2 ripe tomatoes, chopped

¼ cup (1 oz/30 g) chopped white onion

2 tsp finely chopped, seeded, and deribbed jalapeño chile

1 Tbsp fresh lime juice

Salt and freshly ground pepper

½ cup (2 oz/60 g) shredded Monterey jack cheese

3 big handfuls of tortilla chips, crushed

1 avocado, pitted, peeled, and cubed

Preheat the oven to 325°F (165°C). In a Dutch oven or a large baking dish, combine the tomatoes with their juices and 1 cup (8 fl oz/ 250 ml) water. Generously season the brisket on both sides with salt and pepper and nestle in the tomato sauce. Submerge the ancho chiles in the sauce. Cover with a lid or aluminum foil, transfer to the oven, and cook for 1 hour. Using tongs, carefully remove the chiles and place in a bowl. Re-cover the pot, return to the oven, and cook until the brisket shreds easily when pulled apart with a fork, about 2 hours longer. Let cool.

Transfer the brisket to a cutting board, cut into 3 pieces, and shred the meat. Using a large spoon, skim the excess fat off the tomato sauce and transfer the sauce to a food processor or blender. Stem and seed the chiles, add one to the processor, and purée until smooth. Taste the sauce; if you want it spicier, add the second chile and purée. Season with salt and pepper and set aside. ⟩⟩

In a clean, heavy pot, warm the oil over medium-high heat. Add the onion and cook, stirring occasionally, until soft, about 6 minutes. Add the garlic and cook, stirring occasionally, until soft, about 2 minutes. Add the tomato purée and cook, stirring occasionally, until it thickens and deepens in color, about 4 minutes. Stir in the meat and broth, bring to a gentle boil, and cook for 5 minutes. Stir in the cilantro and season with salt and pepper. Keep warm over low heat.

To make the pico de gallo, in a bowl, stir together the tomatoes, onion, jalapeño, and lime juice. Season with salt and pepper.

Serve the stew, topped with a generous dollop of the pico de gallo, cheese, tortilla chips, and avocado.

10

To make the lemon mascarpone, in a small bowl, stir together 4 oz (125 g) room-temperature mascarpone, 1 Tbsp grated lemon zest, 2 tsp lemon juice, and a pinch of salt.

ASPARAGUS-CHERVIL PURÉE WITH LEMON MASCARPONE

serves 4–6

1 Tbsp olive oil

1 small yellow onion, finely chopped

2 cloves garlic, minced

3 cups (24 fl oz/750 ml) chicken or vegetable broth

2 lb (1 kg) asparagus, trimmed and chopped

2 Tbsp minced chervil or flat-leaf parsley

Salt and freshly ground pepper

Lemon Mascarpone (left)

In a large, heavy pot, warm the oil over medium-high heat. Add the onion and garlic and sauté until translucent, about 5 minutes. Add the broth and bring to a boil. Add the asparagus and chervil, reduce the heat to medium-low, and simmer until the asparagus is tender, about 10 minutes. Remove from the heat and let cool slightly.

Working in batches, purée the soup in a blender. Return to the pot and season with salt and pepper. Reheat over low heat.

Serve the soup, garnished with a dollop of the mascarpone.

11

Japanese udon noodles are often served chilled in the summer and hot in the winter, and toppings are chosen to reflect the seasons. Here, they are paired with spinach and green onions and topped, just before serving, with an egg that cooks gently in the hot broth.

UDON NOODLE SOUP WITH CHICKEN & SPINACH

serves 4

⅛ tsp granulated dashi mixed with 1 cup (8 fl oz/250 ml) hot water

1 Tbsp mirin

1 Tbsp dark soy sauce

1 tsp sugar

½ tsp cornstarch

Ground white pepper

¾ lb (375 g) skinless, boneless chicken breast halves, cut into 1-inch (2.5-cm) pieces

FOR THE BROTH

¾ tsp granulated dashi mixed with 6 cups (48 fl oz/1.5 l) hot water

3 Tbsp dark soy sauce

2 Tbsp light soy sauce

2 Tbsp rice vinegar

1 Tbsp sugar

Ground white pepper

1 lb (500 g) udon noodles or thick rice noodles

Salt

3 cups (3 oz/90 g) loosely packed spinach leaves, cut into 2-inch (5-cm) strips, immersed in boiling water for 1 minute, drained, and squeezed dry

4 eggs

4 green onions, white and pale green parts, thinly sliced

1 tsp chili powder

In a saucepan, combine the dashi mixture, mirin, soy sauce, sugar, and cornstarch. Add ⅛ tsp pepper and bring to a boil over high heat. Add the chicken pieces, reduce the heat to medium, and simmer, uncovered, until the chicken is opaque throughout, 10–12 minutes. Remove from the heat.

To make the broth, in a large saucepan, combine the dashi mixture, soy sauces, vinegar, and sugar. Add ⅛ tsp pepper and bring to a boil over medium-high heat. Reduce the heat to medium-low and simmer for 5 minutes. Keep warm.

Bring a saucepan of water to a boil over high heat. Stir in the noodles and 1 tsp salt. Cook until the noodles are just tender, 2–3 minutes. Drain and divide among bowls. ↠

Top each serving of noodles with the chicken mixture and spinach. Crack an egg into each bowl and gently pour the hot broth over the top. Serve, garnished with the green onions and a dusting of chili powder.

12

Roasting root vegetables like carrots caramelizes their natural sugars and concentrates their flavor. Here, roasted carrots are simmered with broth, shallots, and seasonings, then puréed to create a soup that tastes amazingly rich even though it contains no cream or other dairy.

ROASTED CARROT SOUP

serves 8

2½ lb (1.25 kg) carrots, peeled and cut into 1-inch (2.5-cm) pieces

3 Tbsp olive oil

Salt and freshly ground pepper

1½ cups (5½ oz/170 g) thinly sliced shallot

1 tsp minced garlic

½ cup (4 fl oz/125 ml) dry white wine

1 tsp chopped thyme

7 cups (56 fl oz/1.75 l) chicken broth

Preheat the oven to 450°F (230°C).

In a large bowl, stir together the carrots and 1 Tbsp of the oil, and season with salt and pepper. Transfer to a baking sheet. Roast, stirring once halfway through, until the carrots are golden brown and tender, about 45 minutes. Set aside.

In a large, heavy pot, warm the remaining 2 Tbsp oil over medium heat. Add the shallot and cook, stirring occasionally, until tender and translucent, about 6 minutes. Add the garlic and cook, stirring occasionally, for 30 seconds. Add the wine and cook, stirring occasionally, until almost evaporated, about 2 minutes. Add the carrots, thyme, and broth and bring to a simmer. Reduce the heat to medium-low and simmer for 15 minutes. Let cool slightly.

Working in batches, purée the soup in a food processor or blender. Return to the pot, season with salt and pepper, and serve.

SHRIMP & SPINACH NOODLE SOUP

serves 4–6

2 Tbsp olive oil

1 yellow onion, thinly sliced

2 cloves garlic, minced

¼ lb (125 g) white mushrooms, thinly sliced

5 cups (40 fl oz/1.25 l) chicken broth

½ lb (250 g) udon noodles

½ lb (250 g) shrimp, peeled and deveined

1 small bunch spinach, tough stems removed

3 green onions, white and tender green parts, thinly sliced

Salt and freshly ground pepper

This quick-cooking soup is perfect for a busy weeknight. You can substitute nearly any similar green for the spinach; tender pea shoots, available at many farmers' markets in the springtime, would be delicious.

In a large, heavy pot, warm the oil over medium-high heat. Add the onion, garlic, and mushrooms and sauté until the mushrooms release their liquid and begin to turn golden brown, 5–7 minutes. Add the broth and bring to a boil. Add the udon noodles and cook for 4 minutes. Add the shrimp and cook until they turn bright pink, 2–3 minutes. Stir in the spinach and cook just until wilted. Stir in the green onions, season with salt and pepper, and serve.

LAMB & DRIED APRICOT STEW

serves 6–8

2 Tbsp olive oil

1½ lb (750 g) boneless lamb shoulder, trimmed and cut into 1-inch (2.5-cm) cubes

1 large yellow onion, chopped

3 cloves garlic, minced

2 tsp ground cumin

½ tsp ground coriander

¼ tsp cayenne pepper

Salt and freshly ground black pepper

2 cups (16 fl oz/500 ml) chicken broth

1 can (14½ oz/455 g) diced tomatoes

1 can (8¾ oz/270 g) chickpeas, rinsed

¼ cup (2 oz/60 g) dried apricots, halved

1 cinnamon stick

3 Tbsp chopped flat-leaf parsley

This aromatic stew is even better the next day, once the spices have had time to really infuse the meat with flavor. Serve with a simple green salad dressed with a lemony vinaigrette.

In a large, heavy pot, warm the oil over medium-high heat. Cook the lamb in 2 batches until browned on all sides, 6–8 minutes per batch. Transfer to a bowl.

Add the onion and garlic and sauté until soft, 5–7 minutes. Add the cumin, coriander, and cayenne, season with ¼ tsp black pepper, and cook, stirring constantly, for 2 minutes. Add the broth and bring to a simmer, stirring to scrape up any browned bits on the bottom of the pot. Add the tomatoes, chickpeas, apricots, cinnamon stick, and lamb and bring to a boil. Reduce the heat to low, cover partially, and simmer, stirring occasionally, until the lamb is tender and the stew thickens, about 1¼ hours.

Stir in the parsley, season with salt and pepper, and serve.

15

GRILLED ASPARAGUS & GREEN ONION SOUP WITH POACHED EGGS

serves 4

Charring the asparagus and green onions before chopping them and simmering them in broth delivers smoky, complex flavors to the finished soup. Grilling the bread for the poached egg, rather than toasting it in the oven, doubles up on those smoky flavors and makes any brunch or lunch at which this soup is served a special occasion.

2 lb (1 kg) asparagus, trimmed

1 bunch green onions, trimmed

3 Tbsp olive oil

Salt and freshly ground pepper

4 slices baguette, cut on the diagonal

1 Tbsp unsalted butter

½ yellow onion, chopped

5 cups (40 fl oz/1.25 l) vegetable or chicken broth

½ cup (4 oz/125 g) crème fraîche

1 tsp white wine vinegar

4 eggs

Prepare a charcoal or gas grill for direct-heat cooking over medium-high heat. Alternatively, preheat a stove-top grill pan over medium-high heat. In a large bowl, toss together the asparagus, green onions, 2 Tbsp of the oil, ½ tsp salt, and ¼ tsp pepper. Place on the grill rack or in the grill pan and cook, turning often, until lightly golden and tender, about 6 minutes total. Transfer to a cutting board and coarsely chop, keeping the asparagus and green onions separate. Set aside. Brush the baguette slices on both sides with the remaining 1 Tbsp oil. Grill, turning once or twice, until golden, 4–5 minutes total. Transfer to a plate and set aside.

In a large, heavy pot, melt the butter over medium heat. When it foams, add the yellow onion and cook, stirring occasionally, until soft, about 2 minutes. Add the green onions and the broth and bring to a simmer. Reduce the heat to low and simmer for 15 minutes to allow the flavors to blend. Add the asparagus and the crème fraîche and simmer for 2–3 minutes. Let cool slightly.

Working in batches, purée the soup in a food processor or blender. Pour into the same pot, cover, and keep warm over low heat. ↠

In a frying pan, heat 1 inch (2.5 cm) of water over medium-high heat. Add the vinegar and reduce the heat to keep the water at a gentle simmer. Break an egg into a small bowl and, using a large spoon, place the egg gently in the water. Repeat with the remaining 3 eggs.

Cover and simmer until the whites are firm and opaque and the yolks are cooked but still soft, about 4 minutes.

Ladle the soup into bowls. Top each crouton with a poached egg and place one on each bowl. Sprinkle the eggs with ¼ tsp pepper and serve.

16

CHICKEN-LEMONGRASS SOUP

serves 6

This soup, filled with the flavors of Thailand, is easy to make and very addictive. Do not eat the galangal, lemongrass, and lime leaves; they deliver flavor, but are too tough to consume.

1 lb (500 g) skinless, boneless chicken breasts, cut into 1-inch (2.5-cm) pieces

2 cups (16 fl oz/500 ml) chicken broth

3 cups (24 fl oz/750 ml) coconut milk

10 slices galangal

4 lemongrass stalks, center white part only, smashed and cut into 2-inch (5-cm) lengths

6 green Thai chiles or 8 green serrano chiles, cut in half crosswise

8 kaffir lime leaves, spines removed

½ cup (3½ oz/105 g) drained canned straw mushrooms

½ cup (2 oz/60 g) sliced bamboo shoots

3 Tbsp Asian fish sauce

¼ cup (2 fl oz/60 ml) fresh lime juice

¼ cup (¼ oz/7 g) cilantro leaves

In a large saucepan, combine the chicken pieces, broth, coconut milk, galangal, lemongrass, chiles, and lime leaves. Bring to a boil over high heat, reduce the heat to maintain a gentle boil, and cook, uncovered, until the chicken is opaque, about 20 minutes.

Stir in the mushrooms and bamboo shoots, raise the heat to high, and bring to a boil. Add the fish sauce and lime juice, then taste and adjust the seasonings. Serve, garnished with the cilantro.

17

A trio of earthy mushrooms, dried and fresh, creates deep flavor and a variety of textures. Sherry lends a touch of acidity to brighten the palate. Dry to very dry sherries, like golden fino or the slightly darker manzanilla, are best for soups.

THREE-MUSHROOM PURÉE WITH SHERRY

serves 4–6

1½ oz (45 g) dried mushrooms such as porcini or shiitake

3 Tbsp olive oil

1 yellow onion, finely chopped

1 lb (500 g) fresh white mushrooms, thinly sliced

½ lb (250 g) shiitake mushrooms, stemmed and thinly sliced

3 Tbsp all-purpose flour

Salt and freshly ground pepper

4 cups (32 fl oz/1 l) beef, chicken, or vegetable broth

½ cup (4 fl oz/125 ml) half-and-half

¼ cup (2 fl oz/60 ml) dry sherry

2 Tbsp finely chopped flat-leaf parsley

In a heatproof bowl, combine the dried mushrooms and 3 cups (24 fl oz/750 ml) very hot water. Soak for 30 minutes. Drain well, reserving 2 cups (16 fl oz/500 ml) of the soaking liquid. Strain the soaking liquid through a coffee filter into another bowl and set aside.

In a large, heavy pot, warm the oil over medium heat. Add the onion and sauté until softened, 5–7 minutes. Add the fresh mushrooms and cook, stirring, until slightly softened, about 3 minutes. Sprinkle with the flour and season with salt and pepper. Stir to coat the mushrooms and to cook the flour, about 1 minute. Add the broth and the reserved mushroom soaking liquid. Add the drained dried mushrooms and reduce the heat to medium-low. Simmer until all the mushrooms are completely softened, about 15 minutes. Remove from the heat and let cool slightly.

Working in batches, purée the soup in a blender or food processor, making sure to leave a little texture. Return to the pot and place over medium heat. Add the half-and-half and sherry and cook for about 3 minutes to blend the flavors. Serve, garnished with the parsley.

18

This beef-and-potato stew will warm you up—and also fill you up—on a chilly spring evening. It goes perfectly with a glass of red wine or bottle of dark ale. Use good-quality balsamic vinegar for drizzling.

BALSAMIC BEEF STEW

serves 6

3 Tbsp all-purpose flour

Salt and freshly ground pepper

2 lb (1 kg) boneless beef chuck, trimmed and cut into 1½-inch (4-cm) pieces

3 Tbsp canola oil

1 large red onion, sliced

2 bay leaves

1 cup (8 fl oz/250 ml) full-bodied red wine

2 cups (16 fl oz/500 ml) beef broth

1 lb (500 g) red or Yukon Gold potatoes, unpeeled, cut into 1½-inch (4-cm) chunks

3 large carrots, peeled and cut into 1-inch (2.5-cm) chunks

2 Tbsp balsamic vinegar

In a resealable plastic bag, combine the flour, ½ tsp salt, and ½ tsp pepper. Add the beef, seal the bag, and shake to coat the beef. In a large, heavy pot, warm the oil over medium-high heat. Working in batches, remove the beef from the bag, shaking off the excess flour, and add to the pot in a single layer. Cook, turning as needed, until the meat is browned on all sides, 6–8 minutes. Transfer to a plate. Add the onion, reduce the heat to medium, and sauté until golden, about 5 minutes. Stir in the bay leaves, wine, and broth.

Return the meat and any accumulated juices to the pot. Bring to a simmer, then reduce the heat to low. Cover and cook until the meat is nearly fork-tender, 1½–2 hours. Add the potatoes and carrots, cover, and cook until the vegetables are tender, about 30 minutes. Remove and discard the bay leaves.

Season the stew with salt and pepper, stir in the vinegar, and serve.

19

Among the various seafood chowders, Manhattan clam chowder stands out because it includes tomatoes in its clear broth instead of the more typical base of milk or cream. The result is a bright, fresh flavor that supports the briny taste of the clams.

MANHATTAN CLAM CHOWDER

serves 4

FOR THE CLAM BROTH

1 thick slice yellow onion

½ celery rib with leaves

1 bay leaf

1 clove garlic, lightly crushed

Salt

3 lb (1.5 kg) cherrystone or littleneck clams, scrubbed

1 slice thick-cut lightly smoked bacon, cut into ¼-inch (6-mm) dice

1 Tbsp olive oil

1 small onion, finely chopped

1 celery rib, finely chopped

1 large clove garlic, minced

1 can (15½ oz/485 g) crushed tomatoes

1 Tbsp minced flat-leaf parsley, plus whole leaves for garnish

1 tsp thyme leaves

3 Tbsp pearl barley

To make the broth, in a large saucepan over high heat, combine the onion, celery, bay leaf, and garlic. Add 3 cups (24 fl oz/750 ml) water and 1 tsp salt and bring to a boil over high heat. Reduce the heat to low, cover, and cook for 20 minutes to blend the flavors.

Add the clams to the broth, discarding any that do not close to the touch. Raise the heat to medium-high, cover, and cook until the clams open, 3–4 minutes for littlenecks, 4–5 minutes for cherrystones. Transfer the opened clams to a large bowl. Discard any unopened clams.

Strain the broth through a fine-mesh sieve lined with cheesecloth into a heatproof bowl. Working over the sieve to capture any juices, pull the clam meats from the shells and return to the bowl. Cut the clams into ½-inch (12-mm) pieces and refrigerate. Measure the broth; you will need 4 cups (32 fl oz/1 l). Add water if necessary.

In a large, heavy pot, combine the bacon and oil. Warm over medium-low heat until they sizzle. Add the onion, celery, and garlic and sauté until soft, about 12 minutes. Add the strained broth, tomatoes, minced parsley, and thyme. Season with ½ tsp salt and ⟶

⅛ tsp pepper. Bring to a boil over medium-high heat. Stir in the barley, reduce the heat to low, cover, and cook until the barley is very soft, about 50 minutes.

Add in the clams and cook, stirring often, until heated through, about 3 minutes. Serve, garnished with parsley leaves.

20

Celebrate spring—and the arrival of fava beans—with this Italian-inspired soup. You can substitute any small- to medium-sized pasta shape for the farfalle. Serve immediately, so the pasta doesn't overcook.

FAVA BEAN & FARFALLE SOUP

serves 6

2½ lb (1.25 kg) fava beans in the pods, shelled

9 cups (72 fl oz/2.1 l) chicken broth

6 oz (185 g) farfalle

1 Tbsp fresh lemon juice

Salt and freshly ground pepper

½ cup (2 oz/60 g) grated Parmesan cheese

Bring a pot of water to a boil. Add the fava beans and cook for 20 seconds. Drain, rinse under cold running water, and drain again. Split open the skin of each bean along its edge and slip the bean from the skin. Discard the skins.

In a large, heavy pot, bring the broth to a boil. Add the farfalle and cook until al dente, 10–12 minutes or according to the package directions. Add the fava beans and lemon juice. Season with salt and pepper.

Serve the soup, passing the Parmesan at the table.

21

Parsnips are at their best—their sweetest—if they are harvested after the first hard frost of the season. For this soup, they are seasoned with garam masala, an Indian spice blend that varies from region to region but typically includes cumin, coriander, cinnamon, cloves, and cardamom. The soup is accompanied with naan, a popular leavened Indian bread stocked in the fresh bread section of most supermarkets. If you don't have a grill pan, you can toast the naan before brushing it with olive oil and adding salt and parsley.

INDIAN-SPICED PARSNIP PURÉE WITH GRILLED NAAN

serves 4–6

2 Tbsp olive oil, plus more for brushing

2 leeks, white and pale green parts, chopped

2 cloves garlic, chopped

2 tsp garam masala

5 cups (40 fl oz/1.25 l) vegetable or chicken broth

6 parsnips (about 2½ lb/1.25 kg total weight), peeled and chopped

Salt and freshly ground pepper

3 Tbsp heavy cream

6 pieces fresh naan

¼ cup (¼ oz/7 g) flat-leaf parsley leaves, chopped

In a large, heavy pot, warm the oil over medium-high heat. Add the leeks and cook, stirring occasionally, until soft, about 5 minutes. Add the garlic and garam masala and cook, stirring occasionally, until the garlic is soft and the spice is toasted, about 2 minutes. Add the broth and parsnips, season with salt, and bring to a boil. Reduce the heat to low and simmer until the parsnips are soft, 30–35 minutes. Let cool slightly.

Working in batches, purée the soup in a food processor or blender. Return to the pot and place over medium heat. Stir in the cream and cook until warmed through, 3–5 minutes. Season with salt and pepper and keep warm over low heat.

Lightly brush each piece of naan on both sides with oil. Heat a stove-top grill pan over high heat. Grill the naan, turning once, until toasted and grill-marked, about 3 minutes per side. Transfer to a cutting board. While the naan is still hot, lightly brush one side with more oil, season with salt, and sprinkle with the parsley.

Serve the soup with the naan on the side for dipping.

22

Bright coriander harmonizes with two kinds of sweetness in this soup—a familiar, earthy sweetness from the carrots and a more exotic, tropical sweetness from the coconut. Serve as a first course preceding a simple roast chicken or rack of lamb.

CARROT & COCONUT PURÉE WITH CURRIED ALMONDS

serves 6–8

1½ tsp sugar

Salt and freshly ground pepper

¼ tsp ground coriander, plus 1 Tbsp

½ tsp curry powder

1½ tsp unsalted butter, plus 3 Tbsp

½ cup (2 oz/60 g) toasted sliced almonds

1 yellow onion, chopped

2 lb (1 kg) carrots, peeled and thinly sliced

¼ cup (1 oz/30 g) unsweetened shredded coconut, toasted

½ tsp ground ginger

4 cups (32 fl oz/1 l) chicken broth

2 cans (14 fl oz/440 ml each) coconut milk

2 tsp rice vinegar

Stir together ½ tsp of the sugar, ¼ tsp salt, the ¼ tsp coriander, and the curry powder.

In a nonstick frying pan, melt the 1½ tsp butter with 1 Tbsp water and the remaining 1 tsp sugar over medium-high heat. Bring to a boil, swirling the pan to blend. Add the almonds, stir to coat, and cook until the liquid is almost evaporated, about 45 seconds. Transfer to the bowl with the spice mixture and toss to coat the almonds evenly. Pour onto a piece of parchment paper, spread in a single layer, and let cool.

In a large, heavy pot, melt the 3 Tbsp butter over medium-high heat. Add the onion, carrots, coconut, ginger, and the 1 Tbsp coriander and stir to combine. Reduce the heat to low, cover, and cook until the vegetables give off some of their liquid, about 10 minutes. Add the broth, raise the heat to high, and bring to a boil. Reduce the heat to low, cover, and simmer until the carrots are tender, about 20 minutes. Remove from the heat and let cool slightly.

Working in batches, purée the soup in a blender. Pour into a clean pot. Add the coconut milk (reserve some for serving), the vinegar, and 1 tsp salt. Cook gently over medium-low heat, stirring occasionally, until heated through, about 10 minutes. Serve, sprinkled with the spiced almonds and swirled with coconut milk.

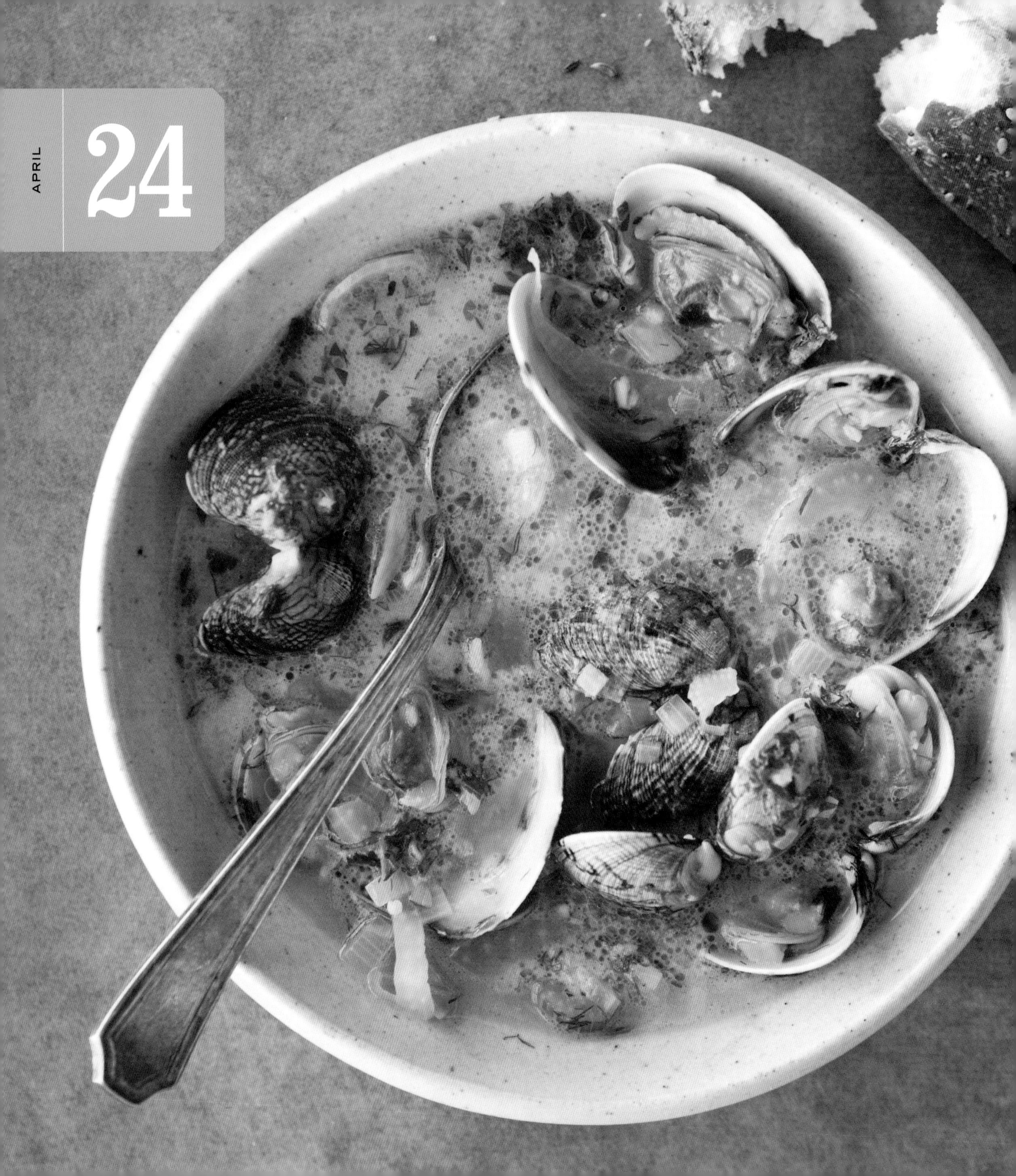

23

You may need to take a trip to an Asian market to source the classic Thai ingredients in this fragrant soup. If you can't find kaffir lime leaves, substitute the grated zest of 1 lime. Adjust the amount of chiles and lime juice according to your taste.

THAI HOT & SOUR SOUP

serves 6

¾ lb (375 g) large shrimp, peeled and deveined, tail segments intact and shells reserved

3 lemongrass stalks, center white part only, smashed and cut into 1-inch (2.5-cm) lengths

5 thin slices galangal, about ¼ inch (6 mm) thick

3 fresh or dried kaffir lime leaves

2 Tbsp Asian fish sauce

5 oz (155 g) white mushrooms, stem ends trimmed and caps quartered

1 tomato, peeled and cut into thin wedges

¼ small yellow onion, cut lengthwise into thin slivers

4 tsp Thai red or green chile paste

2 small red or green chiles such as Thai or serrano

¼ cup (2 fl oz/60 ml) fresh lime juice, or to taste

¼ cup (⅓ oz/10 g) chopped cilantro

In a large saucepan, combine the shrimp shells with 5 cups (40 fl oz/1.25 l) water. Add the lemongrass to the pan. Bring to a simmer over medium heat, cover partially, and simmer gently for 15 minutes to blend the flavors. Strain the broth through a fine-mesh sieve into a clean saucepan.

Add the galangal, lime leaves, fish sauce, mushrooms, tomato, onion, and chile paste. Remove the stems from the chiles, then quarter the chiles lengthwise. Add as many of the quarters to the broth as you like; you may want to start with just a few.

Bring the soup to a simmer over medium heat, cover partially, and simmer gently until the mushrooms are barely tender, about 2 minutes. Taste halfway through and add more chile quarters if the soup is not spicy enough. Stir in the shrimp and simmer just until they turn pink, about 2 minutes. Remove from the heat.

Stir in the ¼ cup lime juice and the cilantro. Taste and adjust the seasoning with more lime juice, if desired, and serve.

24

You can use cockles or mussels in place of the clams in this recipe. Serve with crusty country-style bread to soak up the broth. The parsley vinaigrette is also delicious drizzled on sliced grilled chicken or fish.

CLAMS IN FENNEL BROTH WITH PARSLEY VINAIGRETTE

serves 4

FOR THE VINAIGRETTE

⅓ cup (½ oz/15 g) minced flat-leaf parsley

Grated zest and juice of 1 lemon

1 Tbsp extra-virgin olive oil

1 Tbsp Dijon mustard

1 clove garlic, minced

Salt and freshly ground pepper

1 Tbsp unsalted butter

1 Tbsp olive oil

2 cloves garlic, sliced

2 small fennel bulbs, including stalks and fronds, sliced

2 shallots, minced

½ cup (4 fl oz/125 ml) dry white wine

1 cup (8 fl oz/250 ml) chicken broth

2 lb (1 kg) manila clams, scrubbed

To make the vinaigrette, in a small bowl, stir together the parsley, lemon zest and juice, oil, mustard, and garlic. Season with salt and pepper and let stand at room temperature.

In a large, heavy pot, melt the butter with the oil over medium-high heat. Add the garlic, fennel, and shallots and sauté until soft, about 5 minutes. Add the wine and cook for 2 minutes. Add the broth and bring to a boil. Add the clams to the pot, discarding any that do not close to the touch. Cover and cook until the clams open, 6–8 minutes. Discard any unopened clams.

Ladle the clams and broth into bowls, drizzle with the vinaigrette, and serve.

25

APRIL

You can make this soup ahead and refrigerate it, but you will need to add more broth when you rewarm it, as the lentils will have absorbed most of the liquid. Kielbasa can be substituted for the andouille.

LENTIL & ANDOUILLE SOUP

serves 8–10

1 lb (500 g) andouille sausage, cut into ¼-inch-thick (6-mm-thick) slices

2 Tbsp olive oil

2 carrots, peeled and chopped

1 large yellow onion, chopped

4 large cloves garlic, minced

1 lb (500 g) lentils, picked over and rinsed

8 cups (64 fl oz/2 l) chicken broth, plus more as needed

1 Tbsp heavy cream

¼ cup (⅓ oz/10 g) chopped flat-leaf parsley

Salt and freshly ground pepper

In a large, heavy pot, cook the sausage slices over medium-high heat until browned on both sides, about 8 minutes. Transfer to a plate and set aside.

Add the oil, carrots, onion, and garlic to the same pot and sauté until the vegetables are softened, about 8 minutes. Add the lentils and broth and bring to a boil. Reduce the heat to low and simmer, uncovered, stirring occasionally, until the lentils are tender, 20–30 minutes. Remove from the heat and let cool slightly.

Purée half of the soup in a food processor. Return to the pot and stir to combine. Stir in the sausage, cream, and parsley, and reheat over low heat. Season with salt and pepper and serve.

26

APRIL

A favorite in the kitchens of the Old World, fava beans have been found in sites as disparate as Egyptian tombs and Swiss lake dwellings. They are especially popular in the Mediterranean, where the dried beans are used in soups and stews, the fresh beans are eaten raw or cooked, and the young leaves are used in salads. Here, they are paired with two typical Spanish pantry items, chorizo and paprika, in a full-bodied, flavorful soup.

SPANISH FAVA BEAN SOUP WITH PAPRIKA & CHORIZO

serves 6

2 cups (about ¾ lb/375 g) dried fava beans, picked over and rinsed

1 Tbsp olive oil

1 yellow onion, chopped

2 cloves garlic, chopped

1 Tbsp sweet paprika

2 dried red chiles, such as Colorado or New Mexico

3 tsp dried oregano

Salt and freshly ground pepper

2 bay leaves

¾ lb (375 g) smoked Spanish chorizo, cut into slices ½ inch (12 mm) thick

Put the fava beans in a large bowl, cover with water by 3 inches, and let soak in the refrigerator for 8 hours or overnight.

In a large, heavy pot, warm the oil over medium-high heat. Add the onion and garlic and cook, stirring occasionally, until the onion is softened, about 2 minutes. Sprinkle in the paprika and stir until combined, about 1 minute. Drain the fava beans. Add the fava beans, 8 cups (64 fl oz/2 l) water, the chiles, 1½ tsp of the oregano, ½ tsp salt, and the bay leaves and bring to a boil. Reduce the heat to medium-low, cover, and simmer for 1 hour. Stir in ½ tsp salt, ¼ tsp pepper, and the remaining 1½ tsp oregano. Cover and cook until the beans are tender but still hold their shape, about 1 hour longer, adding more water if needed.

Drain the beans, reserving the broth. Taste the broth and adjust the seasoning; it should be richly flavored. Remove and discard the chiles and bay leaves. Return the beans and broth to the pot and bring to a simmer over medium-high heat. Add the chorizo, simmer for 5 minutes, and serve.

LOTUS ROOT IN
TWO-MUSHROOM BROTH

serves 4

A member of the water lily family, lotus root is native to the Asian tropics, where it has been cultivated for more than three millennia. Every part—seeds, leaves, flowers, rhizomes—is edible. The rhizomes are valued for their crunchy texture, and although their flavor is bland, like that of jicama, they readily absorb other flavors, as they do in this rich, earthy broth. When the rhizomes are sliced, a series of holes are revealed that form a lovely flower-like design.

3 or 4 dried shiitake mushrooms

1 cup (8 fl oz/250 ml) boiling water

¼ lb (125 g) fresh shiitake mushrooms

2 green onions, white and tender green parts, cut into 2-inch (5-cm) lengths

1 carrot, cut into 2-inch (5-cm) lengths

1-inch (2.5-cm) piece fresh ginger, peeled and thinly sliced, plus 4 tsp peeled and grated fresh ginger

¼ cup (2 fl oz/60 ml) dry sherry

1 star anise

3½ cups (28 fl oz/875 ml) chicken broth

1 small lotus root (about ½ lb/250 g)

Ice water, as needed

½ tsp soy sauce (optional)

¼ cup (⅓ oz/10 g) chopped cilantro

Put the dried mushrooms in a bowl and pour the boiling water over them. Let stand until softened, about 20 minutes. Squeeze the mushrooms to release all of the liquid and then chop. Set the mushrooms aside. Strain the soaking liquid through a fine-mesh sieve lined with cheesecloth. Set the liquid aside.

Reserve 1 large fresh mushroom and quarter the remaining ones, including the stems. In a large, heavy pot, combine the green onions, carrot, sliced ginger, sherry, star anise, broth, reserved mushroom soaking liquid, chopped rehydrated mushrooms, and quartered fresh mushrooms. Place over medium-high heat and bring to a boil. Reduce the heat to medium-low, cover, and simmer for 35 minutes.

Meanwhile, using a paring knife, peel the lotus root and cut crosswise into slices ¼ inch (6 mm) thick. You will need about 16 slices. Place in a bowl of ice water to keep them crisp until ready to use.

Strain the broth through a fine-mesh sieve lined with cheesecloth, discarding the solids. Pour the broth into a large, heavy pot. Drain the lotus root slices and add to the broth. ↠

Cut the reserved fresh mushroom into paper-thin slices and add to the broth. Place over medium heat and bring to a simmer, then reduce the heat to low and simmer for 5 minutes. Taste and add soy sauce, if desired.

Ladle into bowls, dividing the lotus root and mushroom slices evenly. Garnish with the grated ginger and cilantro and serve.

SPINACH SOUP WITH
SUMAC & FETA

serves 6–8

Sumac, a tart Middle Eastern spice, brightens up this spinach soup, as does a sprinkle of feta cheese. This is a great recipe to have in your arsenal because it calls for frozen spinach, but you can substitute fresh spinach if you have some on hand.

2 Tbsp unsalted butter

1 Tbsp olive oil

1 large yellow onion, finely chopped

4 cloves garlic, minced

2 tsp sumac

1½ tsp ground cumin

1 tsp ground coriander

¼ tsp cayenne pepper

2 bags (1 lb/500 g each) frozen chopped spinach, thawed

4½ cups (36 fl oz/1.1 l) chicken broth, plus more as needed

Grated zest and juice of 1 lemon

3 Tbsp heavy cream

Salt and freshly ground black pepper

6 oz (185 g) feta cheese, crumbled

In a large, heavy pot, melt the butter with the oil over medium-high heat. Add the onion and garlic and sauté until translucent, about 5 minutes. Add the sumac, cumin, coriander, and cayenne, and cook for 2 minutes. Stir in the spinach, broth, and lemon zest and juice. Bring to a boil. Reduce the heat to low and simmer, stirring frequently, for 10 minutes. Remove from the heat and let cool slightly.

Purée half of the soup in a blender. Return to the pot, thin with additional chicken broth, if desired, then stir in the cream. Season with salt and pepper, and reheat over low heat. Serve, topped with the crumbled feta.

29

CREAM OF MUSHROOM SOUP

serves 6–8

6 cups (48 fl oz/1.5 l) chicken broth

2 oz (60 g) dried porcini mushrooms

4 Tbsp (2 oz/60 g) unsalted butter

3 Tbsp minced shallot

1½ lb (750 g) white mushrooms, coarsely chopped

¼ cup (2 fl oz/60 ml) Madeira (optional)

2 Tbsp all-purpose flour

½ cup (4 fl oz/125 ml) heavy cream, plus ¼ cup (2 fl oz/60 ml) for drizzling (optional)

Salt and freshly ground pepper

Deep-fried sage leaves for garnish (optional)

A mix of dried and fresh mushrooms delivers a welcome depth of flavor to this pleasantly creamy soup. If you opt to include the Madeira, an amber-hued fortified wine from Portugal, choose a modestly priced bottle (blended Madeiras are typically less expensive than single-varietal types). Serve as a first course for an autumn meal with roast beef or lamb on the menu.

In a small saucepan, warm 2 cups (16 fl oz/500 ml) of the broth over medium-high heat. Add the porcini, remove from the heat, and let stand for about 20 minutes. Using a slotted spoon, transfer the porcini to a cutting board and coarsely chop. Strain the soaking liquid through a fine-mesh sieve lined with a double layer of cheesecloth. Set aside.

In a large, heavy pot, melt the butter over medium heat. Add the shallot and cook, stirring occasionally, until soft, about 5 minutes. Add the porcini and white mushrooms and cook, stirring occasionally, until most of the liquid has evaporated, 5–7 minutes. Add the Madeira, if using, and cook until the liquid has evaporated, about 2 minutes. Sprinkle with the flour and stir to coat. Stir in the mushroom soaking liquid and the remaining 4 cups (32 fl oz/1 l) broth. Reduce the heat to low and simmer, stirring occasionally, for about 30 minutes. Let cool slightly.

Working in batches, purée the soup in a food processor or blender. Return to the pot, stir in the ½ cup (4 fl oz/125 ml) cream, and season with salt and pepper. Serve, garnished with fried sage leaves and drizzled with the ¼ cup (2 fl oz/60 ml) cream, if desired.

30

KIELBASA & SAUERKRAUT SOUP

serves 8–10

1 lb (500 g) kielbasa sausage, sliced

2 Tbsp olive oil

2 yellow onions, thinly sliced

4 cloves garlic, minced

1 sweet potato (about 10 oz/315 g), peeled and shredded

6 cups (48 fl oz/1.5 l) chicken broth

1 lb (500 g) sauerkraut, drained

2 Tbsp tomato paste

Salt and freshly ground pepper

Germany is to thank for this genius combination of sausages and pickled cabbage, a sour-savory comfort food. This soup feeds a crowd, but it also freezes well if you have any left over. Serve with hunks of freshly baked rye or pumpernickel bread.

Warm a large, heavy pot over medium-high heat. Add the kielbasa slices and sauté until browned on both sides, about 8 minutes. Transfer to a bowl and set aside.

Put the oil in the same pot. Add the onions and garlic and cook, stirring often and scraping up the brown bits on the bottom of the pot, until softened, 5–7 minutes. Add the sweet potato, the broth, and 1 cup (8 fl oz/250 ml) water and bring to a boil. Reduce the heat to low and simmer, uncovered, for 10 minutes. Add the sauerkraut, tomato paste, and kielbasa, stir well to combine, and simmer, uncovered, for 10 minutes. Season with salt and pepper and serve.

5

WONTON SOUP
page 109

6

RED MISO SOUP WITH
SHIITAKE MUSHROOMS & RAMPS
page 109

7

PEA & MINT PURÉE
WITH LEMON
page 111

12

ED LENTIL & DANDELION GREEN SOUP
page 113

13

SPICY COCONUT CURRY
SEAFOOD SOUP
page 114

14

RAMEN NOODLE SOUP
WITH SUGAR SNAP PEAS
page 114

19

ISRAELI COUSCOUS SOUP WITH
CURRY, CHICKEN & SPINACH
page 119

20

WATERCRESS SOUP
page 119

21

RED PEPPER SOUP WITH
MINI CRAB CAKES
page 120

26

EGG-LEMON SOUP WITH
FAVA BEANS & FRIED GARLIC CHIPS
page 124

27

STRAWBERRY-LEMON SOUP
page 125

28

CREAMY SPINACH-LEEK SOUP
page 125

May heralds high spring, when brisk but ever-sunnier days welcome bowls full of tender shoots and leaves. Enjoy the season's last asparagus, artichokes, and sweet peas, and if a few residual rain showers linger, take advantage of short-season greens—such as ramps and watercress—while you still can. As the weather continues to warm, welcome bell peppers and berries, as more vibrant hues grace our tables.

may

1

This light and bright soup, which can be served cold or hot, is a fitting welcome to spring. Try replacing the ginger with 2 tsp cumin seed or coriander seed and the orange zest with lime zest or lemon zest. Use chicken broth in place of the vegetable broth for a richer taste.

CHILLED CARROT SOUP WITH GINGER & ORANGE ZEST

serves 4–6

2 Tbsp olive oil

1 yellow onion, chopped

2 cloves garlic, minced

2-inch (5-cm) piece fresh ginger, peeled and minced

2 lb (1 kg) carrots, thinly sliced

4 cups (32 fl oz/1 l) vegetable broth

Salt and freshly ground pepper

Grated zest of 1 orange

In a large, heavy pot, warm the oil over medium-high heat. Add the onion, garlic, and ginger and sauté until soft, about 5 minutes. Add the carrots, stir, and cook for 5 minutes. Add the broth and bring to a boil. Reduce the heat to low and simmer until the carrots are very tender, about 35 minutes. Remove from the heat and let cool slightly.

Working in batches, purée the soup in a blender or food processor and return to the pot. Season with salt and pepper.

Stir in the orange zest and let the soup cool to room temperature. Cover and refrigerate until well chilled, at least 3 hours or up to overnight. Serve.

2

For a stunning presentation, serve this soup in shallow bowls so the salmon doesn't sink to the bottom. The dill can be replaced by chopped chervil or chives, if you prefer.

POTATO-LEEK PURÉE WITH SMOKED SALMON & DILL

serves 6

2 Tbsp olive oil

2 leeks, white and pale green parts, chopped

2 russet potatoes, peeled and finely diced

4 cups (32 fl oz/1 l) chicken broth

1/2 cup (4 fl oz/125 ml) heavy cream

1 Tbsp chopped dill

Salt and freshly ground pepper

1/4 lb (125 g) smoked salmon, chopped

In a large, heavy pot, warm the oil over medium-high heat. Add the leeks and sauté until soft, about 5 minutes. Add the potatoes and the broth and bring to a boil. Reduce the heat to low and simmer until the potatoes are very soft, about 20 minutes. Remove from the heat and let cool slightly.

Working in batches, purée the soup in a blender. Return to the pot and stir in the cream and dill. Return the soup to a gentle boil, turn off the heat, and season with salt and pepper.

Serve, garnished with the smoked salmon.

3

CHICKEN & SPRING VEGETABLE SOUP

serves 4–6

1 Tbsp olive oil

1 yellow onion, diced

2 celery ribs, diced

2 carrots, peeled and diced

1 large clove garlic, minced

1 Tbsp chicken demi-glace

2 skinless, boneless chicken breast halves (about 6 oz/185 g each)

6 large flat-leaf parsley sprigs

1 bay leaf

Salt and freshly ground pepper

¼ lb (125 g) cremini mushrooms, thinly sliced

½ bunch asparagus, trimmed and thinly sliced on the diagonal

1 cup (5 oz/155 g) fresh or thawed frozen peas

Asparagus and peas, two signature vegetables of spring, are only briefly cooked in this light, delicate chicken soup. The addition of just a tablespoon of chicken demi-glace creates a savory, flavorful stock in no time, making this a good menu choice for a busy weeknight. Look for the demi-glace in well-stocked grocery stores, specialty food stores, or online.

In a large, heavy pot, warm the oil over medium heat. Add the onion, celery, and carrots and cook, stirring occasionally, until softened, 8–10 minutes. Add the garlic and demi-glace and cook, stirring occasionally, until fragrant, about 1 minute.

Add 12 cups (3 qt/3 l) water, the chicken, parsley, and bay leaf and bring to a simmer. Reduce the heat to medium-low and simmer until the chicken is cooked through, about 20 minutes. Using tongs, transfer the chicken to a plate and, when cool enough to handle, shred into bite-sized pieces.

Strain the broth through a fine-mesh sieve, discarding the solids. Return the broth to the pot and season with salt and pepper. Place over medium-high heat and bring to a simmer. Add the chicken, mushrooms, asparagus, and peas and cook until the vegetables are just tender, 2–3 minutes. Remove and discard the bay leaf. Taste and adjust the seasoning and serve.

4

MOROCCAN-SPICED VEGETARIAN CHILI

serves 6

4 large ancho chiles

4 large whole cloves garlic, plus 6 large cloves, sliced

1 yellow onion, chopped

1½ tsp ground turmeric

1½ tsp ground cinnamon

1½ tsp ground cumin

1½ tsp ground coriander

1 can (28 oz/875 g) diced tomatoes

1 butternut squash (about 1¼ lb/625 g), halved, seeded, peeled, and cut into ½-inch (12-mm) cubes

2 cans (15½ oz/485 g each) chickpeas

2 zucchini, cut into ½-inch (12-mm) dice

⅓ cup (2 oz/60 g) sliced dried apricots

⅓ cup (2 oz/60 g) sliced pitted prunes

Serve this richly spiced vegetarian chili with toasted pita bread or on a bed of steamed couscous or rice. Hubbard or acorn squash may be used in place of the butternut squash.

In a saucepan, combine the chiles and 3 cups (24 fl oz/750 ml) water and bring to a boil. Remove from the heat. Cover and let stand for 15 minutes. Using tongs or a slotted spoon, transfer the chiles to a work surface; reserve the liquid. Discard the stems and seeds from the chiles. In a blender or food processor, combine the chiles with the 4 whole cloves garlic and ½ cup (4 fl oz/125 ml) of the chile soaking liquid. Process until smooth and set aside.

Heat a large, heavy pot over medium heat. Coat the pan with nonstick cooking spray. Add the onion, the sliced garlic cloves, turmeric, cinnamon, cumin, and coriander and sauté until the onion and garlic have softened, about 5 minutes. Stir in the tomatoes and their juices, the butternut squash, and the chile purée. Cover and simmer, stirring occasionally, until the butternut squash is just tender, about 25 minutes.

Stir in the chickpeas with their liquid, the zucchini, and the dried apricots and prunes. Simmer, uncovered, until the zucchini is tender, about 15 minutes. Serve.

5

Simmered in broth, stuffed wontons plump and tenderize for a satisfying soup. Triangles are easy to fold, but also try little bundles or half moons, as you like.

WONTON SOUP

serves 4–6

FOR THE WONTONS

¼ lb (125 g) diced pork, chicken, or shrimp

1½ tsp peeled and grated fresh ginger

2 Tbsp chopped water chestnuts

1½ Tbsp chopped green onion, white part only

1 Tbsp chopped cilantro

1 Tbsp light soy sauce

1 tsp rice wine (optional)

1 small egg

Salt and ground white pepper

24 wonton wrappers

2–3 dried shiitake mushrooms, soaked in hot water to cover for 30 minutes and drained

6 cups (48 fl oz/1.5 l) chicken broth

¾ cup (1¾ oz/50 g) small bok choy leaves

1½-inch (4-cm) piece carrot, peeled and cut into thin matchsticks

1 green onion, tender green part only, cut into thin matchsticks

To make the wontons, in a food processor, combine the pork and the ginger and process to a smooth paste. Add the water chestnuts, green onion, cilantro, soy sauce, rice wine (if using), and egg. Season with salt and pepper and process again until a smooth paste forms.

Working with 1 wonton wrapper at a time, place it on a work surface and moisten any 2 edges with cold water. Place 2–3 tsp of the filling in the center and fold in half into a triangle. Press the edges firmly to seal, then fold the two outer points across the top of the mound and pinch the edges together. If they do not stick, moisten with a little water. Repeat until all the dumplings are filled.

To prepare the soup, remove and discard the stems from the mushrooms and slice the caps. In a saucepan, bring the broth to a boil over medium heat. Add the bok choy leaves, carrot, and mushrooms and simmer for 2 minutes.

Meanwhile, bring a saucepan three-fourths full of water to a boil over high heat. Add the wontons, reduce the heat to medium, and simmer gently until they float to the ⇒⇒

surface and the skins are tender, about 3 minutes. Using a wire skimmer, carefully lift out the wontons and divide evenly among individual bowls.

Ladle the soup over the wontons, garnish with the green onion tops, and serve.

6

Granulated dashi and miso, both staples of the Japanese kitchen, are carried in well-stocked grocery stores and Asian markets. You will likely have a choice of red, white, or yellow miso, and any one of them will work here. For a lighter flavor, choose white or yellow over the red. A springtime treat, ramps, a type of wild onion, look like green onions but with broad green leaves. Fiddleheads, another spring favorite, or a combination of green onions and watercress can be substituted.

RED MISO SOUP WITH SHIITAKE MUSHROOMS & RAMPS

serves 6

1 Tbsp canola oil

¼ lb (60 g) shiitake mushrooms, stemmed and halved

1 bunch ramps, roots trimmed

Salt and freshly ground pepper

2 tsp granulated dashi

2 Tbsp red miso paste

In a frying pan, warm the oil over medium-high heat. Add the mushrooms and cook, stirring frequently, until they begin to soften, about 4 minutes. Cut the greens from the ramps and coarsely chop. Slice the remainder of the ramps. Add the greens and sliced ramps to the pan, and season lightly with salt and pepper. Cook, stirring frequently, until softened, about 3 minutes. Set aside.

In a heavy pot, combine the dashi and 4 cups (32 fl oz/1 l) water and bring to a boil over high heat. Whisk in the miso paste and simmer for 2–3 minutes. Add the mushrooms and ramps and cook until warmed through, about 2 minutes. Serve.

PEA & MINT PURÉE WITH LEMON

serves 4–6

2 Tbsp unsalted butter

2 shallots, minced

3 cups (24 fl oz/750 ml) chicken broth

3 cups (15 oz/470 g) fresh or frozen peas, plus more for garnish

½ cup (¾ oz/20 g) chopped mint, plus small leaves for garnish

1 Tbsp sour cream

Grated zest of 1 lemon

Salt and freshly ground pepper

Extra-virgin olive oil for drizzling

7

MAY

This quintessential spring soup is simply divine, showcasing tender fresh peas. You can substitute frozen peas if necessary, or to enjoy this dish throughout the year. For an elegant and flavorful garnish, swirl crème fraîche or olive oil on top.

In a large, heavy pot, melt the butter over medium-high heat. Add the shallots and cook until soft, 5 minutes. Add the broth and bring to a boil. Add the peas, reserving a few for the garnish, and cook until tender, 3–5 minutes. Stir in the chopped mint. Remove from the heat and let cool slightly.

Working in batches, purée the soup in a blender or food processor. Return to the pot, stir in the sour cream, and warm over medium heat. Turn off the heat and stir in the lemon zest. Season with salt and pepper and serve, garnished with mint leaves and peas and drizzled with oil.

MUSHROOM & WHEAT BERRY SOUP WITH SHRIMP

serves 4

Salt and freshly ground pepper

1 cup (6 oz/185 g) wheat berries, rinsed and drained

4 Tbsp (2 fl oz/60 ml) olive oil

½ lb (250 g) cremini or white mushrooms, thickly sliced

1 Tbsp unsalted butter

2 leeks, white and pale green parts, halved and thinly sliced

2 cloves garlic, chopped

5 cups (40 fl oz/1.25 l) chicken broth

¾ lb (375 g) medium shrimp, peeled and deveined

2 tsp grated lemon zest

8

MAY

Wheat berries are a wonderful nutty-tasting whole grain packed with protein, fiber, and B vitamins. Here, they star in a healthful soup, but they are also an excellent base for salads and side dishes. To make this soup the centerpiece of a lunch or a light dinner, accompany it with a spinach or kale salad with ricotta salata and toasted walnuts.

Bring a large saucepan of salted water to a boil over medium-high heat. Add the wheat berries and cook, stirring occasionally, until tender, about 1 hour. Drain, rinse under cold water, and drain again. Set aside.

Meanwhile, in a frying pan, warm 2 Tbsp of the oil over medium-high heat. Add the mushrooms and season with salt and pepper. Cook, stirring occasionally, until the mushrooms deepen in color and soften, but still hold their shape, about 5 minutes. Set aside.

In a large, heavy pot, melt the butter with the remaining 2 Tbsp oil over medium-high heat. Add the leeks and cook, stirring frequently, until soft and golden around the edges, about 5 minutes. Add the garlic, season with salt and pepper, and cook, stirring occasionally, until soft, about 2 minutes. Add the broth and bring to a boil. Stir in the mushrooms, reduce the heat to low, and simmer for 10 minutes.

Stir in the wheat berries, raise the heat to medium, and bring to a simmer. Add the shrimp and cook until opaque throughout, about 3 minutes. Stir in the lemon zest, season with salt and pepper, and serve.

9

CHICKEN, RICE & CELERY SOUP
serves 4–6

1 Tbsp unsalted butter

½ cup (3 oz/90 g) minced shallot

1 clove garlic, minced

4 celery ribs, chopped, plus celery leaves for garnish

6 cups (48 fl oz/1.5 l) chicken broth

1 skinless, boneless chicken breast half (about ⅓ lb/150 g)

¼ cup (1¾ oz/55 g) white or brown rice

Salt and freshly ground pepper

This is old-fashioned comfort food, thick and hearty with familiar flavors. It can be considered a sister of chicken noodle soup, since many of the same ingredients are used, with only the starch being different. You can use this same recipe to make turkey soup with the leftovers from a holiday meal.

In a large, heavy pot, melt the butter over medium heat. When it foams, add the shallot and garlic and cook, stirring occasionally, until the shallot is softened, about 2 minutes. Add the chopped celery and cook, stirring occasionally, until softened, about 2 minutes. Add the broth and bring to a boil. Add the chicken, reduce the heat to medium-low, cover, and simmer until the chicken is opaque throughout, about 20 minutes. Using tongs, transfer the chicken to a cutting board.

Add the rice, salt, and pepper. Reduce the heat to low, cover, and cook until the rice is tender and the water has been absorbed, about 20 minutes for white rice, about 40 minutes for brown. Set aside.

Shred or chop the chicken, add to the pot, and simmer until warmed through, about 5 minutes.

Serve, garnished with the celery leaves.

10

RED BEAN & ANDOUILLE SOUP
serves 6–8

4 cups (28 oz/875 g) dried red kidney beans, picked over and rinsed

1 meaty ham bone, about 1 lb (500 g), trimmed of excess fat

1 yellow onion, chopped

1 celery rib, chopped

2 cloves garlic, chopped

1 large bay leaf

½ tsp dried thyme

Hot sauce, such as Tabasco

Salt and freshly ground pepper

½ lb (250 g) andouille or other lean smoked sausage, cut into slices ¼ inch (6 mm) thick

Chopped green onions, white and tender green parts, for garnish

This New Orleans–style soup is easy to vary; use a different kind of bean, chicken or vegetable broth, or another lean sausage. Serve with a side of corn bread and hot sauce for dousing.

Soak the dried beans in cold water to cover for at least 4 hours or overnight.

In a large, heavy pot, combine the ham bone and 6 cups (48 fl oz/1.5 l) water and bring to a boil over high heat. Reduce the heat to medium-low and simmer briskly for 1 hour, skimming frequently to remove any foam that rises to the surface.

Remove from the heat. Using tongs, carefully lift the bone from the pot and set aside. When cool enough to handle, remove the meat from the bone, discarding any fat. Skim any fat from the surface of the broth and return the bone to the broth.

Drain the beans and add to the broth along with the yellow onion, celery, garlic, bay leaf, and thyme. Return to high heat and bring to a boil. Reduce the heat to low, cover, and simmer, stirring frequently, until the beans are tender, about 2 hours.

Remove and discard the ham bone and bay leaf and let the soup cool slightly. Scoop out 3 cups (21 oz/655 g) of the beans with a little liquid and purée in a blender or food processor. Return to the pot. Cut the reserved ham into bite-sized pieces and add to the pot. Season with a few drops of hot-pepper sauce, salt, and pepper.

In a large frying pan, brown the andouille over medium-high heat, 2 minutes per side.

Serve, topped with sausage and green onions.

11

LEEK & ASPARAGUS VICHYSSOISE

serves 6–8

Vichyssoise is usually served chilled, but if you prefer it warm, reheat slightly after blending and serve. For a healthier, brighter green soup, omit the half-and-half or use yogurt instead.

5 leeks (about 2½ lb/1.25 kg total), white and pale green parts

2 Tbsp unsalted butter

2 Tbsp canola oil

1 tsp minced thyme

5 cups (40 fl oz/1.25 l) chicken broth

1 small russet potato, peeled and coarsely chopped

2 lb (1 kg) asparagus, trimmed and coarsely chopped

1 cup (1 oz/30 g) packed baby spinach leaves

1 cup (8 fl oz/250 ml) half-and-half, plus 3 Tbsp

Salt and freshly ground pepper

Cut the leeks in half lengthwise and then cut each half crosswise into pieces ¼ inch (6 mm) thick. Rinse well and drain.

In a large, heavy pot, melt 1 Tbsp of the butter with 1 Tbsp of the oil over medium-heat. Set aside 1 cup (4 oz/125 g) of the leeks and add the rest to the pot along with the thyme. Reduce the heat to low, cover, and cook, stirring occasionally, until the leeks are softened, about 10 minutes. Add the broth and potato, raise the heat to medium-high, cover, and bring to a boil. Reduce the heat to medium-low and simmer until the potato is tender, about 10 minutes.

When the potato is tender, add the asparagus, cover the pot, and cook until the asparagus is bright green and just tender, about 3 minutes. Stir in the spinach and cook just until it wilts, about 45 seconds. Remove from the heat and let cool slightly.

Working in batches, purée the soup in a blender. Pour the purée into a bowl, add the 1 cup (8 fl oz/250 ml) half-and-half, 1 tsp salt, and pepper to taste. Stir to blend and let cool to room temperature. Transfer to a covered container and refrigerate until well chilled, at least 3 hours or up to overnight.

When ready to serve, in a frying pan, melt the remaining 1 Tbsp butter with the remaining 1 Tbsp oil over medium heat. Add the reserved 1 cup (4 oz/125 g) leeks ⟶

and ¼ tsp salt and sauté until the leeks are crisp, about 8 minutes. Transfer to paper towels to drain.

Taste the soup and season with salt and pepper. Serve, drizzled with the remaining 3 Tbsp half-and-half and topped with the fried leeks.

12

RED LENTIL & DANDELION GREEN SOUP

serves 6

A member of the sunflower family and loaded with vitamins K and A, dandelion greens are both good for you and delicious. If you cannot find dandelion greens, beet greens or even baby arugula can be used in their place. Red lentils, which are typically more orange than red, cook more quickly than their brown, green, and black cousins, making them the ideal candidate for this puréed soup.

2 Tbsp olive oil

1 small yellow onion, chopped

3 carrots, peeled and cut into ½-inch (12-mm) pieces

2 cloves garlic, chopped

Salt and freshly ground pepper

1 Tbsp tomato paste

1½ cups (10½ oz/330 g) red lentils, picked over and rinsed

5 cups (40 fl oz/1.25 l) vegetable or chicken broth

1 bunch (¾ lb/375 g) dandelion greens, tough stems trimmed, leaves cut in half crosswise

In a large, heavy pot, warm the oil over medium-high heat. Add the onion and carrots and cook, stirring occasionally, until the vegetables soften, about 6 minutes. Add the garlic, season with salt and pepper, and cook, stirring occasionally, until soft, about 2 minutes. Stir in the tomato paste, lentils, and broth and bring to a boil. Reduce the heat to low, cover, and simmer, stirring a couple of times to prevent sticking, until the lentils are soft, 25–30 minutes. Let cool slightly.

Purée half of the soup in a food processor or blender. Return to the pot and stir to combine. Place over medium heat, stir in the dandelion greens, and cook just until they wilt, about 3 minutes. Season with salt and pepper and serve.

13

A rich coconut curry, fresh egg noodles, and briny-sweet shellfish blend into citrus and spice notes. Substitute thinly sliced cooked chicken or beef for the seafood, stirring them into the soup toward the end of cooking to warm through.

SPICY COCONUT CURRY SEAFOOD SOUP
serves 4–6

2 Tbsp canola oil

½ cup (5 oz/155 g) Asian chile paste

3 cups (24 fl oz/750 ml) coconut milk

¼ cup (2 fl oz/60 ml) Asian fish sauce

2 Tbsp fresh lime juice

2 Tbsp brown sugar

1 Tbsp tamarind paste

Salt

1 lb (500 g) fresh Chinese egg noodles

½ lb (250 g) large shrimp, peeled and deveined

½ lb (250 g) cleaned squid bodies, cut into rings ½ inch (12 mm) wide

1 lb (500 g) mussels, scrubbed and debearded

2 green onions, white and tender green parts

Mung bean sprouts, cilantro sprigs, Thai basil sprigs, and sliced serrano chile for garnish

1 lime, cut into wedges

In a large, heavy pot, warm the oil over medium-high heat. Add the chile paste and sauté until fragrant, about 2 minutes. Add the coconut milk, fish sauce, lime juice, sugar, tamarind paste, and 2 cups (16 fl oz/500 ml) water and bring to a boil. Cook for 2 minutes, then reduce the heat to low and simmer the soup for 10 minutes to blend the flavors.

Meanwhile, bring a large saucepan three-fourths full of water to a boil over high heat. Stir in 1 tsp salt. Add the noodles and cook until just tender, 2–3 minutes. Drain and divide them among bowls.

In the same pan, bring 4 cups (32 fl oz/1 l) water to a boil. Reduce the heat to low, add the shrimp, and cook until they just turn pink, about 1 minute. Using a slotted spoon, transfer the shrimp to a large bowl. Add the squid to the same simmering water and cook until they turn opaque, about 1 minute. Transfer to the bowl with the shrimp. Add the mussels to the simmering water, discarding any that do not close to the touch. ⟫

Cook just until the shells open, 2–3 minutes. Transfer the cooked mussels to the bowl of seafood, discarding any unopened mussels. Discard the cooking liquid.

Just before serving, thinly slice the green onions on the diagonal and ready all of the garnishes. Add all of the seafood to the simmering soup and cook just to heat through, about 3 minutes. Use tongs to top each bowl of noodles with a variety of seafood, and then ladle the hot soup over the seafood. Generously top each bowl with the green onions and other garnishes, and serve. Pass lime wedges at the table.

14

Ramen noodles are a fast, easy, and inexpensive staple to keep on hand. Sugar snap peas and diced tomatoes add depth, flavor, and nutritional value to this perfect weeknight soup.

RAMEN NOODLE SOUP WITH SUGAR SNAP PEAS
serves 4–6

2 Tbsp olive oil

2 shallots, chopped

4 cloves garlic, minced

6 cups (48 fl oz/1.5 l) chicken broth

3 oz (90 g) dried ramen noodles

1 can (14½ oz/455 g) diced tomatoes

1½ cups (5 oz/155 g) sugar snap peas, trimmed and halved diagonally

4 green onions, white and tender green parts, thinly sliced

Salt and freshly ground pepper

Hot sauce, such as Sriracha, for serving

In a large, heavy pot, warm the oil over medium-high heat. Add the shallots and garlic and sauté for 3 minutes. Add the broth and bring to a boil. Add the ramen noodles and tomatoes and cook, stirring occasionally, for 5 minutes. Add the sugar snap peas and green onions and cook for 2 minutes. Season with salt and pepper and serve, passing the hot sauce at the table.

15

CURRIED CARROT PURÉE

serves 4

1 Tbsp olive oil, plus more for drizzling

1 large shallot, minced

1½ lb (750 g) carrots, peeled and coarsely chopped

1 tsp curry powder

6 cups (48 fl oz/1.5 l) chicken broth

2 Tbsp fresh orange juice

Salt and freshly ground pepper

Here, curry powder and orange juice add flavor and vibrancy to an earthy carrot soup. To mix it up, try a touch of ground cinnamon or ginger in place of or in addition to the curry powder.

In a large, heavy pot, warm the 1 Tbsp oil over medium heat. Add the shallot and sauté until translucent, about 2 minutes. Add the carrots, curry powder, and broth. Raise the heat to medium-high and bring to a boil. Reduce the heat to low, cover, and cook until the carrots are tender, about 20 minutes. Remove from the heat and add the orange juice. Let cool slightly.

Working in batches, purée the soup in a blender or food processor. Season with salt and pepper.

The soup can be served warm or chilled. To serve warm, return to the pot and gently warm over medium heat. To serve chilled, let cool, transfer to a covered container, and refrigerate for at least 3 hours or up to overnight. Serve, drizzled with oil.

16

PEA SHOOT & PASTA SOUP

serves 4

Salt and freshly ground pepper

½ cup (3½ oz/105 g) stelline or other small soup pasta

2 eggs

4 cups (32 fl oz/1 l) chicken broth

1 small carrot, peeled and chopped

2 cups (2 oz/60 g) chopped pea shoots

¼ cup (1 oz/30 g) grated Parmesan cheese

Look for fresh pea shoots at farmers' markets in early spring, or at Asian markets year-round. Tender and sweet, they deliver the flavor of fresh peas without the effort of shelling. If pea shoots are unavailable, baby spinach can substitute.

Bring a small saucepan of salted water to a boil. Add the pasta and cook until al dente, about 8 minutes or according to the package directions. Drain and rinse under cold running water. In a small bowl, beat the eggs lightly and season with salt and pepper.

In a large saucepan, combine the broth with 1 cup (8 fl oz/250 ml) water. Bring to a simmer over medium-high heat. Add the carrot and simmer, uncovered, until crisp-tender, 5–6 minutes. Add the pea shoots and simmer until tender, 2–3 minutes. Remove from the heat. Slowly drizzle in the beaten eggs, stirring the soup gently in one direction to form even threads of cooked egg. Gently stir in the pasta and cheese. Season with salt and pepper and serve.

17

ARTICHOKE & ROASTED GARLIC SOUP WITH TOASTED HAZELNUTS

serves 4

Artichokes turn up in the market in the early spring and again, in smaller numbers, in the late fall. Here, they are paired with roasted garlic in a rich puréed soup that can be made with or without a little cream. The garnish of toasted nuts adds both crunch and a wonderful earthy flavor. You can toast the nuts on a rimmed baking sheet in a preheated 375°F (190°C) oven or in a dry frying pan over medium-low heat on the stove top. Either way, check on them every few minutes and stir them so they do not burn.

1 head garlic

1 tsp olive oil

Juice of 1 lemon

6 artichokes

2 Tbsp unsalted butter

2 shallots, chopped

Salt and freshly ground pepper

2½ cups (20 fl oz/625 ml) vegetable or chicken broth, plus more as needed

3 Tbsp heavy cream (optional)

¼ cup (1¼ oz/40 g) hazelnuts, skinned, toasted, and chopped

Preheat the oven to 500°F (260°C). Cut off the top of the garlic head, exposing the tops of the cloves, and place on a piece of aluminum foil. Drizzle the garlic with the oil and loosely wrap in the foil. Roast until golden and very soft, about 45 minutes. Let cool.

Fill a large bowl with water and add half of the lemon juice. Cut off the stem of each artichoke flush with the bottom. Snap off the outer leaves until you reach the tender inner leaves. Cut off the top one-third of each artichoke to remove the pointed tips. Quarter the artichoke lengthwise. Cut out the choke from each quarter. As you work, add the quarters to the lemon water.

In a large, heavy pot, melt the butter over medium-high heat. Add the shallots and cook, stirring frequently, until soft, about 4 minutes. Drain the artichokes, add them to the pot, and season with salt and pepper. Cook, stirring occasionally, until they start to soften, about 4 minutes. Using your hands, squeeze the garlic cloves from their papery skin and add to the pot along with the broth. Bring to a boil, reduce the heat to low, and simmer until the artichokes are fork-tender, 12–15 minutes. Let cool slightly. ⤏

Working in batches, purée the soup in a food processor or blender. Return to the pot, place over medium heat, and add more broth if needed to thin the soup. Stir in the remaining lemon juice, cream (if using), and season with salt and pepper.

Serve, garnished with the hazelnuts.

18

BEAN & ELBOW PASTA SOUP WITH BASIL PESTO

serves 6–8

To make the pesto, finely grind ⅓ cup (2 oz/60 g) pine nuts and 3 cloves garlic in a food processor. Add 2 cups (2 oz/ 60 g) packed basil leaves and purée. With the motor running, add ½ cup (4 fl oz/125 ml) extra-virgin olive oil in a steady stream. Stop and add ½ cup (2 oz/60 g) grated Parmesan and purée. Season with salt and pepper.

Salt and freshly ground pepper

1 cup (3½ oz/105 g) elbow pasta

2 Tbsp olive oil

1 yellow onion, chopped

4 cloves garlic, minced

2 Tbsp tomato paste

5 cups (40 fl oz/1.25 l) chicken broth

1 can (14½ oz/455 g) diced tomatoes, drained

1 can (15 oz/470 g) butter beans, drained

1 can (15 oz/470 g) cannellini beans, drained

¼ cup (⅓ oz/10 g) chopped basil

Basil Pesto (left)

In a saucepan, bring 4 cups (32 fl oz/1 l) water to a boil. Add ¼ tsp salt and the pasta and cook until al dente, about 8 minutes, or according to the package directions. Drain and set aside.

In a large, heavy pot, warm the oil over medium-high heat. Add the onion and garlic and sauté for 5 minutes. Add the tomato paste and stir to combine. Add the broth and tomatoes and bring to a boil. Reduce the heat to low and simmer for 20 minutes. Add the pasta, butter beans, and cannellini beans and simmer for 5 minutes. Stir in the basil and season with salt and pepper.

Serve, topping each bowl with a dollop or swirl of pesto.

19

ISRAELI COUSCOUS SOUP WITH CURRY, CHICKEN & SPINACH

serves 4–6

This soup is a great way to use leftover rotisserie or grilled chicken. When reheating, you may need to add more broth or water, as the couscous will absorb the liquid as it sits.

1 cup (6 oz/185 g) Israeli couscous

2 small skinless, boneless chicken breast halves (about ¾ lb/375 g total)

3 Tbsp olive oil

Salt and freshly ground pepper

1 small yellow onion, chopped

2 cloves garlic, minced

½ tsp curry powder

¼ tsp ground turmeric

6 cups (48 fl oz/1.5 l) chicken broth

2 cups (2 oz/60 g) baby spinach leaves

Preheat the oven to 375°F (190°C).

In a small saucepan, bring 1¼ cups (10 fl oz/310 ml) water to a boil. Add the couscous, stir once, and cover. Reduce the heat to low and cook until all the water is absorbed, 8–10 minutes. Set aside.

Place the chicken breasts on a baking sheet, brush with 1 Tbsp of the oil, and season with salt and pepper. Bake the chicken until it is cooked all the way through, 18–20 minutes. When it is cool enough to handle, shred the chicken and set aside.

In a large, heavy pot, warm the remaining 2 Tbsp oil over medium-high heat. Add the onion and the garlic and sauté until soft, about 5 minutes. Add the curry powder and turmeric, stir to combine, and cook for 2 minutes. Add the broth and bring to a boil. Reduce the heat to low, add the couscous and chicken and simmer, stirring occasionally, until the couscous is al dente, about 10 minutes. Stir in the spinach and cook just until it wilts, about 45 seconds. Season with salt and pepper and serve.

20

WATERCRESS SOUP

serves 4

Watercress may bring visions of delectable finger sandwiches, but this favorite salad ingredient also has a tradition in British soups. The peppery green leaves are popular in creamy soups that can be eaten hot or chilled; hot watercress soup is often topped with crisp croutons, while cold soup is given a swirl of cream.

¼ cup (2 fl oz/60 ml) olive oil

1 yellow onion, coarsely chopped

2 large Yukon Gold potatoes, peeled and diced

1 lb (500 g) leeks, white and pale green parts, thinly sliced

4 cups (32 fl oz/1 l) chicken broth or water

Salt and freshly ground pepper

2 bunches watercress

1 cup (8 fl oz/250 ml) heavy cream

In a large saucepan, warm the oil over medium heat. Add the onion and sauté until softened, 5–7 minutes. Stir in the potatoes and cook for 2 minutes. Add the leeks, raise the heat to medium-high, and cook, stirring occasionally, until the leeks begin to soften and wilt, about 4 minutes. Add the broth and season with salt and pepper. Raise the heat to high, bring to a boil, then reduce the heat to medium-low and simmer, uncovered, until the vegetables are very soft, about 25 minutes.

Strip the watercress leaves from the stems and discard the stems. Add the leaves to the saucepan and cook just until they are tender, about 3 minutes. Remove from the heat and let cool slightly.

Working in batches, purée the soup in a blender or food processor. Stir in the cream. Taste and adjust the seasoning.

To serve the soup hot, gently reheat over medium heat. To serve the soup cold, transfer to a covered container and refrigerate until well chilled, at least 2 hours. Ladle the soup into bowls and serve.

21

For a less sweet and more festive soup, replace the fruity red wine with a dry Prosecco or a sparkling rosé stirred in after chilling to preserve the bubbles. Save a little bubbly for serving alongside.

RED PEPPER SOUP WITH MINI CRAB CAKES

serves 4

FOR THE LEMON AIOLI

1 clove garlic

Salt

1 whole egg plus 1 egg yolk

1 cup (8 fl oz/250 ml) canola or vegetable oil

Grated zest and juice of 1 lemon

FOR THE SOUP

2 Tbsp olive oil

2 shallots, chopped

1 large clove garlic, chopped

6 red bell peppers (2½ lb/1.25 kg total weight), seeded and chopped

Salt and freshly ground pepper

3 cups (24 fl oz/750 ml) chicken broth

FOR THE CRAB CAKES

1 lb (500 g) fresh lump crabmeat, picked over for shell fragments

¼ cup (2 fl oz/60 ml) mayonnaise

¼ cup (⅓ oz/10 g) panko or fresh unseasoned bread crumbs

2 Tbsp finely chopped flat-leaf parsley

1 tsp seeded and finely chopped jalapeño chile

Salt and freshly ground pepper

2 Tbsp unsalted butter

3 Tbsp finely chopped chives

To make the lemon aioli, in a food processor or blender, combine the garlic and a big pinch of salt. Pulse several times until the garlic is finely chopped. Add the whole egg and egg yolk and pulse to combine. With the motor running, slowly add a few drops of the oil, and then follow with a slow and steady stream of oil. Continue to purée until fully combined. Transfer to a bowl, stir in the lemon zest and juice, and adjust the seasoning with salt. Set aside at room temperature.

To make the soup, in a large, heavy pot, warm the oil over medium-high heat. Add the shallots and cook, stirring occasionally, until soft, about 4 minutes. Add the garlic and bell peppers, and season with salt and pepper. Cook, stirring occasionally, until the peppers soften slightly, about 5 minutes. Add the broth and bring to a boil. ⟫

Reduce the heat to low and simmer until the peppers are very soft, about 20 minutes. Let cool slightly.

Working in batches, purée the soup in a food processor or blender. Return to the pot and keep warm over low heat.

To make the crab cakes, in a bowl, stir together the crabmeat, mayonnaise, panko, parsley, and jalapeño, and season with salt and pepper. Using a heaping tablespoon of the mixture, form each mini crab cake in your hands and transfer to a plate. In a large nonstick frying pan, melt 1 Tbsp of the butter over medium-high heat. Add half of the crab cakes and cook until golden brown, about 3 minutes per side. Transfer to a clean plate. Repeat with the remaining 1 Tbsp butter and crab cakes.

Serve the soup, topped with a swirl of the aioli, several crab cakes, and a sprinkling of the chives.

22

Good-quality olive oil and ripe avocados are imperative to the success of this dish. Serve with a shredded carrot, feta, and pine nut salad. This soup can also be served at room temperature.

COLD ZUCCHINI & AVOCADO SOUP

serves 4

⅔ cup (3½ oz/105 g) whole raw almonds

4 zucchini, trimmed and chopped

4 celery ribs, chopped

¼ cup (2 fl oz/60 ml) extra-virgin olive oil

¼ cup (2 fl oz/60 ml) fresh lemon juice

2 ripe avocados, pitted, peeled, and diced

A few dashes of Tabasco sauce

Salt and freshly ground pepper

3 Tbsp chopped basil

Put the almonds into a food processor and pulse until finely ground. Add the zucchini, celery, oil, and lemon juice and purée until very smooth. Add the avocados and 1½ cups (12 fl oz/375 ml) water and continue to purée. If needed, add 1 Tbsp of water at a time to achieve the desired consistency. Add the Tabasco and combine. Season with salt and pepper.

Serve, topped with chopped basil.

23

Fresh peas are treated delicately here, allowing their inherent sweetness to dominate the flavor of the soup. Chives, with their mild onion flavor, are the herb of choice, and if their lavender blossoms are available, use them as well. Fresh peas take a bit of work to shell, but the wonderful taste they deliver is worth the time and effort.

FRESH PEA SOUP WITH CHIVES & CRÈME FRAÎCHE

serves 4

3 cups (24 fl oz/750 ml) chicken broth

2½ cups (12½ oz/390 g) fresh peas

Salt and freshly ground pepper

2 Tbsp crème fraîche

2 Tbsp chopped chives or a combination of chopped chives and chive blossoms

In a large saucepan, bring the broth to a boil over medium-high heat. Add the peas, reduce the heat to medium, cover, and cook until the peas are tender, about 10 minutes for young peas and up to 20 minutes for more mature, starchy peas. Let cool slightly.

Working in batches, purée the soup in a food processor or blender. Return to the pot and season with 1 tsp salt and ½ tsp pepper. If you prefer a lighter soup, strain through a fine-mesh sieve lined with cheesecloth, or serve unstrained for a thicker soup. Serve, topped with the crème fraîche and a sprinkling of the chives or chives and chive blossoms.

24

For this soup, try to catch the moment when your local crab haul overlaps with the spring asparagus harvest. Either lump crabmeat or flake will work, but avoid vacuum-packed, frozen, or imitation—with so few ingredients, freshness is key.

CRAB & ASPARAGUS EGG FLOWER SOUP

serves 4

4 cups (32 fl oz/1 l) chicken broth

1 tsp peeled and minced fresh ginger

½ lb (250 g) asparagus, trimmed and cut on the diagonal into 1-inch (2.5-cm) pieces

1 Tbsp cornstarch

1 egg, well beaten

2 tsp dry sherry

1 tsp Asian sesame oil

1 tsp soy sauce

1 cup (6 oz/185 g) fresh lump or flake crabmeat, picked over for shell fragments

In a large saucepan, combine the broth and ginger over medium-high heat and bring to a rolling boil. Add the asparagus, reduce the heat to medium, cover, and simmer until the asparagus is crisp-tender, about 3 minutes.

Meanwhile, in a bowl, mix together the cornstarch and 2 Tbsp water. Set aside.

Reduce the heat to medium-low. Stir 2 Tbsp of the hot broth into the beaten egg. Slowly pour the egg mixture into the broth, stirring constantly to form even threads of cooked egg. Add the cornstarch mixture, sherry, sesame oil, and soy sauce to the broth. Cook, stirring, until the soup thickens slightly, about 1 minute.

Stir in the crabmeat and cook just until it is warmed through, 2–3 minutes. Taste and adjust the seasoning, then serve.

25

FENNEL VICHYSSOISE

serves 4–6

2 Tbsp unsalted butter

1 Tbsp olive oil

½ yellow onion, chopped

2 fennel bulbs (1½ lb/750 g total), stalks and fronds removed, quartered, cored, and thinly sliced

¼ cup (2 fl oz/60 ml) dry white wine

3 cups (24 fl oz/750 ml) vegetable broth

1 russet potato (¾ lb/375 g), peeled and diced

½ cup (4 fl oz/125 ml) heavy cream

Salt and ground white pepper

Traditional vichyssoise is a cold potato and leek soup. In this version, fennel takes center stage. This soup is just as good warm as it is cold, so you can make that decision based on the weather.

In a large, heavy pot, melt the butter with the oil over medium-high heat. Add the onion and fennel and sauté until the fennel is very soft, 7–9 minutes. Add the wine and cook, stirring often, for 2 minutes. Add the broth, bring to a boil, then add the potato. Reduce the heat to medium-low and simmer until the potato is very soft, 30–35 minutes. Remove from the heat and let cool slightly.

Working in batches, purée the soup in a blender. Return to the pot, stir in the cream, and bring to a gentle boil. Remove from the heat and season to taste with salt and pepper.

If serving cold, let the soup cool to room temperature. Transfer to a covered container and refrigerate until well chilled, at least 3 hours or up to overnight. Serve.

26

EGG-LEMON SOUP WITH FAVA BEANS & FRIED GARLIC CHIPS

serves 6–8

Salt

3 lb (1.5 kg) fava beans in the pods, shelled

1 large lemon

8 cups (64 fl oz/2 l) chicken broth

⅔ cup (4½ oz/145 g) long-grain white rice, such as basmati

1 bay leaf

2 eggs, at room temperature

2 egg yolks, at room temperature

Fried Garlic Chips (left)

To make fried garlic chips, thinly slice 8 cloves of garlic. Warm 2 Tbsp oil in a small frying pan over medium heat. Add the garlic and cook, stirring often, until golden brown, about 3 minutes. Transfer to paper towels to drain.

Bring a large saucepan of water to a boil. Add 1 Tbsp salt and the fava beans and cook for 2 minutes. Drain and rinse under cold water. Pinch open the skin of each bean along its edge and slip the bean from the skin. Discard the skins.

With a vegetable peeler, remove the zest from the lemon in wide strips, then squeeze ¼ cup (2 fl oz/60 ml) juice and set aside.

In a large, heavy pot, bring the broth to a boil over high heat. Stir in the rice, lemon zest, bay leaf, and 1½ tsp salt. Reduce the heat to medium, cover, and simmer until the rice is tender, 15–20 minutes.

Remove the bay leaf and lemon zest from the broth. In a bowl, whisk together the eggs, egg yolks, and lemon juice. Whisking constantly, ladle about one-fourth of the hot broth mixture into the egg mixture and whisk until blended. Stir back into the pot. Add the fava beans, reduce the heat to low, and cook, stirring, until the soup thickens and wisps of steam appear, about 5 minutes. Do not allow the soup to come to a simmer, and remove it from the heat as soon as it has thickened.

Taste and adjust the seasoning. Serve, garnished with the garlic chips.

27

For a special garnish, roll the bottom half of whole strawberries in crème fraîche and sprinkle with lemon zest. Fresh mint also pairs nicely with this summery soup.

STRAWBERRY-LEMON SOUP
serves 4–6

1 lb (500 g) fresh or frozen strawberries

¼ cup (2 oz/60 g) sugar

2 lemons

¼ cup (2 fl oz/60 ml) dry white wine

4–6 tsp crème fraîche or sour cream for serving

If you are using frozen strawberries, let them defrost in a bowl, reserving all their juices. Put the strawberries, sugar, the grated zest and juice of 1 lemon, and the wine into a blender and purée.

Transfer the soup to a nonreactive bowl, cover, and refrigerate until well chilled, at least 3 hours.

Serve, garnished with a dollop of the crème fraîche and the grated zest of the remaining lemon.

28

Here, nutmeg is the secret ingredient that laces this simple spinach soup, mellowing the earthy dark greens.

CREAMY SPINACH-LEEK SOUP
serves 4–6

1 Tbsp unsalted butter

1 Tbsp olive oil

2 leeks, white and pale green parts, chopped

½ tsp grated nutmeg

1½ cups (12 fl oz/375 ml) vegetable broth

2 large bunches spinach, tough stems removed

¼ cup (2 fl oz/60 ml) heavy cream

Salt and freshly ground pepper

In a large, heavy pot, melt the butter with the oil over medium-high heat. Add the leeks and nutmeg and sauté until the leeks are softened, 5–7 minutes. Add the broth and bring to a boil. Add the spinach and cook, stirring often, for 10 minutes. Remove from the heat and let cool slightly.

Working in batches, purée the soup in a blender. Return to the pot, add the cream, and bring just to a boil. Season with salt and pepper. Serve.

29

Fava beans are a favorite in France and Italy, where the esteemed seasonal vegetable is eaten in as many ways as possible throughout its short growing season. If you find some at your market, snatch them up and let them shine in this simple, creamy soup.

FAVA BEAN SOUP
serves 6

3 lb (1.5 kg) fava beans in the pods, shelled

2 mint sprigs

1 thyme sprig, plus more for garnish

Salt and freshly ground pepper

1½ cups (12 fl oz/375 ml) milk

¼ cup (2 oz/60 g) crème fraîche or sour cream

2 Tbsp unsalted butter

In a large saucepan, bring 4 cups (32 fl oz/1 l) water to a boil over medium-high heat. Add the fava beans and cook for 1–2 minutes. Using a slotted spoon, transfer the beans to a colander, reserving the cooking liquid, and rinse the beans under cold running water. Drain. Split open the skin of each bean along its edge and slip the bean from the skin. Discard the skins.

Pour the cooking liquid into a large measuring cup. Return 1 cup (8 fl oz/250 ml) to the pan and reserve the remainder. Add the beans, mint, the thyme sprig, and 1 tsp salt to the pan and bring to a boil over medium-high heat. Reduce the heat to medium, partially cover, and cook until the beans are tender, about 15 minutes. Remove from the heat and let cool slightly.

Working in batches, purée the soup in a blender or food processor. Return to the pan over medium heat. Slowly whisk in 1¼ cups (10 fl oz/310 ml) of the milk. The soup will be creamy but somewhat stiff. Whisk in the crème fraîche and butter. Whisk in more milk or some of the reserved cooking liquid until the soup reaches the desired consistency. Serve, garnished with thyme sprigs and pepper.

30

GINGERY BROTH WITH PRAWNS & GREEN ONIONS

serves 4

The aromatic broth can be made ahead and stored in the refrigerator for up to 3 days. Cook the shrimp and green onions in the broth just before serving.

3 green onions

2 tsp canola oil

3-inch (7.5-cm) piece of fresh ginger, peeled and grated

1 clove garlic, minced

⅛ tsp Chinese five-spice powder

¼ lb (125 g) cremini mushrooms, thinly sliced

½ red bell pepper, seeded and thinly sliced

4 cups (32 fl oz/1 l) chicken broth

2 Tbsp soy sauce

½ lb (250 g) medium shrimp, peeled and deveined

Thinly slice the green onions on the diagonal, reserving the white and pale green parts in one bowl and the dark green parts in a separate bowl.

In a large, heavy pot, warm the oil over medium-high heat. Add the ginger and garlic and cook until fragrant, about 4 minutes. Add the five-spice powder, mushrooms, red pepper, and the white and light green parts of the green onions and cook, stirring often, for 3–4 minutes. Add the broth, 2 cups (16 fl oz/500 ml) water, and the soy sauce and simmer for 20 minutes. Raise the heat to high and return the broth to a boil. Add the shrimp and cook until bright pink, about 3 minutes. Serve, sprinkled with the dark green parts of the green onions.

31

SPINACH & VERMICELLI SOUP WITH FRIED EGG

serves 4

Both kid- and adult-friendly, this soup uses ingredients that you probably already have in your pantry. Substitute chard, kale, or other sturdy cooking greens for the spinach.

1 Tbsp olive oil

½ small yellow onion, thinly sliced

1 clove garlic, minced

5 cups (40 fl oz/1.25 l) chicken broth

½ lb (250 g) vermicelli, broken into 2-inch (5-cm) pieces

1 bunch spinach, stemmed

1 Tbsp unsalted butter

4 eggs

Hot sauce, such as Sriracha, for serving (optional)

In a large saucepan, warm the oil over medium-high heat. Add the onion and garlic and sauté until translucent, about 5 minutes. Add the broth and bring to a boil. Add the vermicelli, return to a boil, and cook, stirring occasionally, for 4 minutes. Add the spinach and stir just until it is wilted, about 2 minutes. Reduce the heat to low to keep the soup warm while you prepare the eggs.

In a nonstick frying pan, melt the butter over medium heat. Fry each egg until it is set but the yolk is still runny, 5–6 minutes.

Ladle the soup into bowls and top each with a fried egg. Serve, passing the hot sauce at the table, if using.

5
ROASTED TOMATO SOUP WITH
SERRANO HAM & BURRATA
page 133

6
CUCUMBER-DILL SOUP
page 133

7
CREAMY CLAM & CELERY
ROOT CHOWDER
page 135

12
SPICY COCONUT BROTH
WITH UDON NOODLES & SHRIMP
page 137

13
ROMAN CHICKPEA SOUP
page 138

14
SOBA NOODLES & SEARED SALMON
IN GINGER–GREEN ONION BROTH
page 138

19
CHICKPEA & DANDELION GREEN SOUP
WITH CROUTONS & FRIED EGGS
page 143

20
COOL HONEYDEW-MINT SOUP
page 143

21
GOLDEN BEET SOUP WITH
DILLED GOAT CHEESE
page 144

26
BLACK BEAN SOUP WITH
CHIPOTLE CHILES
page 148

27
CHILLED YELLOW PEPPER
SOUP WITH CHIVES
page 149

28
MELON & PROSCIUTTO SOUP
WITH MASCARPONE CHEESE
page 149

Warmer weather signals an early harvest of melons, beets, peppers, and summer squash in all shapes and sizes—perfect for light soups fit for the season. As the temperature steadily climbs, chilled vegetable soups like zucchini vichyssoise and creamy yellow pepper join fruity blends of tart-sweet rhubarb, melon, and strawberries in especially refreshing bowls uniquely suited to the June table.

june

1

CORN & ROAST CHICKEN SOUP WITH CHIPOTLE SOUR CREAM

serves 4–6

Puréeing a soup is a great way to add body and creaminess without the addition of cream, as this soup illustrates. Kids will like to eat this soup with tortilla chips for dipping. Chipotle chiles in adobo sauce can vary greatly in their heat, so add the chiles a little at a time to the sour cream, tasting as you go. Any leftover sour cream garnish makes a good sandwich spread.

¾ lb (375 g) skinless, boneless chicken breast halves

3 Tbsp olive oil

Salt and freshly ground pepper

2 poblano chiles

½ yellow onion, chopped

2 cloves garlic, chopped

3½ cups (28 fl oz/875 ml) chicken broth

4 cups (1½ lb/750 g) corn kernels (from about 8 ears)

FOR THE CHIPOTLE SOUR CREAM

1 cup (8 oz/250 g) sour cream

1½ tsp finely chopped chipotle chile in adobo sauce

1 Tbsp fresh lime juice

Salt

1 avocado, pitted, peeled, and cubed

Preheat the oven to 375°F (190°C). Brush the chicken with 1 Tbsp of the oil and season with salt and pepper. Place in a small baking dish and roast until opaque throughout, about 25 minutes. When cool enough to handle, shred the chicken and set aside.

Preheat the broiler. Cut the poblano chiles in half lengthwise and remove the stem and seeds. Place, cut side down, on a baking sheet and broil 5 inches (13 cm) from the heat source until the skin blackens and blisters, about 6 minutes. Remove from the broiler, cover loosely with aluminum foil, and let steam for 10 minutes. Peel away the skin and cut the chiles into ½-inch (12-mm) pieces. Set aside.

In a large, heavy pot, warm the remaining 2 Tbsp oil over medium-high heat. Add the onion and cook, stirring occasionally, until tender and translucent, about 6 minutes. Add the garlic and season with salt and pepper. Cook, stirring occasionally, until soft, about 2 minutes. Add the broth and bring to a boil. Stir in the corn and cook for 5 minutes. Let cool slightly. ⤳

Purée half of the soup in a food processor or blender. Return to the pot and stir to combine. Stir in the cooked chicken and peeled chiles, and season with salt and pepper. Keep warm over low heat.

To make the chipotle sour cream, in a bowl, stir together the sour cream, chipotle chile, and lime juice and season with salt.

Serve the soup, topped with a dollop of the chipotle sour cream and the avocado.

2

STRAWBERRY-RHUBARB SOUP WITH PROSECCO

serves 4

Sweet strawberries and tart rhubarb combine in this party-friendly starter. When using sparkling wine in soups, add it at the last moment to prevent the bubbles from going flat. You can serve this garnished with tiny diced strawberries or a sprig of mint.

¾ lb (375 g) rhubarb, thinly sliced

1 lb (500 g) strawberries, hulled and halved

2 Tbsp fresh orange juice

½ cup (4 oz/125 g) sugar

½ cup Prosecco or other dry, sparkling wine

Put the rhubarb and ½ cup (4 fl oz/125 ml) water in a large saucepan over medium heat. Cook, stirring often, for 10 minutes. Add the strawberries, orange juice, and sugar. Stir to combine and cook for 5 minutes. Remove from the heat and let cool slightly.

Purée the soup in a blender. Let cool to room temperature. Transfer to a covered container and refrigerate until chilled, at least 3 hours or up to overnight. Just before serving, stir in the Prosecco.

RED PEPPER, SUGAR SNAP PEA & TOFU LAKSA

serves 4

This vegetarian riff on laksa, a spicy Malaysian rice noodle soup traditionally made with chicken or seafood, shines a light on summer produce like vitamin C–packed red peppers and fiber-rich sugar snap peas. Other vegetables, such as snow peas, bean sprouts, or mushrooms, can be substituted.

¼ lb (125 g) wide rice noodles

5 oz (155 g) firm tofu, drained

2 Tbsp canola or vegetable oil

2 shallots, halved and thinly sliced

1-inch (2.5-cm) piece fresh ginger, peeled and minced

1 lemongrass stalk, center white part only, thinly sliced

1 small jalapeño chile, seeded, deribbed, and thinly sliced

1 small red bell pepper, seeded and cut into ½-inch (12-mm) pieces

1 tsp ground coriander

½ tsp ground turmeric

1 can (14 fl oz/430 ml) coconut milk (not light)

2 cups (16 fl oz/500 ml) vegetable or chicken broth

2 Tbsp Asian fish sauce

¼ lb (125 g) sugar snap peas, trimmed and halved diagonally

1 lime, cut into wedges

¼ cup (¼ oz/7 g) cilantro leaves, coarsely chopped

¼ cup (¼ oz/7 g) mint leaves, coarsely chopped

3 Tbsp lightly salted peanuts, chopped (optional)

Place the rice noodles in a bowl and cover with very hot water. Let stand until the noodles are soft, about 25 minutes. If they are not yet soft, drain the water and repeat the process a second time.

Meanwhile, cut the tofu in half horizontally. Place 3 paper towels on a plate and lay the tofu slices in a single layer. Top with 3 more paper towels and another plate. Place something heavy, such as a pot, on the top plate. Let stand for 5 minutes. Change the paper towels and repeat the process a second time. Transfer the tofu to a cutting board and cut into ½-inch (12-mm) cubes. Set aside.

In a large, heavy pot, warm the oil over medium-high heat. Add the shallots, ginger, lemongrass, and jalapeño and cook, stirring occasionally, until soft, about 5 minutes. ⟩⟩→

Add the bell pepper, coriander, and turmeric and cook, stirring occasionally, until the pepper begins to soften and the spices are toasted, about 3 minutes. Stir in the coconut milk, including the solid layer of cream on the top, along with the broth and fish sauce. Bring to a boil, then reduce the heat to medium. Add the noodles, tofu, and sugar snap peas and simmer for 5 minutes.

Serve, topped with a lime wedge, a generous helping of the cilantro and mint, and the peanuts, if using.

ZUCCHINI VICHYSSOISE WITH GOAT CHEESE

serves 4–6

Vichyssoise is traditionally a cold potato soup, but this version includes zucchini and can be served either cold or hot. For a beautiful presentation at a summer barbecue, serve it cold in a big glass punch bowl with a ladle and punch glasses for guests to help themselves. Complete the menu with grilled chicken, sliced tomatoes, a plate of warmed focaccia, and peach pie.

1 Tbsp unsalted butter

2 Tbsp olive oil

4 leeks, white part only, chopped

4 small zucchini (about 1 lb/500 g total weight), chopped

1 russet potato, peeled and chopped

Salt and freshly ground pepper

3 cups (24 fl oz/750 ml) chicken or vegetable broth

¼ lb (125 g) goat cheese, at room temperature

In a large, heavy pot, melt the butter with the oil over medium-high heat. Add the leeks and cook, stirring occasionally, until soft, about 6 minutes. Add the zucchini and potato, and season well with salt and pepper. Cook the vegetables, stirring a few times, for about 3 minutes. Add the broth and bring to a boil. Reduce the heat to low and cook until the potato is soft, 15–18 minutes. Let cool slightly.

Working in batches, purée the soup in a food processor or blender. Return to the pot and place over low heat. Add 3 oz (90 g) of the cheese and stir until it melts, about 4 minutes. Season with salt and pepper.

Serve, crumbling the remaining cheese on top.

5

Tomatoes and mozzarella are a classic combination that only gets better with Spain's signature cured ham. Make sure the serrano dries out completely in the oven for the best grinding. Burrata is an especially soft and creamy pulled cheese; slice it just before you are ready to serve, but even if it falls apart, torn pieces will taste delicious melting into the soup.

ROASTED TOMATO SOUP WITH SERRANO HAM & BURRATA

serves 4

4 thin slices serrano ham

2½ lb (1.25 kg) small tomatoes, such as plum or Campari, halved

4 Tbsp (2 fl oz/60 ml) olive oil

Salt and freshly ground pepper

1 yellow onion, chopped

4 cloves garlic, minced

2 cups (16 fl oz/500 ml) chicken broth

6 oz (185 g) burrata or fresh mozzarella cheese, sliced

1 Tbsp finely chopped chives

Preheat the oven to 200°F (95°C). Place the ham in a single layer on a baking sheet and bake until completely dried, about 1 hour and 45 minutes. Transfer the ham to paper towels and blot it to remove any excess oil. Tear the ham into small pieces, transfer to a spice grinder, and grind into a fine dust. Set aside.

Raise the oven temperature to 450°F (230°C). Arrange the tomatoes in a single layer on a baking sheet, drizzle with 2 Tbsp of the oil, and season with salt and pepper. Roast the tomatoes until very soft and caramelized, 25–30 minutes. Set aside.

In a large, heavy pot, warm the remaining 2 Tbsp oil over medium-high heat. Add the onion and garlic and sauté until translucent, about 5 minutes. Add the tomatoes with all their juices and stir to combine. Using a wooden spoon, break up the tomatoes a bit and sauté for 3 minutes. Add the broth and bring to a boil. Reduce the heat to low and simmer for 20 minutes. Remove from the heat and let cool slightly.

Purée half of the soup in a blender. Return to the pot, stir in the ham dust, and season with salt and pepper.

Ladle the soup into bowls. Garnish each bowl with a slice of burrata and let it sit for a minute or two so that the cheese begins to melt into the soup. Top each bowl with chopped chives and serve.

6

A chilled soup is a welcome start to the summer, and easy to pack for outdoor day trips. Select a container with a tight-fitting lid that permits easy pouring. Pack over ice, and to serve, pour the soup into wide-mouthed glasses or cups for sipping.

CUCUMBER-DILL SOUP

serves 6

3 English cucumbers, peeled, halved lengthwise, and seeded

1 cup (8 oz/250 g) plain whole-milk Greek yogurt

1 Tbsp fresh lemon juice

3 green onions, white and tender green parts, chopped

3 Tbsp chopped dill

1 clove garlic, chopped

1 tsp caraway seeds, crushed

Salt and ground white pepper

1 cup (8 fl oz/250 ml) vegetable broth

2 Tbsp extra-virgin olive oil

Coarsely chop 5 of the cucumber halves and transfer to a large bowl. Add the yogurt, lemon juice, green onions, dill, garlic, caraway seeds, 1 tsp salt, and ¼ tsp white pepper. Stir to combine, cover, and set aside at room temperature for 1 hour to blend the flavors. Dice the remaining cucumber half and set aside.

Working in batches, purée the cucumber-yogurt mixture in a blender. With the machine running, slowly add the broth and purée until fully incorporated. Transfer to a covered container and refrigerate until well chilled, about 2 hours.

Just before serving, stir in the diced cucumber and oil. Pour the soup into wide-mouthed glasses and serve.

7

Clam chowder is an American classic, and like most classic dishes, it has many versions. This one includes celery root in addition to the more usual celery and potato. Mottled brown, pockmarked, and starchy celery root has a texture similar to potatoes, and is often paired with them in dishes such as gratins and mashes.

CREAMY CLAM & CELERY ROOT CHOWDER

serves 4

2 cans (6½ oz/200 g each) chopped clams with juices, or 1½ cups (8 oz/240 g) shucked fresh clams with juices

2 Tbsp unsalted butter

½ cup (3 oz/90 g) minced yellow onion

1 celery rib and leaves, chopped

1 celery root (about 1 lb/500 g), peeled and cut into ½-inch (12 mm) cubes

2 Tbsp all-purpose flour

2 cups (16 fl oz/500 ml) milk, heated

1 tsp red pepper flakes

Salt

Drain the clams and set aside, reserving the clam juices and adding enough water to total 2 cups (16 fl oz/500 ml).

In a large, heavy pot, melt the butter over medium heat. Add the onion, celery and leaves, and celery root. Cook, stirring occasionally, until the onion and celery are translucent and the celery root begins to change color, 3–4 minutes. Sprinkle the flour over the vegetables and cook, stirring occasionally, for 1–2 minutes. Slowly stir in the reserved clam juices and ½ cup (4 fl oz/125 ml) water. Bring to a simmer, then reduce the heat to low and simmer until the celery root is tender, 8–10 minutes. Using the back of a wooden spoon, mash some of the celery root to thicken the soup.

Add the clams and cook for 2–3 minutes. Pour in the hot milk, add the red pepper flakes, and stir well. Taste and adjust the seasoning with salt. Simmer for 1–2 minutes and serve.

8

The combination of fresh vegetables gives this soup an intense green color as well as a sweet flavor and satisfying texture—all of which becomes even more pleasing with a swirl of sour cream and a dollop of pesto at serving time.

LIMA BEAN, PEA & ZUCCHINI PURÉE WITH PESTO

serves 4

2 Tbsp olive oil

2 small yellow onions, thinly sliced

4 zucchini, thinly sliced

4 cups (32 fl oz/1 l) chicken broth

2 cups (12 oz/375 g) fresh or frozen lima beans

1 cup (5 oz/155 g) fresh or frozen peas

Salt and freshly ground pepper

2 Tbsp sour cream

¼ cup (2 fl oz/60 ml) Basil Pesto (page 118)

In a large, heavy pot, warm the oil over medium-high heat. Add the onions and zucchini and sauté until they are just turning golden, 6–7 minutes. Add the broth and bring to a boil. Add the lima beans and peas. When the soup returns to a boil, reduce the heat to medium-low and simmer until the vegetables are soft, 20–25 minutes. Stir in ¼ tsp salt and ⅛ tsp pepper. Remove from the heat and let cool slightly.

Working in batches, purée the soup in a blender or food processor until completely smooth. Transfer to a clean pan and reheat gently. Stir in the sour cream.

Serve, topped with pesto.

9

Anellini, or "little rings" in Italian, resemble just that. Choosing pasta shapes is no exact science, but one way is to match the other elements in the dish: here, the anellini are a good size relative to the diced veggies, and easy to scoop up with an eager soup spoon.

VEGETABLE SOUP WITH ANELLINI

serves 4–6

Salt and freshly ground pepper

½ cup (3½ oz/105 g) anellini or other small soup pasta such as tubetti, pastina, orzo, or stelline

6 Tbsp (3 fl oz/90 ml) olive oil

3 leeks, white part only, thinly sliced

1 fennel bulb, stalks and fronds removed, finely diced, plus a handful of feathery fronds, chopped

1 bay leaf

1 Tbsp chopped thyme

2 cloves garlic, crushed

1 cup (6 oz/185 g) fresh corn kernels (from about 2 ears)

2 small zucchini, finely diced

3 large tomatoes, peeled, seeded, and finely diced

5 drained oil-packed sun-dried tomatoes, finely diced

6 cups (48 fl oz/1.5 l) vegetable broth

Basil Pesto (page 118) for serving

Bring a saucepan of water to a boil. Generously salt the boiling water, add the pasta, and cook until not quite al dente, 6–8 minutes. (It will cook further in the soup.) Drain and toss with 2 Tbsp of the oil. Set aside.

In a large, heavy pot, heat the remaining 4 Tbsp (2 fl oz/60 ml) oil over medium heat. Add the leeks, fennel bulb and fronds, bay leaf, and thyme. Season with salt and pepper and sauté until all the vegetables are fragrant and just starting to soften, about 5 minutes. Add the garlic and sauté for 1 minute. Add the corn and zucchini, season with a bit more salt, and sauté for 2–3 minutes. Add the fresh and sun-dried tomatoes and the broth. Raise the heat to high and bring to a boil. Reduce the heat to medium and cook, uncovered, at a lively simmer until all the vegetables are tender, 15–20 minutes. Skim the surface if necessary to remove any foam. Add the cooked pasta. Taste and adjust the seasoning. Cook briefly just to reheat the pasta.

Serve, garnished with pesto.

10

A lemony broth is the perfect base for soups in the spring and summer. The broth brightens the flavor of garden-fresh vegetables and also tastes great with the grain, cheese, and bread toppings in this recipe.

QUINOA IN LEMON BROTH WITH GREENS & PARMESAN

serves 4

6 cups (48 fl oz/1.5 l) chicken or vegetable broth

1 cup (8 oz/250 g) quinoa

1 small bunch lacinato (dinosaur) kale or Swiss chard, stems and tough ribs removed, leaves cut crosswise into ribbons

1 bunch green onions, white and green parts, chopped

Salt and freshly ground pepper

½ cup (4 fl oz/125 ml) fresh lemon juice, plus more to taste

Extra-virgin olive oil for drizzling

Parmesan cheese shavings for garnish

Garlic Croutons (page 61)

In a large, heavy pot, bring the broth to a boil over high heat. Stir in the quinoa, reduce the heat to medium-high, and boil, uncovered, until tender, about 15 minutes or according to the package directions.

Stir in the kale, green onions, 1 tsp salt, and a grinding of pepper, and cook until the kale is crisp-tender, about 5 minutes. Stir in the ½ cup (4 fl oz/125 ml) lemon juice and cook for 5 minutes to blend the flavors and warm through.

Season to taste with salt and pepper and more lemon juice, if desired. Serve, drizzled with olive oil and garnished with the cheese shavings and garlic croutons.

11

This German-inspired soup makes a light, pretty first or last course on a hot summer evening. If sour cherries are unavailable, use fresh or frozen Bing cherries and dried cranberries and reduce the amount of honey to 1 tablespoon, or to taste. If you like, garnish with a splash of cream.

SOUR CHERRY–RIESLING SOUP

serves 6

2 cups (16 fl oz/500 ml) dry Riesling wine

2 cups (16 fl oz/500 ml) cherry juice

2¼ lb (1.1 kg) fresh sour cherries, pitted, or 2 lb (1 kg) pitted frozen sour cherries

½ cup (3 oz/90 g) dried sour cherries

1 cinnamon stick, about 2 inches (5 cm) long

¼ cup (3 oz/90 g) honey

¼ cup (2 fl oz/60 ml) fresh orange juice

2 Tbsp cornstarch

1 Tbsp grated orange zest

½ cup (4 oz/125 g) sour cream or plain yogurt

¼ tsp ground cardamom

In a large, heavy pot, combine the wine, cherry juice, half of the fresh or frozen cherries, the dried cherries, and the cinnamon stick and bring to a simmer over medium heat. Reduce the heat to low and cook, uncovered, until the cherries are soft, about 15 minutes. Remove from the heat and remove the cinnamon stick and discard. Let cool slightly.

Working in batches, purée the soup in a blender or food processor until the cherries are finely chopped but retain their texture. Return to the pot.

In a small bowl, stir together the honey, orange juice, cornstarch, and orange zest to make a paste. Whisk the paste into the soup and place over low heat. Cook, stirring occasionally, until thickened, about 5 minutes. Stir in the remaining cherries. Transfer to a covered container and refrigerate until well chilled, at least 2 hours.

In a small bowl, stir together the sour cream and cardamom. Serve, topped with a dollop of the cardamom-spiced cream.

12

For a spicier soup, add another sliced fresh chile and some more red curry paste. Substitute cubes of firm tofu and use vegetable broth for a vegetarian version.

SPICY COCONUT BROTH WITH UDON NOODLES & SHRIMP

serves 4

Salt

5 oz (155 g) udon noodles

1 Tbsp canola oil

2-inch (5-cm) piece fresh ginger, peeled and minced

2 lemongrass stalks, center white part only, smashed and thinly sliced

1 small red chile, seeded and sliced

2 Tbsp red curry paste

2 cans (14 fl oz/440 ml each) light coconut milk

2 cups (16 fl oz/500 ml) chicken broth

½ lb (250 g) medium shrimp, peeled and deveined

2 green onions, white and tender green parts, thinly sliced on the diagonal

Bring a pot of water to a boil. Add ¼ tsp salt and the udon noodles. Cook for 4 minutes, drain, and rinse under cold water. Set aside.

In a large, heavy pot, warm the oil over medium-high heat. Add the ginger, lemongrass, and chile and sauté until soft, about 5 minutes. Add the red curry paste, coconut milk, and broth and whisk to combine. Bring to a boil, reduce the heat to low, and simmer for 10 minutes. Return the soup to a boil, add the shrimp, and cook until bright pink, about 2 minutes. Add the noodles and stir to combine.

Using tongs, divide the noodles among 4 bowls. Ladle the soup over the noodles and serve, garnished with the green onions.

13

ROMAN CHICKPEA SOUP
serves 4

1½ cups (10½ oz/330 g) dried chickpeas, picked over and rinsed

½ tsp baking soda

1 large clove garlic, unpeeled, plus 2 cloves garlic, minced

1 celery rib with leaves

1 small rosemary sprig

Salt and freshly ground pepper

3 Tbsp extra-virgin olive oil

2 oz (60 g) sliced pancetta, finely diced

2 Tbsp tomato paste

½ lb (250 g) dried tagliatelle or fettuccine pasta, broken into 2-inch (5-cm) pieces

The combination of pasta and legumes is common throughout Italy, but a steaming pot of Roman pasta e ceci proves the popularity deserved. Chickpeas mingle happily with pieces of long, flat tagliatelle or fettuccine noodles, but ditalini (thimbles), maltagliati (egg pasta scraps), or quadrucci (pasta squares) would be equally authentic and delicious.

Place the chickpeas in a bowl with cold water to cover by 3 inches (7.5 cm), and stir in the baking soda. Let stand for 24 hours. Drain and rinse well.

In a large saucepan, combine the rehydrated chickpeas, the unpeeled garlic clove, the celery rib, rosemary sprig, and 7 cups (56 fl oz/1.75 l) water. Bring to a gentle boil over medium-high heat. Adjust the heat to maintain a steady simmer, cover partially, and cook until the chickpeas are tender, about 1½ hours.

When the chickpeas are ready, remove the pan from the heat. Measure out ½ cup (4 fl oz/125 ml) of the broth and set aside. Stir in 2 tsp salt and let the chickpeas stand for 5 minutes. Remove and discard the garlic, celery, and rosemary. Remove 1 cup (7 oz/220 g) of the chickpeas and mash them with a fork or potato masher. Return them to the pot and stir to combine.

In a frying pan, warm the olive oil over medium-low heat. Add the pancetta and sauté until golden brown, about 3 minutes. Stir in the minced garlic, reduce the heat to low, and sauté until the garlic is softened, about 1 minute. Add the tomato paste and the reserved chickpea broth and stir well.

Add the pancetta mixture and pasta to the pot and bring to a gentle boil over medium heat. Cook for 10 minutes, or until the pasta is just al dente. Season with salt and pepper and serve.

14

SOBA NOODLES & SEARED SALMON IN GINGER–GREEN ONION BROTH
serves 4

4 green onions

4 cups (32 fl oz/1 l) chicken broth

2-inch (5-cm) piece fresh ginger, peeled and minced

1 star anise

2 Tbsp soy sauce

1 tsp mirin

A few drops of Asian sesame oil

6 oz (185 g) soba noodles, broken in half

¾ lb (375 g) center-cut salmon, cut into 4 equal pieces, skin and pin bones removed

2 Tbsp olive oil

Salt and freshly ground pepper

Even kids (and adults) who are suspicious of fish tend to make an exception for firm-fleshed salmon fillets, especially when served over a bowl of tempting buckwheat noodles and broth. Accompany with an Asian-inspired salad, such as cucumbers dressed in sesame oil.

Thinly slice the green onions, reserving the white and pale green parts in one bowl and the dark green parts in a separate bowl.

In a large, heavy pot, combine the broth, ginger, the white and pale green slices of the green onions, the star anise, soy sauce, mirin, and sesame oil over medium-high heat. Bring the broth to a boil, reduce the heat to low, and simmer for 10 minutes. Turn the heat off, cover the pan, and let steep for 10 minutes.

Strain the soup, discard the solids, and return the broth to the pot. Bring the broth to a boil. Add the soba noodles and cook, stirring once or twice, for 4 minutes. Keep warm over low heat.

Place a small frying pan over high heat until it is very hot. Brush the salmon with the oil and season with salt and pepper. Sear the salmon to medium-rare, 4–5 minutes per side.

To serve, use tongs to divide the soba noodles among 4 shallow bowls. Ladle the hot broth into each bowl and top with a piece of seared salmon. Garnish with the sliced dark green onions and serve.

JUNE

15

15

ROASTED RED PEPPER PURÉE WITH SPICY CORN SALSA

serves 4–6

2 Tbsp olive oil

1 small yellow onion, chopped

2 cloves garlic, minced

1 jar (24 oz/750 g) roasted
red bell peppers, drained

1 russet potato, peeled and diced

4 cups (32 fl oz/1 l) chicken broth

1 Tbsp sour cream

Salt and freshly ground pepper

FOR THE SPICY CORN SALSA

1 Tbsp unsalted butter

1 Tbsp minced jalapeño chile

1 Tbsp thinly sliced green onion,
white and tender green parts

1 cup (6 oz/185 g) fresh corn kernels
(from about 2 ears), or 1 cup frozen corn

Salt and freshly ground pepper

*Guests will be
stunned by this
outrageously
colorful soup.
The recipe calls
for jarred peppers
for convenience, but
you can roast your
own, substituting
3 fresh peppers.
Serve the soup
with simple cheese
quesadillas or
tortilla chips.*

In a large, heavy pot, warm the oil over medium-high heat. Add the onion and garlic and sauté until translucent, about 5 minutes. Add the roasted peppers and potato, stir to coat, and cook for 3 minutes. Add the broth and bring to a boil. Reduce the heat to low and simmer until the potatoes are very tender, 25–30 minutes. Remove from the heat and let cool slightly.

Working in batches, purée the soup in a blender or food processor. Return to the pot, stir in the sour cream, and season with salt and pepper.

Meanwhile, to make the salsa, melt the butter in a small frying pan over high heat. Add the jalapeño and green onion and cook, stirring constantly, until the butter begins to brown, about 2 minutes. Add the corn kernels, stir to combine, and cook for 2 minutes. Season with salt and pepper.

Serve the soup, topped with the corn salsa.

16

EGG DROP SOUP WITH CHARD

serves 3–4

4 cups (32 fl oz/1 l) chicken broth

1 Tbsp cornstarch

1-inch (2.5-cm) piece fresh ginger,
peeled and sliced

2 star anise

3 cloves

1½ Tbsp low-sodium soy sauce,
plus more to taste

1 small bunch chard, ribs removed and
leaves shredded (about 1½ cups/90 g)

3 eggs, beaten

*Chard is a healthful
and pretty
nontraditional
addition to this
classic Chinese soup
that comes together
in about a half hour.
Make sure the soup
is simmering and
not boiling when
you add the eggs
to get the perfect
feathery strands.
Follow the soup
with store-bought
wontons and green
beans stir-fried with
ginger and garlic.*

Pour the broth into a heavy pot and whisk in the cornstarch. Add the ginger, star anise, cloves, and soy sauce. Place over medium-high heat and bring to a boil, then reduce the heat to low and simmer for 20 minutes. Strain the broth through a fine-mesh sieve, discarding the solids.

Return the broth to the pot, place over medium heat, and bring to a gentle simmer. Add the chard and cook just until it wilts, about 2 minutes. Again, make sure the soup is at a gentle simmer.

While whisking continuously, slowly pour the eggs into the simmering broth and cook for about 1 minute. Remove from the heat, add more soy sauce to taste, and serve at once.

17

ROASTED BEET PURÉE WITH FETA

serves 4

This soup couldn't be simpler, but it delivers big color and flavor. Roasting beets concentrates their natural sweetness, and salty feta is a perfect complement.

3 large red or yellow beets, trimmed, leaving 1 inch (2.5 cm) of stem

1½ Tbsp olive oil

1 Tbsp unsalted butter

¼ yellow onion, chopped

4 cups (32 fl oz/1 l) chicken, beef, or vegetable broth

Salt and freshly ground pepper

½ cup (2½ oz/75 g) crumbled feta cheese

2 Tbsp coarsely chopped dill

Preheat the oven to 350°F (180°C). Put the beets in a baking dish and drizzle with the oil, turning to coat. Roast until the beets are easily pierced with a fork, about 1 hour. Remove from the oven. When the beets are cool enough to handle, peel and coarsely chop them.

In a large, heavy pot, melt the butter over medium heat. Add the onion and sauté until translucent, about 2 minutes. Add the beets and broth, bring to a simmer, reduce the heat to low, and cook, uncovered, for 10 minutes. Remove from the heat and let cool slightly.

Working in batches, purée the soup in a blender or food processor. Serve warm or let cool to room temperature, transfer to a covered container, and refrigerate until chilled, at least 2 hours or up to overnight. Season with salt and pepper and serve, garnished with the feta and dill.

18

CREAMY POBLANO CHILE SOUP

serves 4–6

The large poblano chile is extremely versatile. It can be stuffed, cut into rajas (strips), which are used in a variety of ways, or made into this simple yet elegant traditional soup. The cream sweetens the rich spice of the chiles, and the peas lend a bright green hue.

¼ cup (2 oz/60 g) unsalted butter

1 tsp canola oil

4 poblano chiles, roasted, peeled, seeded, and chopped

1 white onion, chopped

3 cloves garlic, chopped

6 cups (48 fl oz/1.5 l) chicken broth

1 cup (5 oz/155 g) fresh or frozen peas

Salt and freshly ground pepper

½ cup (2½ oz/75 g) blanched almonds, finely ground

5 Tbsp (2½ fl oz/75 ml) Mexican crema or sour cream

In a large, heavy pot, melt the butter with the oil over medium heat. Stir in the chiles, onion, and garlic and sauté, stirring, until well softened, about 3 minutes. Add the broth and peas and season with salt and pepper. Simmer, uncovered, for about 10 minutes to blend the flavors. Remove from the heat and let cool slightly.

Working in batches, purée the soup with the ground almonds in a blender. Taste and adjust the seasoning. Return to the pot and reheat the soup gently over medium heat.

Serve, garnished with the crema.

19

CHICKPEA & DANDELION GREEN SOUP WITH CROUTONS & FRIED EGGS

serves 4

2½ Tbsp olive oil

½ cup (2½ oz/75 g) chopped yellow onion

1 clove garlic, minced

1 can (15 oz/470 g) chickpeas, drained

½ tsp ground cumin

Salt and freshly ground pepper

1 bunch dandelion greens or spinach, tough stems trimmed, leaves chopped

5 cups (40 fl oz/1.25 l) vegetable or chicken broth

8 slices baguette, cut on the diagonal

1½ Tbsp unsalted butter

4 eggs

In parts of the Mediterranean, in areas of the United States, and other places where wild dandelions are abundant, people gather the tall, slender greens for making soup. If foraging isn't possible in your area, cultivated dandelions, sometimes labeled Italian dandelion, are sold in markets and at farmers' markets. The cultivated leaves are larger than the wild, and the flavor is slightly milder. Here, the greens create a rich background flavor for chickpeas, and the soup is tastily finished off with a fried egg– topped crouton.

In a large, heavy pot, warm 1 Tbsp of the oil over medium-high heat. Add the onion and garlic and cook, stirring occasionally, until the onion is softened, about 2 minutes. Add half of the chickpeas and cook, stirring occasionally, until lightly golden, about 1 minute. Sprinkle with the cumin, ¼ tsp salt, and ¼ tsp pepper and stir. Add the dandelion greens and stir, then add the broth. Reduce the heat to medium-low and simmer until the dandelion greens are soft but still bright green, about 5 minutes. Let cool slightly.

Purée half of the soup in a food processor or blender. Return to the pot and stir to combine. Place over medium-high heat, add the remaining chickpeas, and cook for 3–4 minutes. Keep warm over low heat.

Meanwhile, in a large frying pan, warm the remaining 1½ Tbsp oil over medium-high heat. Add the baguette slices and fry until golden, about 2 minutes. Turn and fry until golden on the other side, about 1 minute. Transfer to a plate.

In the same frying pan, melt the butter over medium heat. When it foams, break the eggs into the pan and fry until the whites are opaque and the yolks are slightly firm, about 3 minutes. ⟫

Ladle the soup into bowls. Top 4 of the croutons with a fried egg and place one atop each bowl. Serve, accompanied by the remaining croutons.

20

COOL HONEYDEW-MINT SOUP

serves 6

½ large honeydew melon (about 2 lb/1 kg), seeded, peeled, and chopped

¼ cup (¼ oz/7 g) loosely packed mint leaves, plus mint sprigs for garnish

3 Tbsp fresh lime juice, plus more as needed

1 Tbsp honey

Salt

Paper-thin lime slices for garnish

Long summer days coax the sweetest flavor from melons. Green-fleshed honeydew makes a pretty purée, but Casaba, Crenshaw, Persian, or other cantaloupe melons can be substituted with equally pleasing results. With a squeeze of lime and a lift from mint, this makes a simple and refreshing starter for a grilled dinner.

Working in batches, place the melon, ¼ cup (¼ oz/7 g) mint leaves, 3 Tbsp lime juice, and honey in a blender. Purée on high speed until smooth and light, about 2 minutes for each batch. Transfer to a covered container and refrigerate until chilled, at least 2 hours.

Before serving, season with more lime juice, if needed, and salt. Serve, garnished with lime slices and mint sprigs.

21

GOLDEN BEET SOUP WITH DILLED GOAT CHEESE

serves 6–8

With its distinct caraway nuances and celery-like flavor, feathery dill complements both earthy beets and tangy fresh goat cheese. Golden beets are as sweet as red, but they have a finer, milder taste that lightens this silky, summery soup.

5 golden beets (about 2½ lb/ 1.25 kg total), trimmed

1 Yukon Gold potato

¼ lb (125 g) fresh goat cheese, crumbled

¾ cup (6 fl oz/180 ml) half-and-half

½ tsp fresh lemon juice

3 Tbsp minced dill, plus leaves for garnish

Salt and freshly ground pepper

2 Tbsp unsalted butter

1 yellow onion, chopped

2 cloves garlic, minced

6 cups (48 fl oz/1.5 l) chicken broth

1 tsp white wine vinegar

Preheat the oven to 400°F (200°C). Wrap the beets and potato in foil and place on a baking sheet. Roast until tender when pierced with a knife, about 1 hour. Open the foil and let cool, then peel and chop the beets and potato.

Meanwhile, in a small bowl, combine the goat cheese, ¼ cup (2 fl oz/60 ml) of the half-and-half, the lemon juice, minced dill, ¼ tsp salt, and pepper to taste. Using a fork, vigorously beat until blended and pourable but still thick. Set aside.

In a large, heavy pot, melt the butter over medium heat. Add the onion and garlic and sauté until softened, about 5 minutes. Add the broth and bring to a boil over medium-high heat. Add the beets and potato, reduce the heat to low, cover partially, and cook for 15 minutes. Remove from the heat and let cool slightly.

Working in batches, purée the soup in a blender. Return to the pot and add the vinegar, 1½ tsp salt, pepper to taste, and the remaining ½ cup (4 fl oz/125 ml) half-and-half and stir. Place over medium-low heat and cook gently, stirring occasionally, until heated through, about 10 minutes.

Season with salt and pepper. Serve, garnished with a dollop of the goat cheese mixture and the dill leaves.

22

CHEESE & ARUGULA RAVIOLI SOUP

serves 4

This soup is best eaten fresh, as the delicate ravioli may threaten to come apart with reheating. Feel free to vary the ravioli filling according to your likes; goat cheese and pancetta, or artichoke, garlic, and ricotta, for instance, could be equally delicious.

FOR THE RAVIOLI

1 tsp olive oil

½ cup (½ oz/15 g) arugula

⅓ cup (3 oz/90 g) ricotta cheese

2 Tbsp grated Parmesan cheese

Pinch of grated nutmeg

Salt and freshly ground pepper

20 wonton wrappers

2 Tbsp olive oil

2 shallots, thinly sliced

4 cloves garlic, thinly sliced

4 cups (32 fl oz/1 l) chicken broth

1 can (14½ oz/455 g) diced tomatoes

1 Tbsp tomato paste

Salt and freshly ground pepper

1 cup (1 oz/30 g) arugula

¼ cup (⅓ oz/10 g) chopped basil

Grated Parmesan cheese for garnish

To make the ravioli, warm the oil in a small frying pan over medium heat. Add the arugula and sauté until wilted, 1 minute. Transfer the arugula to a cutting board, let cool slightly, and finely chop.

In a small bowl, combine the ricotta, Parmesan, nutmeg, and chopped arugula and season with salt and pepper. Place 1 tsp of the cheese mixture in the middle of each wonton wrapper. Moisten all sides of a wrapper with water and fold the wrapper diagonally, forcing out air bubbles as you press to seal. Repeat for all the ravioli.

To make the soup, in a large, heavy pot, warm the oil over medium-high heat. Add the shallots and garlic and cook until soft, about 4 minutes. Add the broth, tomatoes, and tomato paste and bring to a boil. Reduce the heat to low and simmer for 10 minutes. Season with salt and pepper.

Return the soup to a gentle boil. Carefully add the ravioli and cook for about 2 minutes. Add the arugula and basil and cook just until the greens are wilted, about 1 minute. Serve, passing Parmesan at the table.

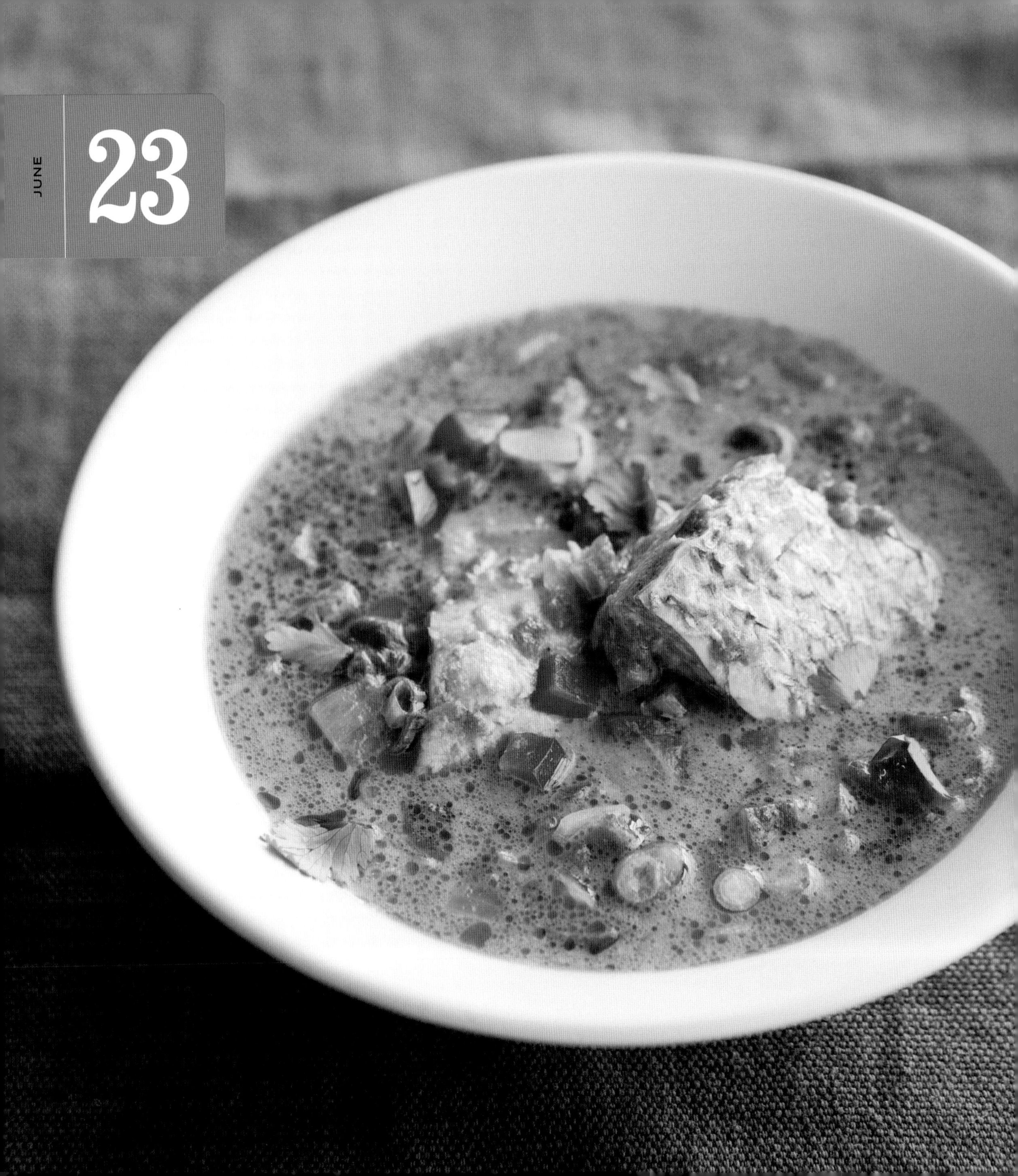

23

BRAZILIAN FISH STEW

serves 4

1 can (14½ oz/455 g) diced tomatoes

1 white onion, chopped

2 cloves garlic, minced

1 bay leaf

2 limes, 1 juiced and 1 cut into wedges

1 lb (500 g) red snapper, cut into 2-inch (5-cm) pieces

2 Tbsp olive oil

1 small red bell pepper, seeded and diced

1 can (14 fl oz/440 ml) coconut milk

1 cup (8 fl oz/250 ml) chicken broth

1 cup (8 fl oz/250 ml) bottled clam juice

3 green onions, white and tender green parts, chopped

2 Tbsp minced cilantro

Hot sauce, such as Tabasco

Salt and freshly ground pepper

Moqueca is a traditional Brazilian fish stew that varies from region to region. This version includes tomatoes, peppers, plenty of seasoning, and a dose of creamy coconut milk. Feel free to replace the red snapper with whichever firm white fish looks freshest that day at the market.

In a bowl, combine the tomatoes, onion, garlic, bay leaf, and the juice of 1 lime. Add the fish to the bowl and gently spoon the marinade over to cover the fish. Cover the bowl and refrigerate for 1 hour.

Remove the fish from the bowl, brushing off the marinade, and set aside. In a large, heavy pot, warm the oil over medium-high heat. Add all of the marinade and the bell pepper to the pot and sauté until the vegetables are very soft, 8–10 minutes. Add the coconut milk, broth, and clam juice and bring to a boil. Reduce the heat to low and add the fish. Cook until the fish begins to flake, 4–5 minutes. Gently stir in the green onions and cilantro. Season with a few drops of hot sauce and salt and pepper. Serve, passing the lime wedges at the table.

24

CORN & SPINACH CHOWDER WITH AVOCADO

serves 8

4 ears of corn, husks and silk removed

2 slices thick-cut bacon, chopped

1 celery rib, chopped

½ large yellow onion, diced

2 cups (16 fl oz/500 ml) chicken broth

1 lb (500 g) red new potatoes cut into ½-inch (12-mm) cubes

2 Tbsp fresh thyme leaves

2 bay leaves

Salt and freshly ground pepper

2 cups (16 fl oz/500 ml) milk, heated

1 cup (1 oz/30 g) spinach, chopped

2 avocados, pitted, peeled, and thinly sliced

This chunky chowder, with fresh corn kernels stripped from the cob, potatoes, and the classic chowder base of celery and onions, is studded with bright green pieces of cut spinach. The avocado garnish adds a Southwestern twist and a creamy contrast to the chunky texture of the chowder. If you like, set out a bowl of tortilla chips as an accompaniment.

Working with one ear of corn at a time, hold it, stem end down, on a cutting board. Carefully cut off the kernels, rotating the ear after each cut until all the kernels are stripped from the cob. Set the kernels aside.

Heat a large, heavy pot over medium-high heat until hot. Reduce the heat to low and fry the bacon, stirring occasionally, until it is crispy and the fat is rendered, 7–8 minutes. Using a slotted spoon, transfer the bacon to a bowl and reserve for another use. Leave the bacon fat in the pot.

Add the celery and onion to the pot and cook over low heat, stirring occasionally, until almost translucent, about 2 minutes. Raise the heat to medium-high and add the broth, stirring to scrape up the browned bits from the bottom of the pot. Add the potatoes, thyme, bay leaves, ½ tsp salt, and ¼ tsp pepper and bring to a boil. Reduce the heat to low, cover, and simmer until the potatoes are fork-tender, 12–15 minutes.

Add the hot milk and simmer for 5 minutes. Add the corn kernels and spinach, and simmer just until the spinach wilts but still retains its bright green color, 3–4 minutes. Taste and adjust the seasoning. Remove and discard the bay leaves. Serve, garnished with the avocado slices.

25

RAMEN NOODLES WITH EDAMAME & MUSHROOMS

serves 6

4 cups (32 fl oz/1 l) chicken broth

¼ cup (2 fl oz/60 ml) soy sauce

3 Tbsp ketchup

⅛ tsp hot chile oil

9 oz (280 g) ramen noodles

½ lb (250 g) Chinese mushrooms, thinly sliced

½ cup (2½ oz/75 g) cooked and shelled edamame

4 green onions, white and tender green parts, chopped

Hot sauce, such as Sriracha, for serving (optional)

Packaged versions can't compare with the freshness of this simple noodle soup, which really couldn't be easier to assemble. You can use any vegetables you have on hand. Chinese mushrooms include shiitake, enoki, and straw varieties, but even white mushrooms will be delicious.

In a large, heavy pot, bring the broth, 2 cups (16 fl oz/500 ml) water, the soy sauce, ketchup, and chile oil to a boil over medium-high heat. Add the ramen noodles, mushrooms, and edamame. Reduce the heat to medium-low and simmer for 5 minutes. Stir in the green onions.

Serve, passing the hot sauce, if using, at the table.

26

BLACK BEAN SOUP WITH CHIPOTLE CHILES

serves 6–8

4 slices bacon, cut into 1-inch (2.5-cm) pieces

½ cup (2 oz/60 g) chopped yellow onion

3 cloves garlic, minced

1 large tomato, diced

2 bay leaves

1 tsp ground cumin

1 tsp ground chili powder

2 chipotle chiles in adobo, finely chopped

½ cup (¾ oz/20 g) chopped cilantro, plus sprigs for garnish

1 Tbsp red wine vinegar

6 cups (48 fl oz/1.5 l) chicken broth

2 cans (15 oz/470 g each) black beans, drained

Salt

¼ lb (125 g) cotija cheese, crumbled

Creaming the beans spreads the flavors not only of the beans but also of the other vegetables and herbs with which they were cooked. The result is a sophisticated backdrop for the poblano and bright white cheese toppings. Poblano chiles are large, heart shaped, and dark, glossy green. Their flavor is mild, with a hint of sharp green bite that mellows when they are roasted.

In a large, heavy pot, fry the bacon over medium-high heat, stirring occasionally, until soft and translucent, about 5 minutes. Add the onion and cook, stirring occasionally, until translucent, about 2 minutes. Add the garlic, tomato, bay leaves, cumin, chili powder, chipotle chiles, ½ cup (¾ oz/20 g) cilantro, and vinegar and stir to combine. Add the broth, beans, and ½ tsp salt and bring to a simmer. Reduce the heat to medium-low and simmer for 20 minutes. Remove and discard the bay leaves. Let cool slightly.

Working in batches, purée the soup in a food processor or blender. Return to the pot, place over medium-high heat, and reheat until the soup is simmering. Serve, garnished with the cheese and cilantro sprigs.

27

CHILLED YELLOW PEPPER SOUP WITH CHIVES

serves 4

2 Tbsp olive oil

2 cloves garlic, minced

½ yellow onion, chopped

1 small carrot, peeled and thinly sliced

1 Tbsp peeled and minced fresh ginger

3 yellow bell peppers, roasted, peeled, seeded, and chopped

1 cup (8 fl oz/250 ml) chicken broth

1 Tbsp heavy cream

Salt and freshly ground pepper

2 Tbsp chopped chives

This soup is sweet from the yellow bell peppers and carrots, but packed with a spicy punch from fresh ginger. Serve with toasted peasant bread topped with melted cheese and thinly sliced prosciutto.

In a large, heavy pot, warm the oil over medium-high heat. Add the garlic, onion, and carrot and sauté until the carrot begins to soften, 5–7 minutes. Add the ginger and bell pepper and cook for 3 minutes, stirring often. Add the broth and bring to a boil. Reduce the heat to low and simmer for 25 minutes. Remove from the heat and let cool slightly.

Working in batches, purée the soup in a blender. Return to the saucepan, add the cream, and bring just to a boil. Remove from the heat, season with salt and pepper, and let the soup cool completely.

Transfer to a covered container and refrigerate until well chilled, at least 3 hours or up to overnight. Serve, garnished with chives.

28

MELON & PROSCIUTTO SOUP WITH MASCARPONE CHEESE

serves 4–6

2 oz (60 g) prosciutto, thinly sliced

1 very ripe cantaloupe, peeled, seeded, and cut into chunks

2 Tbsp Champagne vinegar

Salt and freshly ground pepper

¼ cup (2 oz/60 g) mascarpone cheese

1 lime, cut into wedges, for serving

This is a very sweet soup, but the intensity of summer melons is cut with salty crumbled prosciutto, their well-loved sidekick on the antipasti plate. The ham adds a savory note, and a dollop of creamy mascarpone rounds out the flavors.

In a small frying pan, cook the prosciutto over medium-high heat, turning once, until very crisp, about 10 minutes. Transfer to paper towels to drain. Let cool, then crumble.

Put the cantaloupe chunks in a food processor and pulse until puréed. Add the vinegar and pulse 3 more times. Season with salt and pepper. Transfer to a covered container and refrigerate until well chilled, at least 3 hours.

Serve, topped with a dollop of the mascarpone, the crumbled prosciutto, and a squeeze of lime.

29

Usually served chilled, this Latin American soup is also delicious at room temperature. The zesty tomato salsa provides a lively contrast to the rich and creamy flavor of the avocado. Chopped grapefruit segments or tropical fruits could substitute for the tomatoes.

AVOCADO SOUP WITH SHRIMP & SALSA

serves 6–8

3 large avocados, peeled, pitted, and coarsely chopped

3 cups (24 fl oz/750 ml) chicken broth

1 cup (8 fl oz/250 ml) heavy cream

2 Tbsp fresh lemon juice

Salt and freshly ground pepper

FOR THE SALSA

3 tomatoes (about 1 lb/500 g), finely chopped

1 small red onion, minced

2 or 3 jalapeño chiles, minced

2 cloves garlic, minced

3 Tbsp fresh lemon or lime juice

¼ cup (⅓ oz/10 g) chopped cilantro

¼ cup (2 fl oz/60 ml) olive oil

Salt and freshly ground pepper

12–16 cooked shrimp, peeled and diced

Working in batches, purée the avocados, broth, and cream in a blender. Transfer to a bowl. Add the lemon juice and season with salt and pepper. Cover and refrigerate until cold but not overly chilled, about 1 hour.

Meanwhile, to make the salsa, stir together the tomatoes, onion, chiles, garlic, lemon juice, cilantro, and oil. Season with salt and pepper.

Serve the soup, topped with the shrimp and garnished with the salsa.

30

To make pistou, in a blender, combine 3–4 cloves garlic, ¼ teaspoon coarse sea salt, and 1 cup (1 oz/30 g) basil leaves and process until a paste forms. With the motor running, add ⅓ cup (3 fl oz/80 ml) extra-virgin olive oil in a slow, steady stream, processing until the mixture is thick and green. Refrigerate in an airtight container for up to 5 days. Makes ½ cup (4 fl oz/125 ml).

PROVENÇAL MINESTRONE

serves 4–6

2 cups (16 fl oz/500 ml) chicken broth

3 small boiling potatoes, peeled and diced

2 carrots, peeled and diced

1 tsp fresh thyme leaves, or ½ tsp dried

1 tsp minced fresh winter savory, or ½ tsp dried

Salt and freshly ground pepper

1 large zucchini, diced

1 small yellow onion, diced

½ lb (250 g) young, slender green beans, trimmed and cut into 1-inch (2.5-cm) pieces

1 lb (500 g) fresh cranberry beans in the pod, shelled, or 1 cup (7 oz/220 g) canned butter beans

½ cup (3 oz/90 g) spaghetti broken into 2-inch (5-cm) pieces

Pistou (left)

In a large, heavy pot, bring the broth and 6 cups (48 fl oz/1.5 l) water to a boil over medium-high heat. Add the potatoes, carrots, thyme, winter savory, 2 tsp salt, and ½ tsp pepper. Reduce the heat to medium and cook until the carrots are tender when pierced with a fork, about 20 minutes.

Add the zucchini, onion, green beans, and shelling beans and cook until the shelling beans are tender to the bite, 15–20 minutes.

Add the spaghetti and cook until al dente, 10–11 minutes, or according to the package directions. Taste and adjust the seasoning. Stir 2 Tbsp of the pistou into the soup.

Ladle the soup into bowls and serve, passing the remaining pistou at the table.

5

SOBA NOODLE SOUP
page 157

6

**INDONESIAN-STYLE CURRIED
EGGPLANT STEW**
page 157

7

**PORTUGUESE FISH & SAUSAGE STEW
WITH CHIVE AIOLI**
page 159

12

CALAMARI STEW
page 161

13

**VEGETABLE SOUP
WITH BASIL OIL**
page 162

14

**MISO SOUP WITH BLACK COD
& GREEN ONIONS**
page 162

19

BURMESE CHICKEN CURRY SOUP
page 167

20

**CARROT-GRUYÈRE SOUP
WITH PISTACHIOS**
page 167

21

**CHIPOTLE-CORN PURÉE WITH
BAY SHRIMP & AVOCADO SALSA**
page 168

26

**CHAYOTE SOUP WITH POBLANO
& JALAPEÑO CHILES**
page 172

27

**ROASTED NECTARINE
SOUP WITH MINT**
page 173

28

CRAB & AVOCADO SOUP
page 173

July's warming sun ripens tomatoes on the vine, whose sweet flavor is showcased in light, brothy soups with herbs and pastina, grains, or meats added for heartiness. Toasted chiles enliven summer corn and beans, offering fire that mimics the summer heat. Chilled soups made from fresh fruits and vegetables, enhanced with sparkling wine, vibrant mint, or bracing vinegar, are perfect to begin an alfresco brunch or a backyard barbecue.

july

1

CHILLED CUCUMBER-YOGURT SOUP WITH LEMON & MINT

serves 8–10

6 large English cucumbers (about 5 lb/2.5 kg), peeled and seeded

8 Tbsp (¾ oz/20 g) minced mint

4 Tbsp (2 fl oz/60 ml) extra-virgin olive oil

Grated zest and juice of 1 large lemon

4 cups (32 fl oz/1 l) chicken broth

4 cups (2 lb/1 kg) plain yogurt

2 small cloves garlic, minced

Salt and freshly ground pepper

Serve this soup as a refreshing starter before a Mediterranean-inspired dinner of grilled cumin-spiced lamb and herbed couscous.

Finely chop 1 cucumber. Place half of the pieces between layers of paper towels, pressing to absorb excess moisture. Transfer to a small bowl, add 2 Tbsp of the mint and 1 Tbsp of the oil, and toss to combine. Cover and refrigerate. Cut the remaining 5 cucumbers into large chunks.

Working in batches, coarsely purée the cucumber chunks, the remaining mint, the lemon zest, and 2 cups (16 fl oz/500 ml) of the broth in a food processor or blender. Transfer to a large nonreactive bowl. Add the remaining 2 cups broth along with the finely chopped cucumber and mint mixture, the remaining 3 Tbsp oil, the lemon juice, the yogurt, and the garlic. Add 1½ tsp salt and season with pepper. Stir to blend well, cover, and refrigerate until well chilled, at least 4 hours or up to 12 hours. Serve.

2

SIMPLE ZUCCHINI SOUP

serves 4

1½–2 lb (750 g–1 kg) small zucchini, shredded

Salt and freshly ground pepper

2 Tbsp unsalted butter

2 yellow onions, chopped

2 cups (16 fl oz/500 ml) chicken broth

Grated nutmeg

2 tsp finely chopped mint

3 cups (24 fl oz/750 ml) milk

½ tsp fresh lemon juice

4 thin lemon slices

It's worth it to salt and drain the shredded zucchini to remove a slight edge of bitterness. Don't worry about the salt: most of it washes away in the squeezing and rinsing.

Layer half of the zucchini in a colander set over a bowl. Sprinkle with salt, then top with the remaining zucchini and again sprinkle with salt. Let drain for 25–30 minutes. Pick up the drained zucchini by small handfuls and squeeze out the released juice. Return the zucchini to the colander and rinse quickly under cold running water to remove the salt. Again squeeze out the moisture, then set aside.

In a large, heavy pot, melt the butter over medium-low heat. Add the onions and sauté until translucent, 3–4 minutes. Add the broth, cover, and simmer until the onions are tender, 15–20 minutes. Remove from the heat and let cool slightly.

Working in batches, purée the mixture in a blender. Return to the pot. Add the zucchini, a pinch of nutmeg, and 1 tsp of the mint. Bring to a simmer, cover, and cook for 6–8 minutes. Add the milk and lemon juice, and season with salt and pepper. Heat until the soup is very hot, but do not let it boil. Serve, sprinkled with the remaining mint and garnished with the lemon slices.

3

SPICY CORN SOUP

serves 4

3 slices bacon, chopped

1 small yellow onion, chopped

1 celery rib, chopped

1 poblano chile, seeded and chopped

2 cloves garlic, minced

4 cups (32 fl oz/1 l) milk

1 cup (8 fl oz/250 ml) heavy cream

2 boiling potatoes, peeled and cut into bite-sized cubes

3 cups (18 oz/560 g) fresh corn kernels (from about 6 ears) or 3 cups frozen

½ tsp red pepper flakes

Salt and freshly ground black pepper

Sweet meets heat in this reinvented chowder. The traditional creamy base gets a kick with the addition of both fresh and dried chile. Make it in high summer, when fresh corn kernels need only a brief simmer in the pot, emerging sweet and tender.

In a large, heavy pot, sauté the bacon over medium heat until it begins to crisp, about 5 minutes. Transfer to paper towels to drain. Add the onion, celery, chile, and garlic and sauté just until lightly browned, 6–7 minutes.

Raise the heat to medium-high, add the milk, cream, and potatoes, and bring to a boil. Reduce the heat to low and simmer, uncovered, until the potatoes are tender, about 15 minutes. Stir in the corn and red pepper flakes and simmer until the corn is tender, about 5 minutes. Remove from the heat and let cool slightly.

Purée about 2 cups (16 fl oz/500 ml) of the solids in a blender or food processor. Return to the pot and reheat. Season with salt and pepper and serve, garnished with the bacon.

4

MEDITERRANEAN FISH STEW

serves 6

¼ cup (2 fl oz/60 ml) olive oil

½ small yellow onion, finely chopped

1 celery rib including leaves, chopped

1 carrot, peeled and chopped

3 cloves garlic, minced

1 tsp dried thyme

½ tsp red pepper flakes

2 oil-packed anchovies

1 cup (8 fl oz/250 ml) dry white wine

1 can (14½ oz/455 g) diced tomatoes

4 cups (32 fl oz/1 l) fish broth

Pinch of saffron threads dissolved in 1 Tbsp hot water

1 bay leaf

1 rosemary sprig

2 lb (1 kg) firm white-fleshed fish fillets, cut into bite-sized pieces

12 littleneck or Manila clams, scrubbed

12 mussels, scrubbed and debearded

¾ lb (375 g) large shrimp, peeled and deveined

Salt

3 Tbsp minced flat-leaf parsley

Pungent garlic and sunny saffron define the Mediterranean mood of this shellfish-rich stew, which features a trio of clams, mussels, and prawns. Serve with warm, crusty bread, and lemon wedges for squeezing into the broth.

In a large, heavy pot, warm the oil over medium heat. Add the onion, celery, and carrot and sauté until the onion is translucent, 3–5 minutes. Add the garlic, thyme, red pepper flakes, and anchovies and sauté until the mixture is fragrant and the anchovies have melted, about 3 minutes. Add the wine and simmer until reduced by half, about 10 minutes. Add the tomatoes with their juices, broth, saffron mixture, bay leaf, and rosemary sprig. Pour in 1 cup (8 fl oz/250 ml) water. Reduce the heat to medium-low and simmer for 15 minutes.

Add the fish, cover, and simmer just until opaque, about 2 minutes. Add the clams, cover, and simmer until most of them open, about 6 minutes. Add the mussels, cover, and cook until they open, 3–4 minutes. Discard any unopened clams or mussels. Add the shrimp and cook, uncovered, just until pink, about 2 minutes. Remove from the heat and season with salt. Discard the bay leaf and rosemary. Serve, garnished with the parsley.

5

SOBA NOODLE SOUP

serves 4

2 Tbsp canola oil

2 boneless pork loin chops, cut into slices ¼ inch (6 mm) thick

1 Tbsp peeled and grated ginger

2 cloves garlic, thinly sliced

¼ yellow onion, finely chopped

1 Tbsp soy sauce

6 cups (48 fl oz/1.5 l) chicken broth

½ lb (250 g) soba noodles

4 white mushrooms, sliced

4 green onions, white and tender pale green parts, sliced

Salt and freshly ground pepper

This simple soup features wheat noodles and slices of pork, seasoned with the classic Asian trio of garlic, ginger, and soy. To slice the pork, place the chops in the freezer for half an hour. Firmed, the meat will be much easier to slice very thinly.

In a small frying pan, warm the oil over medium heat. Add the pork and sauté until golden brown, about 4 minutes. Add the ginger, garlic, yellow onion, and soy sauce and sauté until the onion is translucent, about 2 minutes. Remove from the heat.

In a large, heavy pot, bring the broth to a boil over medium-high heat. Add the soba, stir to separate the noodles, and cook just until tender, about 5 minutes. Add the pork mixture, mushrooms, and green onions and cook for 1 minute to heat through. Season with salt and pepper and serve.

6

INDONESIAN-STYLE CURRIED EGGPLANT STEW

serves 4

¼ cup (2 fl oz/60 ml) coconut oil

2 shallots, chopped

1 Tbsp chopped garlic

2-inch (5-cm) piece lemongrass, center white part only, crushed, or 1 tsp dried lemongrass

2 small fresh chiles, such as Thai or serrano, seeded and chopped

1 tsp ground coriander

1 tsp ground turmeric

2 tsp tamarind paste dissolved in 2 Tbsp cold water

1 lb (500 g) round Thai eggplants, stemmed and quartered

1½ cups (12 fl oz/375 ml) unsweetened coconut milk

½ cup (4 fl oz/125 ml) chicken broth

2 Tbsp chopped cilantro

Steamed white rice for serving

Small, green-striated Thai eggplants are used to make this rich, boldly flavored stew. Widely used in Southeast Asian cuisines, they belong to the same family as the familiar purple eggplants but have a slightly bitter flavor that is valued in curries, stews, and soups. They can be found in Asian markets and sometimes at farmers' markets from vendors who specialize in Asian vegetables.

In a large, heavy pot, warm the coconut oil over medium-high heat. Add the shallots and garlic and cook, stirring occasionally, until the shallots are translucent, about 1 minute. Add the lemongrass, chiles, coriander, and turmeric and cook, stirring occasionally, for 1 minute. Add the tamarind mixture, eggplants, coconut milk, and broth and bring to a simmer. Cook until the eggplants are fork-tender, about 20 minutes.

Transfer the stew to a serving bowl, garnish with the cilantro, and serve with steamed rice.

7

Cataplana is the name for both an array of Portuguese seafood dishes and for the clam shell–shaped vessel in which they are cooked. Here, a saucepan with a tight-fitting lid stands in for the more traditional pan. If you cannot find linguiça, a mildly spicy smoked Portuguese pork sausage, any high-quality fresh spicy Italian sausage can be substituted. Make sure the aioli is at room temperature just before serving, as it will blend into the soup better and will not cool the bowl.

PORTUGUESE FISH & SAUSAGE STEW WITH CHIVE AIOLI

serves 4

FOR THE CHIVE AIOLI

1 clove garlic

Salt

1 whole egg plus 1 egg yolk

1 cup (8 fl oz/250 ml) canola or vegetable oil

3 Tbsp finely chopped chives

1 lb (500 g) littleneck clams, scrubbed

2 Tbsp olive oil

½ lb (250 g) linguiça or spicy Italian sausage, cut into ½-inch (12-mm) slices

1 yellow onion, halved and thinly sliced

4 cloves garlic, chopped

1 jar (5 oz/155 g) piquillo peppers, drained and quartered

1 bay leaf

1 tsp smoked paprika

Salt and freshly ground pepper

1 bottle (8 fl oz/250 ml) clam juice

2 cups (16 fl oz/500 ml) chicken broth

½ lb (250 g) small Yukon Gold potatoes, halved

¾ lb (375 g) fresh cod, cut into 2-inch (5-cm) pieces

2 Tbsp chopped flat-leaf parsley

To make the chive aioli, in a food processor or blender, combine the garlic and a big pinch of salt. Pulse several times until the garlic is finely chopped. Add the whole egg and egg yolk and pulse to combine. With the motor running, slowly add a few drops of the oil, and then follow with a slow and steady stream of oil. Continue to purée until fully combined. Transfer to a bowl, stir in the chives, and adjust the seasoning with salt. Set aside at room temperature.

Fill a large bowl or clean sink with cold water and add the clams so that the sand can escape. Let them sit in the water while you prepare the broth.

In a large, heavy pot, warm 1 Tbsp of the oil over medium-high heat. Add the linguiça and cook, stirring occasionally, until browned on all sides and the fat is rendered, 6–8 minutes. Add the onion and cook, stirring occasionally, until soft, about 6 minutes. ⟫

Add the garlic, piquillo peppers, bay leaf, and paprika, and season with salt and pepper. Cook, stirring frequently, until the garlic is soft and the spices are toasted, about 2 minutes. Add the clam juice, broth, and potatoes and bring to a boil. Reduce the heat to low and simmer until the potatoes are tender, about 12 minutes. Add the cod and clams and raise the heat to medium-high. Cover and steam until the fish is opaque throughout and the clams open, about 10 minutes.

Remove and discard the bay leaf and any unopened clams. Gently stir in the parsley.

Serve, topped with a dollop of the aioli.

8

This soup is great hot or cold. Serve with grilled ready-made naan: brush the naan with olive oil, cook in a very hot grill pan, and sprinkle with sea salt.

CHILLED RED PEPPER & FENNEL SOUP WITH INDIAN SPICES

serves 6

3 Tbsp unsalted butter

1 yellow onion, chopped

2 cloves garlic, minced

3 red bell peppers, seeded and chopped

1 fennel bulb, stalks and fronds removed, chopped

2 carrots, peeled and thinly sliced

1½ tsp garam masala

4 cups (32 fl oz/1 l) chicken broth

2 Tbsp sour cream

Salt and freshly ground pepper

In a large, heavy pot, melt the butter over medium-high heat. Add the onion and garlic and sauté until translucent, about 5 minutes. Add the red peppers, fennel, and carrots and cook, stirring often, until the vegetables soften, 10–12 minutes. Stir in the garam masala and cook for 1 minute. Add the broth and bring to a boil. Reduce the heat to low and simmer for 30 minutes. Remove from the heat and let cool slightly.

Working in batches, purée the soup in a blender. Return to the pot, stir in the sour cream, and bring to a gentle boil. Remove from the heat and season with salt and pepper. Let cool completely, cover, and chill in the refrigerator for at least 3 hours. Serve.

9

JULY

A good-quality olive oil, green and peppery, will really make a difference in a soup that isn't cooked, such as this one. Salted crispy croutons add a nice counterpoint to this sweet, smooth soup.

CUCUMBER & GREEN GRAPE GAZPACHO

serves 4–6

1 cup sweet baguette pieces

1 Tbsp fresh lemon juice

2 tsp white wine vinegar, plus more to taste

½ cup (3 oz/90 g) raw almonds

3 small English cucumbers, peeled, seeded, and chopped

2 cups (12 oz/375 g) green grapes

1 clove garlic, coarsely chopped

¼ cup (2 fl oz/60 ml) extra-virgin olive oil

Salt and freshly ground pepper

Put the baguette pieces, lemon juice, and 2 tsp white wine vinegar in a bowl and stir to combine.

Put the almonds into a food processor and pulse until finely ground. Add the cucumbers, grapes, and garlic and pulse to purée. Add the bread mixture, oil, and ⅓ cup (3 fl oz/80 ml) water. Purée. Season to taste with salt, pepper, and additional white wine vinegar, if needed. Transfer to a covered container and refrigerate until chilled, at least 2 hours. Serve.

10

JULY

Classic pork and beans is even better when made with garden-fresh beans and bubbling ham-and-cheese toasts. Lima beans are available fresh from June to September. Choose pods that are firm, plump, and dark green.

SILKEN LIMA BEAN SOUP WITH HAM CROÛTES

serves 6

4 lb (2 kg) fresh lima beans in the pod, shelled (about 4 cups), or 2 bags (1 lb/500 g each) frozen lima beans, thawed

8 cups (2 qt/2 l) chicken broth

1 russet potato, peeled and cut into ½-inch (12-mm) pieces

1 yellow onion, chopped

2 cloves garlic, chopped

1 carrot, peeled and chopped

Salt and freshly ground pepper

6 slices French bread, each 1 inch (2.5 cm) thick

½ cup (4 fl oz/125 ml) heavy cream

½ cup (3 oz/90 g) chopped country ham

⅓ cup (1½ oz/45 g) shredded Cheddar cheese

2 Tbsp cream cheese, at room temperature

1 Tbsp mayonnaise

1 Tbsp thyme leaves

In a large, heavy pot, combine the beans, broth, potato, onion, garlic, and carrot. Add ½ tsp salt and ½ tsp pepper. Bring to a boil over high heat, then reduce the heat to low, cover partially, and cook, stirring occasionally, until the vegetables are very soft, about 1 hour.

Meanwhile, preheat the oven to 400°F (200°C). Arrange the bread slices on a baking sheet and toast until golden brown, about 10 minutes. Remove from the oven and turn on the broiler. Position a rack 6 inches (15 cm) from the heat source.

Remove the soup from the heat and let cool slightly. Working in batches, purée in a blender. Return to the saucepan and stir in the cream. Reheat the soup over low heat.

In a small bowl, stir together the ham, Cheddar cheese, cream cheese, and mayonnaise. Season with pepper. Spread evenly on the toasted bread. Broil until the topping is bubbly and golden, about 2 minutes.

Serve the soup sprinkled with the thyme, and pass the croûtes at the table.

160

11

CORN & ZUCCHINI SOUP WITH CRUMBLED BACON

serves 4–6

6 slices thick-cut bacon

1 Tbsp olive oil

1 yellow onion, chopped

3 cloves garlic, minced

2 zucchini, trimmed, halved lengthwise, and thinly sliced

4 cups (32 fl oz/1 l) chicken broth

3 cups (18 oz/560 g) fresh corn kernels (from about 6 ears) or 3 cups frozen

Salt and ground white pepper

1 Tbsp unsalted butter

¼ tsp minced thyme leaves

The texture of the fried corn, bacon, and thyme garnish elevates this humble dish. You can make the soup ahead of time, but prepare the garnish just before serving. Serve with buttermilk biscuits.

In a large, heavy pot, cook the bacon over medium heat, turning once, until crispy, about 8 minutes. Transfer to paper towels to drain. Let cool, then cut into bite-sized pieces. Set aside.

Discard all but 1 Tbsp of the bacon fat from the pot. Add the oil, onion, and garlic and sauté over medium-high heat until translucent, about 5 minutes. Add the zucchini and sauté for 5 minutes. Add the broth and bring to a boil. Add 2½ cups (15 oz/470 g) of the corn kernels and cook for 5 minutes. Remove from the heat and let cool slightly.

Working in batches, purée the soup in a blender. Return to the pot and season with salt and pepper.

In a small frying pan, melt the butter over high heat. Add the remaining ½ cup (3 oz/90 g) corn kernels, the bacon, and the thyme. Fry, stirring constantly, for 2 minutes and remove from the heat.

Serve the soup topped with the corn and bacon mixture.

12

CALAMARI STEW

serves 6

2 Tbsp olive oil

1 yellow onion, chopped

4 cloves garlic, minced

½ tsp red pepper flakes

1 can (28 oz/875 g) crushed tomatoes

2 cups (16 fl oz/500 ml) chicken broth

1 red bell pepper, roasted, peeled, seeded, and chopped

¼ cup (⅓ oz/10 g) chopped basil

2 Tbsp chopped oregano

Salt and freshly ground pepper

1 lb (2 kg) calamari, cleaned and bodies thinly sliced, tentacles left whole

The soup can be made ahead and frozen, but add the calamari just before serving, as it only takes a few minutes to cook and it will become rubbery if overdone. It's fine to use frozen calamari for this recipe.

In a large, heavy pot, warm the olive oil over medium-high heat. Add the onion and garlic and sauté until translucent, about 5 minutes. Add the red pepper flakes and cook, stirring constantly, for 2 minutes. Add the tomatoes, broth, and bell pepper and bring to a boil. Reduce the heat to low and simmer for 30 minutes.

Stir in the basil and oregano and cook for 5 minutes. Season with salt and pepper. Raise the heat to medium-high and add the calamari, stirring to combine. Cook just until the calamari is opaque and cooked through, 3–5 minutes. Serve.

13

VEGETABLE SOUP WITH BASIL OIL

serves 6–8

4 Tbsp (2 fl oz/60 ml) olive oil

1 large yellow onion, diced

4 red bell peppers, seeded and cut into strips

2 yellow bell peppers, seeded and cut into strips

8 plum tomatoes, quartered

4 zucchini, halved lengthwise and sliced ¼ inch (6 mm) thick on the diagonal

4 cloves garlic, minced

1 russet potato, peeled and cut into ½-inch (12-mm) dice

3 cups (24 fl oz/750 ml) chicken broth

Salt and freshly ground pepper

1 cup (8 fl oz/250 ml) vegetable oil

1 cup (1 oz/30 g) packed basil leaves

This hearty vegetable soup is the perfect answer to a summertime craving for comfort food. If you like, you can trade out the green zucchini for yellow zucchini, straightneck or crookneck yellow squash, or striped romanesco zucchini. A drizzle of basil oil adds an herbal note to the finished soup.

In a large, heavy pot, warm 2 Tbsp of the olive oil over medium heat. Add the onion and bell peppers and cook, stirring occasionally, until just tender, 10–12 minutes. Transfer to a large bowl.

In the same pot, warm 1 Tbsp of the olive oil over medium heat. Add the tomatoes and cook, stirring occasionally, until they begin to break down, 8–10 minutes. Transfer to the bowl with the onion mixture.

In the same pot, warm the remaining 1 Tbsp olive oil over medium-high heat. Add the zucchini and cook, stirring occasionally, until tender, 8–10 minutes. Add the garlic and cook, stirring occasionally, until fragrant, about 1 minute. Stir in the onion mixture. Transfer 2 cups (8 oz/250 g) of the vegetables to a bowl and set aside.

Add the potato and broth to the pot, bring to a simmer, and cook until the potato is tender, 25–30 minutes. Season with salt and pepper.

In a food processor or blender, combine the vegetable oil, basil, and a large pinch of salt and process on high for 10 seconds. Transfer the basil oil to a small bowl. Wash out the processor or blender.

Working in batches, purée the soup in the food processor or blender. Return to the pot and stir in the reserved vegetables. Serve, drizzled with the basil oil.

14

MISO SOUP WITH BLACK COD & GREEN ONIONS

serves 2

1 piece kombu, about 3 inches (7.5 cm)

½ cup (½ oz/15 g) bonito flakes

2 Tbsp white miso paste

5 oz (155 g) black cod, cut into 2–4 pieces

1 Tbsp olive oil

Salt and freshly ground pepper

1 green onion, white and tender green parts, thinly sliced

This beautiful soup makes a perfect light dinner on a warm summer evening. Serve it in shallow bowls to showcase the caramelized black cod. A cold seaweed or sesame-spinach salad would pair well.

Put 3 cups (24 fl oz/750 ml) cold water and the kombu in a saucepan over medium heat. Bring to a boil and then remove and discard the kombu. Turn off the heat, add the bonito flakes, stir gently once, and let sit for 5 minutes. Strain the soup through a fine-mesh sieve and return the broth to the saucepan.

Put the miso paste in a small bowl and add ¼ cup (2 fl oz/60 ml) of the warm broth. Stir until the mixture is very smooth. Add the miso mixture to the saucepan and warm gently, taking care not to let the soup come to a boil.

Place a small frying pan over high heat until it is very hot. Season the cod with the oil, salt, and pepper and sear until just cooked through, 4 minutes per side.

To serve, ladle the soup into bowls, top with one or two pieces of fish, and sprinkle with green onions.

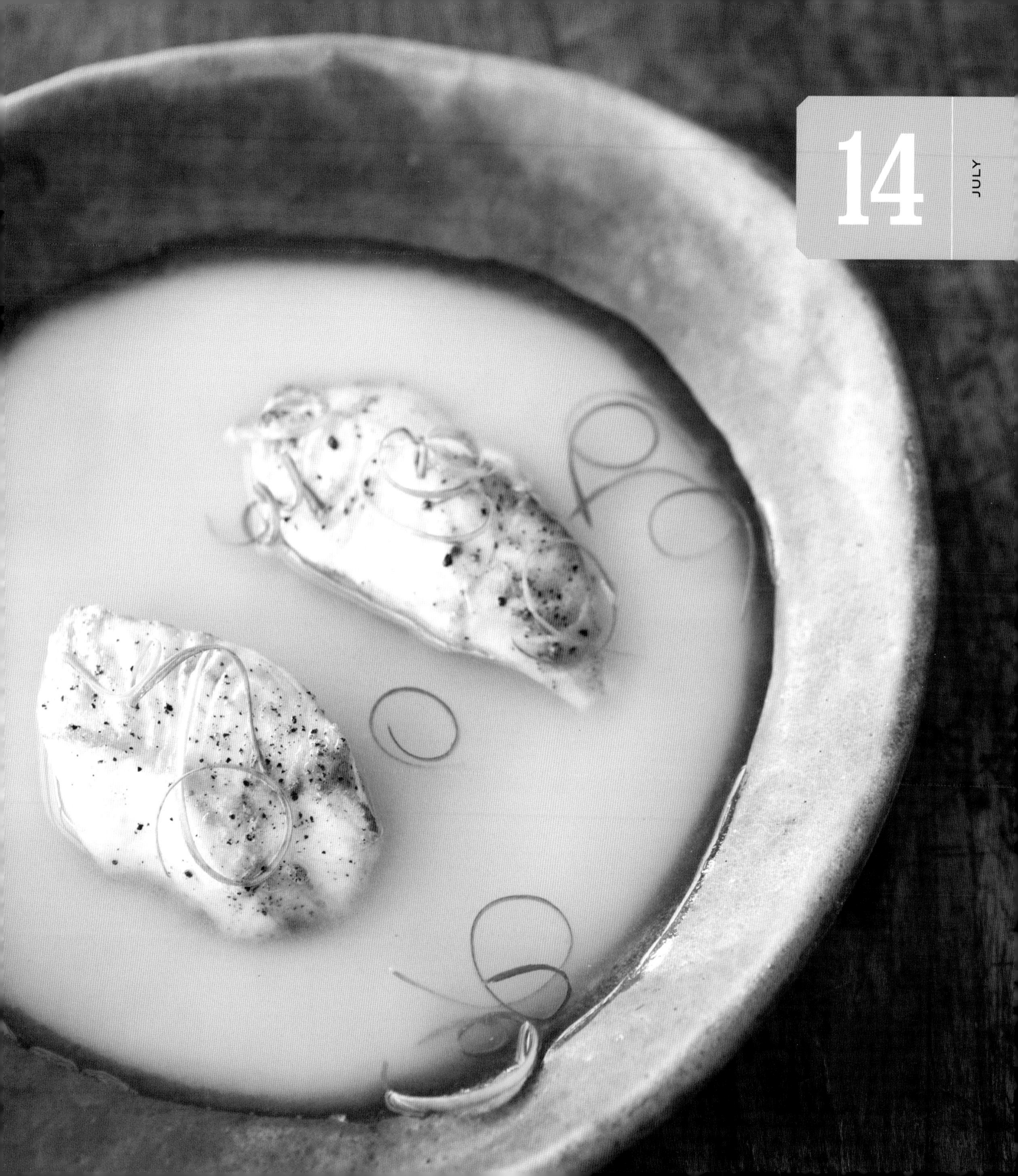

MUSSEL CHOWDER

serves 4–6

JULY

You can adjust the thickness (and therefore the richness) of this soup by adjusting the broth-to-cream ratio. Serve with a simple green salad and plenty of crusty bread for dipping.

1 Tbsp olive oil

1 shallot, thinly sliced

½ cup (4 fl oz/125 ml) dry white wine

2½ cups (20 fl oz/625 ml) chicken broth

2 lb (1 kg) mussels, scrubbed and debearded

6 slices thick-cut bacon

1 small yellow onion, chopped

1 small fennel bulb (about ½ lb/250 g), stalks and fronds removed, quartered and thinly sliced

1 russet potato, peeled and diced

1 cup (8 fl oz/250 ml) heavy cream

1 Tbsp minced flat-leaf parsley

Salt and freshly ground pepper

In a large saucepan over medium-high heat, warm the olive oil. Add the shallot and sauté until soft, 2 minutes. Add the wine and ½ cup (4 fl oz/125 ml) of the broth and bring to a boil. Add the mussels, discarding any that do not close to the touch, cover tightly, and steam until the mussels open, 5–7 minutes. Transfer the mussels to a bowl, discarding any unopened ones. When cool enough to handle, remove them from their shells, coarsely chop, and then refrigerate. Transfer the mussel cooking liquid to a bowl and reserve.

In a large, heavy pot, cook the bacon over medium heat, turning once, until it is crisp, about 8 minutes. Transfer to paper towels to drain. When cool enough to handle, cut into ½-inch (12-mm) pieces. Discard all but 1 Tbsp of the bacon fat from the pot and add the onion and fennel. Sauté until the vegetables are soft, about 7 minutes. Add the reserved mussel cooking liquid and the remaining 2 cups (16 fl oz/500 ml) broth and bring to a boil. Add the potato, reduce the heat to medium-low, and cook until the potato is tender, about 20 minutes. Add the bacon, mussels, and cream and simmer for 5 minutes. Stir in the parsley, season to taste with salt and pepper, and serve.

SUMMER TOMATO SOUP

serves 4

JULY

This summertime soup is flavored with fines herbes, a classic combination of chopped fresh parsley, chervil, tarragon, and chives. Stir in the herbs just before serving, as extended exposure to heat can dull their flavor. Sour cream or plain yogurt can be substituted for the crème fraîche.

2 Tbsp olive oil

1 yellow onion, diced

1 fennel bulb, stalks and fronds removed, diced

2 cloves garlic, minced

¼ cup (2 fl oz/60 ml) dry vermouth (optional)

2 lb (1 kg) plum tomatoes, peeled, seeded, and chopped

2 Tbsp tomato paste

4 cups (32 fl oz/1 l) chicken broth

Salt and freshly ground pepper

2 Tbsp chopped fines herbes (parsley, chervil, tarragon, and chives)

Crème fraîche for garnish

In a large, heavy pot, warm the oil over medium-high heat. Add the onion, fennel, and garlic and cook, stirring occasionally, until tender, about 10 minutes. Add the vermouth, if using, and simmer until evaporated. Add the tomatoes and tomato paste and cook, stirring occasionally, until the tomatoes begin to break down, 8–10 minutes. Add the broth and bring to a boil. Reduce the heat to low and simmer for about 20 minutes. Let cool slightly.

Working in batches, purée the soup in a food processor or blender, leaving some texture. Return to the pot and season with salt and pepper. Stir in the fines herbes and serve, drizzled with crème fraîche.

17

Lemongrass carries a wonderful citrusy scent that gives Thai dishes their signature aromatic quality. Along with the kaffir lime leaves, it beautifully balances the heat of the roasted chile paste in this classic preparation. Succulent shrimp float in the delicious broth.

TOM YUM WITH SHRIMP

serves 6

¾ lb (375 g) large shrimp in the shell

2 Tbsp canola oil

4 lemongrass stalks, center white part only, smashed and cut into 2-inch (5-cm) lengths

6 slices fresh galangal or 3 slices dried galangal

6 green Thai chiles or 8 green serrano chiles, seeded and cut in half crosswise

6 cups (48 fl oz/1.5 l) chicken broth

8 kaffir lime leaves, spines removed

1–2 Tbsp roasted chile paste

1 cup (7 oz/220 g) drained canned straw mushrooms

4-inch (10-cm) piece bamboo shoot, thinly sliced

3 Tbsp Asian fish sauce

¼ cup (2 fl oz/60 ml) fresh lime juice

1 fresh red chile, sliced

¼ cup (¼ oz/7 g) cilantro leaves

Peel and devein the shrimp, reserving the shells. Rinse the shrimp. In a large, heavy pot, warm the oil over medium-high heat. Add the shrimp shells and fry, stirring, until they turn bright orange, about 1 minute. Add the lemongrass, galangal, green chiles, broth, and 4 of the lime leaves. Raise the heat to high and bring to a boil. Reduce the heat to medium and simmer, uncovered, for 15 minutes to blend the flavors. Pour the broth through a sieve placed over a clean pot. Discard the contents of the sieve.

Add the chile paste to taste, the mushrooms, and bamboo shoot, stir well, and bring to a boil over medium heat. Add the shrimp and the remaining 4 lime leaves. Cook until the shrimp turn pink and opaque, 1–2 minutes. Season with the fish sauce and lime juice.

Serve, garnished with the red chile slices and cilantro leaves.

18

This Mexican-inspired version of good old chicken soup gets its zip from lots of puckery lime juice. The uniquely bright, bracing sharpness of the fresh limes is countered by fragrant garlic, herbal oregano, and spicy jalapeño.

MEXICAN LIME SOUP WITH CHICKEN

serves 6

8–10 small limes

2 skin-on, bone-in chicken breast halves (about 10 oz/315 g each)

Salt and freshly ground pepper

1 Tbsp olive oil

1 large white onion, chopped

5 cloves garlic, minced

1 jalapeño chile, seeded and minced

3 cups (24 fl oz/750 ml) chicken broth

1½ tsp dried oregano

1 avocado, pitted, peeled, and diced

2 oz (60 g) queso fresco or ricotta salata cheese, crumbled

Tortilla chips for serving

Cut 2 of the limes into wedges and reserve. Juice as many of the remaining limes as needed to measure out ¼ cup (2 fl oz/60 ml) juice.

Season the chicken breasts with 1 tsp salt and ½ tsp pepper. In a large, heavy pot, warm the oil over medium heat. Add the chicken, skin side down, and cook, turning once, until browned, about 5 minutes. Transfer to a plate. Add the onion and sauté until translucent, about 4 minutes. Stir in the garlic and chile and sauté until fragrant, about 1 minute. Stir in the broth, 3 cups (24 fl oz/750 ml) water, the lime juice, and the oregano. Return the chicken to the pot. Raise the heat to high and bring the liquid to a boil, skimming off any foam on the surface. Reduce the heat to medium-low, cover partially, and simmer gently until the chicken is opaque throughout, about 40 minutes.

Keeping the soup at a simmer, remove the chicken. When it is cool enough to handle, remove and discard the skin and bones and shred the meat into bite-sized pieces. Stir the chicken into the soup. Serve, passing the avocado, cheese, tortilla chips, and lime wedges at the table.

19

BURMESE CHICKEN CURRY SOUP

serves 6

2 Tbsp peanut oil, plus more for frying

1⅛ lb (560 g) fresh thin Chinese egg noodles

3 cloves garlic, minced

2 Tbsp Thai red curry paste

2 tsp Madras curry powder

½ tsp ground turmeric

½ cup (4 fl oz/125 ml) coconut cream

¾ lb (375 g) skinless, boneless chicken thighs, cut into ¼-inch (6-mm) chunks

4 cups (32 fl oz/1 l) chicken broth

3 cups (24 fl oz/750 ml) coconut milk

2 Tbsp Asian fish sauce, or to taste

1 tsp brown sugar

2 Tbsp fresh lemon juice

3 Tbsp chopped pickled Chinese cabbage, rinsed with cold water and drained

3 green onions, white and tender green parts, chopped

½ English cucumber, peeled and thinly sliced

Fried shallots (see note)

2 lemons, cut into wedges

This dish calls for both Madras curry powder, a familiar Indian ingredient, and Thai red curry paste. Although the soup itself has plenty of flavor and texture, the traditional toppings heighten the enjoyment. Look for fried shallots in Asian grocery stores, or make your own by dropping thin slices of fresh shallot into hot oil and frying them until crisp and golden.

Pour 2 inches (5 cm) of peanut oil into a saucepan and heat to 375°F (190°C) on a deep-frying thermometer. Separate out a handful of the noodles and drop them into the hot oil. Fry until golden brown, about 1 minute. Using a wire skimmer, transfer to paper towels to drain.

Bring a large saucepan of water to a boil. Add the remaining noodles, stir well, and return to a boil. Cook for 1 minute. Drain, rinse with cold running water until cool, and drain thoroughly.

In a large, heavy pot, warm the 2 Tbsp oil over medium heat. Add the garlic and sauté until light golden brown, about 2 minutes. Add the curry paste, curry powder, and turmeric and sauté until the oil is fragrant and has a rich yellow hue, about 2 minutes. Add the coconut cream, raise the heat to medium-high, and cook, stirring frequently, until the cream boils gently and oil beads appear on the surface, 5–8 minutes. Add the chicken and stir to coat with the paste. ⟫

Raise the heat to high, add the broth, coconut milk, fish sauce, and sugar, and bring to a boil. Reduce the heat to medium-low and simmer, uncovered, for 10 minutes to blend the flavors. Stir in the lemon juice and remove from the heat.

Divide the boiled noodles among bowls. Ladle the soup over the noodles. Top with the pickled cabbage, green onion, cucumber, shallots, and fried noodles. Serve with the lemon wedges for squeezing over the soup.

CARROT-GRUYÈRE SOUP WITH PISTACHIOS

serves 4–6

2 Tbsp olive oil

2 lb (1 kg) carrots, peeled and chopped

1 yellow onion, chopped

Salt and freshly ground pepper

2 cloves garlic, chopped

⅓ cup (1½ oz/45 g) shelled unsalted pistachios, plus coarsely chopped pistachios for garnish

4 cups (32 fl oz/1 l) chicken broth

¼ lb (125 g) Gruyère cheese, shredded

Gruyère, a semisoft cheese with a hard rind, adds a nutty, earthy flavor and creamy texture to this pale orange soup. Don't throw away that cheese rind! Keep it in the freezer, and the next time you make chicken noodle soup, add the rind to the pot, where it will infuse the broth with flavor. For a classy lunch menu, follow this soup with a shrimp salad or cracked Dungeness crab and a crisp baguette.

In a large, heavy pot, warm the oil over medium-high heat. Add the carrots and onion, season with salt and pepper, and cook, stirring occasionally, until the vegetables soften, about 8 minutes. Add the garlic and ⅓ cup (1½ oz/45 g) pistachios and cook, stirring occasionally, until the garlic is soft, about 2 minutes. Add the broth and bring to a boil. Reduce the heat to low and simmer until the carrots are tender, 20–25 minutes. Let cool slightly.

Working in batches, purée the soup in a food processor or blender. Return to the pot and place over medium heat. Add the cheese and stir until it melts. Season with salt and pepper.

Serve, garnished with chopped pistachios.

21

No recipe ever seems to call for an entire can of chipotle chiles in adobo. Store unused chipotles in the freezer, separated out in an ice cube tray until frozen, and then put in a lock-top plastic bag for easy access.

CHIPOTLE-CORN PURÉE WITH BAY SHRIMP & AVOCADO SALSA

serves 4

2 Tbsp olive oil

1 small yellow onion, chopped

2 cloves garlic, minced

½ small chipotle chile in adobo, chopped

3½ cups (28 fl oz/875 ml) chicken broth

4 cups (24 oz/750 g) fresh corn kernels (from about 8 ears)

Salt and freshly ground pepper

FOR THE SALSA

5 oz (155 g) cooked bay shrimp, coarsely chopped

1 ripe avocado, pitted, peeled, and finely diced

1 Tbsp fresh lime juice

2 tsp chopped cilantro

Salt and freshly ground pepper

In a large, heavy pot, warm the olive oil over medium-high heat. Add the onion and garlic and sauté until translucent, about 5 minutes. Add the chipotle, stir to combine, and sauté for 2 minutes. Add the broth and bring to a boil. Add the corn and cook for 5 minutes. Remove from the heat and let cool slightly. Working in batches, purée the soup in a blender or food processor. Return to the pot and season with salt and pepper.

To make the salsa, put the shrimp and avocado in a small bowl and stir to combine. Stir in the lime juice and cilantro and season with salt and pepper. Serve the soup topped with the salsa.

22

Chilled soups are always welcome on a hot summer day. This soup, dressed up with feta and mint, makes a brightly flavored first course. For variety, you could substitute basil or tarragon for the mint, and crumbled feta or fresh goat cheese for the crème fraîche. Cantaloupe is called for here, but any sweet melon, such as Galia or a deeply ribbed Tuscan-style cantaloupe, can be used.

CHILLED MELON SOUP WITH MINT

serves 6

1 cup (8 fl oz/250 ml) fruity white wine, such as Chenin Blanc, Sémillon, or Gewürztraminer

¼ cup (2 oz/60 g) sugar

1 tsp grated lemon zest

1 cantaloupe (about 2 lb/1 kg), halved, seeded, peeled, cubed, and chilled

1 ice cube

¼ cup (⅓ oz/10 g) chopped mint, plus more for garnish

6 Tbsp crème fraîche

In a saucepan, combine 1½ cups (12 fl oz/375 ml) water, the wine, sugar, and ½ tsp of the lemon zest. Place over medium-high heat and bring to a boil. Continue to boil until the liquid is reduced by about one-third, about 6–7 minutes. Let cool, then place in the freezer for 15 minutes.

In a food processor or blender, combine half of the wine mixture, half of the cantaloupe cubes, and the ice cube and purée until smooth. Pour into a large bowl. Repeat with the remaining wine mixture and cantaloupe cubes and add to the bowl. Stir in the remaining ½ tsp lemon zest and the chopped mint.

Serve, garnished with a swirl of the crème fraîche and a sprinkling of mint.

23

Make this at the height of summer, when tomatoes are their most flavorful. Serve with a simple endive salad with a light buttermilk dressing.

SUMMER PANZANELLA SOUP WITH TINY PASTA

serves 4–6

1 loaf crusty Italian bread

3 Tbsp olive oil

Salt and freshly ground pepper

8 oz (250 g) tiny pasta, such as conchigliette or ditalini

2 shallots, minced

3 cloves garlic, minced

2 lb (1 kg) ripe tomatoes, diced

2 cups (16 fl oz/500 ml) chicken broth

1/3 cup (1/3 oz/10 g) chopped basil

Grated Parmesan cheese for serving

Preheat the oven to 375°F (190°C). Cut enough of the bread up into cubes to measure out 2 cups (2 oz/60 g). Place the bread cubes on a baking sheet, toss with 1 Tbsp of the oil, and season with salt and pepper. Toast in the oven, stirring once, until browned, about 12 minutes. Set aside.

Bring a saucepan of salted water to a boil. Add the pasta and cook until al dente, about 8 minutes or according to the package directions. Drain and set aside.

In a large, heavy pot, warm the remaining 2 Tbsp oil over medium-high heat. Add the shallots and garlic and sauté until translucent, about 5 minutes. Add the tomatoes and sauté until they soften, about 5 minutes. Add the broth and bring to a boil. Reduce the heat to low and simmer for 15 minutes to blend the flavors. Remove from the heat and let cool slightly.

Purée half of the soup in a blender or food processor. Return to the pot and add the toasted bread. Continue to cook for 10 minutes. Stir in the pasta and basil and season with salt and pepper.

Serve, sprinkled with the Parmesan.

24

This is a great family weekday meal. The base is light and brothy, but the chicken and the gnocchi add substance. Use leftover rotisserie or grilled chicken to save time.

CHICKEN SOUP WITH GNOCCHI, BASIL & PARMESAN

serves 4–6

2 small skinless, boneless chicken breast halves

3 Tbsp olive oil

Salt and freshly ground pepper

1/2 small yellow onion, chopped

2 garlic cloves, minced

4 cups chicken broth

1 can (14½ oz/455 g) diced tomatoes

1 package (17½ oz/545 g) potato gnocchi

1 cup (1 oz/30 g) baby spinach

1/4 cup (1/3 oz/10 g) chopped basil

Grated Parmesan cheese for serving

Preheat the oven to 375°F (190°C). Place the chicken breasts on a baking sheet, brush with 1 Tbsp of the oil, and season with salt and pepper. Roast the chicken until opaque throughout, 18–20 minutes. Let the chicken cool to the touch, then shred into bite-sized pieces.

In a large, heavy pot, warm the remaining 2 Tbsp oil over medium-low heat. Add the onion and garlic and sauté until translucent, about 5 minutes. Add the broth and tomatoes with their juices and bring to a boil over medium-high heat. Add the chicken and gnocchi and cook for 5 minutes. Remove from the heat, add the spinach and basil, and stir just until wilted. Season with salt and pepper.

Serve, passing the Parmesan at the table.

HEIRLOOM TOMATO GAZPACHO

serves 4–6

½ red onion, cut into ⅜-inch (1-cm) dice

3 lb (1.5 kg) heirloom tomatoes, cored and cut into ⅜-inch (1-cm) dice

1½ cucumbers, peeled, seeded, and cut into ⅜-inch (1-cm) dice

Salt and freshly ground pepper

5 tsp fresh lemon juice

4 Tbsp (2 fl oz/60 ml) olive oil

2 tsp minced flat-leaf parsley

2 cloves garlic

½ tsp minced thyme

2 Tbsp sherry vinegar

2 cups (4 oz/125 g) cubed French bread

1 large red bell pepper, seeded and cut into ⅜-inch (1-cm) dice

Crème fraîche for garnish

Warm days are made for cold gazpacho. This iconic Spanish soup is perfect served before an array of cured meats and cheeses accompanied with coarse country bread. To ensure that the meal is memorable, take the time to seek out flavorful heirloom tomatoes.

In a bowl, stir together ½ cup (2 oz/60 g) of the onion, 1 cup (6 oz/185 g) of the tomatoes, ¾ cup (3¾ oz/115 g) of the cucumbers, ½ tsp salt, 1 tsp of the lemon juice, 1 Tbsp of the oil, and the parsley. Season with pepper. Cover with plastic wrap and refrigerate until ready to serve.

In a food processor or blender, combine the remaining onion, remaining 4 tsp lemon juice, 1 Tbsp salt, the garlic, thyme, vinegar, and bread and purée until smooth, stopping to scrape down the sides of the bowl as needed. Add the remaining tomatoes and cucumbers along with the bell pepper and purée until the mixture is completely smooth. Season with pepper. Transfer the soup to a large bowl, cover with plastic wrap, and refrigerate for at least 1 hour or up to 1 day.

Just before serving, transfer the soup to the food processor or blender. With the motor running, slowly stream in the remaining 3 Tbsp oil and purée for 1 minute. Taste and adjust the seasoning. Serve, garnished with crème fraîche and a heaping spoonful of the diced vegetables.

CHAYOTE SOUP WITH POBLANO & JALAPEÑO CHILES

serves 4

3 poblano chiles

3 jalapeño chiles

2 Tbsp olive oil

1 yellow onion, chopped

½ tsp dried oregano

2 chayotes (about 1 lb/500 g total weight), or 1 lb (500 g) red potatoes and 2 large carrots

5 cups (40 fl oz/1.25 l) chicken broth

¼ cup (2 oz/60 g) Mexican crema or sour cream

1 avocado, pitted, peeled, and sliced

2 Tbsp chopped cilantro

The chayote, also known as christophene, mirliton, and vegetable pear, originated in Central America. Its firm, bland pale green flesh is ideal for soaking up other flavors, and in Cajun country, cooks prepare it with shrimp, tomatoes, and garlic. Although the skin of the chayote is edible, it is usually a bit tough and should be peeled away. If you can't find chayote, substitute 1 pound (500 g) red potatoes and 2 large carrots.

Place the poblano chiles over an open flame, under a broiler, or on a preheated griddle. Roast, turning often, until the skin is charred, about 5 minutes. Transfer to a plastic bag and let steam for 10 minutes. Repeat with the jalapeño chiles. When cool enough to handle, peel or scrape away the charred skins, cut the chiles in half lengthwise, and remove the stems and seeds. Cut the flesh into ½-inch (12-mm) pieces. Set aside.

Peel the chayotes, remove the seeds, and cut into cubes. If you are using potatoes and carrots, peel and cube them as well. In a large, heavy pot, warm the oil over medium-high heat. Add the chiles, onion, and oregano and cook, stirring occasionally, until the onion is translucent, about 2 minutes. Add the chayotes or the potatoes and carrots and the broth. Bring to a simmer and cook until the vegetables are fork-tender, about 15 minutes for the chayotes and about 20 minutes for the potatoes and carrots. Serve, garnished with a dollop of the crema, a few avocado slices, and a sprinkling of the cilantro.

27

You will have an easy time removing the skins from the nectarines once they've been roasted. Serve for brunch with lemon scones. This soup is also delicious served warm and garnished with a wedge of burrata cheese.

ROASTED NECTARINE SOUP WITH MINT
serves 4

1 lb (500 g) nectarines, pitted and sliced

2 tsp balsamic vinegar

1 tsp olive oil

Salt and freshly ground pepper

½ cup (4 fl oz/125 ml) dry white wine

3 Tbsp fresh lemon juice

2 Tbsp honey

Chopped mint for garnish

Preheat the oven to 400°F (200°C). Toss the nectarine slices with the balsamic vinegar and oil and season with salt and pepper. Spread the nectarines in a single layer on a baking sheet and roast in the oven until caramelized, about 25 minutes. Slip off and discard the peels from the nectarine slices.

Purée the nectarines in a food processor. Add the wine, lemon juice, and honey and pulse several times to combine. Transfer to a covered container and refrigerate until chilled, at least 3 hours. Serve, garnished with the mint.

28

A touch of exotic coconut milk joins buttery avocado in this cool, smooth purée. Choose the freshest lump crabmeat you can find. A sprinkling of chives will be all the embellishment it requires.

CRAB & AVOCADO SOUP
serves 4

3 avocados, peeled, pitted, and coarsely chopped

2 serrano chiles, seeded and chopped

1 cup (8 fl oz/250 ml) coconut milk

Juice from 1 lime, or more as needed

Salt and ground white pepper

½ lb (250 g) fresh lump crabmeat, picked over for shell fragments

In a food processor or blender, combine the avocados, chiles, coconut milk, and lime juice. Add ¾ cup (6 fl oz/180 ml) water and process to a smooth purée. Season with salt, pepper, and additional lime juice to taste.

Transfer to an airtight container and refrigerate for at least 2 or up to 8 hours. Serve, garnished with the crabmeat.

29

Because tofu is stored in liquid, you want to drain it really well before adding it to any dish. This will enhance the flavor of the tofu, and also ensure that it won't dilute the flavor of the broth.

NOODLE SOUP WITH LEMONGRASS & TOFU
serves 4–6

3 oz (90 g) rice noodles

½ lb (250 g) firm tofu

1 tsp canola oil

2 lemongrass stalks, center white part only, smashed and thinly sliced

2 cloves garlic, minced

6 cups (48 fl oz/1.5 l) chicken broth

1 Tbsp fresh lime juice

1 tsp Asian fish sauce

2 green onions, white and tender green parts, chopped

2 Tbsp minced cilantro

In a bowl, combine the rice noodles with hot water to cover. Soak for 10 minutes, then drain.

Cut the tofu in half crosswise. Place both pieces on a plate and top with a second plate. Weigh down the top plate with a can. Let stand for 20 minutes to let the tofu drain. Pour off any water from the plate and cut the tofu into very small cubes.

In a large, heavy pot, warm the oil over medium heat. Add the lemongrass and garlic and sauté until softened, 5–6 minutes. Add the broth and bring to a boil. Reduce the heat and simmer, uncovered, for 20 minutes. Add the tofu, lime juice, and fish sauce and cook for 5 minutes. Stir in the green onions and cilantro. Serve.

30

Because these dumplings are very delicate and fall apart if overcooked, do not cook them until you are just about ready to serve this soup. If you have leftover dumpling filling, it makes a lovely spread on crostini.

SWEET PEA DUMPLINGS IN GINGERY GREEN ONION BROTH

serves 4–6

4 cups (32 fl oz/1 l) chicken broth

2-inch (5-cm) piece fresh ginger, peeled and minced

2 green onions, white and tender green parts, thinly sliced, green tops reserved

1 star anise

2 Tbsp soy sauce

1 tsp mirin

A few drops Asian sesame oil

FOR THE DUMPLINGS

1 cup (5 oz/155 g) fresh or thawed frozen peas

2 Tbsp ricotta cheese

1 Tbsp grated Parmesan cheese

2 tsp canola oil

Salt and freshly ground pepper

24 wonton wrappers

In a large saucepan, combine the broth, ginger, sliced green onions, star anise, soy sauce, mirin, and sesame oil. Bring to a boil over medium-high heat, reduce the heat to low, and simmer for 10 minutes. Remove from the heat, cover the pan, and steep for 10 minutes. Strain the broth, discarding the solids, and return to the saucepan.

Meanwhile, to make the dumplings, combine the peas, ricotta, Parmesan, and oil in a food processor. Add ½ tsp salt and ¼ tsp pepper. Pulse several times to coarsely chop the peas and combine the ingredients. Do not purée. Place 1 tsp of the pea mixture in the middle of each wonton wrapper. Using your fingers, apply a small amount of water on all sides of the wrapper. Fold the wrapper diagonally, forcing out any air bubbles as you press to seal. Take the 2 points on the longest side of the triangle and fold so that the tips meet. Apply a small amount of water on the tips and press firmly to stick together.

Return the broth to a boil, carefully add the dumplings, and cook for 3 minutes. Slice the onion tops. Serve, topped with the sliced onion tops.

31

Meatballs can be heavy and bland, but not when they are made with bright Southeast Asian flavors, as in this recipe, and handled with a light touch.

VIETNAMESE TURKEY MEATBALLS IN BROTH WITH RED ONION & HERBS

serves 6

FOR THE MEATBALLS

1 lb (500 g) ground turkey

1 shallot, minced

2 cloves garlic, minced

2 Tbsp Asian fish sauce

1 Tbsp minced cilantro

Salt and freshly ground pepper

Grated zest of 1 lime

2 Tbsp olive oil

2-inch (5-cm) piece fresh ginger, peeled and grated

2 lemongrass stalks, center white part only, smashed and thinly sliced

6 cups (48 fl oz/1.5 l) chicken broth

Juice of 1 lime

¼ small red onion, thinly sliced

1 Tbsp minced cilantro

2 tsp minced mint

To make the meatballs, preheat the oven to 375°F (190°C). Oil a baking sheet. In a bowl, combine the ground turkey, shallot, garlic, fish sauce, cilantro, 1 tsp salt, ½ tsp pepper, and the lime zest. Using your hands, combine well. For each meatball, scoop up a heaping teaspoonful of the mixture, form into a meatball, and place on the prepared pan. Bake until the meatballs are cooked through, 10–12 minutes.

In a large, heavy pot, warm the oil over medium-high heat. Add the ginger and lemongrass and sauté, stirring constantly, for 4 minutes. Add the broth and lime juice and bring to a boil. Reduce the heat to low and simmer for 10 minutes to blend the flavors. Add the meatballs, red onion, cilantro, and mint and continue to simmer for 5 minutes. Serve.

5
SMOKY RED PEPPER SOUP
page 181

6
**TOMATO SOUP WITH
WHITE WINE & SHALLOTS**
page 181

7
**FIDEO & CHICKEN SOUP
WITH QUESO FRESCO**
page 183

12
PEACH & RIESLING SOUP
page 185

13
**YELLOW GAZPACHO WITH
LEMON-BASIL RICOTTA**
page 186

14
**CREAMY ZUCCHINI SOUP WITH
SUMAC-GRILLED SHRIMP**
page 186

19
ACQUACOTTA
page 191

20
TORTILLA SOUP
page 191

21
BOUILLABAISSE
page 192

26
**ROASTED TOMATO SOUP WITH
CITRUS CRÈME FRAÎCHE**
page 196

27
**MISO SOUP WITH
TOFU & LONG BEANS**
page 197

28
**ANGEL HAIR IN CHICKEN BROTH
WITH TOMATOES & BASIL**
page 197

*During the dog days
of summer, heat-
hungry vegetables
flourish: tomatoes
and peppers
blush deeply red;
cucumbers and green
beans thrive; kernels
of corn plump to
juicy sweetness; and
deep-purple eggplant
has its moment in
the sun. Toss them
together with spices
and the season's
freshest herbs for
lighter fare, or add
summertime salmon,
shellfish, or chicken
for more substantial
warm-weather bowls.*

august

1

AUGUST

When ripe, sweet tomatoes are in season, there's every encouragement to try using them in different ways. As amenable as tomatoes are to basil, they also pair well with other herbs such as tarragon, which has a slight lemon-anise flavor. That anise flavor is echoed in the fennel seeds that stud the croutons.

TOMATO-TARRAGON SOUP WITH FENNEL CROUTONS

serves 6

FOR THE CROUTONS

2 Tbsp olive oil

1 tsp fennel seeds

6 slices baguette, cut on the diagonal

FOR THE SOUP

8 Tbsp (4 oz/125 g) unsalted butter

1 large yellow onion, sliced

4 cloves garlic

½ tsp black peppercorns

1 tsp minced thyme leaves

1 bay leaf

¼ cup (2 oz/60 g) tomato paste

4 cups (24 oz/750 g) canned chopped Italian plum tomatoes, with juices

¼ cup (¼ oz/7 g) chopped tarragon

2 cups (16 fl oz/500 ml) heavy cream

Salt and ground white pepper

Preheat the oven to 375°F (190°C).

To make the croutons, in a small saucepan, warm the oil over medium-high heat. Add the fennel seeds, reduce the heat to low, and heat the seeds, stirring, until fragrant, about 2 minutes. Place the baguette slices on a baking sheet and brush on both sides with the oil, making sure to include some of the fennel seeds. Bake until the slices are lightly golden on top, about 8 minutes. Turn and bake until golden on the other side, about 4 minutes. Remove from the oven and set aside.

To make the soup, in a large, heavy pot, melt 6 Tbsp (3 oz/90 g) of the butter over medium-low heat. Add the onion, garlic, peppercorns, thyme, and bay leaf. Cover and cook, stirring occasionally, until the onion is soft, about 6 minutes; do not let it brown. Add the tomato paste and cook, stirring, for 2 minutes. Add the tomatoes with their juices, reduce the heat to low, cover, and simmer until the vegetables are soft and well blended, about 30 minutes. During the last 5 minutes, add the tarragon. Remove and discard the bay leaf. Let cool slightly. ⤜

Working in batches, purée the soup in a food processor or blender. Strain through a fine-mesh sieve lined with cheesecloth, then pour into the same pot and place over medium-high heat. Add the cream, ½ tsp salt, ½ tsp white pepper, and the remaining 2 Tbsp butter. Bring the soup to a simmer, then serve. Pass the croutons at the table.

2

AUGUST

This soup, inspired by the tropics, must be served right away or the avocado will begin to brown. Serve in clear shot glasses garnished with lime slices as a starter for a brunch or an alfresco cocktail party.

AVOCADO SOUP WITH LIME JUICE & RUM

serves 4–6

2 ripe avocados

4 cups (32 fl oz/1 l) very cold chicken broth

1½ cups (12 fl oz/360 ml) very cold heavy cream

¼ cup (2 fl oz/60 ml) white rum

1 tsp curry powder

Salt

¼ cup (2 fl oz/60 ml) fresh lime juice, plus more to taste

Peel and pit the avocados and chop coarsely. Transfer to a blender along with the chicken broth, cream, rum, curry powder, 1 tsp salt, and the ¼ cup (2 fl oz/60 ml) lime juice. Blend until smooth.

Taste and add more lime juice and salt as needed until the soup is bright-tasting. Serve right away in chilled bowls or glasses.

3

Fish chowders can be made with any firm-fleshed fish, such as halibut, cod, or sea bass, but salmon, because of its fat, adds a special flavor. Potatoes thicken the soup, and onion and herbs flavor it. Salmon chunks specifically for chowder are sometimes offered in fish markets; in their absence, purchase salmon fillet or steak. To preserve its unique flavor and character, the fish is poached separately and then flaked and immersed in the hot chowder just long enough to warm it.

SUMMER SALMON CHOWDER

serves 4–5

1¾ lb (875 g) salmon for chowder or ¾ lb (375 g) salmon fillet or steak

Salt and freshly ground pepper

2 oz (60 g) salt pork or 3 slices bacon, chopped

1 Tbsp unsalted butter

⅓ cup (2 oz/60 g) minced yellow onion

2 celery ribs, diced

2 potatoes, cut into small cubes

1 bay leaf

1 Tbsp minced flat-leaf parsley

½ cup (4 fl oz/125 ml) dry white wine, such as Sauvignon Blanc

2 cups (16 fl oz/500 ml) milk

½ cup (4 fl oz/125 ml) heavy cream

1 Tbsp minced tarragon

Put the salmon in a large saucepan, add water to cover, and sprinkle with 1 tsp salt. Place over medium heat and bring to a simmer. Reduce the heat to low and poach just until the flesh is opaque and flakes with a fork, about 5 minutes. Let cool.

Remove the salmon flesh from the bones, if necessary. Discard the bones. Remove and discard the skin. Flake the flesh into chunks. This can be done a day ahead of time; refrigerate the salmon until ready to use.

In a large, heavy pot, fry the salt pork or bacon over medium-low heat until the fat is rendered, about 5 minutes. If using salt pork, discard the cooked bits; if using bacon, transfer to a paper towel–lined plate.

Increase the heat to medium-high. Add the butter to the fat in the pot. When it has melted, add the onion and cook, stirring occasionally, until soft, about 4 minutes. Add the celery, potatoes, bay leaf, and parsley and cook, stirring occasionally, until the celery is soft, 4–5 minutes. Raise the heat to high and add the wine, stirring to scrape up the browned bits from the bottom of the pot. Add the milk and cream, stir to combine, and reduce the heat to low. Cover and cook until the potatoes are fork-tender, about 20 minutes. Remove and discard the bay leaf. »→

Using the back of a fork or an immersion blender, crush some (but not all) of the potatoes to thicken the soup. Gently stir in the salmon and cook over medium-high heat until heated through, about 2 minutes. Season with salt and pepper. Serve, garnished with the tarragon and bacon.

4

A touch of sparkle and spice makes this an elegant start to a summer supper. Use the sweetest and juiciest cantaloupe or honeydew melon you can find, and garnish with sliced strawberries or whole raspberries, if you like.

ICED MELON SOUP WITH CHAMPAGNE & GINGER

serves 4–6

5 cups (30 oz/940 g) coarsely chopped cantaloupe or honeydew melon

1 Tbsp peeled and grated fresh ginger

1 Tbsp fresh lemon juice

3 cups (24 fl oz/750 ml) dry Champagne or sparkling wine, well chilled

1–2 Tbsp confectioners' sugar

Mint sprigs for garnish

Purée the melon and ginger in a blender, food processor, or food mill. If you use a processor or blender, force the purée through a sieve set inside a bowl, pressing hard on the solids with the back of a wooden spoon. Stir in the lemon juice. Cover tightly and refrigerate until well chilled, at least 2 hours or up to overnight.

Stir in the Champagne. Stir in just enough of the sugar to bring out the melon flavor without making the soup overly sweet. Serve, garnished with the mint sprigs.

5

Thickened with bread crumbs and garnished with capers and anchovies, this coarsely textured puréed soup has a distinctly Spanish leaning. Serve hot or chilled, as desired.

SMOKY RED PEPPER SOUP

serves 8

1 large yellow onion, sliced

4 large cloves garlic, sliced

1 Tbsp chopped marjoram

1 Tbsp paprika, preferably Spanish smoked paprika

Salt and freshly ground pepper

3 Tbsp olive oil

4 red bell peppers, roasted, peeled, seeded, and chopped, any juices reserved

1 cup (2 oz/60 g) coarse fresh bread crumbs

4 anchovy fillets in olive oil

4 cups (32 fl oz/1 l) chicken or vegetable broth

4 tsp capers

Preheat the oven to 450°F (230°C). Place the onion slices on a rimmed baking sheet. Sprinkle with the garlic, marjoram, and paprika. Season lightly with salt and generously with pepper. Drizzle with the oil, then stir to coat the onions completely and spread them out on the baking sheet. Roast, stirring often, until the onions are golden and soft, 15–20 minutes.

Working in batches if necessary, combine the roasted peppers and their juices and the roasted onion mixture in a food processor and process until a coarse purée forms. Add the bread crumbs and 2 of the anchovies, then process again just to a coarse purée. Add 2 cups (16 fl oz/500 ml) of the broth and purée again. Pour into a large, heavy pot along with the remaining 2 cups broth and bring to a simmer over medium heat, stirring often. Taste and adjust the seasoning with salt and pepper and simmer for 1–2 minutes to blend the flavors.

Ladle the soup into bowls. Cut the remaining 2 anchovies lengthwise into 4 pieces each and float 1 slice in each bowl. Sprinkle with the capers and serve.

6

Plum, or Roma, tomatoes can be purchased year-round, but blush deepest in the summer months for incomparable color and flavor. A little wine, a little garlic, and a few leaves of sweet-scented basil showcase the season's finest.

TOMATO SOUP WITH WHITE WINE & SHALLOTS

serves 4

10 plum tomatoes, halved

2 cloves garlic, minced

4 Tbsp (1/3 oz/10 g) chopped basil

5 Tbsp (2½ fl oz/75 ml) olive oil

4 shallots, halved

1½ cups (12 fl oz/375 ml) dry white wine

Salt and freshly ground pepper

Preheat the oven to 400°F (200°C). Arrange the tomato halves, cut side up, in a roasting pan. Sprinkle with the garlic and 1 Tbsp of the basil and drizzle with 4 Tbsp (2 fl oz/60 ml) of the oil. Roast until the tomatoes are soft when pierced with a fork, about 40 minutes. Peel and discard the skins.

In a large, heavy pot, warm the remaining 1 Tbsp oil over medium-high heat. Add the shallots and sauté for about 2 minutes. Add the roasted tomatoes and garlic, wine, and ½ cup (4 fl oz/125 ml) water and bring to a boil. Reduce the heat to medium-low and simmer, uncovered, until the mixture has thickened, about 20 minutes. Season with salt and pepper. Remove from the heat and let cool slightly.

Working in batches, purée the soup in a blender or food processor to the desired consistency. Return to the pot and reheat to serving temperature. Serve, garnished with the remaining 3 Tbsp basil.

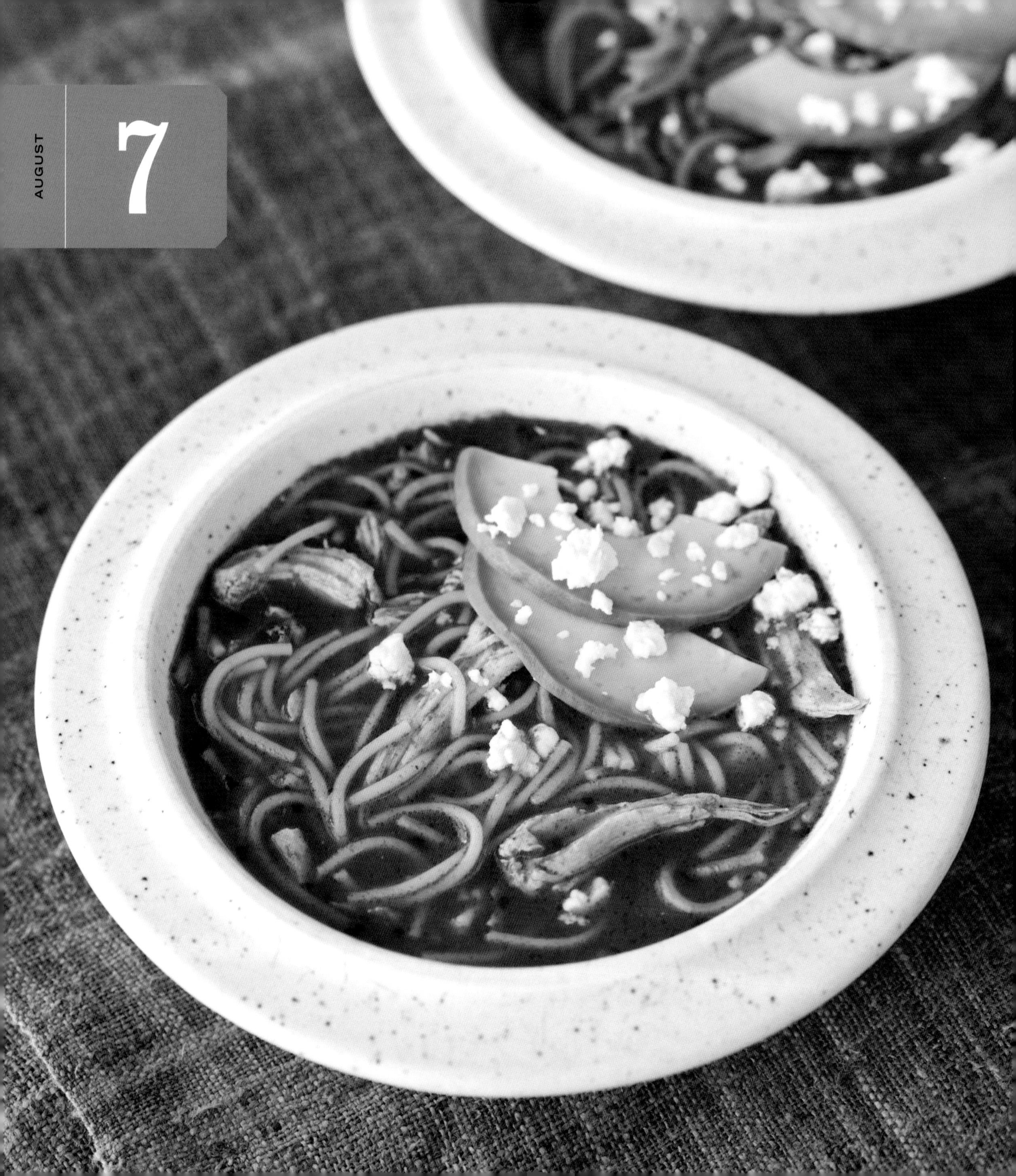

7

*Fideo is a thin
Spanish pasta
similar to vermicelli.
Serve with grilled
corn tortillas
cut into triangles
for dipping.*

FIDEO & CHICKEN SOUP WITH QUESO FRESCO

serves 6

2 small skinless, boneless
chicken breast halves

3 Tbsp olive oil

Salt and freshly ground pepper

1 white onion, chopped

4 cloves garlic, minced

1 tsp dried oregano

2 Tbsp tomato paste

½ chipotle chile in adobo, minced

6 cups (48 fl oz/1.5 l) chicken broth

1½ cups (4 oz/125 g) fideo noodles
or vermicelli pasta broken into
2-inch (5-cm) pieces

2 Tbsp chopped cilantro

1 avocado, pitted, peeled, and sliced

3 oz (90 g) queso fresco, crumbled

Preheat the oven to 375°F (190°C) and put
the chicken breasts on a baking sheet.
Brush the chicken with 1 Tbsp of oil and
season with salt and pepper. Roast the
chicken in the oven until it is cooked
all the way through, about 20 minutes.
When the chicken is cool enough to handle,
shred it and set aside.

In a large, heavy pot, warm the remaining
2 Tbsp oil over medium-high heat. Add
the onion and garlic and sauté until
translucent, about 5 minutes. Add the
oregano, tomato paste, and chipotle and
stir well to combine. Add the broth and
bring to a boil. Add the fideo and cook for
8 minutes. Add the shredded chicken and
cilantro and stir to combine. Season to taste
with salt and pepper.

Serve, topped with sliced avocado and
crumbled queso fresco.

8

*Spanish chorizo
is most commonly
found as cured and
smoked salami-
style links, unlike
Mexican chorizo,
which is typically a
fresh sausage, sold
in links and in bulk.
Using chopped dried
chorizo creates little
bursts of chewy
flavor among the
soft white beans and
the peppers. For a
vegetarian version
of this hearty soup,
omit the chorizo.*

SPANISH WHITE BEAN SOUP WITH CHORIZO & PIQUILLO PEPPERS

serves 6

1 lb (500 g) dried large white beans,
such as Royal Corona, picked over
and rinsed

1 bay leaf

¼ tsp dried winter savory

Salt and freshly ground pepper

¾ lb (375 g) smoked Spanish chorizo,
cut into ¼-inch (6-mm) slices

2 canned Spanish piquillo peppers,
drained and cut into ¼-inch (6-mm) slices

Put the beans in a bowl with cold water to
cover and soak overnight. Drain.

Transfer the beans to a large, heavy pot and
add water to cover by 2½–3 inches (6–7.5 cm)
(these are big beans and will absorb a lot).
Add the bay leaf. Place over medium-high
heat and bring to a boil. Reduce the heat to
low, cover, and simmer for 1 hour. Stir in
the winter savory and 1 tsp salt. Cover and
cook until the beans are almost tender, about
1 hour longer. Add 1 tsp salt, cover, and cook
until the beans are completely tender and
offer no resistance, up to 1 hour longer.

Add the chorizo, season with pepper, and
simmer until the chorizo is warmed through,
about 15 minutes. Taste and adjust the
seasoning. Remove and discard the bay leaf.
Stir in the piquillo peppers and serve.

9

Filé is the olive-green powder made from the dried and pulverized leaves of the sassafras tree. Like okra, it is frequently used as a thickener in Cajun gumbos. Look for it in the spice aisle of well-stocked markets.

CAJUN SHRIMP SOUP

serves 4

2 Tbsp olive oil

¼ cup (1½ oz/45 g) finely chopped yellow onion

2 cloves garlic, minced

½ green bell pepper, seeded and finely chopped

1 serrano chile, seeded and finely chopped

1 can (14½ oz/455 g) diced tomatoes

2 cups (16 fl oz/500 ml) chicken broth

½ tsp minced thyme

¼ tsp cayenne pepper

1 lb (500 g) shrimp, peeled and deveined

½ tsp filé powder

Salt and freshly ground black pepper

In a large, heavy pot, warm the oil over medium-high heat. Add the onion and sauté until translucent, about 2 minutes. Stir in the garlic and bell pepper, then add the chile, tomatoes with their juices, broth, thyme, and cayenne. Bring to a boil, reduce the heat to low, and simmer, uncovered, for 15 minutes to blend the flavors.

Add the shrimp and filé powder and cook just until the shrimp turn pink and opaque, about 3 minutes. Season with salt and pepper and serve.

10

Fresh summer beans star in this Portuguese peasant soup. If possible, use vegetable stock, as it allows the flavors of the vegetables to shine more distinctly than if you use poultry stock.

FRESH GREEN BEAN SOUP

serves 4–6

5 Tbsp (2½ fl oz/75 ml) olive oil

2 yellow onions, chopped

1 lb (500 g) tomatoes, peeled, seeded, and chopped

1 lb (500 g) boiling potatoes, peeled and diced

4 cups (32 fl oz/1 l) vegetable or chicken broth

1 lb (500 g) green beans, trimmed and cut on the diagonal into 1-inch (2.5-cm) pieces

Salt and freshly ground pepper

3 Tbsp chopped mint (optional)

In a large, heavy pot, warm the oil over medium heat. Add the onions and sauté until tender, 8–10 minutes. Add the tomatoes and potatoes and sauté for 3–5 minutes. Add the broth, raise the heat to high, and bring to a boil. Reduce the heat to low and simmer, uncovered, until the potatoes are very tender, about 20 minutes. Remove from the heat and let cool slightly.

Working in batches, purée the soup in a blender or food processor. Return to the pot.

Bring a saucepan three-fourths full of salted water to a boil. Add the green beans and cook until crisp-tender, about 5 minutes. Drain, reserving a bit of the cooking water to add to the purée if it is too thick.

Reheat the purée and season with salt and pepper. Add the green beans and simmer over medium heat until heated through, about 5 minutes. Thin with the reserved cooking water if needed.

Serve, garnished with the chopped mint, if using.

11

MEXICAN PORK STEW WITH NOPALES

serves 6

4–6 dried pasilla chiles

1½–2 cups (12–16 fl oz/375–500 ml) boiling water

3 jalapeño chiles, seeded and chopped

½ large yellow onion, chopped

4 cloves garlic, chopped

2 Tbsp peeled and chopped fresh ginger

1 tsp ground cinnamon

1½ lb (750 g) juicy tomatoes, peeled, seeded, and chopped

2 lb (1 kg) boneless pork shoulder, cut into 2-inch (5-cm) cubes

Salt and freshly ground pepper

1 Tbsp olive oil

2 cups (16 fl oz/500 ml) chicken broth

3 cups (9 oz/280 g) prepared chopped fresh nopales (cactus paddles) or canned nopales, drained and rinsed

Steamed white rice for serving

Cilantro leaves for garnish

Nopales, the fleshy, soft pads of the nopal (prickly pear) cactus, are important ingredients in Mexican cooking, where they are used in scrambled eggs, burritos, and in stews. Look for them already cleaned of their spines, chopped, and packed into plastic bags or tubs at Latin supermarkets. They are also available canned in the international aisle of many supermarkets. Serve this hearty stew over steamed white rice.

Place the pasilla chiles on a hot grill or frying pan and roast, turning several times, until softened, about 3 minutes. Transfer to a bowl, cover with the boiling water, and let stand until pliable, about 30 minutes. Drain the chiles, reserving the soaking water. Cut the chiles in half lengthwise and remove the stems and seeds. Coarsely chop the chiles.

In a food processor or blender, combine the pasillas, jalapeños, onion, garlic, ginger, cinnamon, and ½ cup (4 fl oz/125 ml) of the soaking water and purée, adding more soaking water as necessary to form a smooth paste. Set aside.

Season the pork with ½ Tbsp salt and 1 tsp pepper. In a large, heavy pot, warm the oil over medium-high heat. Working in batches if necessary, add the pork and sear, turning occasionally, until golden, about 5 minutes per batch. Transfer to a large bowl.

Add the chile paste to the pot, stirring to heat it through. Slowly add 1 cup (8 fl oz/250 ml) of the broth, stirring to scrape up the browned bits from the bottom of the pot. Add the remaining 1 cup (8 fl oz/250 ml) broth, the tomatoes, the pork, and the ⟩⟩

accumulated juices and bring to a boil. Reduce the heat to low, cover, and simmer until the pork is fork-tender, about 2 hours. Add the nopales and simmer for 30 minutes for fresh nopales and 10 minutes for canned. Most of the liquid will have evaporated, leaving a thick sauce. Taste and adjust the seasoning.

Serve the stew over rice, garnished with cilantro.

12

PEACH & RIESLING SOUP

serves 4

2 lb (1 kg) ripe peaches, peeled

1½ cups (12 oz/375 g) plain yogurt

2 Tbsp tawny port

⅓ cup (3 fl oz/80 ml) Riesling

¼ tsp ground ginger

Pinch of grated nutmeg

Honey for sweetening (optional)

Mint leaves for garnish

Any variety of peach or nectarine works for this lightly boozy, Bellini-inspired soup. It makes a particularly good starter for an outdoor lunch, but you could also serve it as a refreshing finish to a warm-weather grilled dinner.

Cut the peaches in half and remove the pits. Cut one peach half into small cubes to use for garnishing and place in a bowl. Cover and refrigerate until ready to use.

Coarsely chop the remaining peach halves and purée in a food processor until smooth. Pour the purée into a bowl and stir in the yogurt, port, Riesling, ginger, and nutmeg. Whisk to blend well. Taste and add honey to sweeten, if desired. Cover and refrigerate until well chilled, at least 4 hours.

Serve, garnished with the reserved peach cubes and mint leaves.

13

YELLOW GAZPACHO WITH LEMON-BASIL RICOTTA

serves 6–8

2 yellow bell peppers, seeded and chopped

1 English cucumber, peeled, seeded, and chopped

4 yellow tomatoes (about 2 lb/1 kg total), chopped, with all their juices

1 small yellow onion, chopped

2 cloves garlic, finely minced

2 Tbsp white wine vinegar

¼ cup (2 fl oz/60 ml) olive oil

Salt and freshly ground pepper

Tabasco sauce

FOR THE LEMON-BASIL RICOTTA

1 cup ricotta (8 oz/250 g), at room temperature

Grated zest of 1 lemon

¼ cup (⅓ oz/10 g) chopped basil

Salt

Adjust the spiciness as you like: add more hot sauce or even a fresh jalapeño. Serve the lemon-basil ricotta at room temperature so it incorporates easily. Leftover lemon-basil ricotta is a delicious spread for a vegetable sandwich wrap.

In a food processor, separately pulse the bell peppers, cucumber, tomatoes, and onion until finely chopped but not puréed. After each vegetable, transfer the contents of the food processor to a large bowl. Add the garlic, white wine vinegar, and oil and stir to combine. Season to taste with salt, pepper, and Tabasco.

To make the lemon-basil ricotta, combine the ricotta, lemon zest, basil, and a pinch of salt in a bowl and stir to mix well.

Serve the gazpacho, topped with a dollop of lemon-basil ricotta.

14

CREAMY ZUCCHINI SOUP WITH SUMAC-GRILLED SHRIMP

serves 4

2 Tbsp olive oil

1 yellow onion, chopped

2 cloves garlic, chopped

2 lb (1 kg) zucchini, chopped

Salt and freshly ground pepper

2 cups (16 fl oz/500 ml) chicken broth

4 Tbsp (4 oz/125 g) plain whole-milk Greek yogurt

FOR THE SUMAC-GRILLED SHRIMP

¾ lb (375 g) medium shrimp, peeled and deveined

1½ tsp sumac

Salt

1 tsp olive oil

1 Tbsp fresh lemon juice

A beautiful centerpiece for a summer lunch, this puréed soup gets extra body and creaminess from the addition of just a couple of spoonfuls of Greek yogurt. Serve it with a tray of cucumber tea sandwiches and pour a crisp white wine or sparkling lemonade. Sumac, a Middle Eastern spice with a tart lemony flavor, can be found in most grocery stores.

In a large, heavy pot, warm the oil over medium-high heat. Add the onion and cook, stirring occasionally, until translucent, about 6 minutes. Add the garlic and zucchini, and season with salt and pepper. Cook, stirring occasionally, until soft, about 5 minutes. Add the broth and bring to a boil. Reduce the heat to low and simmer for 15 minutes. Let cool slightly.

Working in batches, purée the soup in a food processor or blender. Return to the pot and place over medium heat. Stir in 2 Tbsp of the yogurt and season with salt and pepper. Keep warm over low heat.

To make the sumac-grilled shrimp, heat a large stove-top grill pan or frying pan over high heat. In a large bowl, toss together the shrimp, sumac, ¼ tsp salt, oil, and lemon juice. Cook the shrimp until opaque throughout, about 2 minutes per side.

Serve the soup, topped with a dollop of the remaining yogurt and the shrimp.

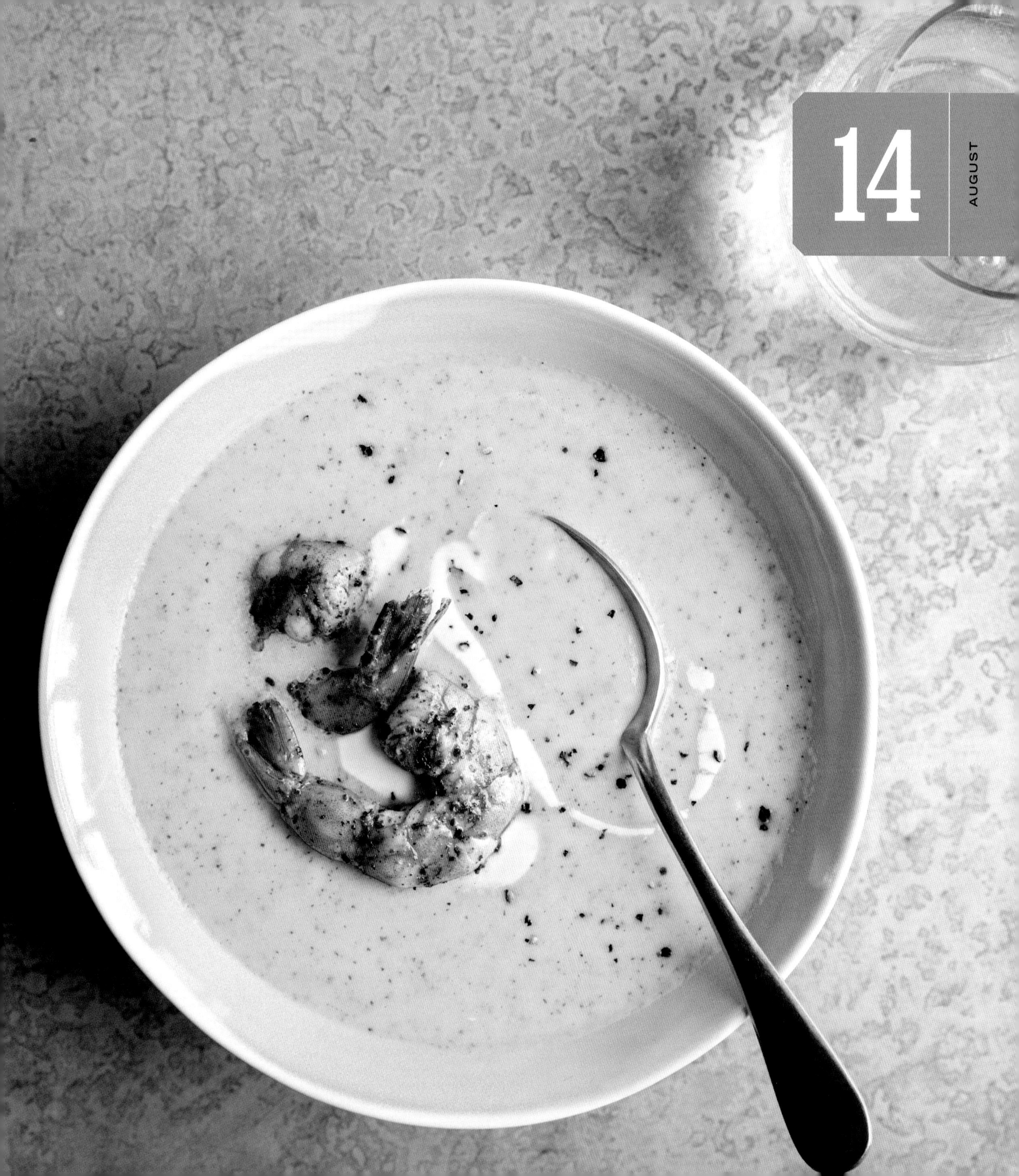

15

This soup can also be served smooth: after cooking the vegetables, purée them in batches in a blender. The charred eggplant turns silky and almost creamy, and the pleasant smoky flavor pervades the soup.

CHARRED EGGPLANT SOUP WITH CUMIN & GREEK YOGURT

serves 6–8

1 Tbsp olive oil, plus more for brushing

2 large eggplants (about 2½ lb/1.25 kg total), peeled and cut crosswise into slices 1 inch (2.5 cm) thick

3 ripe tomatoes (about 1¼ lb/625 g total), cored, halved, and seeded

3 carrots, peeled and finely chopped

5 shallots, finely chopped

3 cloves garlic, minced

¾ tsp minced thyme

¼ tsp ground cumin

1 cup (8 fl oz/250 ml) dry white wine

5 cups (40 fl oz/1.25 l) chicken or vegetable broth

Salt and freshly ground pepper

½ cup (4 oz/125 g) plain Greek yogurt (optional)

Fresh basil leaves for garnish (optional)

Prepare a charcoal or gas grill for direct-heat cooking over medium-high heat. Brush the grate with oil. Brush the eggplant slices and tomato halves with oil and arrange on the grill directly over the heat. Cook, turning as needed, until softened and nicely grill-marked, about 8 minutes for the tomatoes and 10 minutes for the eggplant. Transfer to a cutting board. When cool enough to handle, peel and discard the skins from the tomatoes. Coarsely chop the eggplant slices.

In a large, heavy pot, warm the 1 Tbsp oil over medium-high heat. Add the carrots and sauté until just beginning to soften, about 4 minutes. Add the shallots, garlic, thyme, and cumin and cook, stirring occasionally, until fragrant, about 2 minutes. Add the tomatoes, chopped eggplant, wine, and broth and bring to a boil. Reduce the heat to low, cover partially, and simmer for 20 minutes to blend the flavors. Season with 1½ tsp salt and pepper to taste. Serve, garnished with a dollop of yogurt and basil leaves, if using.

16

This is a soup inspired by the classic side dish of creamed corn. Serve with warm focaccia and a mixed green salad with mandarin oranges and sliced ripe avocado—and a grilled steak, of course.

CREAMY CORN SOUP WITH BACON & SAGE

serves 6

5 slices thick-cut bacon

2 Tbsp unsalted butter

1 Tbsp olive oil

2 leeks, white and pale green parts, chopped

5 sage leaves, chopped

4 cups (32 fl oz/1 l) chicken broth

6 cups (2¼ lb/1 kg) fresh corn kernels (from about 12 ears) or 6 cups frozen

2 Tbsp heavy cream

Salt and freshly ground pepper

In a large, heavy pot, cook the bacon over medium heat, turning once, until crispy, about 8 minutes. Transfer the bacon to paper towels to drain. When it is cool enough to handle, crumble into bite-sized pieces. Set aside.

In the same pot, melt the butter with the oil over medium heat. Add the leeks and sauté until soft, about 4 minutes. Add the sage and cook, stirring to combine, for 1 minute. Add the broth and bring to a boil over medium-high heat. Add the corn and cook for 5 minutes. Remove from the heat and let cool slightly.

Purée half of the soup in a blender. Return to the pot, stir in the cream, and warm through over medium-low heat. Season with salt and pepper and serve, topped with the crumbled bacon.

17

Inspired by France's most beloved peasant dish, this soup features a marriage of hot-weather produce: deep purple eggplants, summer squash, the season's sweetest red peppers and tomatoes, and a handful of basil leaves. It's summer in a bowl.

RATATOUILLE SOUP

serves 4

3 Tbsp olive oil

2 cloves garlic, minced

1 eggplant, peeled and cut into small cubes

1 zucchini, trimmed and chopped

1 yellow onion, quartered

1 red bell pepper, seeded and chopped

4 large tomatoes, peeled and quartered

2–3 cups (16–24 fl oz/500–750 ml) chicken broth

Salt and freshly ground pepper

¼ cup (⅓ oz/10 g) minced basil

In a large, heavy pot, warm 2 Tbsp of the oil over medium heat. Add the garlic and sauté until fragrant, about 1 minute. Add the eggplant, zucchini, onion, and bell pepper and cook, stirring occasionally, until the vegetables have softened, 10–15 minutes. Add the tomatoes and the remaining 1 Tbsp oil. Cook, stirring occasionally, until the tomatoes begin to break down, about 15 minutes. Reduce the heat to low and simmer for 15 minutes.

Add 1 cup (8 oz/250 ml) of the broth to the vegetables. Working in batches if necessary, purée the soup in a blender or food processor. Return to the pot and place over medium heat. Add enough broth to make a thick soup. Simmer until heated through, about 5 minutes. Season with salt and pepper and serve, garnished with the basil.

18

What makes the tomatoes the show-off in this simple soup is their striking gold color, while the ginger adds an unexpected spicy note. Try serving this as an appetizer in a demitasse or shot glass, garnished with a bright, edible nasturtium blossoms to highlight the soup's dramatic hue.

YELLOW TOMATO & GINGER SOUP

serves 4

1 Tbsp unsalted butter

1 clove garlic, minced

2 tsp grated fresh turmeric or 1 tsp ground

1 tsp peeled and grated fresh ginger

5 large yellow tomatoes, peeled, seeded, and chopped, juices reserved

2 cups (16 fl oz/500 ml) chicken broth

Salt and ground white pepper

In a large, heavy pot, melt the butter over medium-high heat. Add the garlic, turmeric, and ginger and cook, stirring frequently, until fragrant, 2–3 minutes. Add the tomatoes with their juices and cook, stirring, until soft, about 5 minutes. Add the broth, ½ tsp salt, and ½ tsp white pepper and bring to a simmer. Reduce the heat to medium and simmer to blend the flavors, about 10 minutes. Let cool slightly.

Working in batches, purée the soup in a food processor or blender. Strain through a fine-mesh sieve lined with cheesecloth, then pour the soup into a clean pot. Place over medium-high heat and reheat, then serve.

19

ACQUACOTTA
serves 8

1/2 cup (4 fl oz/125 ml) olive oil

2 red onions, chopped

3/4 lb (375 g) mixed red and yellow bell peppers, seeded and chopped

3 celery ribs, chopped

1 lb (500 g) tomatoes, peeled, seeded, and chopped

Salt and freshly ground pepper

3 eggs

1/2 cup (2 oz/60 g) grated Parmesan cheese

8 slices day-old country-style bread, toasted

1 clove garlic

There is no single recipe for this Tuscan classic, though it usually includes eggs, bread, and vegetables such as peppers and tomatoes.

In a large, heavy pot, warm the oil over medium heat. Add the onions and sauté until fragrant, about 4 minutes. Add the bell peppers and celery and sauté until soft, about 10 minutes. Stir in the tomatoes. Season with salt and pepper. Reduce the heat to low, cover, and simmer gently, stirring occasionally, until thick, about 1 hour.

Pour in 8 cups (2 qt/2 l) water, return to a simmer, and cook for 10 minutes. In a small bowl, beat together the eggs and cheese and pour into the soup. Stir briskly for a minute, then remove from the heat. Season with salt and pepper.

Rub the toasts with the garlic clove and divide among bowls. Ladle the soup over the toasts and serve.

20

TORTILLA SOUP
serves 6

5 dried ancho chiles, soaked in boiling water, drained, seeded, and chopped

4 fresh Anaheim chiles, seeded and chopped

3 cups (18 oz/560 g) chopped peeled tomato

1 large white onion, diced

7 cloves garlic, minced

2 Tbsp canola oil

6 cups (48 fl oz/1.5 l) chicken broth

1 1/2 lb (750 g) cooked chicken, cut into 1/2-inch (12-mm) dice

2/3 cup (1 oz/30 g) chopped cilantro, plus leaves for garnish

Vegetable oil for deep-frying

6 corn tortillas, cut into strips 2 inches (5 cm) long

6 oz (185 g) crumbled queso fresco or shredded Monterey jack cheese

1 avocado, pitted, peeled, and sliced

Traditional tortilla soups are found in the American Southwest, Mexico, and Central America, where they vary from the simple to the elaborate. Some are as straightforward as a good broth, roasted tomatoes, onion, chiles, and strips of fried tortilla. Here, chunks of cooked chicken are added to the broth, and the garnish of deep-fried tortilla strips is joined by crumbled queso fresco, avocado slices, and cilantro.

In a large bowl, stir together the ancho and Anaheim chiles, tomato, onion, and garlic. Working in batches, coarsely purée in a food processor or blender. Transfer to a separate bowl.

In a large, heavy pot, warm the canola oil over medium-high heat until almost smoking. Add the chile mixture and cook, stirring occasionally, for 15 minutes. Stir in the broth and 2 cups (16 fl oz/500 ml) water and bring to a boil. Reduce the heat to medium-low and simmer for 20 minutes. Stir in the chicken and cilantro.

Meanwhile, in a deep pot, pour in vegetable oil to a depth of 2 inches (5 cm) and heat to 375°F (190°C) on a deep-frying thermometer. Working in batches, fry the tortilla strips until crisp, about 2 minutes. Using a slotted spoon, transfer to a paper towel–lined plate.

Serve the soup, garnished with the tortilla strips, cilantro leaves, cheese, and avocado.

21

To make rouille, in a blender, combine 2 seeded dried chiles, 4 cloves garlic, 1 Tbsp dried bread crumbs, 2 large egg yolks, and ½ teaspoon sea salt and process until a paste forms. With the motor running, drizzle in ½ cup (4 fl oz/125 ml) extra-virgin olive oil in a slow, steady stream, processing until the mixture is creamy and smooth. Store in the refrigerator in an airtight container for up to 1 week. Makes ¾ cup (6 fl oz/180 ml).

BOUILLABAISSE

serves 6–8

¼ cup (2 fl oz/60 ml) olive oil

1 yellow onion, chopped

2 leeks, white parts only, coarsely chopped

1 orange zest strip

2 tomatoes, peeled and coarsely chopped

1 fennel stalk, about 6 inches (15 cm) long, thinly sliced

2 cloves garlic, crushed

2 thyme sprigs

1 bay leaf

Salt and freshly ground pepper

2 cups (16 fl oz/500 ml) dry white wine

5 boiling potatoes (about 1½ lb/750 g), peeled and cut into slices ½ inch (12 mm) thick

¼ tsp saffron threads

2 lb (1 kg) firm-fleshed fish steaks or fillets, cut into 1½-inch (4-cm) chunks

2 lb (1 kg) tender-fleshed whole fish, cleaned, cut into 1½-inch (4-cm) chunks

1 lb (500 g) mussels, scrubbed and debearded

Boiling water as needed

Rouille (left)

8 slices country-style bread, toasted and rubbed with 1 clove garlic

1 Tbsp minced flat-leaf parsley

In a large, heavy pot, warm the oil over medium-high heat. Add the onion and leeks and sauté until translucent, 2–3 minutes. Stir in the orange zest, tomatoes, fennel, garlic, thyme, and bay leaf. Season with ½ tsp salt and ½ tsp pepper. Add the wine, the potatoes, and 1 cup (8 fl oz/250 ml) water and bring to a boil. Reduce the heat to low, cover, and simmer until the potatoes are nearly tender, about 25 minutes.

Raise the heat to medium-high and bring the soup to a rolling boil. Stir in the saffron. Place the firm-fleshed fish on top of the soup, add just enough boiling water as needed to cover, and boil until the fish is just half-cooked, about 7 minutes. Add the tender-fleshed fish, the mussels, discarding any that do not close to the touch, and just enough boiling water as needed to cover. Boil just until the tender-fleshed fish separates easily with a fork and the mussels open, 3–4 minutes. Discard any unopened mussels. »→

Stir 2–3 Tbsp of the broth into the rouille. Place a slice of toasted bread in the bottom of each bowl. Top with the fish, mussels, and potatoes. Ladle the broth over the top and sprinkle with the parsley. Serve, passing the remaining rouille at the table.

22

This colorful soup makes use of the best that summer has to offer. The tomato broth is partially puréed to add satisfying thickness to the soup.

TOMATO, ZUCCHINI & FRESH CORN SOUP

serves 4–6

2 zucchini, trimmed, halved, and sliced

3 Tbsp olive oil

Salt and freshly ground pepper

1 yellow onion, chopped

5 cloves garlic, minced

4 plum tomatoes, chopped

4 cups (32 fl oz/1 l) vegetable or chicken broth

1 cup (6 oz/180 g) corn kernels (from about 2 ears)

⅓ cup (½ oz/15 g) chopped basil

Preheat the oven to 400°F (200°C). Toss the zucchini with 1 Tbsp of the oil and season with salt and pepper. Spread on a baking sheet and roast for 20 minutes. Set aside.

In a large, heavy pot, warm the remaining 2 Tbsp oil over medium-high heat. Add the onion and garlic and sauté until soft, about 5 minutes. Add the tomatoes, stir to combine, and cook for 3 minutes. Add the broth and bring to a boil. Reduce the heat to low and simmer for 20 minutes. Remove from the heat and let cool slightly.

Purée half of the soup in a blender. Return to the pot and season with salt and pepper. Return the soup to a boil, add the corn, and cook for 5 minutes. Add the zucchini and stir in the basil. Serve.

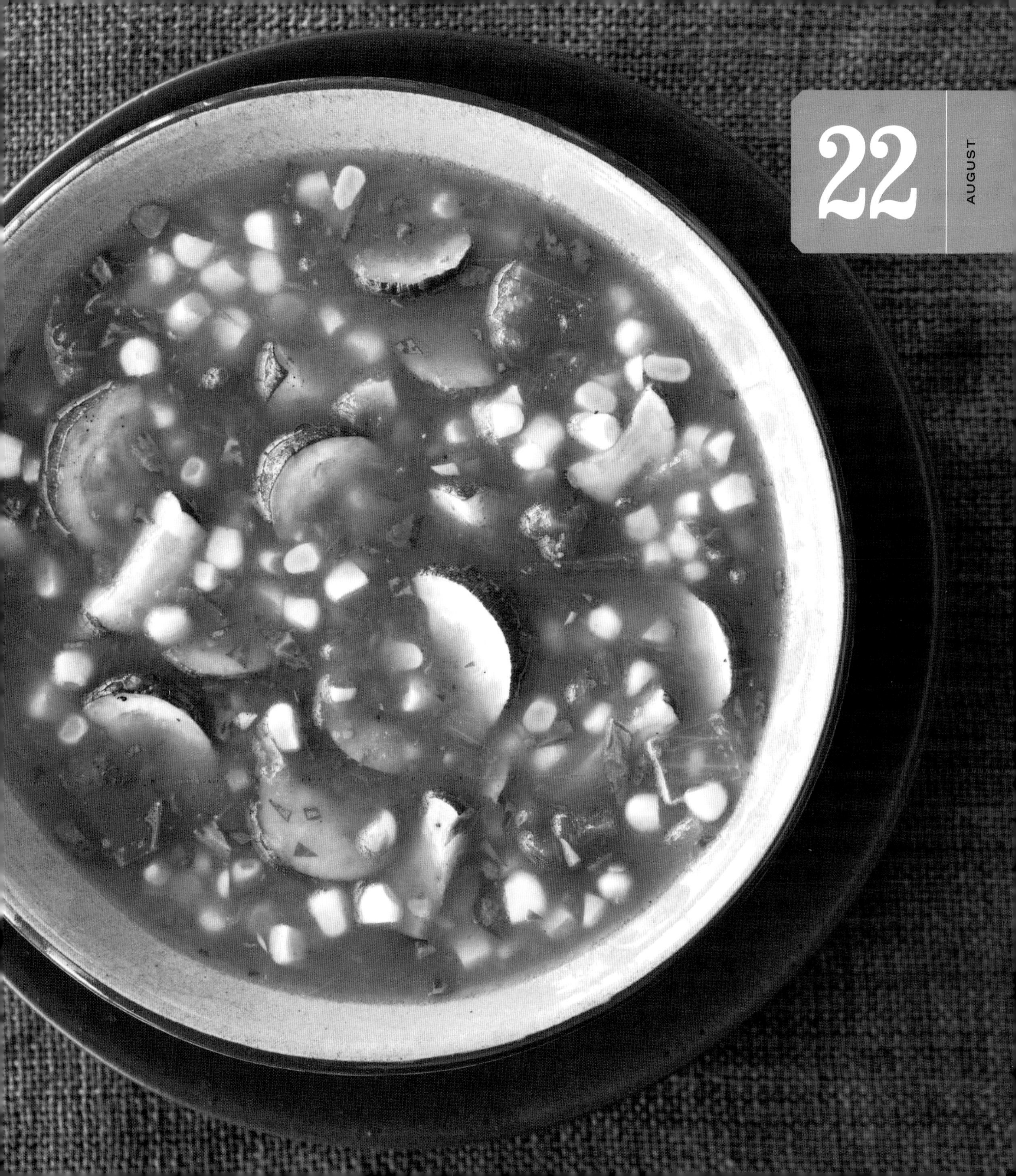

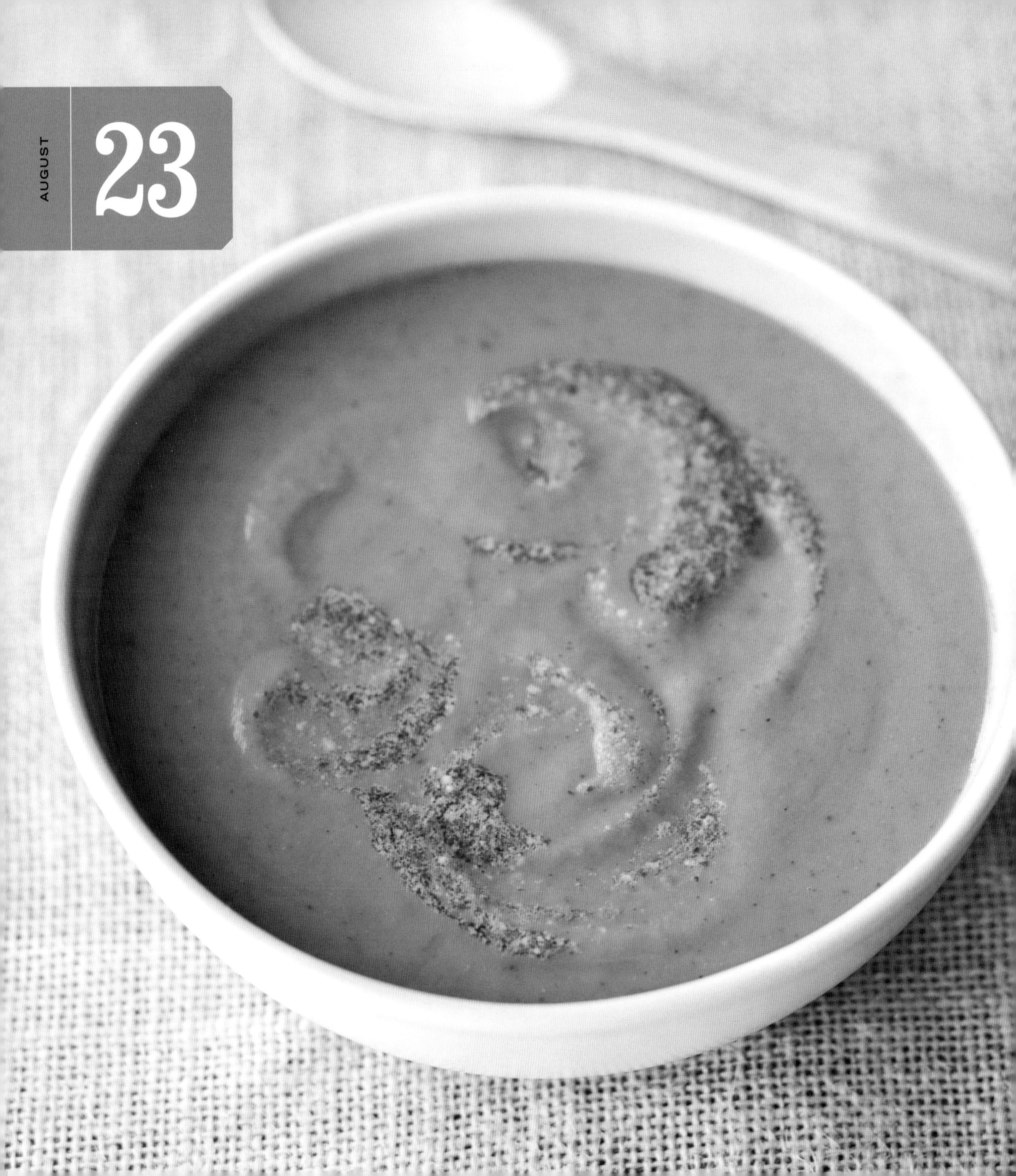

23

To make the sun-dried tomato pesto, in a food processor, mince 1 clove garlic. Coarsely chop and add ½ cup (2½ oz/ 75 g) drained oil-packed sun-dried tomatoes, 2 Tbsp olive oil, 2 Tbsp finely chopped basil, and 2 Tbsp pine nuts. Season with salt and pepper. Process to form a thick paste, adding more oil if needed.

ROASTED SUMMER VEGETABLE SOUP WITH PESTO

serves 4–6

2 leeks, white and pale green parts, finely chopped

4 carrots, peeled and cut into 2-inch (5-cm) pieces

2 zucchini, cut into 2-inch (5-cm) pieces

2 Asian eggplants, cut into 2-inch (5-cm) pieces

2 large tomatoes, quartered

2 potatoes (about 10 oz/315 g), peeled and cut into 2-inch (5-cm) pieces

4½ cups (36 fl oz/1.1 l) chicken broth, or more as needed

2 Tbsp olive oil

Salt and freshly ground pepper

2 Tbsp finely chopped basil

2 Tbsp fresh lemon juice

Basil Pesto (page 118) or Sun-Dried Tomato Pesto (left) for serving

Preheat the oven to 425°F (220°C). In a large, heavy roasting pan, combine the leeks, carrots, zucchini, eggplants, tomatoes, and potatoes. Add ½ cup (4 fl oz/125 ml) of the broth and the oil, season with salt and pepper, and mix until the vegetables are well coated. Roast, turning once, until the vegetables are softened, about 40 minutes. Remove from the oven and let cool slightly.

Working in batches, purée the vegetables with ½ cup (4 fl oz/125 ml) of the broth. Transfer to a large saucepan and stir in the remaining 3½ cups (28 fl oz/875 ml) broth, the basil, and the lemon juice. If needed, add more broth for the desired consistency. Cook over low heat for 3 minutes to blend the flavors. Season with salt and pepper.

Serve, garnished with the pesto.

24

Cinnamon and fresh ginger are unexpected spices to enhance the flavors of ripe summer berries. Serve with a scoop of vanilla ice cream for a gorgeous and unique summertime dessert.

SPICED BERRY SOUP

serves 4

1½ lb (750 g) strawberries, hulled and halved

1 lb (500 g) raspberries

¾ cup (6 fl oz/180 ml) cranberry juice cocktail

1 cinnamon stick

1½ tsp peeled and grated fresh ginger

⅓ cup (3 oz/90 g) sugar

In a large saucepan, combine the strawberries, raspberries, cranberry juice cocktail, cinnamon stick, ginger, and sugar over medium-low heat. Cook, stirring often, for 7 minutes. Remove from the heat, remove and discard the cinnamon stick, and let cool slightly.

Working in batches, purée the soup in a blender. Transfer to a covered container and refrigerate until thoroughly chilled, at least 3 hours. Serve.

25

Serving mussels family style makes such a beautiful presentation and is fun for all at the table. Serve this with plenty of bread, because you will be fighting over the last drop of this flavorful broth.

MUSSELS IN SAFFRON BROTH

serves 4

1 tsp saffron threads

½ cup (4 fl oz/125 ml) dry white wine

2 Tbsp unsalted butter

2 Tbsp olive oil

1 small yellow onion, chopped

3 cloves garlic, sliced

1 cup (8 fl oz/250 ml) chicken broth

Salt and freshly ground pepper

2 lb (1 kg) mussels, scrubbed and debearded

2 Tbsp chopped flat-leaf parsley

Using your fingers, gently crush the saffron into a small bowl and add the white wine. Set aside.

In a large, heavy pot, melt the butter with the oil over medium-high heat. Add the onion and garlic and sauté until soft, about 5 minutes. Add the saffron mixture and cook for 2 minutes. Add the broth and bring to a boil. Season with salt and pepper. Add the mussels, discarding any that do not close to the touch. Cover tightly and cook until the mussels open, 8–10 minutes.

Transfer the mussels and broth to a large bowl, discarding any unopened mussels. Sprinkle with the parsley and serve family style.

26

It's not hard to make your own crème fraîche. Take 1 cup (8 fl oz/250 ml) cream, heat to lukewarm, add 1 Tbsp buttermilk, and let sit at room temperature for 12–48 hours to thicken and become tangy. Once you like the flavor and texture, refrigerate it.

ROASTED TOMATO SOUP WITH CITRUS CRÈME FRAÎCHE

serves 4–6

4 lb (2 kg) plum tomatoes, halved lengthwise and seeded

5 Tbsp (3 fl oz/80 ml) olive oil

Salt and freshly ground pepper

1 yellow onion, chopped

3 cloves garlic, minced

2 cups (16 fl oz/500 ml) chicken broth

FOR THE CITRUS CRÈME FRAÎCHE

¼ cup (2 oz/60 g) crème fraîche or sour cream, at room temperature

Grated zest and juice of 1 lemon

Preheat the oven to 450°F (230°C). Arrange the tomatoes on a baking sheet. Drizzle with 3 Tbsp of the oil and season with salt and pepper. Toss gently and spread out in a single layer. Roast until the tomatoes are caramelized and very soft, about 25 minutes.

In a large, heavy pot, warm the remaining 2 Tbsp oil over medium-high heat. Add the onion and garlic and sauté until very soft, about 5 minutes. Stir in the tomatoes and sauté for 3–4 minutes. Add the broth, bring to a boil, reduce the heat to low, and simmer, uncovered, for 15 minutes to blend the flavors. Remove from the heat and let cool slightly.

Working in batches, purée the soup in a blender. Return to the pot and season with salt and pepper.

To make the citrus crème fraîche, in a bowl, combine the crème fraîche, the lemon zest, and 1 Tbsp of lemon juice. Using a whisk, blend well. Season with additional lemon juice and with salt and pepper.

Serve the soup, topped with a dollop of the citrus crème fraîche.

27

MISO SOUP WITH TOFU & LONG BEANS

serves 2

3 oz (90 g) firm tofu

Salt

¼ lb (125 g) Chinese long beans or green beans, cut into 1-inch (2.5-cm) pieces

1 piece kombu, about 3 inches (7.5 cm)

½ cup (½ oz/15 g) bonito flakes

2 Tbsp white miso paste

1 green onion, white and tender green parts, thinly sliced

In addition to being delicious, miso soup is said to enhance digestion and immunity. This is a very clean and light soup. If you can't find Chinese long beans, use Blue Lake beans or haricots verts. Serve with cold sesame noodles.

Drain the tofu and slice in half crosswise. Place both pieces of tofu on a plate and top with a second plate. Weigh down the top plate with a can. Let stand for 20 minutes to drain the tofu. Pour off any released water from the plate and cut the tofu into tiny cubes. Set aside.

Bring a small saucepan of water to a boil and add 1 Tbsp salt. Add the long beans and cook until crisp-tender, about 3 minutes. Drain the beans and set aside.

Put 3 cups (24 fl oz/750 ml) cold water and the kombu in a saucepan over medium heat. Bring to a boil and then remove and discard the kombu. Turn off the heat, add the bonito flakes, stir gently once, and let sit for 5 minutes. Strain the soup through a fine-mesh sieve and return the broth to the saucepan.

Put the miso paste in a small bowl and add ¼ cup (2 fl oz/60 ml) of the warm broth. Stir until the mixture is very smooth. Add the miso mixture to the saucepan and warm gently, taking care not to let the soup come to a boil. Add the tofu, long beans, and green onion and warm for just a few minutes. Serve.

28

ANGEL HAIR IN CHICKEN BROTH WITH TOMATOES & BASIL

serves 4

2 Tbsp olive oil

½ small yellow onion, thinly sliced

3 cloves garlic, minced

5 cups (40 fl oz/1.25 l) chicken broth

½ lb (250 g) angel hair pasta, broken into 2-inch (5-cm) pieces

4 plum tomatoes, chopped

⅓ cup (⅓ oz/10 g) chopped basil

Salt and freshly ground pepper

Grated Parmesan cheese for serving

A modern version of the classic noodle soup, this summertime recipe is a great way to use leftover grilled chicken and the half-full box of angel hair pasta that's hanging around in your pantry waiting to be cooked.

In a large, heavy pot, warm the oil over medium heat. Add the onion and garlic and sauté until translucent, about 5 minutes. Add the broth and bring to a boil. Add the pasta, return to a boil, and cook, stirring once or twice, for 4 minutes. Add the tomatoes and cook for 3 minutes. Turn off the heat, stir in the basil, and season with salt and pepper. Serve, topped with a generous amount of Parmesan.

29

LENTIL SOUP WITH SORREL

serves 4–6

2 Tbsp olive oil

1 yellow onion, chopped

3 cloves garlic, minced

Salt and freshly ground pepper

1 cup (7 oz/220 g) lentils

5 cups (40 fl oz/1.25 l) vegetable broth

⅓ cup (¾ oz/20 g) chopped sorrel

Grated zest and juice of 1 lemon

Sorrel is an herb that looks and acts a lot like spinach. As sorrel ages it becomes more acidic, so choose younger, smaller leaves for their subtle flavor. As this soup cools it will thicken, so you may need to add more broth when you reheat it. Substitute baby spinach if desired.

In a large, heavy pot, warm the oil over medium-high heat. Add the onion, garlic, 1 tsp salt, and ¼ tsp pepper and sauté until the onion is translucent, about 5 minutes. Add the lentils and broth and bring to a boil. Reduce the heat to low, partially cover, and simmer until the lentils are tender, about 30 minutes. Let cool slightly.

Working in batches, purée the soup in a blender. Return to the pot and stir in the sorrel and lemon zest and juice. Season with salt and pepper and serve.

30

CHICKEN & ACORN SQUASH SOUP WITH BACON & SAGE

serves 4–6

¾ lb (375 g) skinless, boneless chicken breast halves

1½ lb (750 g) acorn squash, peeled, seeded, and cut into 1-inch (2.5-cm) pieces

2 Tbsp olive oil

Salt and freshly ground pepper

4 slices thick-cut bacon

1 yellow onion, chopped

2 cloves garlic, chopped

¼ cup (¼ oz/7 g) packed sage leaves, torn in half

4 cups (32 fl oz/1 l) chicken broth

1 can (15 oz/470 g) white beans, drained

Acorn and other winter squashes are commonly used in soups, but peeling them can be tricky. The easiest way to do it is to lay the squash on its side, trim off the top and bottom, and then cut the squash in half crosswise. Working with one half at a time, stand it up on its new flat bottom and cut from the top to the bottom, removing only the peel and not the flesh and following the contour of the squash.

Place the chicken in a heavy saucepan and cover by 2 inches (5 cm) with cold water. Place over high heat and bring to a boil. Reduce the heat to medium-low and simmer until the chicken is opaque throughout, 15–18 minutes. Using tongs, transfer the chicken to a plate and, when cool enough to handle, shred the meat. Set aside.

Meanwhile, preheat the oven to 400°F (200°C). Line a baking sheet with parchment paper. Pile the squash on the prepared baking sheet and toss with the oil. Spread in a single layer and season with salt and pepper. Roast, stirring once, until the squash is fork-tender and caramelized, about 25 minutes. Set aside.

In a large, heavy pot, fry the bacon over medium-high heat, flipping once, until crispy, about 8 minutes total. Transfer to a paper towel–lined plate. When cool enough to handle, tear into bite-sized pieces. Set aside.

Pour off all but 2 Tbsp of the fat from the pot and return to medium-high heat. Add the onion and cook, stirring occasionally, until translucent, about 5 minutes. Add the garlic and sage, season with salt and pepper, and cook, stirring occasionally, until the garlic is soft, about 2 minutes. Add the broth, beans, chicken, and squash and bring to a boil. Reduce the heat to low and simmer for 15 minutes. Season with salt and pepper.

Serve, topped with the bacon.

31

PORK PHO

serves 2

3 oz (90 g) rice noodles

1 star anise

1 Tbsp coriander seeds

1 cinnamon stick

2 whole cloves

4 cups (32 fl oz/1 l) chicken broth

2-inch (5-cm) piece fresh ginger, peeled and minced

1 Tbsp Asian fish sauce

1 tsp sugar

¼ lb (125 g) pork tenderloin, cut into paper-thin slices

½ lime, cut into 4 wedges

2 Tbsp cilantro or basil leaves

¼ red onion, thinly sliced

1 small red chile, seeded and thinly sliced

1 small greeen chile, thinly sliced

Hot sauce, such as Sriracha

Pho is comfort food, Southeast Asian style. The light-bodied broth and zesty flavors satisfy without weighing you down. To slice the pork paper-thin, chill it in the freezer for half an hour.

In a bowl, combine the noodles with hot water to cover and let soak for 10 minutes. Drain and set aside.

In a small frying pan, combine the star anise, coriander seeds, cinnamon, and cloves. Toast the spices over medium heat, stirring frequently, until fragrant, 2–3 minutes.

In a large saucepan, combine the broth, ginger, fish sauce, sugar, and toasted spices. Bring to a boil over medium-high heat. Reduce the heat to low and simmer for 30 minutes. Strain the soup through a fine-mesh sieve and return to the pan. Return to a boil, add the noodles, and cook for 5 minutes.

Using tongs, remove the noodles from the soup and put in bowls. Top with half of the pork. Ladle the hot soup directly over the pork, adding enough to cover the noodles and cook the meat. Serve, passing the lime wedges, cilantro, red onion, chiles, and hot sauce at the table.

5

SPICY MEATBALL SOUP
page 205

6

BUTTERNUT SQUASH CHOWDER
page 205

7

RIBOLLITA
page 207

12

LAMB & LENTIL SOUP WITH
CILANTRO & PARSLEY
page 209

13

WHITE BEAN & DITALINI SOUP
WITH BASIL PESTO
page 210

14

GREEN CHILE STEW
page 210

19

CHICKEN & FARFALLE
VEGETABLE SOUP
page 215

20

LEEK & POTATO SOUP
WITH FRIED PROSCIUTTO
page 215

21

ROASTED TOMATO SOUP
page 216

26

ITALIAN BEEF STEW
page 220

27

BOURRIDE
page 221

28

ROASTED RED PEPPER
& TOMATO SOUP
page 221

The glorious days of Indian summer are a boon to home cooks, offering late-harvest tomatoes, bell peppers, and eggplant as well as first-of-the-season fall produce. Later in the month, introduce autumn's rich flavor to summer peppers and squash with oven-roasted heat, and add hearty and satisfying cured meats, fresh fish, and sliced sausages to soups and stews as nights become cooler and longer.

september

1

This wonderfully textured soup marries a handful of classic Tuscan flavors. The beans and farro make it hearty enough for a meal. Serve with an Italian red wine such as Chianti or Sangiovese.

TUSCAN FARRO SOUP WITH WHITE BEANS, TOMATOES & BASIL

serves 6

½ cup (3 oz/90 g) farro

Salt and freshly ground pepper

3 Tbsp olive oil

1 large yellow onion, chopped

3 cloves garlic, minced

4 cups (32 fl oz/1 l) chicken broth

1 can (15 oz/470 g) cannellini or other white beans, drained

1 can (14½ oz/455 g) diced tomatoes

2 cups packed (2½ oz/75 g) baby spinach

½ cup (¾ oz/20 g) chopped basil

In a small saucepan, bring 1½ cups (12 fl oz/ 375 ml) water to a boil. Add the farro and a pinch of salt, reduce the heat to low, and cook, partially covered, until all the water is absorbed, 20–25 minutes.

In a large, heavy pot, warm the oil over medium-high heat. Add the onion and garlic and sauté until translucent, about 5 minutes. Add the broth and bring to a boil. Reduce the heat to low and add the beans, tomatoes with their juices, and farro. Bring to a simmer and cook, uncovered, for 10 minutes to blend the flavors. Add the spinach and basil and stir just until the spinach is wilted. Season with salt and pepper and serve.

2

Indian summer's chiles and the last corn of the season combine with fall's first mushrooms in this flavorful Latin-style soup. Crema is a thick, slightly sour cream sold in Mexican markets.

POBLANO CHILE SOUP WITH CORN & MUSHROOMS

serves 6

1 Tbsp canola oil

1 white onion, coarsely chopped

2 cloves garlic

2 cups (12 oz/375 g) fresh or frozen corn kernels

3 poblano chiles, roasted, peeled, seeded, and coarsely chopped

4 cups (32 fl oz/1 l) chicken broth

½ tsp dried oregano

2 Tbsp unsalted butter

½ lb (250 g) chanterelle, cremini, or other flavorful mushrooms, sliced

Salt and freshly ground pepper

½ cup (4 oz/125 g) Mexican crema or sour cream, thinned with milk

3 oz (90 g) Muenster cheese or farmers cheese, cut into ¼-inch (6-mm) cubes, at room temperature

In a large, heavy pot, warm the oil over medium-low heat. Add the onion and garlic and sauté until translucent, about 5 minutes. Raise the heat to medium and add half of the corn, half of the chiles, and 1 cup (8 fl oz/ 250 ml) of the broth. Bring to a simmer, stir in the oregano, and cook, uncovered, until the corn is tender, 10–15 minutes. Remove from the heat and let cool slightly.

Working in batches, purée the soup in a blender with ½ cup (4 fl oz/125 ml) of the remaining broth. Pass through a medium-mesh sieve back into the pot. Add the remaining 2½ cups (20 fl oz/625 ml) broth and bring to a simmer over medium-low heat.

Meanwhile, melt the butter in a frying pan over medium heat. Add the remaining chiles, the remaining corn, and the mushrooms and stir well. Season with salt and pepper and sauté until the mushrooms release their liquid and the liquid evaporates, about 8 minutes.

Add the mushroom mixture and the crema to the soup, stir well, cover, and simmer for 10 minutes to blend the flavors. Season with salt and pepper. Serve, garnished with the cheese.

3

Called pappa al pomodoro *in Italian, this soup combines a handful of favorite Italian ingredients: ripe tomatoes, bread (usually day-old), olive oil, and basil. This version has cosmopolitan flair, with croutons, crisp-fried basil leaves, and a drizzling of basil oil as garnishes.*

TOMATO-BREAD SOUP WITH BASIL OIL

serves 4–6

FOR THE BASIL OIL

1 cup (1 oz/30 g) packed basil leaves

¾ cup (6 fl oz/180 ml) extra-virgin olive oil

1 loaf country-style bread, crusts removed, cut into 1½-inch (4-cm) cubes

Salt and freshly ground pepper

6 Tbsp (3 fl oz/90 ml) extra-virgin olive oil, plus more for drizzling

3 celery ribs, minced

3 white onions, minced

2 carrots, peeled and minced

2 cloves garlic, minced

2 Tbsp tomato paste

2 lb (1 kg) plum tomatoes, peeled, seeded, and coarsely chopped

1 tsp sugar

To make the basil oil, bring a small saucepan of water to a boil. Have ready a bowl of ice water. Set aside 8 to 12 of the basil leaves. Blanch the remaining leaves in the boiling water for about 10 seconds. Drain, then plunge into the ice water. Drain again, and squeeze the leaves to remove as much water as possible. Transfer to a blender, add the oil, and pulse until the mixture is a uniform deep green. Strain the basil oil through a fine-mesh sieve lined with cheesecloth.

Preheat the oven to 350°F (180°C). Arrange the bread cubes in a single layer on a baking sheet, season with salt and pepper, and drizzle with olive oil. Bake until lightly toasted, about 10 minutes.

Meanwhile, in a large, heavy pot, warm 4 Tbsp (2 fl oz/60 ml) of the olive oil over medium heat. Add the celery, onions, carrots, and garlic and sauté until the vegetables are softened but not browned, about 10 minutes. Stir in the tomato paste and cook for 5 minutes. Add the tomatoes and sugar and season with salt and pepper. Simmer, stirring occasionally, until the tomatoes are softened, about 10 minutes.

Add the toasted bread cubes and 6 cups (48 fl oz/1.5 l) water to the pot. Stir to combine with the vegetables, bring to a ⟫→

simmer over medium-high heat, and cook, uncovered and stirring often, until the bread has softened, about 15 minutes. Whisk the soup vigorously to break up the bread cubes. Keep warm.

In a small frying pan, warm the remaining 2 Tbsp olive oil over medium heat. Add the reserved basil leaves and fry, turning once, until crisp and slightly translucent, 30 seconds. Transfer to paper towels to drain and cool.

Serve the soup, garnished with the fried basil and drizzled with basil oil.

4

To make the croutons, remove the crusts from 4–6 slices of coarse country bread and cut the slices into cubes. Warm ⅓ cup (3 fl oz/80 ml) extra-virgin olive oil in a frying pan over medium-high heat. Add the bread cubes to the pan and fry, stirring often, until golden brown on all sides, 5–7 minutes. Transfer to paper towels to drain.

GARLIC-SAGE SOUP WITH POACHED EGGS & CROUTONS

serves 6

20 cloves garlic, coarsely chopped

10 sage leaves

Salt and freshly ground pepper

6 eggs

Croutons (left)

2 Tbsp chopped flat-leaf parsley

6 Tbsp (3 fl oz/90 ml) extra-virgin olive oil

In a large, heavy pot, combine 8 cups (64 fl oz/2 l) water, the garlic, and the sage. Bring to a boil over high heat and boil until the garlic is soft, about 15 minutes. Remove from the heat. Using a slotted spoon, scoop out the sage and garlic. Discard the sage and mash the garlic with a fork. Return the garlic to the pot and season with salt and pepper.

Return the soup to a boil, then reduce the heat so that it gently simmers. Break each egg into a small bowl and slip into the simmering liquid. Cook until the whites are opaque but the yolks are still soft, about 2 minutes.

Using a slotted spoon, quickly and carefully lift the eggs from the soup and place in the bowls. Ladle some of the soup into each bowl, garnish with the croutons, and sprinkle with parsley. Drizzle with the oil and serve.

5

For this simple and filling Spanish-style soup, meatballs are enriched with grated potato and simmered in a base of tomato and parsley, then spiked with chile for a nice little kick.

SPICY MEATBALL SOUP

serves 6

4 large russet potatoes (about 2 lb/1 kg)

1 lb (500 g) ground lean pork

1 white onion, one half minced, one half coarsely chopped

½ tsp dried oregano

Salt and freshly ground pepper

2 eggs, lightly beaten

1 lb (500 g) ripe tomatoes, chopped, or 1 can (14½ oz/455 g) diced tomatoes, drained

4 cups (32 fl oz/1 l) chicken broth

2 Tbsp canola oil

1 Tbsp all-purpose flour

1 jalapeño chile, partially slit open

1 flat-leaf parsley sprig, chopped

¼ cup (¼ oz/7 g) cilantro leaves for garnish

Peel the potatoes and shred on the medium holes of a box grater-shredder. Wrap in a kitchen towel and squeeze out the excess liquid. In a bowl, combine the shredded potatoes, pork, minced onion, and oregano. Add 1 tsp salt and 1 tsp pepper, and toss to mix. Add the eggs and mix again. With your hands, roll the mixture into 1-inch (2.5-cm) balls.

In a blender, process the tomatoes and chopped onion until smooth, adding a little of the broth, if needed, to facilitate blending.

In a large, heavy pot, warm the oil over medium heat. Working in batches, gently add the meatballs and fry until lightly brown on all sides, about 10 minutes per batch. Using a slotted spoon, transfer the meatballs to a plate.

Return the pot to medium heat, sprinkle the flour into the hot oil in the pot, and cook, stirring, for about 4 minutes. Slowly pour in the tomato mixture, then add the chile and parsley. Cook, stirring occasionally, until the mixture thickens and darkens in color, about 3 minutes. Add the remaining broth and the meatballs and let the soup simmer, uncovered, for 10–15 minutes. Discard the chile. Season with salt and pepper and serve, garnished with the cilantro.

6

Chowder was traditionally a communal dish. It is said to have originated centuries ago in French seacoast towns, where local fishermen would contribute part of the day's catch to a stew-like soup that was shared by all of the residents. Over time, chowder became synonymous with a type of thick, hearty soup that can be prepared with a variety of different ingredients, such as the winter squash used here.

BUTTERNUT SQUASH CHOWDER

serves 4–6

2½ lb (1.25 kg) butternut squash, halved

2 tsp olive oil

4 slices bacon, cut into ½-inch (12-mm) pieces

1 yellow onion, diced

2 celery ribs, diced

1 bay leaf

1 tsp chopped sage, plus small sage leaves for garnish

Salt and freshly ground pepper

2 russet potatoes, peeled and cut into ½-inch (12-mm) cubes

¼ cup (2 fl oz/60 ml) dry white wine

3 cups (24 fl oz/750 ml) chicken broth

½ cup (4 fl oz/125 ml) heavy cream

Preheat the oven to 400°F (200°C). Rub the cut sides of the squash with the oil. Place, cut side down, in the pan and roast until a knife easily pierces the skin, 45–50 minutes. Let cool, scoop out and discard the seeds, and scoop out the pulp. Set aside to cool.

Meanwhile, in a large, heavy pot, fry the bacon over medium heat, stirring occasionally, until crispy, about 5 minutes. Using a slotted spoon, transfer to a paper towel–lined plate. Set aside.

Pour off all but 1 Tbsp of the fat from the pot and return to medium heat. Add the onion, celery, bay leaf, sage, 4 tsp salt, and 1 tsp pepper and cook, stirring occasionally, until the vegetables are soft, 5–6 minutes. Stir in the potatoes, cover, and cook, stirring occasionally, for 3 minutes.

Add the wine and simmer, stirring to scrape up the browned bits from the bottom of the pot, 1–2 minutes. Add the broth and bring just to a boil. Reduce the heat to low and simmer until the potatoes are tender, about 12 minutes.

Meanwhile, working in batches, purée the squash in a blender until smooth.

Add the squash purée and bacon to the pot and simmer for 5 minutes, then stir in the cream. Taste and adjust the seasoning. Remove and discard the bay leaf. Serve, garnished with sage leaves.

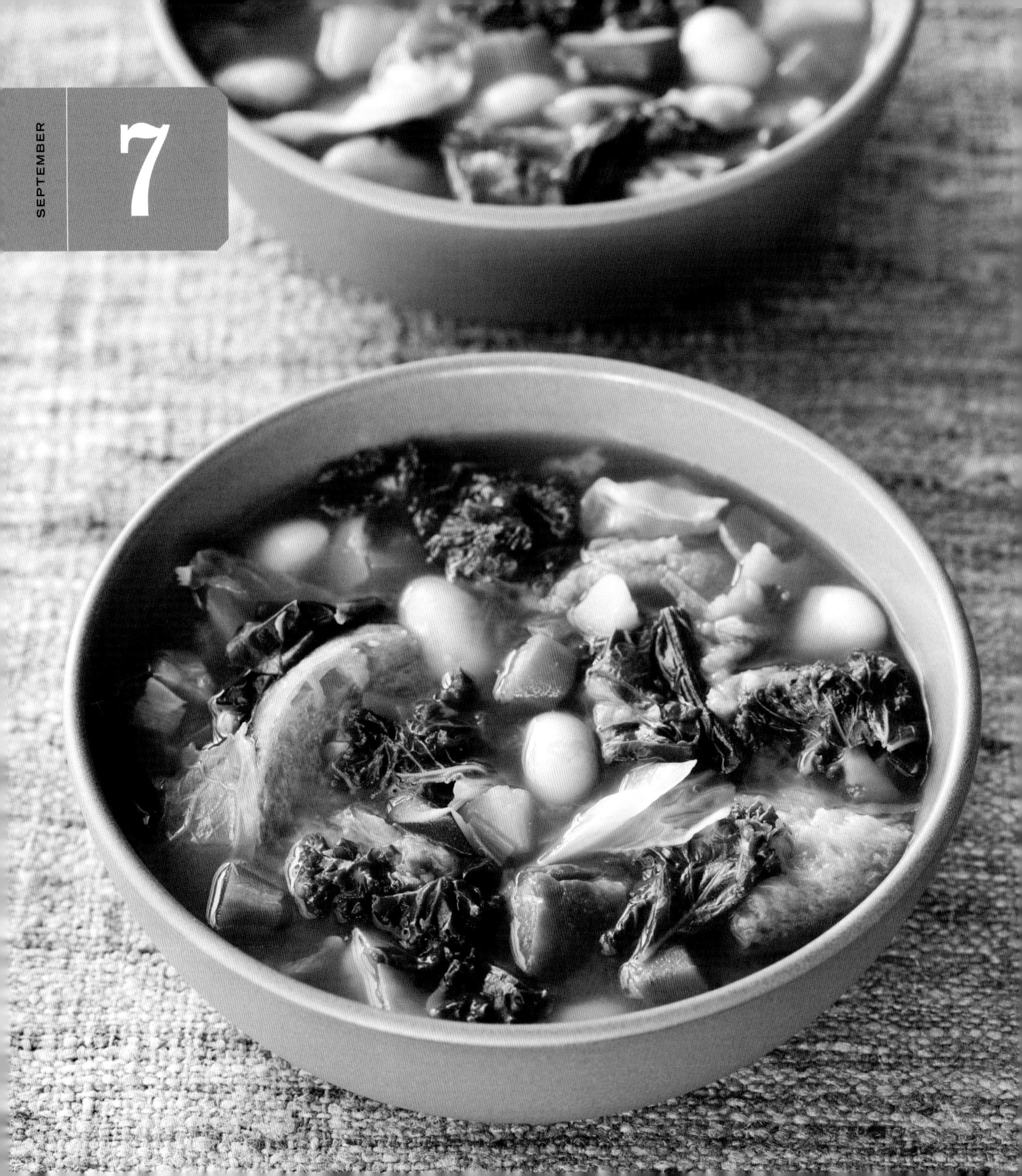

RIBOLLITA

serves 6–8

This dish begins as a typical Tuscan vegetable soup, which you can eat as such on the first day. It becomes ribollita on the second day, when, as its name implies, it is reboiled with toasted bread added to thicken the soup. Because it's denser than most soups, some even serve it with a fork.

½ cup (4 fl oz/125 ml) extra-virgin olive oil, plus more for seasoning

2 carrots, peeled and coarsely chopped

2 celery stalks, chopped

2 yellow onions, coarsely chopped

2 potatoes, peeled and cut into chunks

2 zucchini, coarsely chopped

1 cup (6 oz/185 g) canned diced tomatoes

1 bunch Tuscan kale (lacinato kale), tough center stalks removed, leaves cut into thick strips

½ head savoy cabbage, coarsely chopped

1 bunch spinach, stemmed and coarsely chopped

1½ cans (21 oz/655 g) cannellini or other white beans, drained

Leaves from 3 thyme sprigs

Salt and freshly ground pepper

5 slices day-old country-style bread, toasted

In a large, heavy pot over medium heat, warm the ½ cup oil. Add the carrots, celery, onions, potatoes, and zucchini and sauté until the vegetables are softened, 10–15 minutes. Stir in the tomatoes with their juices and 4 cups (32 fl oz/1 l) water, then add the kale, cabbage, and spinach. Raise the heat to high, bring to a simmer, reduce the heat to low, and let cook until the greens are tender, about 45 minutes.

Stir in the beans and cook over medium heat for 10 minutes. Add the thyme leaves and season with salt and pepper. Remove from the heat and let cool, then cover and refrigerate overnight.

The following day, preheat the oven to 350°F (180°C). Line a 2-qt (2-l) baking dish with the toasted bread slices and ladle the soup over the top. Bake, stirring occasionally with a wooden spoon so that the bread slices break apart and blend with the soup, 20–25 minutes. Continue baking without stirring until a lightly browned crust forms on top of the soup, 5–10 minutes longer.

Season generously with oil and freshly ground pepper and serve.

LINGUINE & CLAM SOUP

serves 4

A classic Italian pasta dish is reinvented as a delicious soup in this simple recipe. Select the clams carefully, passing over any that have a fishy smell or a chipped or cracked shell. Serve this soup with homemade garlic bread: sauté 3 cloves garlic, finely chopped, in 2 tablespoons each olive oil and unsalted butter until translucent and stir in 2 tablespoons chopped fresh flat-leaf parsley; spread on the cut sides of a split baguette-type Italian loaf, wrap in aluminum foil, and heat in a moderate oven until hot.

3 lb (1.5 kg) littleneck clams, scrubbed

2 tsp olive oil

5 oz (155 g) pancetta, chopped

1 fennel bulb, stalks and fronds removed, quartered and sliced

Salt and freshly ground pepper

2 tomatoes, seeded and chopped

4 cups (32 fl oz/1 l) chicken broth

½ lb (250 g) linguine, broken into 2-inch (5-cm) pieces

2 Tbsp chopped flat-leaf parsley

⅓ cup (1½ oz/45 g) grated Parmesan cheese

Fill a large bowl or clean sink with cold water and add the clams so that the sand can escape. Let them sit in the water while you prepare the broth.

In a large, heavy pot, warm the oil over medium-high heat. Add the pancetta and cook, stirring occasionally, until it begins to render its fat and is just golden, about 5 minutes. Add the fennel and season lightly with salt and pepper. Cook, stirring occasionally, until the fennel is soft and the pancetta is cooked through, 8–10 minutes. Stir in the tomatoes and broth and bring to a boil. Add the linguine and cook, stirring occasionally to prevent sticking, until al dente, about 12 minutes.

Meanwhile, pour water into a large saucepan with a steamer insert, just to the bottom of the insert. Place over high heat and bring to a boil. Carefully remove the clams from the cold water so as to not stir up the dirt and sand on the bottom, and place in the steamer insert. Cover and cook until the clams open, about 6 minutes. Discard any unopened clams. Transfer half of the clams to a bowl and remove the meat from the shells. Cover the clams still in their shells to keep warm.

When the pasta is cooked, stir the clam meat and parsley into the soup, and season with salt and pepper.

Serve, topped with the clams in their shells and a generous helping of the cheese.

9

SEPTEMBER

Old-fashioned corn chowder reaches new heights when chunks of rosy lobster meat are added just before serving. For briny-sweet lobster, tender summer corn, buttery potatoes, and silky heavy cream, there's no better match than a crumbling of salty bacon. Ideal for a late-summer supper, serve this with a mixed green salad and warmed bread.

LOBSTER & SWEET CORN CHOWDER

serves 6–8

3 cooked lobsters (about 1½ lb/750 g each)

4 yellow onions

4 ears corn, husked

1 cup (8 fl oz/250 ml) dry white wine

1 can (14½ oz/455 g) diced tomatoes

4 sprigs flat-leaf parsley, plus 4 Tbsp chopped

6 sprigs thyme

2 bay leaves

Salt and freshly ground pepper

6 slices bacon, cut crosswise into thin strips

2 Tbsp unsalted butter

1 tsp sweet paprika

5 Yukon Gold potatoes (2½ lb/1.25 kg), peeled and cut into ¾-inch (2-cm) chunks

1½ cups (12 fl oz/375 ml) heavy cream

Remove the meat from the lobsters, cut into small pieces, and refrigerate. Put the shells in a large, heavy pot. Add 7 cups (56 fl oz/1.75 l) water and bring to a boil over high heat. Thinly slice 2 of the onions and add to the pot. Cut the kernels from the corn cobs and set aside. Add the cobs to the pot along with the wine, the tomatoes with their juices, the parsley sprigs, 4 of the thyme sprigs, the bay leaves, and ½ tsp salt. Reduce the heat to medium and simmer for 1½ hours, skimming off foam on the surface. Strain the lobster broth through a fine-mesh sieve into a large heatproof bowl. Discard the solids.

Finely chop the remaining 2 onions. In a large saucepan, sauté the bacon over medium heat until crisp, about 8 minutes. Transfer to paper towels to drain. Pour off all but 2 Tbsp fat from the pan and return to medium heat. Add the butter and chopped onions and sauté until softened, about 5 minutes. Add the paprika and cook until fragrant, about 1 minute. Add the potatoes, the remaining 2 thyme sprigs, and 6 cups (48 fl oz/1.5 l) of the lobster broth. Raise the heat to high and bring to a boil. Cover and cook until the potatoes just begin to soften, about 8 minutes. Using a wooden spoon, mash a few potato chunks against the side of the pan and stir into the liquid. Cook until ⇥

the potatoes are tender, about 5 minutes. Reduce the heat to low and add the lobster meat, corn kernels, bacon, and cream. Add 2 tsp salt and season with pepper. Cook until the corn is tender and the lobster meat is warmed through, 6–8 minutes. Stir in the chopped parsley and serve.

10

SEPTEMBER

Pearl barley is a barley from which the hard outer hull and germ have been removed, leaving small, cream-colored balls that look like the gems for which they are named. In this recipe, the tiny grains are used to thicken the soup, resulting in a pleasantly chewy texture.

VEGETABLE-BARLEY SOUP

serves 6

2½ qt (2.5 l) chicken or vegetable broth

½ cup (2½ oz/125 g) pearl barley

2 carrots, peeled and diced

2 parsnips, peeled and diced

2 boiling potatoes, unpeeled and diced

1 rutabaga, peeled and diced

1 cup (2 oz/60 g) broccoli florets

1 tsp chopped thyme

1 tsp chopped oregano

1 Tbsp chopped flat-leaf parsley

In a large soup pot, bring the broth to a boil over high heat. Add the barley, reduce the heat to medium-low, cover, and simmer until almost tender, 15–20 minutes.

Raise the heat to medium-high and bring to a vigorous simmer. Add the carrots, parsnips, potatoes, rutabaga, broccoli, thyme, and oregano. Simmer, uncovered, until all the vegetables are tender, about 15 minutes.

Serve, garnished with the parsley.

11

MINESTRONE WITH PESTO

serves 6

1 oz (30 g) dried porcini mushrooms

¼ cup (2 fl oz/60 ml) olive oil

1 yellow onion, chopped

2 carrots, peeled and chopped

1 celery rib, chopped

1 bunch Swiss chard, ribs removed, leaves chopped

3 Yukon Gold or other boiling potatoes, peeled and chopped

1½ cups (8 oz/250 g) peeled, seeded, and diced butternut squash

4 tomatoes, peeled, seeded, and chopped, or 2 cups (12 oz/375 g) canned diced plum tomatoes with juices

2 lb (1 kg) cranberry beans in the pod, shelled, or 2 cups (8 oz/250 g) fresh shelled beans

1 piece Parmesan cheese rind

Salt and freshly ground pepper

1 cup (3½ oz/105 g) macaroni, tubetti, or other small soup pasta

¼ cup (2 fl oz/60 ml) Basil Pesto (page 118), or purchased pesto

Grated Parmesan cheese for serving

The best versions of this soup are made with fresh seasonal vegetables. Don't hesitate to use cabbage, green beans, eggplant, cauliflower, peas, zucchini, leeks, or whatever else looks good at the market or that you might have on hand. Simmering the rind from a wedge of Parmesan in the soup imparts a rich, deep flavor.

In a bowl, combine the mushrooms with 2 cups (16 fl oz/500 ml) hot water and soak for 30 minutes. Drain well, reserving the liquid. Strain the liquid through a coffee filter. Rinse the mushrooms well under cold running water. Drain well and chop.

In a large, heavy pot, warm the oil over medium heat. Add the onion, carrots, and celery and sauté until tender and golden, 10–15 minutes. Stir in the mushrooms, chard, potatoes, squash, tomatoes, beans, and cheese rind. Add the mushroom liquid and enough water to cover the vegetables by ½ inch (12 mm), bring to a simmer, and reduce the heat to low. Season with salt and pepper and cook uncovered, stirring occasionally, until the vegetables are soft, about 1½ hours, adding water as needed if the soup becomes too thick.

Add the pasta and cook, stirring frequently, until al dente, about 15 minutes or according to package directions. Remove the cheese rind from the pot and discard. Serve, topped with the pesto and passing the Parmesan at the table.

12

LAMB & LENTIL SOUP WITH CILANTRO & PARSLEY

serves 8

½ cup (3½ oz/105 g) dried small fava beans, picked over and rinsed

2 Tbsp olive oil

1 yellow onion, chopped

1 lb (500 g) boneless lamb shoulder, trimmed of fat and cut into ½-inch (12-mm) pieces

1 tsp ground ginger

½ tsp ground cinnamon

½ tsp ground turmeric

⅛ tsp caraway seeds, crushed

1 can (14½ oz/455 g) diced tomatoes

1 cup (7 oz/220 g) small green-brown lentils

8 saffron threads, steeped in 2 Tbsp warm water

½ cup (3½ oz/105 g) orzo or other small pasta

¼ cup (⅓ oz/10 g) chopped cilantro

¼ cup (⅓ oz/10 g) chopped flat-leaf parsley

Salt and freshly ground pepper

1 large lemon, cut into 8 wedges

To break the fast at day's end during Ramadan, Moroccans serve this sustaining soup, called harira. It is often made with chickpeas, but this version uses an earthy mix of dried fava beans and lentils. Choose small green-brown lentils, such as those grown in Umbria.

Put the dried beans in a bowl with cold water to cover and soak for at least 4 hours or up to overnight. Drain.

In a large, heavy pot, warm the oil over medium-high heat. Add the onion and lamb and sauté until the onions are soft and the meat is browned on all sides, 6–8 minutes. Add the ginger, cinnamon, turmeric, and caraway and cook, stirring, until the spices are fragrant, about 1 minute. Add the favas and 8 cups (64 fl oz/2 l) water and bring to a boil over high heat. Reduce the heat to medium-low, cover, and simmer until the beans are tender, about 1 hour. Add the tomatoes with their juices, lentils, and saffron with its steeping liquid. Cover and cook until the lentils are tender, about 1 hour, adding more water if needed.

About 10 minutes before serving, bring a large pot of salted water to a boil and cook the pasta until al dente, about 5 minutes, or according to package directions. Drain and add to the soup. Stir in the herbs and cook for 5 minutes to blend the flavors. Season with salt and pepper and serve, accompanied with the lemon wedges.

13

WHITE BEAN & DITALINI SOUP WITH BASIL PESTO

serves 4–6

Freshly made pesto adds a wonderful bouquet of flavor to this hearty fall soup. Take the time to grate the Parmesan for the pesto here, and you will be rewarded with its pleasantly sharp, nutty flavor. Any leftover pesto is delicious spread on sandwiches or served with grilled lamb chops or vegetables. If fresh basil is no longer in the market, look for a good-quality pesto at your local market or deli.

Salt and freshly ground pepper

1 cup (3½ oz/105 g) ditalini or other small soup pasta

2 Tbsp olive oil

½ yellow onion, chopped

2 cloves garlic, chopped

⅓ cup (1½ oz/45 g) drained oil-packed sun-dried tomatoes, chopped

2 cans (15 oz/470 g each) white beans, drained

5 cups (40 fl oz/1.25 l) vegetable or chicken broth

3 Tbsp chopped basil

FOR THE BASIL PESTO

2 cups (2 oz/60 g) packed basil leaves

2 cloves garlic

½ cup (2½ oz/75 g) pine nuts, toasted

½ cup (4 fl oz/125 ml) extra-virgin olive oil

½ cup (2 oz/60 g) grated Parmesan cheese

Salt and freshly ground pepper

Bring a pot of water to a boil over high heat. Salt the water, add the pasta, and cook until al dente, about 8 minutes or according to the package directions. Drain, rinse under cold water, and drain again. Set aside.

In a large, heavy pot, warm the oil over medium-high heat. Add the onion and cook, stirring occasionally, until soft, about 6 minutes. Add the garlic and cook, stirring occasionally, until soft, about 2 minutes. Stir in the sun-dried tomatoes, beans, and broth, and season well with salt and pepper. Bring to a boil, then reduce the heat to low and simmer for 15 minutes. Let cool slightly.

Purée half of the soup in a food processor or blender. Return to the pot and stir to combine. Stir in the pasta and basil, and season with salt and pepper. Keep warm over low heat.

To make the basil pesto, in a food processor or blender, combine the basil, garlic, and pine nuts. Pulse until the ingredients are minced, scraping down the sides of the bowl as needed. With the motor running, slowly add the oil and process until smooth. Transfer to a bowl, stir in the cheese, and season with salt and pepper.

Serve the soup, topped with a generous swirl of the pesto.

14

GREEN CHILE STEW

serves 6

Commonly called simply chile verde, or "green chile," this easy-to-make, delicious dish is one of New Mexico's most popular traditional stews. Regional markets sell the state's green chiles both fresh and frozen. If you cannot find them, substitute Anaheims or poblanos.

3 Tbsp toasted peanut oil or canola oil

2 lb (1 kg) boneless pork shoulder, trimmed and cut into ¾-inch (2-cm) cubes

1 white onion, chopped

2 cloves garlic, minced

½ lb (250 g) white or brown mushrooms, quartered

¾ lb (375 g) small Yukon Gold potatoes, quartered lengthwise

1½ tsp coriander seeds, toasted and ground

1 tsp dried oregano

2 bay leaves

6 cups (48 fl oz/1.5 l) chicken broth

Salt

12–16 New Mexico green chiles (about 2 lb/1 kg), roasted, peeled, seeded, and chopped

6 Tbsp (3 oz/90 g) sour cream

Cilantro leaves for garnish

In a large, heavy pot, warm the oil over high heat. Working in batches, add the pork and brown well on all sides, 6–8 minutes per batch. Transfer to a plate.

Add the onion to the oil remaining in the pot and sauté over medium-high heat until lightly golden, about 4 minutes. Add the garlic and sauté for 1 minute. Add the mushrooms and sauté until the edges are browned, 3–4 minutes. Add the potatoes, coriander, oregano, and bay leaves and return the meat to the pot. Stir well, pour in the broth, and add 1 tsp salt. Bring to a boil, reduce the heat to medium, and simmer, uncovered, until the meat is just tender, about 30 minutes.

Add the chiles and simmer, uncovered, until the meat is very tender, about 20 minutes. Stir in another 1 tsp salt, then taste and adjust with more salt if necessary. Remove and discard the bay leaves. Serve, garnished with the sour cream and cilantro.

SEPTEMBER

16

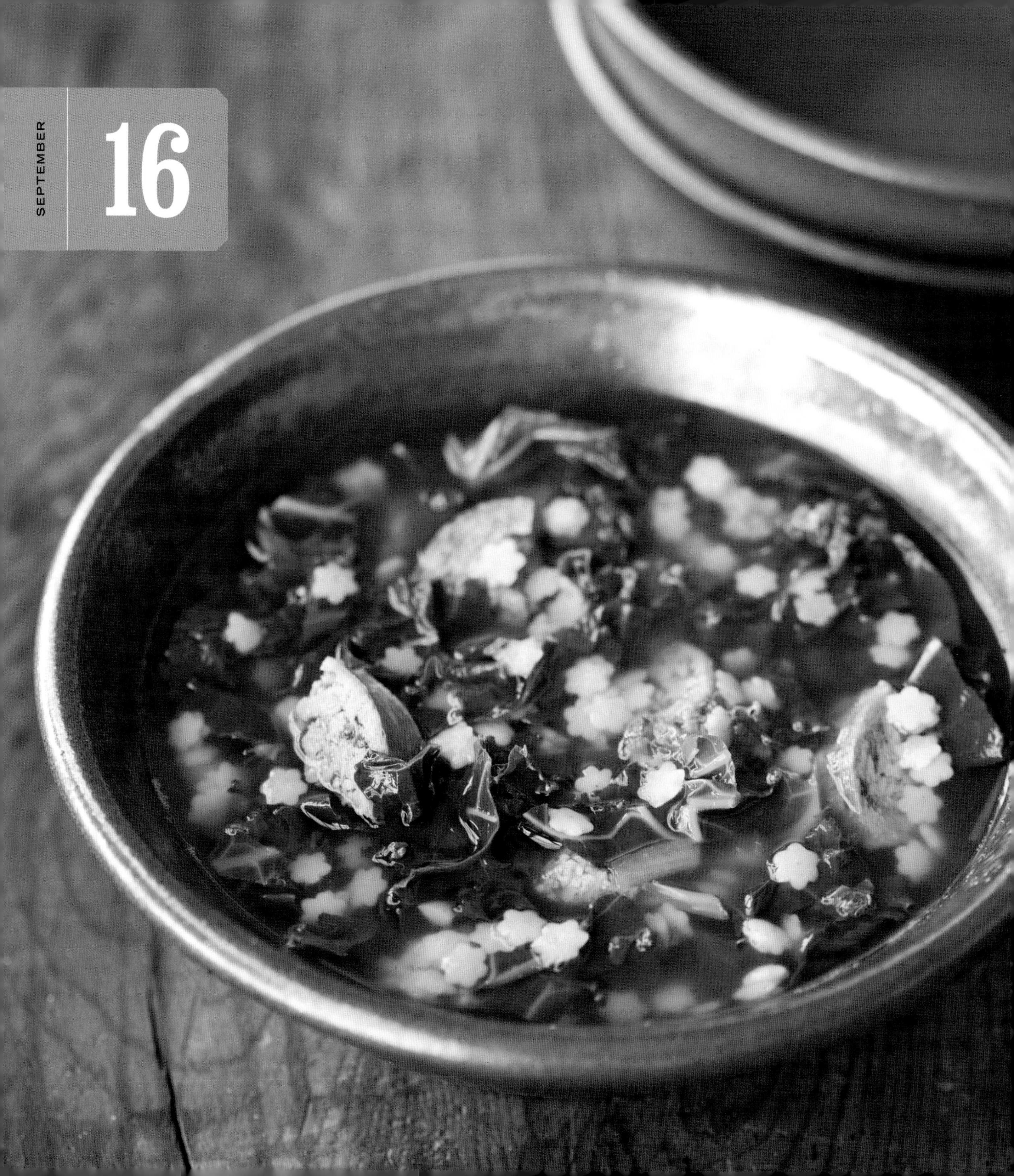

MUSHROOM SOUP WITH CHICKEN

serves 4

1 oz (30 g) dried mushrooms, such as porcini

4 cups (32 fl oz/1 l) chicken broth

4 Tbsp (2 oz/60 g) unsalted butter

1 yellow onion, finely chopped

¾ lb (375 g) fresh cremini mushrooms, thinly sliced

¼ cup (1½ oz/45 g) all-purpose flour

Salt and ground white pepper

2 tsp soy sauce

1 lb (500 g) skinless, boneless chicken breast halves, cut crosswise against the grain into thin slices

1 cup (8 fl oz/250 ml) half-and-half

¼ cup (2 fl oz/60 ml) tawny port

Finely chopped flat-leaf parsley for garnish

Fresh mushrooms contain a lot of moisture, which is why it's important to sauté them well. Browning releases their liquid and softens their texture, and ensures that they won't dilute the soup when they are added to the pot.

In a saucepan, combine the dried mushrooms and broth. Cover, bring to a boil over medium-high heat, and cook for 5 minutes. Remove from the heat.

In a large, heavy pot, melt the butter over medium heat. Add the onion and sauté until softened, about 5 minutes. Add the cremini and sauté until softened, about 3 minutes. Sprinkle with the flour, season with salt and pepper, and cook, stirring, until the flour is incorporated and the mushrooms are coated, about 1 minute. Drain the soaked mushrooms through a coffee filter, reserving the liquid. Add the soaking liquid, drained mushrooms, and soy sauce to the pot and simmer, partially covered, until the mushrooms are tender and the flavors are blended, about 15 minutes. Remove from the heat and let cool slightly.

Working in batches, purée the soup, making sure to leave some texture. Return to the pot, add the chicken, and simmer over medium heat until opaque, 2–4 minutes. Add the half-and-half and port and simmer for about 1 minute to blend the flavors.

Serve, garnished with the parsley.

PASTINA & KALE SOUP WITH ANDOUILLE

serves 4

1 cup (7 oz/200 g) small soup pasta, such as stelline, orzo, or ditalini

3 links andouille sausage (10 oz/315 g)

1 Tbsp olive oil

1 yellow onion, chopped

2 cloves garlic, minced

1 bunch kale, ribs removed, leaves chopped

4 cups (32 fl oz/1 l) chicken broth

1 Tbsp tomato paste

Salt and freshly ground pepper

Grated Parmesan cheese

This soup is flavor-packed, thanks to the spicy andouille, and nutrition-rich, thanks to the kale. Serve with bruschetta rubbed with garlic and topped with chopped ripe tomatoes and chopped fresh basil.

Bring a pot of salted water to a boil over high heat. Add the pasta and cook until al dente, according to package directions. Drain and set aside.

In a large, heavy pot, cook the sausage over medium heat until no longer pink in the center, about 15 minutes. Remove from the pot and cut into slices ¼ inch (6 mm) thick.

Add the oil to the pot and warm over medium-high heat. Add the onion and garlic and sauté until translucent, about 5 minutes. Add the kale, stir to coat, and sauté for 3–4 minutes. Add the broth and bring to a boil. Reduce the heat to low. Add the pasta, sausage, and tomato paste and stir well to combine. Simmer, stirring often, for 5 minutes. Season with salt and pepper and serve, topped with the Parmesan.

17

Oceans and seas around the world yield an array of shellfish and fish that are incorporated into soups and stews with local vegetables, herbs, and spices, creating dishes that mirror the bordering cultures. This medley, which is reflective of the Mediterranean, uses fish and shellfish that are readily available.

SEAFOOD MEDLEY

serves 6

FOR THE BROTH

1 Tbsp olive oil

¼ cup (¼ oz/7 g) shrimp shells
(reserved from soup recipe below)

1 yellow onion, chopped

2 cloves garlic, chopped

2 celery ribs, chopped

2 fennel bulbs, stalks
and fronds removed, chopped

1 carrot, chopped

1 flat-leaf parsley sprig, 2 thyme sprigs, and
1 bay leaf, tied to make a bouquet garni

1 cup (8 fl oz/250 ml) bottled clam juice

4 cups (1½ lb/750 g) chopped canned
tomatoes with juices

Salt and freshly ground pepper

FOR THE SOUP

1 potato, peeled and cut into
½-inch (12-mm) pieces

½ cup (3 oz/90 g) minced celery

1 lb (500 g) firm white fish, such as halibut
or sea bass, cut into 1-inch (2.5-cm) cubes

2 tablespoons chopped flat-leaf parsley

¼ tsp saffron threads dissolved
in 2 Tbsp strained broth

1 lb (500 g) medium shrimp,
peeled and deveined (reserve at least
8 shells for broth above)

½ lb (250 g) squid rings

1 can (6½ oz/185 g) clam meat, drained

To make the broth, in a large, heavy pot, warm the oil over medium-high heat. Add the shrimp shells and cook, stirring occasionally, until fragrant, about 2 minutes. Add the onion and cook, stirring occasionally, until translucent, about 2 minutes. Add the garlic, celery, fennel, carrot, bouquet garni, clam juice, tomatoes with their juices, 2 cups (16 fl oz/500 ml) water, ½ tsp salt, and ½ tsp pepper and bring to a simmer. Reduce the heat to low, cover, and simmer until the flavors are blended, about 15 minutes. Taste and adjust the seasoning. Strain the broth through a chinois or a fine-mesh sieve lined with cheesecloth, discarding the solids. ⟫

To make the soup, pour the broth into a clean large, heavy pot and bring to a simmer over medium-high heat. Add the potato and celery, reduce the heat to low, and simmer until the potato is fork-tender, 10–15 minutes. Add the fish, parsley, and saffron and cook just until the fish is opaque and easily flakes when pulled apart with a fork, 4–5 minutes. Add the shrimp and squid and cook just until opaque, about 3 minutes. Stir in the clam meat, heat until warmed through, and serve.

18

Fresh cranberry beans are beautiful in their red-and-white-striped shells, but if you can't find them, it's fine to use frozen or canned. Serve this brothy soup with a savory focaccia.

SPICY BROCCOLINI & CRANBERRY BEAN SOUP

serves 4–6

2 Tbsp olive oil

1 small yellow onion, finely diced

2 cloves garlic, minced

⅛ tsp red pepper flakes

Salt and freshly ground pepper

5 cups (40 fl oz/1.25 l) vegetable broth

1 lb (500 g) cranberry beans in the pods,
shelled

1 bunch broccolini, tough ends discarded,
cut into ½-inch (12-mm) pieces

In a large, heavy pot, warm the oil over medium-high heat. Add the onion and garlic and sauté until translucent, about 5 minutes. Add the pepper flakes, ½ tsp salt, and ¼ tsp pepper and cook for 1 minute. Add the broth and bring to a boil. Add the beans and cook until they are tender, 15–20 minutes. Add the broccolini and cook for 5 minutes. Season to taste with salt and pepper and serve.

19

CHICKEN & FARFALLE VEGETABLE SOUP

serves 6

1 small chicken (3 lb/1.5 kg), quartered

1 large yellow onion, coarsely chopped

1 carrot, peeled and coarsely chopped

6 flat-leaf parsley sprigs, plus ¼ cup (⅓ oz/10 g) finely chopped parsley

1 tsp finely chopped thyme

2 bay leaves

3 celery ribs with leaves, cut into ½-inch (12-mm) pieces

½ small head savoy cabbage (6 oz/185 g), cored and coarsely chopped

½ lb (250 g) green beans, trimmed and cut into 1-inch (2.5-cm) pieces

2 cups (7 oz/210 g) farfalle pasta

1 Tbsp fresh lemon juice

Salt and freshly ground pepper

¾ cup (3 oz/90 g) grated Parmesan cheese

As the weather starts to cool, it's time for a back-to-school classic: chicken noodle soup. This one's full of healthy veggies and tender bowtie pasta. Simmering the stock requires little effort on busy weeknights, and leftovers are a cinch to pour into insulated containers for work or school the next day.

In a large, heavy pot, combine the chicken, onion, carrot, parsley sprigs, thyme, and bay leaves. Pour in 2½ qt (2.5 l) water and bring to a boil over high heat. Reduce the heat to medium-low and simmer, covered, until the chicken falls from the bone, about 1 hour.

Transfer the chicken to a plate. Strain the broth through a fine-mesh sieve and return to the pot. Discard the solids in the sieve. Once the chicken is cool enough to handle, remove the meat from the bones and discard the bones and skin. Tear the meat into 1-inch (2.5-cm) pieces.

Add the celery, cabbage, green beans, and farfalle to the pot and simmer, covered, until the farfalle is al dente, 10–12 minutes or according to package directions. Add the chicken pieces, chopped parsley, and lemon juice. Season with salt and pepper. Cook, stirring occasionally, until the chicken is warmed through. Remove and discard the bay leaves.

Serve, topped with the Parmesan.

20

LEEK & POTATO SOUP WITH FRIED PROSCIUTTO

serves 6–8

8 leeks (about 4 lb/2 kg), white and pale green parts

¼ cup olive oil

6 slices prosciutto (about 3 oz/90 g), cut into ribbons

Salt and freshly ground pepper

1½ tsp minced thyme

2 Tbsp all-purpose flour

8 cups (2 qt/2 l) chicken broth

5 Yukon Gold potatoes (about 2½ lb/1.25 kg), peeled and cut into 1-inch (2.5-cm) chunks

2 small bay leaves

¼ cup (⅓ oz/10 g) chopped chives

Since they grow in sandy soil and grit becomes trapped within their layers, leeks always need a careful rinse. After slicing them lengthwise, hold them under cold running water and separate the layers with your fingers to clean them thoroughly.

Cut the leeks in half lengthwise and then cut each half crosswise into pieces ½ inch (12 mm) thick. In a large, heavy pot, warm the oil over medium heat. Add the prosciutto and sauté until crisp, about 6 minutes. Transfer to paper towels to drain.

Add the leeks and ½ tsp salt to the pot and stir to coat. Reduce the heat to medium-low, cover, and cook, stirring occasionally, until the leeks begin to soften, about 10 minutes. Add the thyme and flour and cook, stirring constantly, until the flour is incorporated.

Raise the heat to medium-high and, stirring constantly, slowly add the broth. Add the potatoes and bay leaves, season with pepper, cover, and bring to a boil. Reduce the heat to medium-low and simmer until the potatoes just start to become tender, about 6 minutes. Remove from the heat and let stand, covered, until the potatoes are tender all the way through, about 15 minutes. Discard the bay leaves and return the soup to a simmer. If desired, use the back of a large spoon to mash some of the potatoes against the side of the pot and stir them into the soup to thicken it.

Serve, garnished with the fried prosciutto and the chives.

21

Nearly everyone likes tomato soup, and this version won't disappoint. The tomatoes are roasted to intensify their natural sweetness and then puréed with toasted bread to give the soup more body. The garnish of mascarpone and Parmigiano-Reggiano is optional but delicious, or you can top each bowl with a little chopped fresh thyme. For an old-school accompaniment, serve with grilled cheese sandwiches.

ROASTED TOMATO SOUP

serves 6

3 lb (1.5 kg) plum tomatoes, cored and halved lengthwise

8 thyme sprigs

4 cloves garlic

Salt and freshly ground pepper

5 Tbsp (3 fl oz/80 ml) olive oil

½ cup (4 oz/125 g) mascarpone cheese (optional)

½ cup (2 oz/60 g) grated Parmesan cheese (optional)

1 yellow onion, chopped

3 cups (24 fl oz/750 ml) chicken broth

4 slices country-style bread, toasted

Preheat the oven to 275°F (135°C).

Place the tomato halves, cut side up, on a baking sheet, and scatter the thyme sprigs and garlic on top. Season with salt and pepper and drizzle with 3 Tbsp of the oil. Roast until the tomatoes have dried slightly and some of the skins have burst, about 2 hours.

Meanwhile, if using the cheeses, in a small bowl, combine the mascarpone and Parmesan cheeses and stir with a rubber spatula until smooth. Cover and refrigerate until ready to serve.

Pass the roasted tomatoes through a tomato press or food mill. In a large, heavy pot, warm the remaining 2 Tbsp oil over medium heat. Add the onion and cook, stirring occasionally, until tender and translucent, 4–6 minutes. Add the puréed tomatoes, the broth, and bread. Bring to a simmer and cook for 5 minutes. Let cool slightly.

Working in batches, purée the soup in a food processor or blender. Return to the pot and season with salt and pepper. Serve, topped with a dollop of the cheese mixture, if using.

22

Although this recipe includes two components, the soup and the roasted salmon, it comes together quickly. Have the fish ready to slip into the hot oven just before the soup is ready. The pecorino romano cheese pairs well with zucchini, but a different Italian grating cheese, such as Parmesan, Asiago, or grana padano, can be substituted.

ZUCCHINI-PECORINO PURÉE WITH ROASTED SALMON

serves 4

4 Tbsp (2 fl oz/60 ml) olive oil

2 shallots, chopped

2 lb (1 kg) zucchini, chopped

Salt and freshly ground pepper

2 cups (16 fl oz/500 ml) vegetable or chicken broth

¼ cup (1 oz/30 g) grated pecorino romano cheese

Grated zest and juice of 1 lemon

1 lb (500 g) center-cut salmon, preferably wild, cut into 4 equal pieces, skin and pin bones removed

In a large, heavy pot, warm 2 Tbsp of the oil over medium-high heat. Add the shallots and cook, stirring occasionally, until soft, about 4 minutes. Add the zucchini, season with salt and pepper, and cook, stirring occasionally, until the zucchini begins to soften, about 4 minutes. Add the broth and bring to a boil. Reduce the heat to low and cook until the zucchini is tender, about 15 minutes. Let cool slightly.

Working in batches, purée the soup in a food processor or blender. Return to the pot and place over medium heat. Add the cheese and stir until it melts, about 4 minutes. Stir in the lemon juice and season with salt and pepper. Keep warm over low heat.

Preheat the oven to 400°F (200°C). Line a baking sheet with aluminum foil. Brush the salmon with the remaining 2 Tbsp olive oil and season with salt and pepper. Place on the prepared baking sheet and roast until opaque throughout, about 8 minutes.

Serve the soup, topped with a piece of salmon and a sprinkling of the lemon zest.

23

CHORIZO & CHICKEN STEW WITH AVOCADO CREMA

serves 4–6

1 skinless, boneless chicken breast half

½ lb (250 g) Mexican chorizo, cut into slices ½ inch (12 mm) thick

2 Tbsp olive oil

1 yellow onion, chopped

2 cloves garlic, minced

1 red bell pepper, seeded and chopped

4 cups (32 fl oz/1 l) chicken broth

1 Tbsp minced thyme

Salt and freshly ground pepper

FOR THE AVOCADO CREMA

1 avocado, pitted and peeled

¼ cup (2 oz/60 g) sour cream

1 Tbsp fresh lime juice

Salt

For the avocado crema, lime juice and sour cream are added to mashed avocados for a smooth, tangy version of guacamole. It melts into this soup, adding a creamy element and also helping to tame the spiciness of the chorizo.

In a small saucepan, combine the chicken breast with cold water to cover by 1 inch (2.5 cm) and bring to a boil over high heat. Reduce the heat to low and simmer until the chicken is cooked through, 15–18 minutes, skimming off any foam on the surface. Remove the chicken from the pan. When it is cool enough to handle, shred the meat.

Warm a large, heavy pot over medium-high heat. Add the chorizo and cook, stirring often, until browned on both sides, about 8 minutes. Transfer to a bowl. Add the oil and warm over medium-high heat. Add the onion and garlic and sauté until translucent, about 5 minutes. Add the bell pepper, stir to coat, and cook for 3 minutes. Add the shredded chicken, chorizo, broth, and thyme and simmer, uncovered, for about 15 minutes to blend the flavors. Season with salt and pepper.

To make the avocado crema, put the avocado in a small bowl and mash with a fork until creamy and smooth. Add the sour cream, the lime juice, and 2 large pinches of salt and stir to combine.

Serve the soup, accompanied with the avocado crema.

24

SHIITAKE DUMPLINGS IN KAFFIR LIME BROTH

serves 4

4 cups (32 fl oz/1 l) chicken broth

1 tsp peeled and minced fresh ginger

1 green onion, white and tender green parts, thinly sliced

5 kaffir lime leaves, torn in half

2 Tbsp soy sauce

2–3 drops Asian sesame oil

FOR THE SHIITAKE DUMPLINGS

2 oz (60 g) dried shiitake mushrooms

½ tsp peeled and minced fresh ginger

½ tsp soy sauce

¼ tsp toasted Asian sesame oil

1 Tbsp minced green onion, white and light green parts, plus sliced dark green tops

Freshly ground pepper

24 wonton wrappers

Kaffir lime leaves are a popular ingredient in Southeast Asian cooking. They are highly aromatic and can be found in well-stocked grocery stores near other fresh herbs. If you can't find them, substitute grated lime zest and a touch of fresh lime juice.

In a large saucepan, combine the broth, ginger, sliced green onion, kaffir lime leaves, and soy sauce and bring to a boil over medium-high heat. Reduce the heat to low and simmer for 10 minutes. Remove from the heat, add the drops of sesame oil to taste, cover, and let steep for 10 minutes. Strain the broth and return to the saucepan.

To make the dumplings, in a small bowl, combine the mushrooms with very hot water to cover. Soak for at least 30 minutes. Drain and finely chop. In a bowl, stir together the soaked mushrooms, ginger, soy sauce, sesame oil, and minced green onion. Season with a pinch of pepper. Place 1 tsp of the mushroom mixture in the middle of each wonton wrapper. Using your fingers, apply a small amount of water on all sides of the wrapper. Fold the wrapper diagonally, forcing out any air bubbles as you press to seal. Take the 2 points on the longest side of the triangle and fold so that the tips meet. Apply a small amount of water on the tips and press firmly to stick together.

Return the broth to a gentle simmer. Add the dumplings and cook until tender, about 3 minutes. Using a slotted spoon and ladle, transfer the dumplings and broth to bowls. Serve, garnished with the green onion tops.

25

EGGPLANT PARMESAN SOUP
serves 4–6

2 Tbsp olive oil

1 yellow onion, finely chopped

2 cloves garlic, finely chopped

Salt and freshly ground pepper

1 can (28 oz/875 g) crushed tomatoes

1 can (14½ oz/455 g) diced tomatoes with juices

2 cups (16 fl oz/500 ml) vegetable or chicken broth

2 Tbsp heavy cream

½ cup (½ oz/15 g) loosely packed basil leaves, chopped

1 cup (1½ oz/45 g) panko bread crumbs

¼ cup (1 oz/30 g) grated Parmesan cheese

2 eggs, beaten with 1 Tbsp water

1 eggplant, peeled and cut into ½-inch (12-mm) cubes

½ lb (250 g) fresh mini bocconcini, drained, at room temperature

In this imaginative deconstruction of eggplant parmigiana, mozzarella bocconcini, small balls of fresh mozzarella, and fried cubes of breaded eggplant are added to a rustic tomato soup laced with fresh basil. Look for the bocconcini packed in water in tubs. If you cannot find them, buy larger balls of fresh mozzarella and cut them into bite-sized pieces. Be sure to add the cheese and eggplant to the soup bowls just before serving so the eggplant remains crisp.

In a large, heavy pot, warm the oil over medium-high heat. Add the onion and cook, stirring occasionally, until soft, about 6 minutes. Add the garlic, season with salt and pepper, and cook, stirring occasionally, until soft, about 2 minutes. Stir in the crushed and chopped tomatoes with their juices and the broth and bring to a boil. Reduce the heat to low and simmer for 20 minutes. Stir in the cream and basil, and season with salt and pepper. Keep warm over low heat.

Meanwhile, preheat the oven to 375°F (190°C). Line a baking sheet with parchment paper. In a resealable plastic bag, combine the panko and Parmesan cheese, and season generously with salt and pepper. Put the egg mixture in a bowl, add the eggplant, and toss to coat. Remove the eggplant, letting the excess egg drip back into the bowl, and place the eggplant in the bag. Seal the bag and shake until all of the pieces are coated in panko. Spread the eggplant in a single layer on the prepared baking sheet. Roast until fork-tender and golden brown, 20–25 minutes.

Serve the soup, topped with several bocconcini and eggplant pieces.

26

ITALIAN BEEF STEW
serves 4

3 Tbsp olive oil

1 beef chuck steak (about 2 lb/1 kg), trimmed

2 Tbsp red wine vinegar

2 large sweet onions, halved lengthwise, then cut crosswise into slices ½ inch (12 mm) thick

2 red bell peppers, seeded and cut into ½-inch (12-mm) strips

2 green bell peppers, seeded and cut into ½-inch (12-mm) strips

2 cups (16 fl oz/500 ml) beef broth

½ lb (250 g) Romano beans, trimmed and cut into 2-inch (5-cm) pieces

½ lb (250 g) cremini mushrooms, thinly sliced

Salt and freshly ground pepper

Long cooking at a low temperature makes chuck steak wonderfully tender. Look for Italian (Romano) beans at farmers' markets, but if they evade you, regular green beans can easily substitute; just reduce the cooking time to about 15 minutes.

In a large, heavy pot, warm 1 Tbsp of the oil over medium-high heat. Add the steak and cook, turning once, until richly browned on both sides, 4–6 minutes. Transfer to a plate. Add the vinegar and bring to a simmer. Stir to scrape up any browned bits on the bottom of the pot. Pour the liquid over the steak.

In the same pot, warm the remaining 2 Tbsp oil over medium-high heat. Add the onions and bell peppers and sauté until well browned, about 10 minutes. Add 2–3 Tbsp water if necessary to keep the vegetables from sticking. Slowly stir in the broth, scraping up any browned bits on the bottom of the pot. Return the meat to the pot and bring to a simmer. Reduce the heat to medium-low, cover, and simmer gently until the meat is very tender, about 2½ hours.

Add the beans and mushrooms, cover, and simmer until just tender, 20–30 minutes. Transfer the meat to a cutting board and cut it into bite-sized pieces. Return the meat to the pot, raise the heat to medium, and simmer until heated through, 2–3 minutes. Season with salt and pepper and serve.

27

BOURRIDE

serves 6

1½ lb (750 g) heads, tails, backbones, and other trimmings from non-oily fish

2 carrots, peeled and quartered

1 yellow onion, quartered

1 fennel bulb, stalks and fronds removed, quartered and cored

3 cloves garlic

1 celery rib, quartered

4 flat-leaf parsley sprigs

3 thyme sprigs

1 bay leaf

2-inch (5-cm) piece dried orange peel

Salt

2 cups (16 fl oz/500 ml) dry white wine

2 lb (1 kg) monkfish or other firm white-fleshed fish fillets, cut into 1-inch (2.5-cm) cubes

6 slices day-old country-style bread, each about 1 inch (2.5 cm) thick

1 cup (3 fl oz/250 ml) Aioli (left), or purchased aioli

6 egg yolks

Chopped flat-leaf parsley for garnish (optional)

To make aioli, in a blender, combine 8 cloves garlic, 1 tsp coarse sea salt, and 6 large egg yolks and process until a paste forms. With the motor running, add 2 cups (16 fl oz/ 500 ml) extra-virgin olive oil in a slow, steady stream. Process until the mixture is thick and creamy. Store in an airtight container in the refrigerator for up to 5 days. Makes about 2 cups (16 fl oz/500 ml).

In a large, heavy pot, combine the fish bones and trimmings, carrots, onion, fennel, garlic, celery, parsley, thyme, bay leaf, and orange peel. Add 1 tsp salt and 8 cups (64 fl oz/2 l) water. Bring to a boil over medium-high heat, regularly skimming off any scum and froth on the surface. Reduce the heat to low and simmer for 15 minutes. Add the wine, raise the heat to high, and bring to a boil. Reduce the heat to low and simmer for 15 minutes. Using a slotted spoon, remove and discard the solids. Line a colander with several layers of cheesecloth and strain the broth into a large saucepan. You should have about 6 cups (48 fl oz/1.5 l).

Place the pan over medium heat and bring the broth to a simmer. Add the monkfish and cook just until opaque throughout, about 5 minutes. Using the slotted spoon, transfer to a platter and loosely cover with foil to keep warm.

Place a bread slice in the bottom of each bowl. Ladle just enough broth into each bowl for the bread to absorb. ⟫

In a large bowl, whisk together half of the aioli and the egg yolks until well blended. Whisk in the remaining broth, adding it in a slow, steady stream. Pour into a clean saucepan and place over very low heat. Cook, stirring gently and being very careful not to let the mixture boil, until thickened to the consistency of light cream, 6–7 minutes.

Divide the fish among the bowls, ladle the creamy broth over the top, and garnish with the chopped parsley, if using. Serve, passing the remaining aioli at the table.

28

ROASTED RED PEPPER & TOMATO SOUP

serves 4–6

1 Tbsp unsalted butter

1 Tbsp olive oil

½ yellow onion, chopped

2 cloves garlic, minced

2 red bell peppers, roasted, peeled, seeded, and chopped

1 can (28 oz/875 g) diced tomatoes

2 Tbsp heavy cream

Salt and freshly ground pepper

How can you resist serving this classic soup with an old-fashioned grilled cheese sandwich? Use smoked Cheddar on a sliced baguette to make several mini sandwiches. To save time, use store-bought roasted peppers.

In a large, heavy pot, melt the butter with the oil over medium-high heat. Add the onion and garlic and cook until translucent, about 5 minutes. Add the peppers, stir to coat, and cook for 3 minutes. Add the tomatoes with their juices, bring to a boil, reduce the heat to low, and simmer, uncovered, for 20 minutes to blend the flavors. Remove from the heat and let cool slightly.

Working in batches, purée the soup in a blender. Return to the pot, stir in the cream, and bring the soup just to a boil. Remove from the heat, season with salt and pepper, and serve.

29

Two garnishes—crispy pancetta and toasted bread crumbs tossed with parsley and lemon zest—transform this easy cauliflower soup into a special-occasion dish. To make this soup vegetarian, use the suggested vegetable stock and omit the pancetta. It will still be delicious.

CREAMY CAULIFLOWER SOUP WITH CRISPY PANCETTA

serves 6

FOR THE GREMOLATA

1 cup (2 oz/60 g) fresh bread crumbs

4 Tbsp (2 fl oz/60 ml) olive oil

3 Tbsp chopped flat-leaf parsley

1½ tsp grated lemon zest

Salt and freshly ground pepper

6 oz (185 g) pancetta, diced

1 yellow onion, diced

4 shallots, sliced

3 celery ribs, diced

1 head cauliflower (about 2½ lb/1.25 kg), trimmed and cut into florets

Salt and freshly ground pepper

5 cups (40 fl oz/1.25 l) chicken or vegetable broth, plus more as needed

1 Tbsp fresh lemon juice

¾ cup (6 fl oz/180 ml) heavy cream (optional)

Preheat the oven to 350°F (180°C).

To make the gremolata, in a bowl, toss together the bread crumbs and 2 Tbsp of the oil. Transfer to a rimmed baking sheet. Bake, stirring occasionally, until the bread crumbs are golden brown and crisp, 15–20 minutes. Let cool to room temperature. In a bowl, toss together the toasted bread crumbs, parsley, and lemon zest, and season with salt and pepper. Set aside.

In a nonstick frying pan, cook the pancetta over medium heat, stirring occasionally, until crispy and the fat is rendered, 8–10 minutes. Using a slotted spoon, transfer to a paper towel–lined plate. Set aside.

In a large, heavy pot, warm the remaining 2 Tbsp oil over medium heat. Add the onion, shallots, and celery and cook, stirring occasionally, until softened, 8–10 minutes. Add the cauliflower and cook, stirring occasionally, for 1–2 minutes. Season with salt and pepper. Add the broth, raise the heat to medium-high, and bring to a boil. Reduce the heat to medium-low, cover, and simmer until the cauliflower is tender, about 30 minutes. Let cool slightly. ⟫

Working in batches, purée the soup in a food processor or blender. Return to the pot and add more broth if needed to reach the desired consistency. Taste and adjust the seasoning. Stir in the lemon juice and cream, if using. Serve the soup, garnished with the crispy pancetta and gremolata.

30

There is nothing more seasonally satisfying than pumpkin in the fall. You can also swap in butternut squash or sweet potatoes for this soup. Serve with a Waldorf salad of walnuts, raisins, and chopped apples.

ROASTED PUMPKIN SOUP WITH CHINESE FIVE-SPICE

serves 4–6

1 small Sugar Pie pumpkin (about 3 lb/1.5 kg total weight), peeled, seeded, and diced

3 Tbsp olive oil

Salt and freshly ground pepper

2 Tbsp unsalted butter

1 small yellow onion, chopped

2 cloves garlic, minced

½ tsp Chinese five-spice powder

4½ cups (36 fl oz/1.1 l) vegetable broth

Preheat the oven to 400°F (200°C). Line a baking sheet with parchment paper. In a bowl, toss the pumpkin with the oil and season with salt and pepper. Arrange in a single layer on the prepared pan and roast until tender, about 25 minutes.

In a large, heavy pot, melt the butter over medium-high heat. Add the onion and garlic and sauté until translucent, about 5 minutes. Add the five-spice powder, stir to combine, and cook for 1 minute. Add the pumpkin and broth and bring to a boil. Reduce the heat and simmer for about 15 minutes to blend the flavors. Remove from the heat and let cool slightly.

Working in batches, purée the soup in a blender. Return to the pot, season with salt and pepper, and serve.

Hearty roots and winter squash bring warm colors to the autumn kitchen. Seasonal vegetables, from turnips and parsnips to pumpkins and sweet potatoes, are ideal for turning into savory and smooth purées laced with spicy ginger and pungent curry. Fall nuts, seeds, herbs, and cured meats are wonderful additions to the soup pot, subtly adding flavor to autumn's earthy compositions.

october

1

CARROT-GINGER SOUP

serves 4

2 Tbsp unsalted butter

1 large sweet onion such as Vidalia or Walla Walla, finely chopped

2 cloves garlic, minced

1 lb (500 g) carrots, cut into slices ¼ inch (6 mm) thick

Salt and freshly ground pepper

6 cups (1,5 l) chicken broth

1½ tsp peeled and grated fresh ginger

½ tsp freshly grated orange zest

Minced chives for garnish

Fresh carrots are puréed with sweet onions, garlic, and chicken broth for this bright orange soup, made even more vibrant-tasting with the addition of orange zest. Ginger adds a bit of spice to the finished soup, which has a pleasing spoon-coating consistency.

In a large, heavy pot, warm the butter over medium-low heat. When the butter has melted and the foam begins to subside, add the onion and sauté until it softens and is just translucent, 8–10 minutes. Add the garlic and sauté until fragrant, about 30 seconds. Add the carrots and salt to taste and stir to coat the carrots well with the butter.

Add 2 cups (16 fl oz/500 ml) of the broth, increase the heat to high, and bring to a boil. Reduce the heat to a simmer, cover, and cook until the carrots are tender when pierced with the tip of a knife, about 20 minutes. Uncover, remove from the heat, and let cool slightly.

Working in batches, purée the soup in a blender. Return to the pot and warm over medium-low heat, gradually whisking in the remaining 4 cups broth. Stir in the ginger and orange zest. Reheat gently, stirring occasionally, until the soup is hot, about 10 minutes. Season with salt and pepper and serve, garnished with the chives.

2

CHEDDAR & HARD CIDER SOUP WITH FRIED SHALLOTS

serves 6–8

4 Tbsp (2 oz/60 g) unsalted butter

2 yellow onions, chopped

1 celery rib, chopped

1 Yukon Gold potato, peeled and chopped

2 cloves garlic, minced

2 Tbsp all-purpose flour

2½ cups (20 fl oz/625 ml) chicken broth

2½ cups (20 fl oz/625 ml) hard apple cider

1 cup (8 fl oz/250 ml) half-and-half

2 bay leaves

2 thyme sprigs

2 Tbsp applejack or Calvados brandy

¾ lb (375 g) English Cheddar cheese, shredded

Salt and freshly ground pepper

Fried shallots (page 167)

Apples and Cheddar, a classic tart and sharp pairing—does it get any better? In fact it can, when thinly slivered shallot rings take a dive into hot oil for a crispy, crunchy, oniony topping. Serve a lightly dressed salad on the side, and ready yourself for compliments from your dinner companions.

In a large, heavy pot, melt 3 Tbsp of the butter over medium-high heat. Add the onions, celery, potato, and garlic and stir. Reduce the heat to low, cover, and cook, stirring occasionally, until the vegetables are softened, about 12 minutes. Sprinkle the flour over the vegetables and cook, stirring constantly, until the flour is incorporated. While stirring constantly, gradually add the broth, cider, and half-and-half. Raise the heat to medium-high, add the bay leaves and thyme sprigs, and bring to a boil. Reduce the heat to low and simmer to blend the flavors, about 10 minutes.

Remove the bay leaves and thyme sprigs from the soup and discard. Remove the soup from the heat and let cool slightly.

Working in batches, purée the soup in a blender. Pour into a clean pot. Stir in the applejack. Off the heat, while whisking constantly, gradually add the cheese one handful at a time. Continue whisking until all the cheese is melted. Place over medium-low heat, stir in 1 tsp salt and pepper to taste, and cook gently, stirring often, until heated through, about 10 minutes.

Taste and adjust the seasoning. Serve, garnished with the fried shallots.

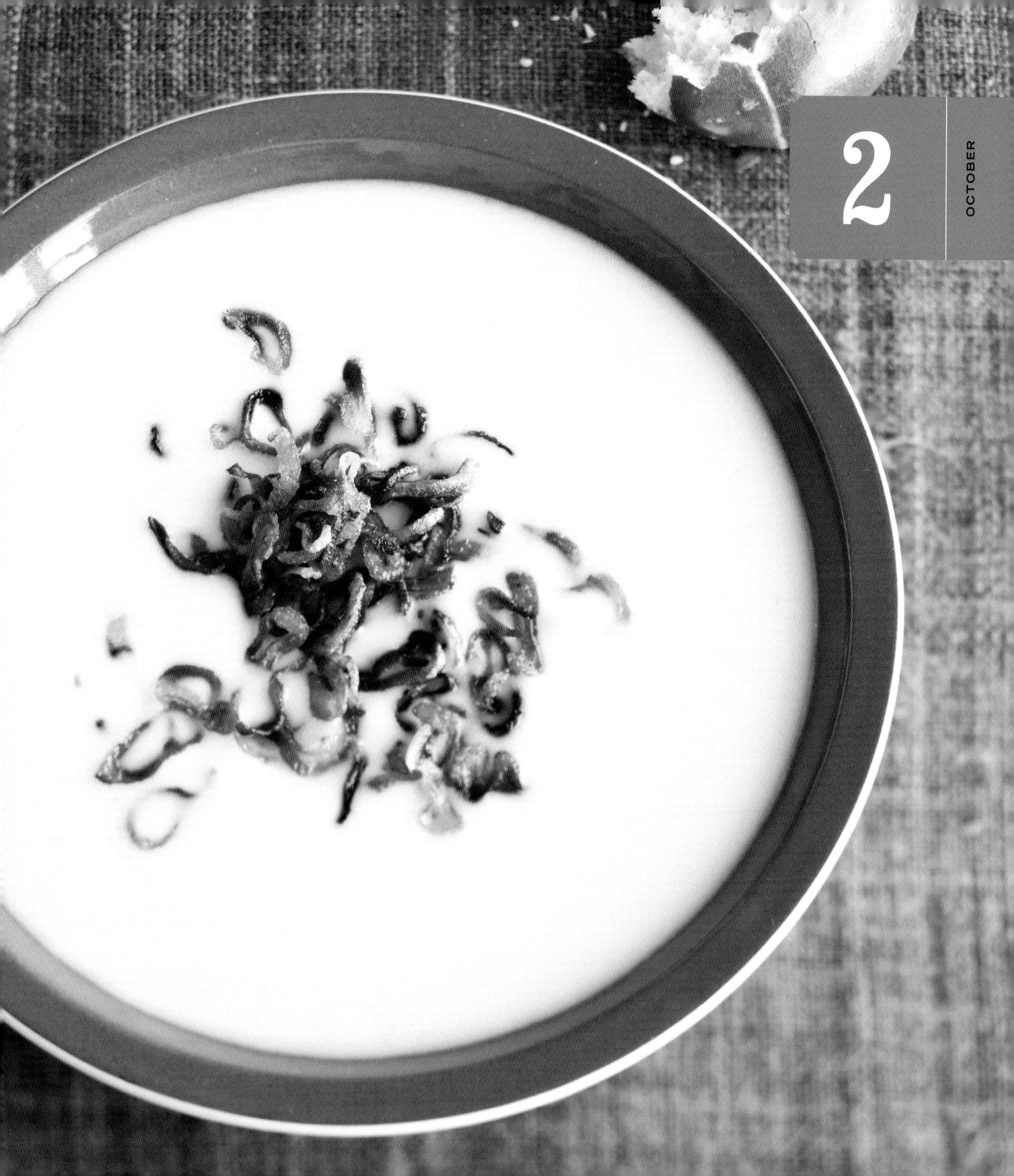
2
OCTOBER

3

This fragrant, savory soup makes excellent cool-weather fare and is the perfect start to any holiday meal. It is also just as tasty when served chilled. Reserve 4–6 thin slices of the tender green portion of the leeks for garnish, if desired.

CURRIED LEEK & APPLE SOUP

serves 6

1 Tbsp unsalted butter

3 large crisp apples, such as Golden Delicious, pippin, or Granny Smith, peeled, cored, and cut into ½-inch (12-mm) dice

2 celery ribs, thinly sliced

2 tsp Madras curry powder

4 large leeks, white part and 2 inches (5 cm) of the green, halved lengthwise and sliced crosswise

4 cups (32 fl oz/1 l) vegetable broth

1 small russet potato, peeled and cut into ½-inch (12-mm) dice

½ cup (4 fl oz/125 ml) milk

Salt and freshly ground pepper

In a large, heavy pot, melt the butter over medium-low heat. Add the apples, celery, curry powder, and leeks and stir well. Cook, stirring occasionally, until the leeks soften, about 5 minutes. Cover the pan and cook for 5 minutes, stirring once. Add the broth and potato and bring to a boil over medium-high heat. Reduce the heat to low, cover, and simmer until the apples and potato are tender when pierced with the tip of a knife, about 20 minutes. Remove from the heat and let cool slightly.

Working in batches, purée the soup in a blender or food processor until smooth. Return to the pot and stir in the milk. Season with salt and pepper. Rewarm over low heat without letting it come to a boil. Serve.

4

Veal is a popular meat in Italy, where it is frequently paired with sweet peppers and onions, as it is here. This stew, which has a thick, rich sauce, can be served Italian style with creamy polenta or pasta, such as tagliatelle or pappardelle, but it is also excellent with buttered boiled potatoes sprinkled with parsley.

VEAL & RED PEPPER STEW

serves 4

1½ lb (750 g) veal stew meat

Salt and freshly ground pepper

1 tsp chopped thyme

1 Tbsp unsalted butter

1 Tbsp olive oil

½ yellow onion, minced

1 clove garlic, minced

2 large red bell peppers, seeded and cut into 1-inch (2.5-cm) pieces

1 can (28 oz/875) whole San Marzano plum tomatoes, coarsely chopped, with juices

Season the veal with 1 tsp salt, ¼ tsp pepper, and the thyme. In a large, heavy pot, melt the butter with the oil over medium-high heat. Add the onion and garlic and cook, stirring occasionally, until the onion is translucent, about 2 minutes. Working in batches if necessary, add the veal and sear on all sides, turning as needed, until golden, about 7 minutes per batch. Using a slotted spoon, transfer the meat to a bowl.

Add the bell peppers to the pot and cook, stirring occasionally, just until slightly limp, about 2 minutes. Transfer to the bowl with the meat.

Add about ½ cup (3 oz/90 g) of the tomatoes with their juices to the pot, stirring to scrape up the browned bits from the bottom of the pot. Add the remaining tomatoes with their juices, the veal, bell peppers, and the accumulated juices and bring to a simmer. Reduce the heat to medium-low, cover, and simmer until the meat is tender, about 1 hour. Taste and adjust the seasoning and serve.

5

To use the seeds from the pumpkin for the pesto (or just for snacking), rinse them under cold water to remove any flesh or strings, then dry them well on a clean kitchen towel. Transfer them to a parchment paper–lined baking sheet, toss with 2 tablespoons olive oil, season generously with salt, and roast in a 250°F (120°C) oven, stirring a few times, until golden brown, about 1 hour. Let cool, then store in an airtight container until using.

ROASTED PUMPKIN & PEAR SOUP WITH PUMPKIN SEED PESTO

serves 4–6

1 Sugar Pie pumpkin or butternut squash (about 2¾ lb/1.35 kg), peeled, seeded, and cut into 2-inch (5-cm) pieces

5 Tbsp (3 fl oz/80 ml) olive oil

Salt and freshly ground pepper

1 yellow onion, chopped

1 large clove garlic, chopped

1 very ripe Bartlett pear, peeled, cored, and chopped

4½ cups (36 fl oz/1.1 l) chicken broth

FOR THE PUMPKIN SEED PESTO

1 clove garlic

¼ cup (1 oz/30 g) roasted and lightly salted pumpkin seeds

¼ cup (1 oz/30 g) grated pecorino romano cheese

2 cups (2 oz/60 g) flat-leaf parsley leaves

½ cup (½ oz/15 g) mint leaves

½ cup (4 fl oz/125 ml) extra-virgin olive oil

Preheat the oven to 400°F (200°C). Line a baking sheet with parchment paper. Pile the pumpkin on the prepared baking sheet and toss with 3 Tbsp of the oil. Spread in a single layer and season with salt and pepper. Roast, stirring once or twice, until very soft, 35–45 minutes. Set aside.

In a large, heavy pot, warm the remaining 2 Tbsp oil over medium-high heat. Add the onion and cook, stirring occasionally, until soft, about 6 minutes. Add the garlic, season with salt and pepper, and cook, stirring occasionally, until soft, about 2 minutes. Add the pear, broth, and pumpkin and bring to a boil. Reduce the heat to low and simmer for 15 minutes. Let cool slightly.

Working in batches, purée the soup in a food processor or blender. Return to the pot, season with salt and pepper, and keep warm over low heat. ⤳

To make the pumpkin seed pesto, in a food processor or blender, combine the garlic, pumpkin seeds, cheese, parsley, and mint and pulse until finely chopped. With the motor running, slowly add the oil and process until combined.

Serve the soup, topped with a dollop of the pesto.

6

Turnips can be a hard sell to non-vegetable-lovers, but whirled with apples and potatoes, their bold flavor is sweetened and mellowed. The important thing to remember is that the smaller and younger the turnip, the more mild and tender it is.

TURNIP, APPLE & POTATO SOUP

serves 4

2 Tbsp unsalted butter

1 small yellow onion, finely diced

1 tsp chopped thyme

1 bay leaf

Salt and ground white pepper

1 lb (500 g) turnips, peeled and cut into ½-inch (12-mm) chunks

2 tart apples, such as Braeburn, Granny Smith, Jonagold, or pippin, peeled, cored, and quartered

½ lb (250 g) Yukon Gold potatoes, peeled and quartered

2 Tbsp crème fraîche or sour cream

2 Tbsp chopped flat-leaf parsley

In a large, heavy pot, melt the butter over medium-low heat. Add the onion, thyme, bay leaf, and a pinch of salt and sauté until the onion is tender, 10–12 minutes. Add the turnips, apples, potatoes, a pinch of salt, and 1 cup (8 fl oz/250 ml) water. Cover and simmer until the vegetables and apples are tender, 10–15 minutes. Add another 4 cups (32 fl oz/1 l) water, raise the heat to high, and bring to a boil. Reduce the heat to low and simmer, uncovered, for 20 minutes. Remove from the heat, remove the bay leaf, and let cool slightly.

Working in batches, purée the soup in a blender. Return to the pot and reheat. Thin the soup with water, if necessary, and season with salt and pepper. Serve, garnished with the crème fraîche and parsley.

OCTOBER

7

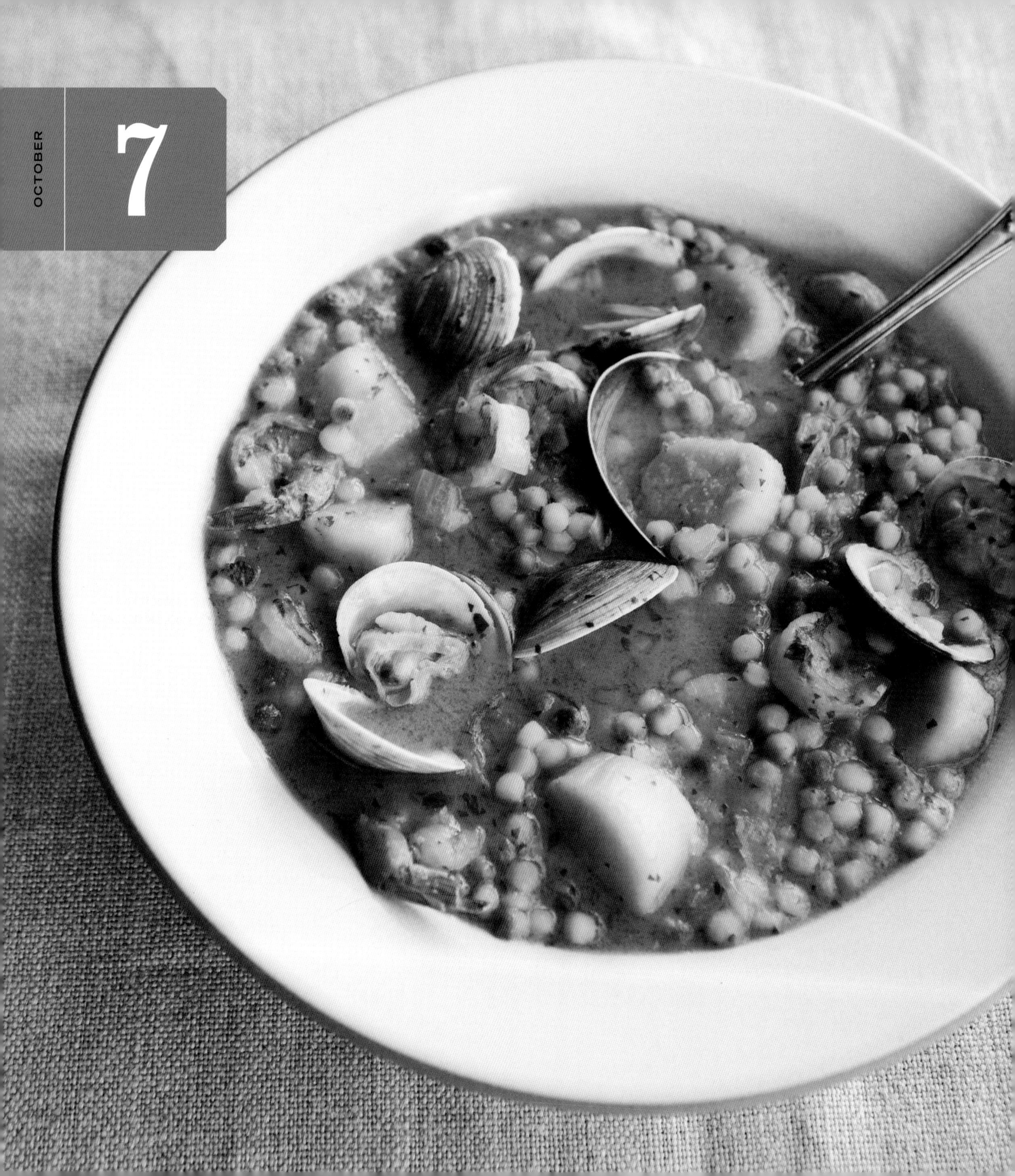

SAFFRON FREGOLA WITH SEAFOOD

serves 4

1 tsp saffron threads

¼ cup (2 fl oz/60 ml) dry white wine

2 Tbsp olive oil

½ lb (250 g) medium shrimp, shelled and deveined

½ lb (250 g) medium scallops, tough muscles removed

1 small yellow onion, chopped

2 cloves garlic, minced

2 cups (16 fl oz/500 ml) chicken broth

1 cup (6 oz/185 g) fregola (Sardinian couscous) or Israeli couscous

Salt and freshly ground pepper

½ lb (250 g) clams, scrubbed

2 Tbsp minced flat-leaf parsley

A bit of culinary exotica, fregola is a type of pasta from the Italian island of Sardinia. The more common Israeli couscous may be substituted. Serve this hearty stew with a refreshing butter lettuce and pear salad and plenty of crusty bread for dipping.

Crush the saffron in a bowl and add the white wine. Set aside.

In a large, heavy pot, warm 1 Tbsp of the oil over high heat. When the pan is very hot, add the shrimp and sear for 1 minute on each side (do not cook all the way through). Transfer to a bowl. Add the scallops and sear for 1 minute on each side, also without cooking all the way through. Transfer to the bowl with the shrimp.

Add the remaining 1 Tbsp oil, onion, and garlic to the same pot and sauté until soft, about 5 minutes. Add the saffron mixture and cook for 2 minutes. Add the broth and bring to a boil. Add the fregola, stir to combine, and reduce the heat to medium-low. Cook for 12 minutes. Season with salt and pepper.

Add the clams, discarding any that do not close to the touch. Cover the saucepan tightly and steam for 3 minutes. Remove the lid and quickly add the shrimp and scallops. Tightly cover the saucepan again and continue to cook just until the clams open and the shrimp and scallops are cooked through, about 3 minutes. Discard any unopened clams. Serve, sprinkled with the parsley.

ROASTED CAULIFLOWER & PARMESAN SOUP

serves 4–6

1 head cauliflower (about 2 lb/1 kg), stemmed and cut into florets

2 Tbsp olive oil

Salt and freshly ground pepper

2 Tbsp unsalted butter

1 yellow onion, chopped

3 cloves garlic, minced

3 cups (24 fl oz/750 ml) chicken broth, plus more as needed

½ cup (2 oz/60 g) grated Parmesan cheese

This soup might be your answer to getting more vegetables on the family table. Roasted cauliflower turns sweet, and Parmesan adds a salty-nutty complement. Use a good-quality Parmesan and serve with garlic bread and a green salad.

Preheat the oven to 400°F (200°C) and line a rimmed baking sheet with parchment paper. Toss the cauliflower with the oil and season with salt and pepper. Spread on the prepared baking sheet and roast in the oven until very tender, 30–35 minutes.

In a large, heavy pot, melt the butter over medium-high heat. Add the onion and garlic and sauté until translucent, about 5 minutes. Add the cauliflower and 3 cups (24 fl oz/ 750 ml) broth and bring to a boil. Reduce the heat to low and simmer for 15 minutes to blend the flavors. Remove from the heat and let cool slightly.

Working in batches, purée the soup in a blender or food processor. Return to the pot over low heat. If needed, add more broth, ¼ cup (2 fl oz/60 ml) at a time, until you achieve the desired consistency. Add the Parmesan and stir until melted. Season to taste with salt and pepper and serve.

9

Autumn brings the alluring sight of market stands featuring baskets piled high with winter squash. In this recipe, butternut, Hubbard, turban, or buttercup squash can be substituted for the acorn squash, as can pumpkin. A pretty round of compound butter melts over the top of the soup, spreading rich walnut flavor.

ACORN SQUASH SOUP WITH TOASTED WALNUT BUTTER

serves 6

4 acorn squash, about 1 lb (500 g) each

1 Tbsp unsalted butter, at room temperature

2 slices bacon, finely chopped

1 large yellow onion, chopped

6 cups (48 fl oz/1.5 l) chicken broth

FOR THE TOASTED WALNUT BUTTER

¼ cup (1 oz/30 g) walnut halves

2 tsp walnut oil

Large pinch of sugar

Salt and freshly ground pepper

2 Tbsp unsalted butter, at room temperature

¼ cup (2 fl oz/60 ml) heavy cream

Large pinch of grated nutmeg

¼ cup (2 fl oz/60 ml) fresh orange juice

Preheat the oven to 375°F (190°C). Lightly oil a baking sheet.

Cut each squash in half through the stem end and place, cut sides down, on the prepared baking sheet. Bake until easily pierced with a knife, about 45 minutes. Remove from the oven and set aside until cool enough to handle, then scoop out the seeds and discard. Spoon the flesh into a bowl and set aside. Leave the oven set at 375°F (190°C).

In a large, heavy pot, melt the butter over medium heat. Add the bacon and onion and sauté until the onion is soft, about 10 minutes. Raise the heat to high, add the squash and broth, and bring to a gentle boil. Reduce the heat to medium and simmer, uncovered, until the squash is very soft, about 30 minutes.

Meanwhile, make the walnut butter. In a small bowl, toss together the walnuts, walnut oil, sugar, and salt and pepper to taste and spread out on a baking sheet. Toast until golden, 5–7 minutes. Remove from the oven, let cool, and chop finely. In a small bowl, using a fork, mash together the walnuts and butter. Season with salt and pepper. Spoon out the butter onto a piece of plastic wrap and, using the plastic wrap, shape into a log about 1 inch (2.5 cm) in diameter. Wrap and refrigerate until serving. ⟶

Remove the soup from the heat and let cool slightly. Working in batches, purée in a blender until smooth. Return to a clean saucepan over medium-low heat. Add the cream, nutmeg, orange juice, and salt and pepper to taste. Serve warm, garnished with slices of the walnut butter.

10

Crispy lardons, small pieces of smoked or unsmoked cured pork belly, are an essential ingredient in every French kitchen, where they are used to garnish salads and soups and to flavor stews and other dishes. In French markets, they come ready-cut and packaged, but you can easily make your own version with bacon. Lardons add welcome flavor and texture to simple soups with just a few ingredients, like this one.

PROVENÇAL CHARD SOUP WITH LARDONS

serves 4

4 slices thick-cut bacon, cut into ½-inch (12-mm) pieces

3 Tbsp olive oil

1 small yellow onion, minced

1 tsp chopped garlic

2 carrots, peeled and cut into ¼-inch (6-mm) rounds

10 medium or 5 large chard leaves, minced, including ribs

2 large red potatoes, peeled if desired and cut into ½-inch (12-mm) cubes

3 cups (24 fl oz/750 ml) chicken broth

Salt and freshly ground pepper

In a frying pan, fry the bacon over medium heat, stirring occasionally, until crispy, about 10 minutes. Transfer to a paper towel–lined plate and set aside.

In a large, heavy pot, warm the oil over medium heat. Add the onion, garlic, and carrots and cook, stirring occasionally, until the onion is translucent, about 2 minutes. Add the chard, potatoes, broth, 3 cups (24 fl oz/750 ml) water, ½ tsp salt, and ¼ tsp pepper and bring to a boil. Reduce the heat to medium-low, cover partially, and simmer until the potatoes are very soft, almost dissolving, about 45 minutes. Taste and adjust the seasoning. Serve, garnished with the crispy bacon lardons.

11

ROASTED VEGETABLE STEW WITH COUSCOUS

serves 6

This is a vegetarian feast to tempt carnivores, with hearty roasted veggies and chickpeas simmered into a stew thick enough to serve over a bed of couscous. Purplish-black Kalamata olives impart full, briny flavor and a meaty texture.

8 carrots, peeled

1 eggplant, peeled

4 yellow crookneck squash

2 leeks, white and pale green parts, finely chopped

½ lb (250 g) small Brussels sprouts, halved

3 Tbsp olive oil

4 cups (32 fl oz/1 l) chicken or vegetable broth

1 tsp finely chopped thyme leaves

Salt and freshly ground pepper

6 cloves garlic, minced

1 tomato, peeled and diced

1 can (15 oz/470 g) chickpeas, drained

1 cup (5 oz/155 g) Kalamata olives, pitted and chopped

6 Tbsp finely chopped mixed herbs such as flat-leaf parsley, chives, and basil

¼ cup (1 oz/30 g) grated Parmesan cheese

1¼ cups (10 oz/315g) cooked couscous

Preheat the oven to 400°F (200°C).

Cut the carrots, eggplant, and squash into 1½-inch (4-cm) chunks. In a large roasting pan, combine with the leeks and Brussels sprouts. Pour in the oil and 1 cup (8 fl oz/250 ml) of the broth. Add the thyme and salt and pepper to taste and mix to coat the vegetables evenly.

Roast, stirring occasionally, for 30 minutes. Add another 1 cup (8 fl oz/250 ml) broth, the garlic, and tomato to the pan and continue roasting, stirring every 15 minutes, until the vegetables are very tender, about 30 minutes.

Add the remaining 2 cups (16 fl oz/500 ml) broth, the chickpeas, olives, and herbs to the pan and stir to combine. Taste and adjust the seasoning, and return to the oven for 5 minutes.

Spoon the vegetables into a large serving bowl and garnish with the Parmesan. Spoon the couscous into bowls, ladle the stew on top, and serve.

12

CAULIFLOWER SOUP WITH CHEDDAR & BLUE CHEESE

serves 4–6

Cauliflower has a mild flavor that marries nicely with cheese. Sharp Cheddar is stirred directly into this vegetable purée, and a few crumbles of potent blue cheese on top make the perfect cheese-lover's garnish.

2 Tbsp olive oil

1 yellow onion, sliced

3 cloves garlic, minced

½ tsp caraway seeds

2 lb (1 kg) cauliflower, stemmed and cut into florets

4 cups (32 fl oz/1 l) vegetable broth

1 cup (4 oz/125 g) shredded sharp Cheddar cheese

Salt and ground white pepper

¼ cup (1 oz/30 g) crumbled blue cheese

1 Tbsp finely chopped flat-leaf parsley

In a large, heavy pot, warm the oil over medium-high heat. Add the onion and sauté until softened, about 5 minutes. Add the garlic and caraway seeds and sauté for 1 minute.

Add the cauliflower and broth and bring to a simmer. Reduce the heat to medium and cook until the cauliflower is softened, 20–25 minutes. Remove from the heat and let cool slightly.

Working in batches, purée the soup in a blender or food processor until smooth. Return to the pot. Whisk in the Cheddar until completely incorporated. Season with salt and pepper.

Return the soup to medium heat and cook until heated through, about 2 minutes. Serve, sprinkled with the blue cheese and parsley.

13

Do yourself a favor and make a double recipe of these homemade meatballs and cook and freeze the extra batch for up to a couple of months. You are then halfway to a great soup supper on a busy weeknight. A different meat—chicken, beef, pork, lamb—can be used in place of the turkey, and Swiss chard or kale can be substituted for the mustard greens.

CHICKPEA & TURKEY MEATBALL SOUP WITH MUSTARD GREENS

serves 4–6

FOR THE TURKEY MEATBALLS

¾ lb (375 g) ground turkey

1 clove garlic, minced

3 Tbsp panko bread crumbs

2 Tbsp grated Parmesan cheese

1 egg, lightly beaten

1 Tbsp tomato paste

2 Tbsp chopped oregano

Salt and freshly ground pepper

2 Tbsp olive oil

1 small yellow onion, chopped

2 cloves garlic, chopped

2 Tbsp tomato paste

2 cans (15 oz/470 g each) chickpeas, drained

Salt and freshly ground pepper

4 cups (32 fl oz/1 l) chicken broth

1 bunch mustard greens, thick stems and ribs removed, leaves cut into 2-inch (5-cm) pieces

Preheat the oven to 375°F (190°C). Line a baking sheet with aluminum foil and spray with nonstick cooking spray.

To make the meatballs, in a bowl, combine the ground turkey, garlic, panko, cheese, egg, tomato paste, and oregano. Season with salt and pepper and stir just until combined. Using a heaping teaspoon of the mixture, form each mini meatball and place about ½ inch (12 mm) apart on the prepared baking sheet. Roast until the meatballs are cooked through, 15–18 minutes. Set aside.

In a large, heavy pot, warm the oil over medium-high heat. Add the onion and cook, stirring occasionally, until soft, about 6 minutes. Add the garlic and cook, stirring occasionally, until soft, about 2 minutes. Stir in the tomato paste and chickpeas, and season with salt and pepper. Add the broth and bring to a boil. Reduce the heat to low and simmer for 15 minutes. Let cool slightly.

→→

Purée half of the soup in a food processor or blender. Return to the pot and stir to combine. Season with salt and pepper. Place over medium-low heat and add the meatballs and the mustard greens. Cook until the meatballs are warmed through and the mustard greens wilt, about 4 minutes, then serve.

14

Cinnamon and nutmeg add an intriguing dimension to this soup, but parsnips are so sweet and flavorful that they could pull it off all on their own. For a fresh garnish, top with chopped parsley. This soup freezes well.

CREAM OF PARSNIP SOUP

serves 4–6

2 Tbsp unsalted butter

1 Tbsp olive oil

1 small yellow onion, chopped

2 celery ribs, chopped

2 cloves garlic, minced

½ tsp grated nutmeg

Pinch of ground cinnamon

6 parsnips (about 2½ lb/1.25 kg total), peeled and diced

6 cups (48 fl oz/1.5 l) chicken broth

½ cup (4 fl oz/125 ml) heavy cream

Salt and ground white pepper

In a large, heavy pot, melt the butter with the oil over medium-high heat. Add the onion, celery, and garlic and sauté until the vegetables are very soft, about 7 minutes. Add the nutmeg and cinnamon, stir to combine, and cook for 1 minute. Add the parsnips and the broth and bring to a boil. Reduce the heat to low and simmer until the parsnips are very soft, 45–55 minutes. Remove from the heat and let cool slightly.

Working in batches, purée the soup in a blender. Return to the pot, stir in the cream, and bring to a boil. Turn off the heat. Season to taste with salt and pepper and serve.

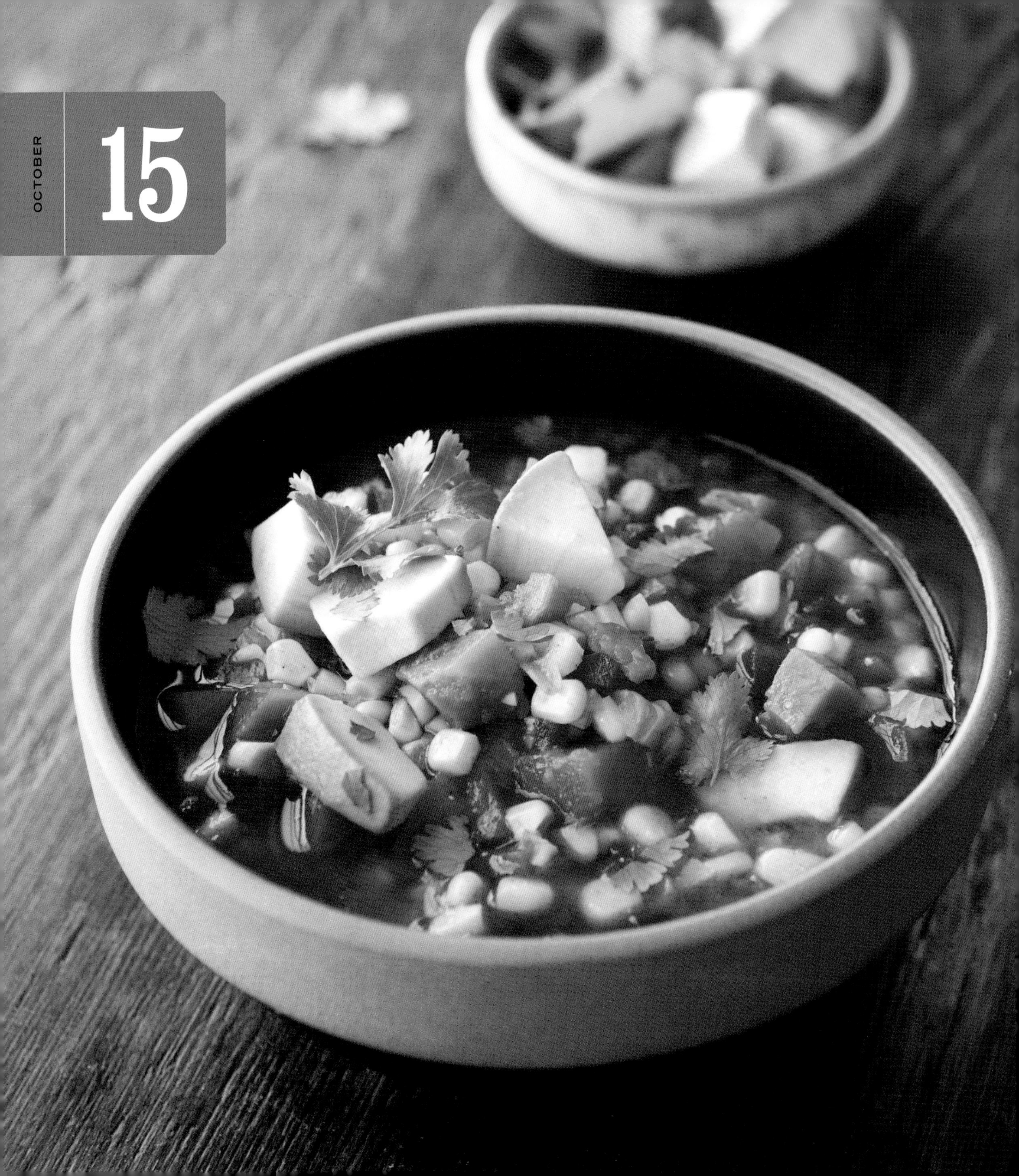

OCTOBER

15

15

SWEET POTATO–CORN CHOWDER WITH AVOCADO

serves 6

2 Tbsp olive oil

1 small white onion, finely diced

2 cloves garlic, minced

2 tsp ground cumin

½ tsp ground coriander

Salt and freshly ground pepper

2 sweet potatoes (about 1½ lb/750 g total), peeled and diced

3 cups (24 fl oz/750 ml) vegetable or chicken broth

1 red bell pepper, seeded and finely diced

8 ears fresh corn, husks and silk removed and kernels cut from cobs, or 3½ cups (1 lb/500 g) thawed frozen corn kernels

2 Tbsp minced cilantro

1 ripe avocado, pitted, peeled, and diced

½ cup (4 oz/125 g) sour cream (optional)

Southwestern ingredients mingle in this surprisingly light chowder. It gets its creamy consistency not from dairy but by puréeing half of the soup. Serve with fresh tortilla chips and salsa.

In a large, heavy pot, warm the oil over medium-high heat. Add the onion and garlic and sauté until translucent, about 5 minutes. Add the cumin, coriander, and salt and pepper to taste and cook for 1 minute. Add the sweet potatoes, stir to coat, and cook for 3 minutes.

Add the broth, bring to a boil, and reduce the heat to low. Simmer until the sweet potatoes are tender, about 20 minutes. Add the red pepper and corn and cook until the vegetables are tender, 10 minutes. Remove from the heat and let cool slightly.

Purée half of the soup in a blender. Return to the pot. Stir in the cilantro and season with salt and pepper. Serve, garnished with the avocado and the sour cream, if desired.

16

ROASTED PUMPKIN SOUP WITH CIDER CREAM

serves 6–7

2 baking pumpkins or kabocha squash (about 2 lb/1 kg each), quartered and seeded

1½ Tbsp olive oil, plus more for drizzling

Salt and freshly ground pepper

¼ cup (2 fl oz/60 ml) apple cider

2 carrots, peeled and thickly sliced

3 shallots, thickly sliced

1 celery rib, thickly sliced

2 cloves garlic, minced

¼ tsp ground nutmeg

½ Tbsp minced sage

6 cups (48 fl oz/1.5 l) chicken broth

½ cup (4 fl oz/125 ml) heavy cream

When shopping for pumpkins for this recipe, pass up field pumpkins, which are too fibrous for cooking (but are ideal for jack-o'-lanterns). Use a small, sweet pumpkin variety with a thick flesh and a fairly small seed cavity, such as the Sugar Pie, Baby Bear, or Cheese pumpkin. Kabocha squash, which has pale orange flesh and bright green skin marked with pale green stripes, can also be used here.

Place 1 rack in the upper third of the oven and 1 rack in the lower third and preheat to 425°F (220°C).

Divide the pumpkins among 2 baking sheets. Drizzle with oil and season with salt and pepper. Place, cut side down, on the baking sheets. Roast, turning the pumpkins occasionally and rotating the baking sheets halfway through cooking, until the pumpkins are tender and beginning to brown, about 45 minutes. Let cool, then scoop the flesh into a bowl.

Meanwhile, in a small saucepan, simmer the apple cider over medium-high heat until reduced to about 2 Tbsp. Let cool.

In a large, heavy pot, warm the 1½ Tbsp oil over medium-high heat. Add the carrots, shallots, and celery, and season with salt and pepper. Cover and cook, stirring occasionally, until the vegetables begin to soften, about 6 minutes. Add the garlic, nutmeg, and sage and cook, stirring frequently, for 1 minute. Add the pumpkin flesh and broth, cover, and bring to a boil. Reduce the heat to medium-low and simmer for 15 minutes. Let cool slightly.

Working in batches, purée the soup in a food processor or blender. Return to the pot and keep warm over low heat.

In a bowl, whisk the cream until slightly thickened, then whisk in the reduced apple cider until blended. Serve the soup, drizzled with the cider cream.

17

WHITE BEAN SOUP WITH BELL PEPPER CROSTINI

serves 6

A food processor makes fast work of two steps in this easy recipe. It is used to purée the soup and to whip up the red bell pepper spread that tops the crostini that are served alongside. If you are pressed for time, you can skip the crostini and accompany the soup with crusty French or Italian bread.

¼ cup (2 fl oz/60 ml) olive oil, plus more for brushing

¼ cup (½ oz/15 g) chopped pancetta

½ yellow onion, chopped

1 carrot, peeled and chopped

1 celery rib, chopped

4 cloves garlic, minced

3 cans (15 oz/470 g each) cannellini beans, drained

5 cups (40 fl oz/1.25 l) chicken broth

¾ tsp minced thyme

½ cup (2 oz/60 g) grated Parmesan cheese

Salt and freshly ground black pepper

12 slices baguette, each 4 inches (10 cm) long and ½ inch (12 mm) thick

1 cup (6 oz/185 g) jarred roasted red bell peppers

2 Tbsp minced flat-leaf parsley

1 tsp sherry vinegar

⅛ tsp red pepper flakes

½ tsp honey

In a large, heavy pot, warm 2 Tbsp of the oil over medium heat. Add the pancetta and cook, stirring occasionally, until crispy, about 5 minutes. Add the onion, carrot, and celery and cook, stirring occasionally, until the vegetables are beginning to soften, about 8 minutes. Add the garlic and cook, stirring occasionally, for 1 minute. Add the beans, broth, and thyme and bring to a simmer. Reduce the heat to low, cover, and cook until the vegetables are tender, about 10 minutes. Let cool slightly.

Working in batches, purée the soup in a food processor or blender. Return to the pot, stir in the cheese, and season with salt and black pepper. Keep warm over low heat. Wash out the processor or blender.

Brush the baguette slices on both sides with oil and season lightly with salt. Heat a stove-top grill pan over medium-high heat. Grill the bread, turning once, until nicely grill-marked, about 2 minutes per side. Set aside. ⇥

In the food processor or blender, chop the bell peppers. Transfer to a bowl. Stir in ½ tsp salt, the remaining 2 Tbsp oil, the parsley, vinegar, red pepper flakes, and honey. Spread the baguette slices with the bell pepper spread. Serve the soup with the crostini alongside.

18

VEGETABLES IN COCONUT-LIME BROTH

serves 4

This aromatic and creamy broth makes a great base for almost any combination of vegetables. You could also add thinly sliced poached chicken, prawns, or scallops.

1 Tbsp canola oil

1 shallot, minced

2 cloves garlic, minced

1-inch (2.5-cm) piece fresh ginger, peeled and minced

2 cans (14 fl oz/430 ml each) coconut milk

4 cups (32 fl oz/1 l) vegetable broth

½ lb (250 g) small Yukon Gold potatoes, quartered

3 oz (90 g) green beans, trimmed and halved on the diagonal

1 small red bell pepper, seeded and thinly sliced

Juice of 2 limes

Salt

In a large, heavy pot, warm the oil over medium-high heat. Add the shallot, garlic, and ginger and sauté until translucent, 2–3 minutes. Add the coconut milk and broth and bring to a boil. Add the potatoes and cook until tender, about 10 minutes. Add the green beans, red pepper, and lime juice and simmer for 4 minutes. Season to taste with salt and serve.

19

In France, a pinch of freshly grated nutmeg accents many a béchamel sauce, used in gratins and all things creamy. Here, it is the secret ingredient lacing a simple spinach soup, creating a perfect foil for the dark greens.

CREAM OF SPINACH SOUP

serves 4

3 lb (1.5 kg) spinach, tough stems removed

2 cups (16 fl oz/500 ml) milk, plus more as needed

2 cups (16 fl oz/500 ml) chicken or vegetable broth

3 Tbsp unsalted butter

3 Tbsp all-purpose flour

Salt and freshly ground pepper

½ tsp grated nutmeg

½ cup (4 fl oz/125 ml) heavy cream

Put the spinach, with the rinsing water still clinging to the leaves, in a saucepan over medium heat, cover, and cook until wilted and tender, about 3 minutes. Drain the spinach and squeeze to extract as much water as possible. Using a food processor, process until finely chopped. Set aside.

Pour the 2 cups (16 fl oz/500 ml) milk and the broth into separate small saucepans and place over low heat. Heat both just until small bubbles form around the edge of the pan, then remove from the heat.

In a large, heavy pot, melt the butter over medium-low heat. When the foam begins to subside, add the flour and stir until smooth, about 2 minutes. Gradually add the hot milk while whisking gently. Cook, stirring often, until the mixture bubbles vigorously and has thickened, about 3 minutes. Gradually add the hot broth, whisking, and bring to a low boil. Cook until pale beige and opaque, about 3 minutes. Let cool slightly.

Add the spinach purée to the milk-broth mixture and stir until blended. Add 1 tsp salt, ⅛ tsp pepper, and the nutmeg. Reduce the heat to a bare simmer, cover, and cook for 10 minutes, stirring occasionally. Remove from the heat and let cool slightly.

Working in batches, purée the soup in a blender or food processor. Return to the pot and stir in the cream. Reheat gently over low heat. If the soup seems too thick, thin it with milk, adding ¼ cup (2 fl oz/60 ml) at a time. Season with salt and pepper and serve.

20

The French call it velouté *when broth and cream are combined to make a "velvety" soup or sauce. This recipe yields only 2 cups (8 fl oz/250 ml), but a little goes a long way—it's a very rich soup meant to be served as a small first course. The recipe can be doubled easily.*

ROASTED GARLIC & SHALLOT VELOUTÉ WITH CRISPY PANCETTA

serves 2

2 heads garlic

10 shallots

2 tsp olive oil

4 thyme sprigs, plus ¼ tsp minced leaves

2 oz (60 g) thinly sliced pancetta

2 Tbsp unsalted butter

1¼ cups (10 fl oz/310 ml) chicken broth

2 Tbsp heavy cream

Salt and freshly ground pepper

Preheat the oven to 400°F (200°C). Cut off the tops of the garlic heads and the shallots to expose the bulbs. Place the garlic heads and shallots on a sheet of aluminum foil. Sprinkle with the olive oil and place the thyme sprigs on top. Loosely close the foil. Roast in the oven until very tender, about 1 hour and 10 minutes. When cool enough to handle, squeeze all the pulp from the skins of the garlic and shallots into a bowl.

In a saucepan, cook the pancetta over medium-high heat until crispy. Transfer to paper towels to drain. When cool enough to handle, crumble the pancetta. Add the butter to the saucepan and when melted, add the roasted garlic and shallots and the minced thyme and cook until translucent, about 6 minutes. Add the broth and bring to a boil. Stir in the cream and return to a boil. Reduce the heat to a simmer and cook for 5 minutes. Remove from the heat and let cool slightly.

Working in batches, purée the soup in a blender. Return to the pot and warm through over medium-low heat. Season with salt and pepper and serve, garnished with the crumbled pancetta.

21

INDIAN-SPICED CHICKPEA STEW

serves 6

¾ cup (5 oz/155 g) dried chickpeas, picked over and rinsed

5 cups (40 fl oz/1.25 l) vegetable broth

1 lb (500 g) russet potatoes, peeled and diced

1 lb (500 g) tomatoes, peeled and chopped

2 tsp garam masala

½ tsp ground ginger

½ tsp ground turmeric

Salt and freshly ground pepper

3 Tbsp chopped cilantro

Well seasoned but not too spicy, this cold-weather chickpea stew is an excellent source of protein. To save time, substitute 1 can (15 oz/470 g) chickpeas, drained and well rinsed, for the dried ones, decreasing the stock to 3 cups (24 fl oz/750 ml).

Put the chickpeas in a bowl with cold water to cover and soak for 3 hours. Drain.

In a large, heavy pot, bring the broth to a boil over high heat. Add the chickpeas, reduce the heat to medium, and simmer, uncovered, until almost tender, about 1½ hours. Add the potatoes, tomatoes, garam masala, ginger, and turmeric and continue to cook until the chickpeas and potatoes are tender, about 30 minutes. Remove from the heat and let cool slightly.

Purée half of the broth and vegetables in a blender or food processor. Return to the pot and season with salt and pepper. Reheat to serving temperature. Serve, garnished with the cilantro.

22

SQUASH SOUP WITH SAGE BROWN BUTTER

serves 4–6

1 butternut squash (2 lb/1 kg), peeled and diced

3 Tbsp olive oil

Salt and freshly ground pepper

2 Tbsp unsalted butter

1 yellow onion, chopped

2 cloves garlic, minced

4 cups (32 fl oz/1 l) vegetable broth

FOR THE SAGE BROWN BUTTER

¼ cup (2 oz/60 g) unsalted butter

6 sage leaves

Heavy cream for garnish (optional)

Butternut squash is the quintessential fall vegetable. Roasting the squash brings out its naturally nutty taste. When serving, drizzle the brown butter over the top of the soup, but do not stir, for an elegant presentation. Add a swirl of cream, if you like, along with the sage leaves.

Preheat the oven to 400°F (200°C) and line a baking sheet with parchment paper. Toss the squash with the oil and season with salt and pepper. Place on the prepared baking sheet and roast until tender, about 25 minutes.

In a large, heavy pot, melt the butter over medium-high heat. Add the onion and garlic and sauté until translucent, about 5 minutes. Add the roasted squash and broth and bring to a boil. Reduce the heat to low and simmer for 20 minutes to blend the flavors. Remove from the heat and let cool slightly.

Working in batches, purée the soup in a blender. Return to the pot and season with salt and pepper.

To make the sage brown butter, melt the butter in a small frying pan over low heat. Add the sage leaves and cook until the butter begins to brown and the sage is very aromatic, 3–4 minutes.

Serve the soup, drizzled with the brown butter, 1–2 sage leaves, and a swirl of cream, if desired.

23

CORN SOUP WITH CHANTERELLES & THYME

serves 4

3 Tbsp unsalted butter

2 Tbsp olive oil

2 shallots, minced

4 cloves garlic, minced

4 cups (32 fl oz/1 l) chicken broth

2 packages (1 lb/500 g each) frozen corn kernels

¼ cup (2 fl oz/60 ml) heavy cream

Salt and freshly ground pepper

2 oz (60 g) chanterelle mushrooms, thinly sliced

½ tsp minced thyme leaves

Slice the mushrooms crosswise to retain their shape. Chanterelles are beautiful, and you want diners to be able to see that you are serving a really special mushroom. Serve with warm croissants.

In a large, heavy pot, warm 2 Tbsp of the butter and the oil over medium-high heat. Add the shallots and garlic and sauté until soft, about 3 minutes. Add the broth and bring to a boil. Add the corn and cook for 5 minutes. Remove from the heat and let cool slightly.

Purée half of the soup in a blender. Return to the pot and stir in the cream. Season with salt and pepper.

In a small frying pan, melt the remaining 1 Tbsp butter over medium-high heat. Add the mushrooms and thyme and sauté, stirring often, until the mushrooms release their liquid and caramelize slightly, about 4 minutes. Serve the soup, garnished with the chanterelles.

24

CURRIED YELLOW SPLIT PEA SOUP WITH KABOCHA SQUASH

serves 4–6

1 kabocha squash (about 2¼ lb/1.15 kg), peeled, seeded, and cut into 1-inch (2.5-cm) pieces

4 Tbsp (2 fl oz/60 ml) olive oil

Salt and freshly ground pepper

1 yellow onion, chopped

2 cloves garlic, chopped

1 Tbsp curry powder

1½ cups (10½ oz/330 g) yellow split peas, picked over and rinsed

5 cups (40 fl oz/1.25 l) chicken or vegetable broth

½ cup (2 oz/60 g) roasted and salted sunflower seeds

½ cup (4 oz/125 g) sour cream (optional)

High in protein and nutrient-dense, split peas come in yellow and green, and either can be used in this recipe. Curry powder varies from country to country and from region to region. If you have a favorite curry powder, use it here. If not, a Madras-style powder is a good middle-of-the-road choice. Serve this soup with thick slices of crusty bread covered with shredded Monterey jack and run under the broiler.

Preheat the oven to 400°F (200°C). Line a baking sheet with parchment paper. Pile the squash on the prepared baking sheet and toss with 2 Tbsp of the oil. Spread in a single layer and season with salt and pepper. Roast, stirring once, until golden, about 30 minutes. Set aside.

In a large, heavy pot, warm the remaining 2 Tbsp oil over medium-high heat. Add the onion and cook, stirring occasionally, until soft, about 6 minutes. Add the garlic, season with salt and pepper, and cook, stirring occasionally, until soft, about 2 minutes. Stir in the curry powder and split peas and allow them to toast, about 2 minutes. Add the broth and bring to a boil. Reduce the heat to low, cover, and simmer, stirring a couple of times to prevent sticking, until the split peas are soft, 25–35 minutes. Let cool slightly.

Purée half of the soup in a food processor or blender. Return to the pot and stir to combine. Stir in the squash and season with salt and pepper.

Serve, garnished with the sunflower seeds and a dollop of sour cream, if using.

BUTTERNUT SQUASH-CARROT SOUP WITH PORK BELLY "CROUTONS"

serves 6–8

The garnish of pork "croutons" adds a surprising savory note to this cool-weather soup. For the best result, select a slab of skin-on center-cut pork belly that includes wide bars of silky white fat and streaks of reddish meat. Serve this beautiful golden soup with a green salad and a cheese plate for an autumn lunch.

1 large butternut squash (about 3 lb/1.5 kg), peeled, seeded, and cut into 1-inch (2.5-cm) cubes

3 large carrots, peeled and cut into 1-inch (2.5-cm) pieces

2 Tbsp olive oil, plus 1 tsp

Salt and freshly ground pepper

10-oz (315-g) slab pork belly, cut into batons about ½ by 1 inch (12 mm by 2.5 cm)

2 Tbsp unsalted butter

1 large yellow onion, thinly sliced

1 large Granny Smith apple, peeled, cored, and thinly sliced

2 cloves garlic, minced

6 cups (48 fl oz/1.5 l) chicken broth

2 thyme sprigs

1 bay leaf

1 cup (8 fl oz/250 ml) heavy cream

2 Tbsp chopped flat-leaf parsley

Preheat the oven to 450°F (230°C).

In a large bowl, stir together the squash, carrots, and the 2 Tbsp oil, and season with salt and pepper. Transfer to a baking sheet. Roast, stirring occasionally, until the vegetables are browned and tender, about 45 minutes. Set aside.

In a large, heavy pot, warm the 1 tsp oil over medium heat. Add the pork belly and cook, stirring occasionally, until browned and the fat is rendered, 15–20 minutes. Transfer to a paper towel–lined plate. Discard the fat in the pot and wipe it out with paper towels.

In the same pot, melt the butter over medium heat. Add the onion and apple and cook, stirring occasionally, until tender and caramelized, 25–30 minutes. Add the garlic and cook, stirring occasionally, until fragrant, about 1 minute. Add the broth, thyme sprigs, and bay leaf, raise the heat to medium-high, and bring to a boil. Reduce the heat to medium-low and simmer, stirring occasionally, for 10 minutes. Remove and discard the thyme sprigs and bay leaf. Let cool slightly. ⟶

Working in batches, purée the apple-broth mixture with the roasted vegetables in a food processor or blender. Return to the pot, place over medium heat, and simmer for 10 minutes. Stir in the cream. Taste and adjust the seasoning. Serve, garnished with the parsley and pork belly croutons.

PEANUT-GINGER SWEET POTATO SOUP

serves 4–6

Peanut butter ensures that this soup is a kid-pleaser. You can garnish with chopped peanuts for a little crunch. This would make a satisfying and nutritious dinner on Halloween night before you send the kids out for their sugar rush.

2 Tbsp unsalted butter

1 small yellow onion, chopped

2 cloves garlic, minced

1 Tbsp peeled and minced fresh ginger

2 sweet potatoes (1½ lb/750 g total), peeled and diced

4½ cups (36 fl oz/1.1 l) vegetable broth

3 Tbsp creamy peanut butter

2 Tbsp minced cilantro

Salt and freshly ground pepper

In a large, heavy pot, melt the butter over medium-high heat. Add the onion, garlic, and ginger and sauté until very soft, about 5 minutes. Add the sweet potatoes, stir to combine, and cook for 5 minutes. Add the broth and bring to a boil. Reduce the heat to low and simmer until the sweet potatoes are very tender, 30–35 minutes. Remove from the heat and let cool slightly.

Working in batches, purée the soup in a blender or food processor. Return to the pot over low heat, add the peanut butter, and stir until melted, about 4 minutes. Add the cilantro and season to taste with salt and pepper. Serve.

27

This delicate soup is seasoned primarily with kombu or wakame (dried seaweed) and miso (fermented soybean paste), two Asian staples now commonly stocked by many grocers. Light and flavorful, this soup comes together very easily.

MISO SOUP

serves 4–6

3 oz (90 g) wakame

¾ tsp granulated dashi mixed with 6 cups (48 fl oz/1.5 l) hot water

6 Tbsp white miso paste

1 tsp rice vinegar

2 oz (60 g) soft tofu, cut into small cubes

3 green onions, white and tender green parts, thinly sliced on the diagonal

Soak the wakame in hot water to cover until soft, about 10 minutes. Drain and cut into thin strips.

In a large, heavy pot, bring the dashi mixture to a bare simmer over low heat. Whisk in the miso and vinegar and simmer for 5 minutes to blend the flavors. Stir in the wakame, tofu cubes, and green onions and serve.

28

Garam masala is a classic blend of Indian spices that adds beautiful depth to this sweet purée. Sautéing the spice mixture before adding the liquid toasts the spices, further enhancing their flavors.

CARROT & ASIAN PEAR PURÉE

serves 4–6

2 Tbsp olive oil

1 small yellow onion, chopped

2 cloves garlic, minced

2 tsp garam masala

8 carrots, peeled and chopped

2 ripe Asian pears, peeled, cored, and chopped

4 cups (32 fl oz/1 l) vegetable broth

Salt and ground white pepper

In a saucepan, warm the oil over medium-high heat. Add the onion and garlic and sauté until translucent, about 5 minutes. Add the garam masala, stir to combine, and cook for 1 minute. Add the carrots and pears, stir, and cook until the carrots begin to soften, 5–7 minutes. Add the broth and bring to a boil. Reduce the heat to low and simmer until the carrots are very tender, about 30 minutes. Remove from the heat and let cool slightly.

Working in batches, purée the soup in a blender. Return to the saucepan and heat through over medium-low heat. Season to taste with salt and pepper and serve.

29

A great way to use up leftover baguette, this is a very different take on classic tomato and bread soup. Because this soup, featuring earthy artichokes, is so hearty, serve it with a simple green salad topped with fresh figs and a balsamic vinaigrette.

ARTICHOKE & TOASTED BREAD SOUP WITH SAGE

serves 4

1 small loaf day-old Italian peasant bread, cut into ½-inch (12-mm) cubes (about 2 cups/2 oz/60 g)

3 Tbsp olive oil

Salt and freshly ground pepper

1 Tbsp unsalted butter

1 leek, white and pale green parts, chopped

2 cloves garlic, minced

7 sage leaves, chopped

2 cups (16 fl oz/500 ml) chicken broth

12 oz (375 g) frozen artichoke hearts

Preheat the oven to 350°F (180°C). Spread the bread cubes on a baking sheet, toss with 2 Tbsp of the oil, and season with salt and pepper. Bake until golden brown and toasted, about 10 minutes. Set aside.

In a large, heavy pot, melt the butter with the remaining 1 Tbsp oil over medium-high heat. Add the leek and garlic and sauté for 4 minutes. Add the sage and continue to sauté for 1 minute. Add the broth and 2 cups (16 fl oz/500 ml) water and bring to a boil. Add the artichoke hearts, reduce the heat to medium-low, and simmer until the artichokes are soft and heated through, about 10 minutes. Add the toasted bread, stir to combine, and cook for 5 minutes. Remove from the heat and let cool slightly.

Working in batches, purée the soup in a blender. Return to the pot and warm through over medium-low heat. Season with salt and pepper and serve.

30

CREAMY BLACK BEAN PURÉE WITH CHEESE STRAWS

serves 4–6

FOR THE CHEESE STRAWS

1 sheet puff pastry, thawed

½ cup (2 oz/60 g) finely shredded Cheddar cheese

2 Tbsp olive oil

1 yellow onion, chopped

3 cloves garlic, minced

1 small jalapeño chile, seeded and minced

1½ tsp ground cumin

4 cans (15 oz/470 g each) black beans, drained

2¾ cups (22 fl oz/680 ml) chicken broth

Salt and freshly ground pepper

¼ cup (2 oz/60 g) sour cream

For a creative appetizer at a cocktail party, serve this as "soup sips." Put the soup into clear shot glasses and balance a cheese straw across the top rim of each glass. Encourage guests to dip their straws and then sip their soup.

To make the cheese straws, preheat the oven to 400°F (200°C) and line a baking sheet with parchment paper. Roll out the puff pastry to ⅛ inch (3 mm) thick on a floured surface. Cut the pastry into 9 squares, each about 3½ by 3½ inches (9 by 9 cm). Cut each square in half diagonally to make 18 triangles. Starting with the longest side, tightly roll up each triangle and place, seam side down, on the prepared baking sheet. Brush each roll with water and sprinkle with cheese, gently pressing with your fingers to help the cheese stick to the pastry. Bake until the straws turn golden brown, 18–20 minutes.

Meanwhile, in a large, heavy pot, warm the oil over medium-high heat. Add the onion and garlic and sauté until soft, about 5 minutes. Add the jalapeño and cumin and cook, stirring often, for 2 minutes. Add the black beans and broth and bring to a boil. Reduce the heat to low and simmer for 15 minutes. Remove from the heat and let cool slightly.

Working in batches, purée the soup in a blender or food processor. Return to the pot and warm through over medium-low heat. Season to taste with salt and pepper and serve, topping each with a dollop of sour cream. Serve with cheese straws on the side for dipping. Pass the extra straws at the table.

31

FARRO, KIELBASA & BROCCOLI RABE SOUP

serves 4–6

2 Tbsp olive oil

½ yellow onion, chopped

2 cloves garlic, chopped

¾ lb (375 g) kielbasa, cut into ½-inch (12-mm) slices

Salt and freshly ground pepper

8 cups (64 fl oz/2 l) chicken broth

1¼ cups (7½ oz/235 g) farro, rinsed and drained

½ bunch broccoli rabe (about ¾ lb/375 g), thick stems removed, cut into 1-inch (2.5-cm) pieces

2 oz (60 g) pecorino romano cheese, shaved

One of the most important steps when making many soups is to sweat the aromatic vegetables properly. For example, take the time to sauté the onions and garlic in this recipe so they develop a complex flavor. When shopping for the farro used here, be sure to select a package labeled "semipearled" (semiperlato), as whole-grain farro takes much longer to cook.

In a large, heavy pot, warm the oil over medium-high heat. Add the onion and cook, stirring occasionally, until translucent, about 6 minutes. Add the garlic and kielbasa, season with salt and pepper, and cook, stirring occasionally, until the kielbasa is golden brown on the edges, about 6 minutes. Add the broth and bring to a boil. Stir in the farro and cook until tender but still holding a slight crunch, about 20 minutes. Add the broccoli rabe and cook until the stems are fork-tender, about 4 minutes. Season with salt and pepper.

Serve, topped with the shaved cheese.

5

PORK & PUMPKIN STEW
page 253

6

CHESTNUT–CELERY ROOT SOUP
WITH BACON & SAGE CROUTONS
page 253

7

CELERY ROOT PURÉE
WITH CARAMELIZED APPLES
page 255

12

CHEDDAR CHEESE SOUP WITH ALE
page 257

13

SAVORY BARLEY SOUP WITH
WILD MUSHROOMS & THYME
page 258

14

APPLE, LEEK &
BUTTERNUT SQUASH SOUP
page 258

19

SALSIFY & MUSHROOM CHOWDER
WITH ROSEMARY OIL
page 263

20

TOMATO-FENNEL BROTH
WITH CLAMS
page 263

21

TOMATO BISQUE
page 264

26

GARLICKY GREENS, ROAST PORK
& WHITE BEAN SOUP
page 268

27

CARROT SOUP WITH BACON
& CHESTNUT CREAM
page 269

28

SPICED BROTH WITH
ROASTED ACORN SQUASH & KALE
page 269

This month's bracing winds and touches of frost call for making robust, long-simmered dishes. Slow-cooked stews of succulent pork or chicken are just the thing for cozy evenings at home, as is hearty vegetarian fare featuring earthy grains, beans, and mushrooms. When the harvest wanes toward the end of the month, it's a good time to take advantage of leftover roasts and make easy rice and noodle soups.

november

1

It may be difficult to find fresh udon for this homey Asian-inspired soup, but 1 pound (500 g) dried udon can be substituted. Just follow the cooking instructions on the package. You can also use fresh Chinese egg noodles in place of the udon. If you don't have time to roast the pork belly and you live near a Chinese delicatessen, purchase a piece of crispy skin pork, a Cantonese specialty, and ask the clerk to slice it for you.

UDON NOODLE SOUP WITH PORK BELLY & SOFT EGGS

serves 4–6

8 cups (2 qt/2 l) chicken broth

1 pork belly (2¼–2½ lb/1.1–1.25 kg)

2 Tbsp olive oil

Salt and freshly ground pepper

7 cloves garlic

4 star anise

2 cinnamon sticks

2 Tbsp unsalted butter

1 Tbsp light sesame oil

2-inch (5-cm) piece fresh ginger, peeled and grated

1 jalapeño chile, seeded, deribbed, and finely chopped

5 Tbsp (3 fl oz/80 ml) low-sodium soy sauce

1½ oz (45 g) dried shiitake mushrooms

3 packages (7 oz/220 g each) fresh udon noodles (flavor packets discarded if included)

4 eggs

3 green onions, white and tender green parts, thinly sliced

Preheat the oven to 500°F (260°C). In a roasting pan, combine 2 cups (16 fl oz/500 ml) of the broth and 1 cup (8 fl oz/250 ml) water. Place the pork belly, fat side up, in the pan. Brush with the olive oil and season with salt and pepper. Cut 4 of the garlic cloves in half lengthwise and scatter into the broth along with the star anise and cinnamon sticks. Roast until the top is golden and beginning to bubble, about 15 minutes. Reduce the oven temperature to 325°F (165°C) and continue to roast until an instant-read thermometer inserted into the thickest part of the pork belly registers 145°F (63°C), about 1 hour longer. Remove from the oven, tent the pan with aluminum foil, and keep the pork warm in the braising juices.

Mince the remaining 3 garlic cloves. In a large, heavy pot, melt the butter with the sesame oil over medium-high heat. Add the garlic, ginger, and jalapeño and cook, stirring occasionally, until soft, about 2 minutes. Add the remaining 6 cups (48 fl oz/1.5 l) broth and the soy sauce and bring to a boil. Reduce the heat to low, stir in the dried mushrooms, and simmer until very soft, about 15 minutes. ⟫

Raise the heat to high and return the broth to a boil. Add the udon noodles and cook until al dente, about 4 minutes or according to the package directions.

Meanwhile, bring a saucepan of water to a boil over medium-high heat. Gently lower the eggs into the pan and cook for exactly 8 minutes. Drain, rinse the eggs under cold water, and peel. Cut the eggs in half lengthwise.

Transfer the pork belly to a cutting board and cut crosswise into ¾-inch (2-cm) slices.

Using tongs, fill bowls with the udon noodles. Ladle the broth over the noodles and top each with a few slices of pork and 2 egg halves. Garnish with the green onions and serve.

2

Serve this hearty pasta soup as a starter or main course, using orecchiette or other medium-sized pasta shapes. For a more authentic Italian touch, use broccoli rabe, a robust, pleasantly bitter cousin to broccoli.

ORECCHIETTE, SAUSAGE & BROCCOLI IN BROTH

serves 6

8 cups (64 fl oz/2 l) chicken broth

½–1 tsp red pepper flakes

1 lb (500 g) spicy Italian sausage

1½ lb (750 g) broccoli, trimmed and cut into florets

Salt and freshly ground pepper

12 oz (375 g) orecchiette pasta

In a large, heavy pot, bring the broth and red pepper flakes to a boil over medium heat. Reduce the heat to low and simmer for 20 minutes.

Using a fork, prick the skins of the sausages. In a frying pan, cook the sausages over medium heat until lightly browned on all sides and cooked through, 15–20 minutes. Transfer to paper towels to drain and cool. Cut the sausages into rounds and add to the broth. Add the broccoli and simmer until tender, about 15 minutes.

In a large pot, bring 5 quarts (5 l) water to a boil over high heat. Add 1 Tbsp salt and the orecchiette and cook until al dente, about 12 minutes, or according to package directions. Drain well.

Add the orecchiette to the broth and season to taste with salt and pepper. Stir to mix well and serve.

3

A relative of cabbage, kohlrabi, which looks a bit like a knobby turnip and can be purple or green, most often turns up roasted or sautéed and sometimes shredded in salads or slaw. But it is also wonderful in soups, here simmered together with carrots and potatoes and then puréed until smooth. The potato adds body to the soup, and the garnish of roasted chickpeas contributes both crunch and spiciness. You can roast the chickpeas—which also make a great snack—a couple of days in advance and store them in an airtight container.

KOHLRABI SOUP WITH SPICED CHICKPEAS

serves 4

2 Tbsp olive oil

½ yellow onion, chopped

2 carrots, peeled and chopped

3 kohlrabi, peeled and chopped

1 russet potato, peeled and chopped

Salt and freshly ground pepper

3 cups (24 fl oz/750 ml) vegetable or chicken broth

FOR THE SPICED CHICKPEAS

1 can (15 oz/470 g) chickpeas

1 Tbsp olive oil

1 tsp ground cumin

½ tsp chili powder

Salt

In a large, heavy pot, warm the oil over medium-high heat. Add the onion and cook, stirring occasionally, until soft, about 5 minutes. Add the carrots, kohlrabi, and potato, and season with salt and pepper. Cook, stirring frequently, until the vegetables to begin to soften, about 10 minutes. Add the broth and bring to a boil. Reduce the heat to low and simmer until the vegetables are very soft, 30–35 minutes. Let cool slightly.

Working in batches, purée the soup in a food processor or blender. Return to the pot, season with salt and pepper, and keep warm over low heat.

Meanwhile, make the spiced chickpeas: Preheat the oven to 400°F (200°C). Drain and rinse the chickpeas, wrap them in a kitchen towel, and gently pat dry. Transfer to a bowl, add the oil, cumin, chili powder, and ¼ tsp salt, and toss to coat. Spread the chickpeas in a single layer on a baking sheet and roast, stirring once, until crispy, 30–35 minutes.

Serve the soup, topped with the spiced chickpeas.

4

Inspired by the classic French soupe à l'oignon, this flavor-packed, hearty onion soup includes a healthy measure of mushrooms. You will probably have bread cubes left over. Toss them with olive oil or melted butter, toast them in the oven, and use as a crunchy garnish for salads.

CARAMELIZED ONION & MUSHROOM SOUP

serves 6

3 Tbsp olive oil

1 lb (500 g) yellow onions, thinly sliced

1 carrot, peeled and thinly sliced

1 celery rib, thinly sliced

2 cloves garlic, crushed

¼ cup (2 fl oz/60 ml) Marsala, plus 1 Tbsp

1¾ lb (875 g) cremini mushrooms, thinly sliced

1 bay leaf

7 cups (56 fl oz/1.75 l) chicken broth

Salt and freshly ground pepper

2 Tbsp chopped flat-leaf parsley

1 tsp fresh lemon juice

1 loaf country-style bread, crusts removed, bread cut into ½-inch (12-mm) cubes

6 oz (185 g) Gruyère cheese, shredded

In a large, heavy pot, warm the oil over medium heat. Add the onions and cook, stirring occasionally, until soft and caramelized, 25–30 minutes. Add the carrot, celery, and garlic and cook, stirring occasionally, until the vegetables are soft, about 6 minutes. Add the ¼ cup (2 fl oz/ 60 ml) Marsala and cook until evaporated, about 2 minutes. Add the mushrooms and cook, stirring occasionally, until soft and the liquid evaporates, about 15 minutes. Add the bay leaf and broth, raise the heat to high, and bring just to a boil. Reduce the heat to medium and simmer for 20–25 minutes. Season with salt and pepper. Remove and discard the bay leaf. Let cool slightly.

Working in batches, purée the soup in a food processor or blender. Return to the pot and stir in 1 Tbsp of the parsley, the lemon juice, and the 1 Tbsp Marsala.

Preheat the broiler.

Place 6 ovenproof soup bowls on a baking sheet and ladle about 1½ cups (12 fl oz/ 375 ml) soup into each one. Top each with 4 or 5 bread cubes and sprinkle with the cheese. Broil until the bread is lightly toasted and the cheese is bubbly and golden brown, 5–6 minutes. Sprinkle each serving with ½ tsp parsley and serve.

5

PORK & PUMPKIN STEW

serves 6

2 lb (1 kg) boneless pork shoulder, cut into 1-inch (2.5-cm) cubes

Salt and freshly ground black pepper

3 Tbsp olive oil

1 yellow onion, diced

1½ tsp minced garlic

1 tsp peeled and minced fresh ginger

2 tsp chicken demi-glace

2 tsp tomato paste

¾ tsp ground cinnamon

¼ tsp ground coriander

¼ tsp red pepper flakes

⅛ tsp ground nutmeg

⅛ tsp ground cloves

1½ Tbsp cider vinegar

3 Tbsp applesauce

9 oz (280 g) canned diced tomatoes with juices

1 lb (500 g) pumpkin or winter squash, such as kabocha, peeled, seeded, and cut into ¾-inch (2-cm) dice

2 tsp chopped fresh sage

2 cups (16 fl oz/500 ml) chicken broth

Loaded with tender pork and pumpkin and seasoned with a medley of fragrant spices, this warming dish can be made a couple of days in advance, cooled, covered, and refrigerated, and then reheated for a quick and easy dinner. Spoon it over mashed potatoes or egg noodles and accompany it with broccoli rabe sautéed with garlic and red pepper flakes.

Preheat the oven to 325°F (165°C).

Season the pork with salt and black pepper. In a large, heavy pot, warm 2 Tbsp of the oil over medium-high heat. Working in batches, add the pork and brown on all sides, 8–10 minutes per batch. Using a slotted spoon, transfer the meat to a plate.

Reduce the heat to medium and warm the remaining 1 Tbsp oil. Add the onion and cook, stirring occasionally, until tender, 6–8 minutes. Add the garlic, ginger, demi-glace, tomato paste, cinnamon, coriander, red pepper flakes, nutmeg, and cloves and cook, stirring constantly, until fragrant, about 1 minute. Add the vinegar, applesauce, tomatoes with their juices, pumpkin, sage, broth, and pork. Bring to a boil and season with salt and black pepper. Transfer the pot to the oven and cook until the pork is fork-tender, 2–2½ hours. Skim the excess fat off the sauce and serve the stew.

6

CHESTNUT–CELERY ROOT SOUP WITH BACON & SAGE CROUTONS

serves 6–8

6 slices bacon

1 yellow onion, chopped

3 celery ribs, chopped

¼ tsp celery seed

6 cups (48 fl oz/1.5 l) chicken broth

1 celery root (about 1 lb/500 g), peeled and chopped

1 jar (15 oz/470 g) steamed peeled chestnuts, chopped

½ cup (4 fl oz/125 ml) half-and-half

Salt and freshly ground pepper

Sage Croutons (page 261)

Fresh sage just hints at bitterness, but asserts woodsy flavor. Here, with salty bacon, it accents the mellow sweetness of chestnuts and celery root. Try sage in other fall soups. Even a single leaf, browned in butter until fragrant and floated atop a serving, will add distinction.

In a large, heavy pot, cook the bacon over medium heat, turning once, until crisp, about 8 minutes. Transfer to paper towels to drain. Let cool, then crumble.

Pour off all but 2 Tbsp of the bacon fat from the pot and return to medium heat. Add the onion and celery and sauté until softened, about 7 minutes. Add the celery seed and cook, stirring often, until fragrant, about 1 minute. Add the broth, raise the heat to medium-high, and bring to a boil. Add the celery root and chestnuts and return to a boil, then reduce the heat to low, cover partially, and simmer until the celery root is tender when pierced with the tip of a knife, about 25 minutes. Remove from the heat and let cool slightly.

Working in batches, purée the soup in a blender. Transfer to a clean pot. Add the half-and-half, 1½ tsp salt, and pepper to taste and place over medium-low heat. Cook gently, stirring occasionally, until heated through, about 10 minutes. Season with salt and pepper. Serve, garnished with the bacon and croutons.

7

CELERY ROOT PURÉE WITH CARAMELIZED APPLES

serves 4

2 Tbsp unsalted butter

1 leek, white and pale green parts, chopped

2 celery roots (2 lb/1 kg total), peeled and chopped

3½ cups (28 fl oz/875 ml) vegetable broth

FOR THE CARAMELIZED APPLES

1 Tbsp unsalted butter

1 small Granny Smith apple, peeled, cored, and cut into tiny cubes

¼ tsp dark brown sugar

2 Tbsp half-and-half

Salt and ground white pepper

Celery root is just what it sounds like, the root of a variety of celery plant. It's sometimes labeled celeriac. Its subtle flavor stands out best in simple preparations like this one. This soup freezes well, without the caramelized apples.

In a large, heavy pot, warm the butter over medium-high heat. Add the leek and sauté until soft, about 4 minutes. Add the celery roots, stir to coat, and sauté for 2 minutes. Add the broth and bring to a boil. Reduce the heat to low and simmer until the celery root is very tender, 25–30 minutes. Remove from the heat and let cool slightly.

While the soup is cooling, make the caramelized apples. In a frying pan, melt the 1 Tbsp butter over medium-high heat until it foams. Add the apple and sauté for 4 minutes. Sprinkle with the brown sugar, stir to combine, and cook until the apples begin to caramelize, about 3 minutes. Remove from the heat and set aside.

Working in batches, purée the soup in a blender. Return to the pot over medium heat, add the half-and-half, and return just to a gentle boil. Turn off the heat and season with salt and pepper. Serve, garnished with the caramelized apples.

THAI SHRIMP & BUTTERNUT SQUASH SOUP

serves 8–10

2 Tbsp olive oil

2 yellow onions, diced

2 Tbsp minced garlic

3 tsp Thai curry powder

3 tsp Chinese ginger powder or regular ground ginger

½ tsp ground turmeric

½ serrano chile, seeded

2 pieces lemongrass, each about 3 inches (7.5 cm) long, lightly bruised in a mortar with a pestle

1 kaffir lime leaf (optional)

4 cups (32 fl oz/1 l) chicken broth

3 Tbsp Asian fish sauce

1½ lb (750 g) butternut squash, peeled, seeded, and cut into ½-inch (12-mm) cubes

2 cups (16 fl oz/500 ml) coconut milk

½ lb (250 g) green beans, trimmed and cut into 1-inch (2.5-cm) pieces

1½ lb (750 g) medium shrimp, peeled and deveined

Thai or regular basil, cut into thin strips, for garnish

Lime wedges for garnish

An aromatic herb used throughout Southeast Asia, lemongrass is shaped like a green onion, has long, thin, gray-green leaves, and has a light lemon flavor. Kaffir lime leaves, which are dark green on top and pale green on the underside, have a light citrus flavor and a distinctive shape: they are attached in pairs, end to end. Both ingredients can be found in well-stocked supermarkets and in Asian markets.

In a large, heavy pot, warm the oil over medium heat. Add the onions and cook, stirring occasionally, until soft and translucent, about 5 minutes. Add the garlic, curry powder, ginger powder, turmeric, chile, lemongrass, and kaffir lime leaf (if using). Cook, stirring frequently to prevent the ingredients from burning, for about 3 minutes. Add the broth and fish sauce, cover, and simmer for 5 minutes.

Add the squash, cover, and cook until the squash is tender, 5–7 minutes. Add the coconut milk and green beans, cover, and cook until the beans are tender, about 5 minutes. Add the shrimp, re-cover the pot, and cook until opaque, 3–5 minutes.

Remove the pot from the heat. Remove and discard the chile, lemongrass, and kaffir lime leaf (if using). Serve, garnished with basil and lime wedges.

9

NOVEMBER

A rich base for the broth provides depth of flavor in this soup: chipotle chiles add smokiness and heat, the adobo sauce lends a sweet-tartness, and tangy tomatillos balance with a bright, almost citrusy, flavor. The garnishes offer an inviting range of fresh colors and textures.

CHICKEN-TOMATILLO SOUP WITH CHIPOTLE CHILES

serves 6–8

8 cups (2 qt/2 l) chicken broth

1½ lb (750 g) skinless, boneless chicken breast halves

1 oregano sprig

10 cilantro sprigs

9 cloves garlic, crushed

1 lb (500 g) tomatillos, husked, rinsed, and chopped

1 white onion, chopped

2 large chipotle chiles in adobo, minced, plus 1 Tbsp adobo sauce

1½ Tbsp canola oil

Salt and freshly ground pepper

4 tsp fresh lime juice

1 ripe avocado

Tortilla chips for serving

1½ cups (9 oz/280 g) cherry or grape tomatoes, quartered

½ lb (250 g) cotija or feta cheese, crumbled

In a large, heavy pot, combine the broth, chicken breasts, oregano and cilantro sprigs, and 3 of the garlic cloves and bring to a boil over medium-high heat. Reduce the heat to low, cover, and simmer until the chicken is opaque throughout, 15–20 minutes.

Transfer the chicken to a plate. Strain the broth through a fine-mesh sieve into a large heatproof bowl. Discard the solids in the sieve. Wipe out the pot and set aside. Once the chicken is cool enough to handle, shred the meat into bite-sized pieces and set aside.

In a food processor, combine the tomatillos, onion, chipotle chiles and adobo sauce, and the remaining 6 garlic cloves and process to a smooth purée. In the clean pot, heat the oil over high heat. Add the tomatillo mixture and fry, stirring occasionally, until the liquid evaporates, the color darkens, and the mixture is fragrant, about 15 minutes. ⟫→

Add the broth and bring to a simmer. Cook, stirring occasionally, to blend the flavors, about 10 minutes. Add 1½ tsp salt, 3 tsp of the lime juice, the shredded chicken, and pepper to taste and simmer until the chicken is heated through, about 5 minutes.

Meanwhile, pit, peel, and dice the avocado and toss with the remaining 1 tsp lime juice.

Taste the soup and adjust the seasoning. Serve, garnished with the tortilla chips, avocado, tomatoes, and cheese.

10

NOVEMBER

Crushing the cooked potatoes instead of puréeing them gives this soup an interesting texture. There is no milk or cream here, but the soup is satisfying nonetheless. Fresh thyme can be substituted for the rosemary.

POTATO-ROSEMARY SOUP

serves 4–6

2 tsp olive oil

½ small shallot, minced

6 cups (48 fl oz/1.5 l) chicken broth

1 lb (500 g) Yukon Gold or other all-purpose potatoes, peeled and cut into large pieces

1 tsp minced rosemary

1 bay leaf

Salt and freshly ground pepper

In a large, heavy pot, warm the oil over medium heat. Add the shallot and sauté until translucent, 1–2 minutes. Pour in the broth and bring to a boil. Add the potatoes, half of the rosemary, the bay leaf, and ¼ tsp pepper. Cover partially, reduce the heat to low, and simmer until the potatoes are tender when pierced with a fork, 15–20 minutes.

Remove the pot from the heat and discard the bay leaf. Using a fork or potato masher, crush the potatoes into small chunks. Season with salt and serve, garnished with the remaining rosemary.

256

11

In eastern Europe, cooks take pride in their family recipes for homey, hearty stews. In this oven-braised version of Hungary's famed paprikás csirke, both sweet and hot paprika is used to give the dish a beautiful reddish-orange color and a memorable bold flavor. Although this rich dish is traditionally served with spaeztle-like nokedli, here easier-to-source egg noodles are used.

CHICKEN PAPRIKA STEW

serves 4–6

1 chicken (about 4 lb/2 kg), cut into 8 serving pieces

Salt and freshly ground pepper

2 Tbsp vegetable oil

1 yellow onion, chopped

2 cloves garlic, minced

½ lb (250 g) mushrooms, such as oyster or cremini, chopped (optional)

1½ Tbsp sweet paprika

1 tsp hot paprika

1 tsp caraway seeds, lightly crushed

1 red bell pepper, seeded and chopped

1 can (14½ oz/455 g) diced tomatoes with juices

1 tsp red wine vinegar

¾ cup (6 oz/185 g) sour cream

Cooked egg noodles for serving

Preheat the oven to 325°F (165°C).

Season the chicken with salt and pepper. In a large, heavy pot, warm the oil over medium-high heat. Working in batches, add the chicken and brown on both sides, 8–10 minutes per batch. Transfer to a plate.

Add the onion and garlic to the pot, season with salt, and cook, stirring occasionally, until softened, about 5 minutes. Add the mushrooms (if using) and cook, stirring frequently, until beginning to soften, about 5 minutes. Add the paprikas and caraway seeds and stir for 1 minute. Add the bell pepper and cook, stirring occasionally, until beginning to soften, about 5 minutes. Stir in the tomatoes with their juices, ½ cup (4 fl oz/125 ml) water, and the vinegar, scraping up any browned bits that cling to the bottom of the pan. Bring to a simmer. Return the chicken to the pot and bring to a simmer. Cover the pot, transfer to the oven, and cook until the meat is fork-tender, about 2 hours.

Transfer the chicken to a warm serving platter. Skim the excess fat off the sauce. Stir in the sour cream until combined. Taste and adjust the seasoning. Remove the skin from the chicken, if desired, and spoon the sauce over the chicken. Serve with egg noodles.

12

This soup brings together a classic pub combination. Compared to American-style lagers, British ales have a heavier body and a more assertive taste. To match that flavor, the sharper the Cheddar, the better. Serve with beer bread or warm pretzels.

CHEDDAR CHEESE SOUP WITH ALE

serves 4–6

½ cup (4 oz/125 g) unsalted butter

1 leek, white and pale green parts, thinly sliced

1 carrot, peeled and cut into ½-inch (12-mm) dice

1 celery rib, cut into ½-inch (12-mm) dice

Salt and freshly ground black pepper

½ cup (2½ oz/75 g) all-purpose flour

½ tsp dry mustard

4 cups (32 oz/1 l) chicken broth

1 bottle (12 fl oz/375 ml) good-quality ale such as Bass or Newcastle

2 cups (8 oz/250 g) shredded sharp Cheddar cheese

¼ cup (1 oz/30 g) grated Parmesan cheese

Pinch of cayenne pepper

1 tsp Worcestershire sauce

In a large, heavy pot, melt the butter over medium heat. Add the leek, carrot, and celery and sauté until softened, about 10 minutes. Season with salt and pepper.

Stir in the flour and mustard until incorporated and cook for about 1 minute. Add the broth and ale and bring to a simmer over high heat. Reduce the heat to medium and cook, whisking to break up any lumps of flour, until the mixture is slightly thickened, about 5 minutes.

Add the cheeses and whisk constantly until completely melted, 3–5 minutes. Do not let the soup boil, or it may develop a stringy texture. Stir in the cayenne and Worcestershire sauce. Season with salt and pepper and serve.

13

Barley, an excellent source of minerals and fiber, deserves its renaissance in the modern kitchen. Thanks to a partial puréeing, this creamy soup supports meaty fall mushrooms. Add a Parmesan rind to the broth as it simmers for a boost in flavor.

SAVORY BARLEY SOUP WITH WILD MUSHROOMS & THYME

serves 4

½ oz (15 g) dried porcini mushrooms

½ cup (4 fl oz/125 ml) dry white wine

1 Tbsp olive oil

½ cup (2 oz/60 g) chopped shallots

2 cloves garlic, minced

8 oz (250 g) cremini mushrooms, chopped

1 tsp minced fresh thyme, or ½ tsp dried

Salt and freshly ground pepper

3 cups (24 fl oz/750 ml) chicken broth

¾ cup (6 oz/185 g) pearl barley

1 Tbsp tomato paste

2 tsp fresh lemon juice

Rinse the porcini well to remove any dirt or grit. In a small saucepan, bring the wine to a simmer. Remove from the heat and add the porcini. Let stand for 15 minutes, then drain the porcini over a bowl, reserving the liquid, and finely chop.

In a large, heavy pot over medium-high heat, warm the oil. Add the shallots and garlic. Sauté until the shallots are wilted, 3–5 minutes. Add the cremini, thyme, ¼ tsp salt, and ¼ tsp pepper. Cook until the cremini release their liquid and begin to brown, 4–5 minutes. Add the reserved mushroom soaking liquid and bring to a boil, scraping up any browned bits from the pan bottom.

Add the broth, barley, tomato paste, 3 cups (24 fl oz/750 ml) water, and the chopped porcini to the pot. Cover and simmer until the barley is tender to the bite, 45–50 minutes. Remove from the heat and let cool slightly.

Purée about 1 cup (8 fl oz/250 ml) of the soup in a blender. Return to the pot, heat until just hot, and stir in the lemon juice. Season with salt and pepper and serve.

14

Apples, leeks, and cider create a complexity of flavor that makes this winter squash purée rich in character and in little need of embellishment. To save time, substitute 2½ lb (1.25 kg) butternut squash chunks from the produce section. Accompany with a warm baguette and a bottle of dry French cider.

APPLE, LEEK & BUTTERNUT SQUASH SOUP

serves 8

1 or 2 butternut squash (about 4 lb/2 kg total), halved, seeded, peeled, and cut into chunks

1 lb (500 g) tart apples, peeled, cored, and quartered, plus 1 small tart apple, unpeeled, halved, cored, and thinly sliced

1 large leek, white and pale green parts, thickly sliced

4 large cloves garlic

2 Tbsp chopped sage, plus whole leaves for garnish (optional)

2 tsp ground cumin

Salt and freshly ground pepper

3 Tbsp olive oil

4 cups (32 fl oz/1 l) chicken broth

1 cup (8 fl oz/250 ml) hard cider or dry white wine

8 Tbsp (4 oz/125 g) crème fraîche or sour cream

Preheat the oven to 425°F (220°C). Place the squash, quartered apples, leek, and garlic on a rimmed baking sheet. Sprinkle with 1 Tbsp of the chopped sage and 1 tsp of the cumin. Season with salt and pepper. Drizzle with the oil, stir to coat, and spread the apples and vegetables in a single layer.

Roast, stirring 2 or 3 times, until the squash is fork-tender and all the vegetables and apples are golden, 20–25 minutes. Remove from the oven.

Working in batches, process in a food processor until a coarse purée forms. With the motor running, pour in 1–1½ cups (8–12 fl oz/250–375 ml) of the broth and process until nearly smooth. Transfer the purée to a large, heavy pot over medium heat. Stir in the remaining broth, the cider, and the remaining 1 Tbsp chopped sage and 1 tsp cumin and bring just to a simmer, stirring often. Season with salt and pepper.

Ladle the soup into shallow bowls and top each serving with 1 Tbsp crème fraîche. Float a few apple slices in each bowl. Garnish with sage leaves, if using, and serve.

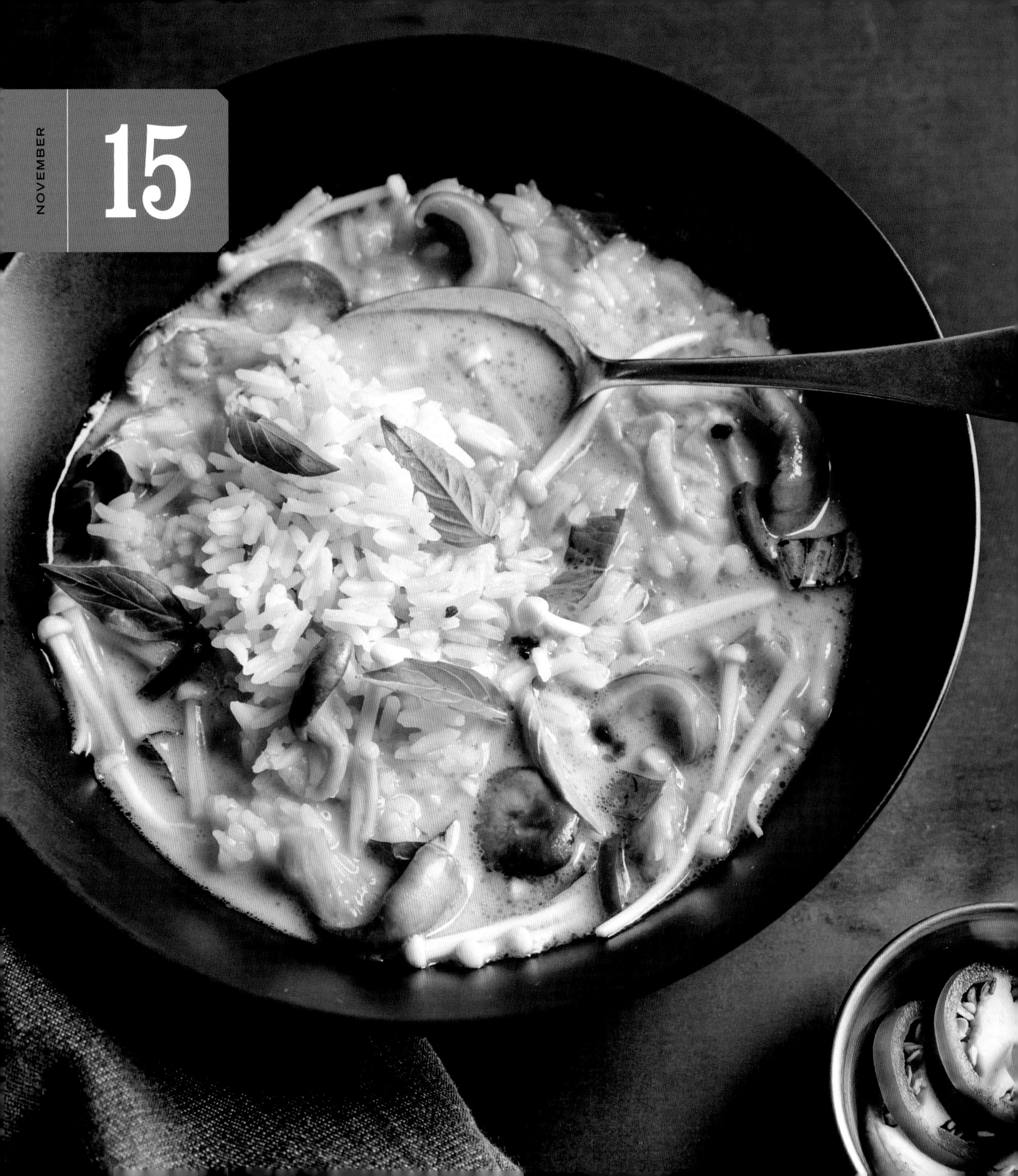

NOVEMBER

15

15

SPICY COCONUT-MANDARIN
SOUP WITH MUSHROOMS

serves 6

1 cup (7 oz/220 g) long-grain white
or brown rice

1 cup (8 fl oz/250 ml) chicken broth

1 can (14 fl oz/430 ml) coconut milk

1 Tbsp grated mandarin orange zest

½ cup (4 fl oz/125 ml) mandarin orange juice,
strained (from about 3 oranges)

1 Tbsp Asian fish sauce

1 tsp Thai chile paste

1 serrano chile, seeded and minced

2 cups (6 oz/185 g) enoki mushrooms or
quartered button mushrooms

½ cup (1½ oz/45 g) chopped
oyster mushrooms

½ cup (¾ oz/20 g) chopped basil

Salt and freshly ground pepper

The combination of citrus and coconut milk is common in Southeast Asian dishes, especially in curries and soups. Mandarins are typically a little sweeter than oranges, but oranges could be used here, as well. This soup is served over rice for a main dish, but it would also make a satisfying appetizer without the rice.

In a saucepan, bring 2 cups (16 fl oz/500 ml) water to a boil over medium-high heat. Add the rice, reduce the heat to low, cover, and cook until the rice is tender and the water has been absorbed, about 20 minutes for white rice and about 40 minutes for brown rice. Remove from the heat and keep covered.

In a large, heavy pot, combine the broth, coconut milk, mandarin orange zest and juice, fish sauce, chile paste, and serrano chile. Place over medium-high heat and bring to a boil. Reduce the heat to medium and simmer for about 5 minutes. The soup will be slightly foamy and will have turned a golden-orange color. Add the mushrooms and cook until tender, about 5 minutes. Remove from the heat and stir in the basil, ½ tsp salt, and ¼ tsp pepper.

Spoon the rice into bowls, ladle the soup over the rice, and serve.

16

PENNE & SQUASH SOUP
WITH SAGE CROUTONS

serves 6

1 Tbsp plus 1 tsp olive oil

2 lb (1 kg) butternut squash, halved
lengthwise and seeded

Salt and freshly ground pepper

6 oz (185 g) penne pasta

1 Tbsp unsalted butter

3 slices bacon, coarsely chopped

1 large yellow onion, coarsely chopped

6 cups (48 fl oz/1.5 l) chicken broth

Pinch of grated nutmeg

¾ cup (3 oz/90 g) coarsely shredded
Gruyère cheese

18 flat-leaf parsley leaves

Sage Croutons (left)

To make the sage croutons, in a large bowl, toss together ½ lb (250 g) cubed crustless country-style bread, 2 Tbsp olive oil, and 1 Tbsp chopped sage. Season with salt and pepper. Bake in a preheated 350°F (190°C) oven for about 10 minutes, until crisp and golden.

Preheat the oven to 375°F (190°C). Coat a baking sheet with the 1 tsp olive oil. Place the squash on the baking sheet cut side down. Bake the squash until soft, about 1 hour. With a large spoon, scoop the squash pulp from the skin and discard the skin.

In a large pot, bring 4 qt (4 l) water to a boil over high heat. Add 2 tsp salt and the penne and cook until al dente, 10–12 minutes, or according to package directions. Drain the penne and toss it immediately with the 1 Tbsp oil.

In a large, heavy pot, melt the butter over medium heat. Add the bacon and onion and cook, uncovered, until the onion is soft, about 10 minutes. Add the squash and broth and simmer, uncovered, until the squash falls apart, about 30 minutes. Remove from the heat and let cool slightly.

Working in batches, purée the soup in a blender or food processor. Return to the pot. Add the penne, nutmeg, and salt and pepper to taste. Stir to mix well and serve, garnished with the Gruyère, parsley, and croutons.

17

KALE & SWEET POTATO SOUP WITH LAMB SAUSAGE

serves 6–8

3 sweet potatoes (about 2 lb/1 kg total), cut into 1½-inch (4-cm) chunks

2 Tbsp olive oil

Salt and freshly ground pepper

½ lb (250 g) lamb sausage, such as merguez

1 large yellow onion, finely chopped

4 cloves garlic, minced

2 tsp minced thyme

8 cups (64 fl oz/2 l) chicken broth

1 large red potato, peeled and cut into ¾-inch (2-cm) pieces

1 small bunch kale (about 1 lb/500 g), ribs removed, leaves cut crosswise into ¼-inch (6-mm) pieces

North African in origin, merguez is a lamb or beef sausage spiced with chiles or harissa. Starchy sweet potatoes and leafy kale make perfect foils for the spicy sausage.

Preheat the oven to 450°F (230°C). Line a rimmed baking sheet with foil. In a large bowl, toss together the sweet potatoes, 1½ Tbsp of the oil, and salt and pepper to taste. Spread in a single layer on the prepared baking sheet and roast until barely tender, about 20 minutes.

In a large, heavy pot, heat the remaining ½ Tbsp oil over medium heat. Add the sausage and cook, turning occasionally, until browned all over, about 8 minutes. Transfer to paper towels to drain. Add the onion to the pot and sauté until softened, about 5 minutes. Stir in the garlic and thyme and cook until fragrant, about 45 seconds. Add 3 cups (24 fl oz/750 ml) of the broth, raise the heat to high, and bring to a boil, using a wooden spoon to scrape up any browned bits from the bottom of the pot. Add the red potato, cover, and cook until tender, about 25 minutes. Meanwhile, cut the sausage into slices ½ inch (12 mm) thick.

Use a wooden spoon to mash the potatoes against the side of the pot, then stir them into the soup to thicken it. Add the sausage and remaining 5 cups (40 fl oz/1.25 l) broth and bring to a boil. Reduce the heat to low and simmer for 10 minutes to blend the flavors. Raise the heat to medium, add salt and pepper to taste, the roasted sweet potatoes, and the kale and cook, stirring often, until the kale is tender, about 8 minutes. Taste and adjust the seasoning and serve.

18

MUSTARD GREENS & WILD RICE SOUP WITH GRUYÈRE

serves 4

1 cup (6 oz/185 g) wild rice

3 Tbsp unsalted butter

½ lb (250 g) white mushrooms, thinly sliced

Salt and freshly ground pepper

½ cup (4 fl oz/125 ml) dry sherry

1 Tbsp olive oil

1 yellow onion, chopped

5 cloves garlic, minced

5 cups (40 fl oz/1.25 l) chicken broth, plus more as needed

1 bunch mustard greens, coarsely chopped

¼ lb (125 g) Gruyère cheese, coarsely shredded

It takes only minutes to cook mustard greens, so be careful not to let the peppery leaves get soggy. Melted Gruyère on top brings the soup together. Serve with warm herbed popovers (simply add chopped fresh herbs such as chives or thyme to popover batter).

In a small saucepan, cook the wild rice according to package directions.

In a frying pan, melt 2 Tbsp of the butter over medium-high heat. Add the mushrooms and season with salt and pepper. Sauté until the mushrooms release their liquid and turn golden, about 5 minutes. Add the sherry and bring to a simmer, stirring to scrape up any browned bits on the pan bottom, and cook for 2 minutes. Remove from the heat and set aside.

In a large, heavy pot, melt the remaining 1 Tbsp butter with the oil over medium-high heat. Add the onion and garlic and sauté until translucent, about 5 minutes. Add the 5 cups broth (40 fl oz/1.25 l) and the mushrooms with all their juices, and bring to a boil. Reduce the heat to medium-low and simmer for 10 minutes. Add the wild rice and mustard greens and simmer, stirring occasionally, for 5 minutes. Season with salt and pepper and serve, topped with the shredded cheese.

19

SALSIFY & MUSHROOM CHOWDER WITH ROSEMARY OIL

serves 4–6

6 Tbsp (3 fl oz/90 ml) olive oil

2 shallots, chopped

2 celery ribs, chopped

2 salsifies, peeled and sliced

¾ lb (375 g) small Yukon Gold potatoes, cut into ¼-inch pieces

Salt and freshly ground pepper

4 cups (32 fl oz/1 l) vegetable or chicken broth

4 rosemary sprigs

½ lb (250 g) cremini mushrooms, thickly sliced

1 cup (8 fl oz/250 ml) half-and-half

Salsify is a root vegetable with the shape of a slender parsnip. It has dark, thick skin and a creamy white interior. Salsify is particularly meaty, so it adds some real substance to this chowder. Once it is peeled and cut, it must be immersed in acidulated water (lemon juice or white vinegar is fine) to prevent it from discoloring. After you fry the rosemary, crumble it, combine it with kosher salt, and rub it on pork chops or steaks for the grill.

In a large, heavy pot, warm 2 Tbsp of the oil over medium-high heat. Add the shallots and celery and cook, stirring occasionally, until soft, about 5 minutes. Add the salsifies and potatoes, season with salt and pepper, and toss to coat in the oil. Cook, stirring occasionally, until the vegetables soften, about 8 minutes. Add the broth and bring to a boil. Reduce the heat to low and simmer until the vegetables are fork-tender, about 15 minutes.

Meanwhile, in a frying pan, warm the remaining 4 Tbsp (2 fl oz/60 ml) oil over medium heat. Add the rosemary and cook, flipping once, until crispy but not burned, about 4 minutes. Add the mushrooms and season with salt and pepper. Cook, stirring frequently, until the mushrooms deepen in color and soften but still hold their shape, about 5 minutes. Remove and discard the rosemary sprigs.

Stir the mushrooms into the chowder, including all of the rosemary oil from the pan. Stir in the half-and-half, raise the heat to medium-high, bring to a gentle boil, and cook until thickened, about 3 minutes. Season with salt and pepper and serve.

20

TOMATO-FENNEL BROTH WITH CLAMS

serves 4

1 cup (6 oz/180 g) cherry tomatoes

2 Tbsp olive oil

Salt and freshly ground pepper

1 Tbsp unsalted butter

2 cloves garlic, sliced

2 small fennel bulbs, stalks and fronds removed, cored, and sliced

2 shallots, minced

½ cup (4 fl oz/125 ml) dry white wine

1 cup (8 fl oz/250 ml) chicken broth

2 lb (1 kg) clams, scrubbed

¼ cup (⅓ oz/10 g) chopped flat-leaf parsley

For a soup with a milder licorice flavor, replace one of the fennel bulbs with 1 chopped yellow onion and 2 chopped celery ribs.

Preheat the oven to 500°F (260°C). Spread the cherry tomatoes on a rimmed baking sheet, toss with 1 Tbsp of the oil, and season with salt and pepper. Roast the tomatoes just until they soften and begin to split, about 7 minutes.

In a large, heavy pot, warm the butter and the remaining 1 Tbsp oil over medium-high heat. Add the garlic, fennel, and shallots and sauté until soft, about 5 minutes. Add the white wine and cook for 2 minutes. Add the broth and tomatoes and bring to a boil. Season with salt and pepper.

Add the clams to the pot, discarding any that do not close to the touch. Cover tightly and cook until the clams open, 8–10 minutes, discarding any unopened clams. Transfer the clams and broth to a serving bowl, sprinkle with the parsley, and serve family style.

21

A generous addition of cream turns this tomato bisque a warm, deep pink. With minimal hands-on cooking time, it makes a good weeknight supper. Serve with warmed crusty French or Italian bread.

TOMATO BISQUE

serves 4–6

2 Tbsp unsalted butter

⅓ cup (1½ oz/45 g) chopped shallots

2 cloves garlic, minced

2½ cups (20 fl oz/625 ml) vegetable broth

3 Tbsp long-grain white rice

Salt and ground white pepper

1 can (28 oz/875 g) crushed plum tomatoes

1 Tbsp torn basil leaves

1 cup (8 fl oz/250 ml) heavy cream

3 drops Tabasco sauce

Croutons for garnish

In a large saucepan, melt the butter over medium-low heat. Add the shallots and garlic and sauté until softened, about 3 minutes. Add the broth, rice, and ½ tsp salt and bring to a boil. Reduce the heat to low, cover, and cook until the rice is soft, 20–25 minutes.

Add the tomatoes and basil. Cover and simmer for 10 minutes. Remove from the heat and let cool slightly.

Purée in a blender until smooth, then push through a sieve with the back of a ladle and return to the saucepan over low heat. Whisk in the cream, ¼ tsp salt, ⅛ tsp pepper, and the Tabasco and reheat gently. Taste and adjust the seasoning and serve, garnished with the croutons.

22

An ancient preparation—the biblical "mess of pottage" for which Esau sold his birthright—red lentil soup remains common today in Egypt and Lebanon. Red lentils cook more quickly than other varieties, so are ideal for soups and puréeing.

LEMONY RED LENTIL SOUP WITH FRIED SHALLOTS

serves 4

2 Tbsp olive oil

1 yellow onion, chopped

1 tsp ground cumin

½ tsp ground coriander

Pinch of red pepper flakes

1 cup (7 oz/220 g) split red lentils, picked over and rinsed

1 carrot, peeled and finely chopped

1 tomato, peeled, seeded, and chopped

4 cups (32 fl oz/1 l) vegetable broth

Salt and freshly ground pepper

Juice of ½ lemon, plus 1 lemon cut into 4 wedges

Fried shallots (page 167)

In a large, heavy pot, warm the oil over medium-high heat. Add the onion and sauté until soft, about 5 minutes. Add the cumin, coriander, and red pepper flakes and cook, stirring, until the spices are fragrant, about 30 seconds.

Add the lentils, carrot, tomato, and broth. Season with 1 tsp salt and a few grinds of pepper. Bring to a boil, reduce the heat to medium, cover, and simmer until the lentils fall apart and the carrots are soft, about 40 minutes. Remove from the heat and let cool slightly.

Working in batches, purée the soup in a blender. Return to the pot, add the lemon juice, and warm through over medium heat, stirring occasionally.

Serve, garnished with the fried shallots and accompanied with the lemon wedges.

23

The best part about this recipe is that it uses almost the entire pumpkin, and the seeds from the pumpkin are roasted to use for the garnish. You can also add a swirl of crème fraîche to each serving, if you like. Pack leftover toasted pumpkin seeds in your child's lunchbox for a fun snacktime treat.

PUMPKIN SOUP WITH SPICY PUMPKIN SEEDS

serves 6

1 small pumpkin (about 3 lb/1.5 kg), such as Sugar Pie, peeled, seeded, and chopped

2 Tbsp olive oil

Salt and freshly ground pepper

3 Tbsp unsalted butter

1 yellow onion, chopped

2 cloves garlic, minced

1 tsp ground cumin

½ tsp ground coriander

4 cups (32 fl oz/1 l) chicken broth

FOR THE SPICY PUMPKIN SEEDS

½ cup (2 oz/60 g) pumpkin seeds, cleaned

1 tsp canola oil

Salt

¼ tsp cayenne pepper

¼ tsp ground cumin

Pinch of ground cinnamon

Preheat the oven to 400°F (200°C) and line a baking sheet with parchment paper. Toss the pumpkin with the oil, season with salt and pepper, and spread on the prepared baking sheet. Roast the pumpkin until soft and caramelized, 30–35 minutes.

In a large, heavy pot, warm the butter over medium-high heat. Add the onion and garlic and sauté until translucent, about 5 minutes. Add the cumin and coriander and cook for 1 minute. Add the broth and pumpkin and bring to a boil. Reduce the heat to low and simmer for 25 minutes. Remove from the heat and let cool slightly.

Working in batches, purée the soup in a blender or food processor. Return to the pot and season with salt and pepper.

To make the spicy pumpkin seeds, lower the oven temperature to 350°F (180°C) and line a rimmed baking sheet with parchment paper. In a bowl, toss the seeds with the oil. In another bowl, combine 1 tsp salt, the cayenne, cumin, and cinnamon. Add the pumpkin seeds to the spice mixture and stir to coat. Spread the seeds in a single layer on the prepared baking sheet and bake, stirring once, until golden brown, 10–12 minutes. Serve the soup garnished with the pumpkin seeds.

24

Sunchokes are very curious-looking vegetables that are usually available from the end of October through March. It takes some time to peel them, but they produce a very mellow and delicious flavor similar to that of artichokes.

CREAM OF SUNCHOKE SOUP WITH PORCINI MUSHROOMS

serves 4

4 Tbsp (2 oz/60 g) unsalted butter

2 Tbsp olive oil

2 leeks, white and pale green parts, chopped

2 lb (1 kg) sunchokes (Jerusalem artichokes), peeled and thinly sliced

3 cups (24 fl oz/750 ml) vegetable broth

2 Tbsp heavy cream

Salt and ground white pepper

2 oz (60 g) porcini mushrooms, thinly sliced

1 Tbsp finely chopped chives

In a large saucepan, melt 2 Tbsp of the butter with the oil over medium-high heat. Add the leeks and sauté until soft, about 4 minutes. Add the sunchokes and sauté for 4 minutes. Add the broth and bring to a boil. Reduce the heat to low and simmer for 25 minutes, until the sunchokes are very tender. Remove from the heat and let cool slightly.

Working in batches, purée the soup in a blender. Return to the saucepan and stir in the cream. Bring to a gentle boil. Turn off the heat and season with salt and pepper.

In a small frying pan, melt the remaining 2 Tbsp butter over medium-high heat. Add the porcini and season with salt and pepper. Sauté until soft and golden, about 4 minutes.

Serve, topped with the porcini and chives.

25

TURKEY & JASMINE RICE SOUP WITH LEMONGRASS

serves 6–8

Lemongrass is citrusy and lightly herbal in taste, with a crisp, refreshing aroma. The fragrant herb shines new light on a familiar turkey soup that also receives a flavor boost from ginger, garlic, hot chiles, and jasmine rice.

1-inch (2.5-cm) piece fresh ginger

3 serrano chiles

2 tsp canola oil

1 yellow onion, finely chopped

3 cloves garlic, minced

4 lemongrass stalks, center white part only, smashed and minced

3 carrots, peeled and thinly sliced

8 cups (2 qt/2 l) chicken or turkey broth

1 cup (8 fl oz/250 ml) dry white wine

¾ cup (5 oz/155 g) jasmine rice or other long-grain white rice

Leftover shredded cooked turkey meat

Salt and freshly ground pepper

Peel the ginger, cut it into 4 equal slices, and crush each piece with the flat side of a chef's knife. Seed and mince 2 of the serrano chiles; cut the remaining chile crosswise into very thin rings and set aside.

In a large, heavy pot, warm the oil over medium heat. Add the onion and sauté until softened, about 5 minutes. Stir in the garlic, minced chiles, and lemongrass and cook until fragrant, about 45 seconds. Raise the heat to high, add the ginger, carrots, broth, and wine and bring to a boil. Stir in the rice, turkey, 2 tsp salt, and pepper to taste. Reduce the heat to low and simmer until the rice is tender, about 15 minutes. Remove and discard the ginger pieces.

Season the soup with salt and pepper and serve, garnished with the reserved chile slices.

26

GARLICKY GREENS, ROAST PORK & WHITE BEAN SOUP

serves 4–6

The next time you roast a pork tenderloin for dinner, roast two and then you'll be halfway to this soup for another night. Serve with warmed crusty bread and a glass of Pinot Noir.

1 small pork tenderloin (about ¾ lb/375 g)

4 Tbsp (2 fl oz/60 ml) olive oil

7 cloves garlic, minced

Salt and freshly ground pepper

½ yellow onion, chopped

1 bunch kale, ribs removed, leaves chopped

3 cups (24 fl oz/750 ml) chicken broth

4 plum tomatoes, seeded and chopped

1 can (15 oz/470 g) cannellini or other white beans, drained

Preheat the oven to 400°F (200°C). Place the pork tenderloin on a baking sheet and drizzle with 2 Tbsp of the oil. Rub about 2 cloves' worth of the minced garlic over the meat and season with salt and pepper. Roast in the oven until the pork is cooked through and a thermometer inserted into the thickest part registers 140°–150°F (60°–65°C), about 25 minutes. Transfer to a cutting board, let rest for at least 10 minutes, then cut into small cubes.

In a large, heavy pot, warm the remaining 2 Tbsp oil over medium-high heat. Add the remaining garlic and the onion and sauté until translucent, about 5 minutes. Add the kale and sauté for 4 minutes. Add the broth, tomatoes, beans, and pork and stir to combine. Simmer over low heat for 10 minutes to blend the flavors. Season with salt and pepper and serve.

27

CARROT SOUP WITH BACON & CHESTNUT CREAM

serves 8–10

For convenience, look for vacuum-packed steamed peeled chestnuts. The hard outer shells and bitter inner skins have already been peeled away, saving you from a labor of love. Avoid chestnuts packed in water in cans—they have poor texture and lack flavor.

4 slices bacon

¼ cup (2 oz/60 g) unsalted butter

1 yellow onion, chopped

1 leek, white and pale green parts, chopped

2 lb (1 kg) carrots, peeled and thinly sliced

1 russet potato, peeled and diced

6–8 cups (48–64 fl oz/1.5–2 l) chicken broth

FOR THE CHESTNUT CREAM

½ cup (2 oz/60 g) purchased steamed peeled chestnuts

¼ cup (2 fl oz/60 ml) chicken broth

⅓ cup (3 oz/90 g) crème fraîche or sour cream

Pinch of grated nutmeg

Salt and freshly ground pepper

2 Tbsp minced chives

In a large, heavy pot, fry the bacon over medium heat, turning once, until crisp, 6 minutes. Transfer to paper towels to drain. When cool, crumble the bacon and set aside.

Pour off the bacon fat from the pot, return the pan to medium heat, and add the butter. When the butter has melted, add the onion and leek and sauté until golden, about 10 minutes. Add the carrots, potato, and 6 cups (48 fl oz/1.5 l) of the broth and bring to a boil over high heat. Reduce the heat to low, cover partially, and simmer until all the vegetables are tender, about 45 minutes.

Meanwhile, make the chestnut cream. In a small saucepan, combine the chestnuts and broth over low heat. Bring to a simmer, cover, and cook until the chestnuts are tender, about 15 minutes. Remove from the heat and let cool slightly. Transfer to a blender, add the crème fraîche and nutmeg, and purée. Transfer to a small bowl and set aside.

Remove the vegetables from the heat and let cool slightly. Working in batches, purée in a blender. Return to the pot. If the soup is too thick, add broth as needed to thin to the desired consistency. Season with salt and pepper. Reheat the soup to serving temperature over low heat. Serve, topped with a swirl of the chestnut cream and the chives and bacon.

28

SPICED BROTH WITH ROASTED ACORN SQUASH & KALE

serves 4–6

Lining a baking sheet with parchment paper will ensure that roasted vegetables keep their flavorful caramelized outer layer and won't end up stuck to the sheet. Plus, it makes cleanup a whole lot easier.

1 acorn squash, peeled, seeded, and cubed

3 Tbsp olive oil

Salt and freshly ground pepper

¼ lb (125 g) thick-cut bacon, cut into ½-inch (12-mm) pieces

1 white onion, finely diced

2 cloves garlic, minced

1 tsp allspice

½ tsp grated nutmeg

¼ tsp ground cinnamon

1 bunch kale, ribs removed, and leaves cut crosswise into ½-inch (12-mm) strips

6 cups (48 fl oz/1.5 l) chicken broth

Preheat the oven to 400°F (200°C) and line a baking sheet with parchment paper. Toss the squash with 2 Tbsp of the oil, season with salt and pepper, and spread on the prepared baking sheet. Roast the squash until tender but not mushy, about 20 minutes.

In a large, heavy pot, cook the bacon over medium-high heat until crispy, about 10 minutes. Transfer the bacon to paper towels to drain. Add the remaining 1 Tbsp oil to the bacon fat in the pot. Add the onion, garlic, allspice, nutmeg, and cinnamon and cook, stirring frequently, until the onion is soft, 5–7 minutes. Add the kale and squash, stir to coat, and cook for 3 minutes. Add the broth, bring to a simmer, and cook for 10 minutes to blend the flavors. Stir in the bacon, season with salt and pepper, and serve.

SHRIMP BISQUE

serves 8

5 thyme sprigs

5 flat-leaf parsley sprigs

1 small yellow onion, quartered

1 small carrot, peeled and quartered

8 peppercorns

2 bay leaves

1½ lb (750 g) shrimp in the shell, preferably with the heads on

⅓ cup (3 fl oz/80 ml) olive oil

1 bottle (24 fl oz/750 ml) dry white wine

Salt and freshly ground pepper

4 cups (32 fl oz/1 l) heavy cream

Shells are the secret to many a great seafood soup. For this bisque, you cook the shrimp, peel them, and then sauté the shells alone before returning them to the simmering stock. This concentrates the rich flavors.

In a large, heavy pot, combine 6 cups (48 fl oz/1.5 l) water, the thyme, parsley, onion, carrot, peppercorns, and bay leaves. Bring to a boil over medium-high heat. Add the shrimp and cook just until opaque, 1–2 minutes. Using a slotted spoon, transfer the shrimp to a colander and rinse under cold running water. Reduce the heat to low so the broth simmers.

Cover and refrigerate 8 shrimp in the shell. Peel the remaining shrimp, reserving the heads and shells. Chop the shrimp, cover, and refrigerate.

In a frying pan, warm the oil over medium-high heat. When hot, add the shrimp heads and shells and sauté until fragrant and beginning to brown, 5–8 minutes. Reduce the heat to medium and sauté for 15 minutes. Add the shells to the broth and cook until reduced to 2 cups (16 fl oz/500 ml), about 45 minutes. Using the slotted spoon, remove the herbs, vegetables, and shells and heads and discard. Add the wine, raise the heat to high, and bring to a boil. Reduce the heat to low and simmer, uncovered, until reduced to 3 cups (24 fl oz/750 ml), 30–40 minutes. Season with 1 tsp salt.

Add the cream, raise the heat to medium-high, and heat, stirring, until small bubbles form along the edge of the pan. Reduce the heat to medium and simmer, stirring frequently, until reduced to about 4 cups (32 fl oz/1 l) and the soup is thick and ⟩⟩

creamy, about 20 minutes. Taste and adjust the seasoning with salt. Strain the soup through a fine-mesh sieve. Pour into a clean pot and heat over medium heat, stirring, until small bubbles form along the edge of the pan. Remove from the heat and cover.

To serve, divide the chopped shrimp among bowls. Ladle the soup on top, float a reserved unpeeled shrimp in the center of each bowl, sprinkle with pepper, and serve.

TURKEY NOODLE SOUP WITH SPINACH

serves 8–10

2 Tbsp olive oil

1 yellow onion, chopped

3 cloves garlic, minced

3 carrots, peeled and finely diced

4 celery ribs, finely diced

1½ Tbsp minced thyme

8 cups (64 fl oz/2 l) chicken broth

½ lb (250 g) wide egg noodles

2½ cups (15 oz/470 g) shredded cooked turkey meat

2 cups (2 oz/60 g) packed spinach leaves

Salt and freshly ground pepper

A noodle soup is the perfect way to finish off the last bits of meat from a turkey roast. If you just can't take one more day of the bird, stick this in your freezer and save it for another time.

In a large, heavy pot, warm the oil over medium-high heat. Add the onion, garlic, carrots, celery, and thyme and sauté until the carrots begin to soften, about 8 minutes. Add the broth and bring to a boil. Add the egg noodles and cook until al dente, about 5 minutes. Add the turkey and spinach and stir to combine. Simmer the soup for 5 minutes to blend the flavors. Season to taste with salt and pepper and serve.

5

JERUSALEM ARTICHOKE SOUP
WITH HAZELNUT-ORANGE BUTTER
page 277

6

ASIAGO, FONTINA & STOUT SOUP
WITH SPICY CARAMELIZED PEARS
page 277

7

ORZO, DELICATA SQUASH &
CHICKEN SOUP WITH SAGE
page 279

12

ITALIAN-STYLE CLAM
SOUP WITH PASTA
page 281

13

CHICKEN & HOMINY SOUP
WITH ANCHO CHILES
page 282

14

KOREAN KIMCHI & TOFU SOUP
page 282

19

SHIITAKE BROTH WITH
BUTTER-POACHED LOBSTER & CHIVES
page 287

20

CHICKPEA SOUP
page 287

21

WEDDING SOUP
page 288

26

LINGUIÇA & POTATO STEW
WITH TWO PAPRIKAS
page 292

27

GINGER CHICKEN SOUP
page 293

28

CURRIED CREAM OF CELERY SOUP
page 293

With the winter holidays in full swing, soups become festive party fare that can often be made ahead. Luxurious ingredients such as crab and lobster star in creamy bisques and elegant broths. Dress up bowls to suit the season with citrusy butters, spiced creams, or caviar toasts. Between parties, nourish and rebuild yourself with heartwarming soups of roots, grains, vegetables, and meats.

december

1

TOMATO SOUP WITH SMOKED PAPRIKA & BACON

serves 4–6

4 slices thick-cut bacon

1 Tbsp unsalted butter

1 yellow onion, chopped

2 cloves garlic, minced

2 cans (28 oz/875 g each) crushed tomatoes

3 Tbsp heavy cream

1¼ tsp smoked paprika

Salt and freshly ground pepper

Classic tomato soup gets a punch with smoked paprika and crumbled bacon. Serve with savory panini, such as provolone and arugula or Cheddar and sage.

In a large, heavy saucepan, fry the bacon over medium heat, turning once, until crispy, 8–10 minutes. Transfer to paper towels. Let cool, then crumble.

Add the butter to the pan and melt over medium heat. Add the onion and garlic and sauté until very soft, about 5 minutes. Add the tomatoes and bring to a boil. Reduce the heat to low and simmer for 20 minutes. Remove from the heat and let cool slightly.

Working in batches, purée the soup in a blender. Return to the saucepan and add the cream, paprika, and ½ tsp salt. Return just to a boil, turn off the heat, taste, and adjust the seasoning.

Serve, topped with the crumbled bacon and a generous grinding of pepper.

2

CREAM OF ONION SOUP

serves 4

5 Tbsp (2½ oz/75 g) unsalted butter

1½ lb (750 g) sweet onions, such as Vidalia or Walla Walla, thinly sliced

2 cups (16 fl oz/500 ml) milk, plus more if needed

2 cups (16 fl oz/500 ml) chicken or vegetable broth

3 Tbsp all-purpose flour

Salt and freshly ground pepper

½ cup (4 fl oz/125 ml) heavy cream

½ cup (4 fl oz/125 ml) dry sherry

Onions, the aromatic base of so many silky cream soups, are allowed to shine on their own in this preparation. Favorite varieties such as Walla Walla, Maui, or Vidalia (named after the places they are grown) deliver a natural sweetness. This soup complements a savory roast.

In a large frying pan, melt 2 Tbsp of the butter over medium heat. Add the onions, reduce the heat to low, cover, and sauté until softened, about 5 minutes. Uncover and continue sautéing until golden, 10–12 minutes. Let cool slightly, then finely chop the onions in a food processor.

Pour the 2 cups (16 fl oz/500 ml) milk and the broth into separate small saucepans and place over low heat. Heat both just until small bubbles form around the edge of the pan, then remove from the heat.

In a large, heavy pot, melt the remaining 3 Tbsp butter over medium-low heat. When the foam begins to subside, sprinkle in the flour and whisk until smooth, about 2 minutes. Gradually add the hot milk while whisking and cook, stirring often, until the mixture bubbles vigorously and has thickened, about 3 minutes. Gradually add the hot broth, whisking, and bring to a low boil. Cook until pale beige and opaque, about 3 minutes. Let cool slightly.

Add the chopped onions to the pot and season with salt and pepper. Reduce the heat to a bare simmer, cover, and cook for 10 minutes, stirring occasionally. Remove from the heat and let cool slightly.

Working in batches, purée the soup in a blender or food processor. Return to the pot and stir in the cream. Place over low heat and reheat gently, stirring constantly. If the soup seems too thick, thin it with a little milk to the desired consistency. Taste and adjust the seasoning. Stir in the sherry, heat through, and serve.

3

SPLIT PEA SOUP

serves 4

1 Tbsp olive oil

1 yellow onion, finely diced

1 celery rib, thinly sliced

2 small carrots, peeled and thinly sliced

1 cup (7 oz/220 g) dried green or yellow split peas, picked over and rinsed

4 cups (32 fl oz/1 l) chicken or vegetable broth

6 slices bacon

2 Tbsp finely chopped flat-leaf parsley

½ tsp finely chopped marjoram

½ tsp finely chopped thyme

Salt and freshly ground pepper

You can substitute the fresh marjoram and thyme with dried in this recipe; just use half as much. Always use fresh parsley in recipes; it is easy to find and tastes infinitely better than dried parsley.

In a large, heavy pot, warm the oil over medium heat. Add the onion and sauté until softened, 3–5 minutes. Add the celery and carrots and sauté just until slightly softened, 3 minutes.

Add the split peas, broth, 2 slices of the bacon, parsley, marjoram, and thyme. Reduce the heat to medium-low and bring to a simmer. Cover partially and cook until the peas are tender, 50–60 minutes. Remove from the heat, discard the bacon, and let cool slightly.

Meanwhile, in a frying pan, fry the remaining 4 slices bacon over medium heat, turning once, until crisp, 8–10 minutes. Transfer to paper towels to drain. Let cool, then crumble.

Coarsely purée 2 cups (16 fl oz/500 ml) of the soup in a food processor and return to the pot. Season with salt and pepper to taste, return the soup to medium heat, and simmer for 5 minutes. Taste and adjust the seasoning.

Serve, garnished with the crumbled bacon.

4

CHESTNUT SOUP WITH SPICED CREAM

serves 4–6

FOR THE SPICED CREAM

½ cup (4 fl oz/125 ml) heavy cream

¼ tsp sugar

Pinch of ground cinnamon

Pinch of ground nutmeg

Pinch of ground ginger

Salt

FOR THE SOUP

4 Tbsp (2 oz/60 g) unsalted butter, cut into small pieces

1 yellow onion, diced

1 celery rib, diced

15 oz (470 g) peeled roasted chestnuts

4 cups (32 fl oz/1 l) chicken broth

2 Tbsp Marsala

½ cup (4 fl oz/125 ml) heavy cream

Salt and freshly ground pepper

Unlike most nuts, chestnuts contain little fat, making them a healthful and delicious addition to holiday menus, where calories can typically add up. With their subtle, nutty taste, they offer the perfect balance to richer ingredients, such as the butter and cream in this soup. You can alter the spices here as you like, trading out the cinnamon for cardamom, for example.

To make the spiced cream, in a small bowl, combine the cream, sugar, cinnamon, nutmeg, ginger, and a pinch of salt and stir until the sugar has dissolved. Refrigerate for 1 hour.

To make the soup, in a large, heavy pot, melt the butter over medium heat. Add the onion and celery and cook, stirring occasionally, until tender and translucent, 3–5 minutes. Add the chestnuts and broth, raise the heat to high, and bring to a boil. Reduce the heat to low and simmer until the chestnuts are very soft, about 20 minutes. Let cool slightly.

Working in batches, purée the soup in a food processor or blender. Return to the pot and add the Marsala and cream. Season with salt and pepper and stir to combine. Place over medium heat and gently reheat the soup.

Whisk the spiced cream until lightly foamy. Serve the soup, garnished with a swirl of the spiced cream.

5

JERUSALEM ARTICHOKE SOUP WITH HAZELNUT-ORANGE BUTTER

serves 6

Jerusalem artichokes, also known as sunchokes, are a favorite of the cold-weather months. To make the hazelnut-orange butter, finely chop ¼ cup (1¼ oz/37 g) toasted and skinned hazelnuts. Mix with 2 Tbsp softened butter and 1 tsp grated orange zest and season to taste with salt and pepper. Roll into 6 teaspoon-sized balls and refrigerate until ready to serve.

3 Tbsp unsalted butter

3 celery ribs with leaves, diced

3 large yellow onions, diced

2½ tsp ground coriander

3 lb (1.5 kg) Jerusalem artichokes, unpeeled, cut into 1-inch (2.5-cm) pieces

2 large strips orange zest

9 cups (2¼ qt/2.25 l) chicken broth

3 Tbsp fresh orange juice

Salt and freshly ground pepper

Hazelnut-Orange Butter (left)

In a large, heavy pot, melt the butter over medium heat. Add the celery and onions and sauté until the vegetables are soft, about 10 minutes. Add the coriander and sauté for about 1 minute. Add the Jerusalem artichokes, orange zest, and broth and bring to a boil over high heat. Reduce the heat to medium-low and simmer, uncovered, until the Jerusalem artichokes are soft, about 30 minutes.

Remove the Jerusalem artichokes from the broth and let cool slightly. Remove the orange zest and discard. Working in batches, purée the soup in a blender. Strain the purée through a fine-mesh sieve into a clean saucepan. Add the orange juice and mix well. Season with salt and pepper.

Reheat the soup to serving temperature over medium heat. Serve, placing a piece of the flavored butter in the center of each helping.

6

ASIAGO, FONTINA & STOUT SOUP WITH SPICY CARAMELIZED PEARS

serves 6–8

Stout is a particularly hoppy dark beer. Guinness is probably the best-known brand, but any good-tasting stout will work here. This soup is quite rich, so the rest of the menu should be simple and refreshing, such a crisp green salad with apple slices and a warmed baguette.

4 Tbsp (2 oz/60 g) unsalted butter

2 shallots, finely chopped

2 celery ribs, finely chopped

Salt and freshly ground pepper

⅓ cup (2 oz/60 g) all-purpose flour

1 bottle (12 fl oz/375 ml) stout beer

1½ cups (12 fl oz/375 ml) half-and-half

2 cups (16 fl oz/500 ml) chicken broth

½ lb (250 g) Asiago cheese, shredded

½ lb (250 g) fontina cheese, shredded

2 Tbsp Worcestershire sauce

1 Tbsp Dijon mustard

FOR THE SPICY CARAMELIZED PEARS

3 Tbsp unsalted butter

2 pears, such as Anjou or Bosc, peeled, cored, and cut into very small pieces

1 small jalapeño chile, seeded, deribbed, and finely chopped

Salt and freshly ground pepper

In a large, heavy pot, melt the butter over medium-high heat. Add the shallots and celery, season with salt and pepper, and cook, stirring occasionally, until very soft, about 8 minutes. Stir in the flour and cook, stirring frequently, until it turns golden brown, about 4 minutes. Whisk in the beer, half-and-half, and broth and bring to a boil. Reduce the heat to medium-low and simmer, whisking frequently, until the soup thickens, about 8 minutes. Add the Asiago and fontina cheeses a handful at a time, stirring each addition until completely melted. Stir in the Worcestershire sauce and mustard, and season with salt and pepper. Keep warm over low heat.

To make the spicy caramelized pears, in a nonstick frying pan, melt the butter over high heat. Allow the butter to brown, but not burn, and then add the pears and jalapeño. Cook, stirring a few times, until the pears are golden brown, about 5 minutes. Season lightly with salt and pepper.

Serve the soup, topped with the spicy caramelized pears.

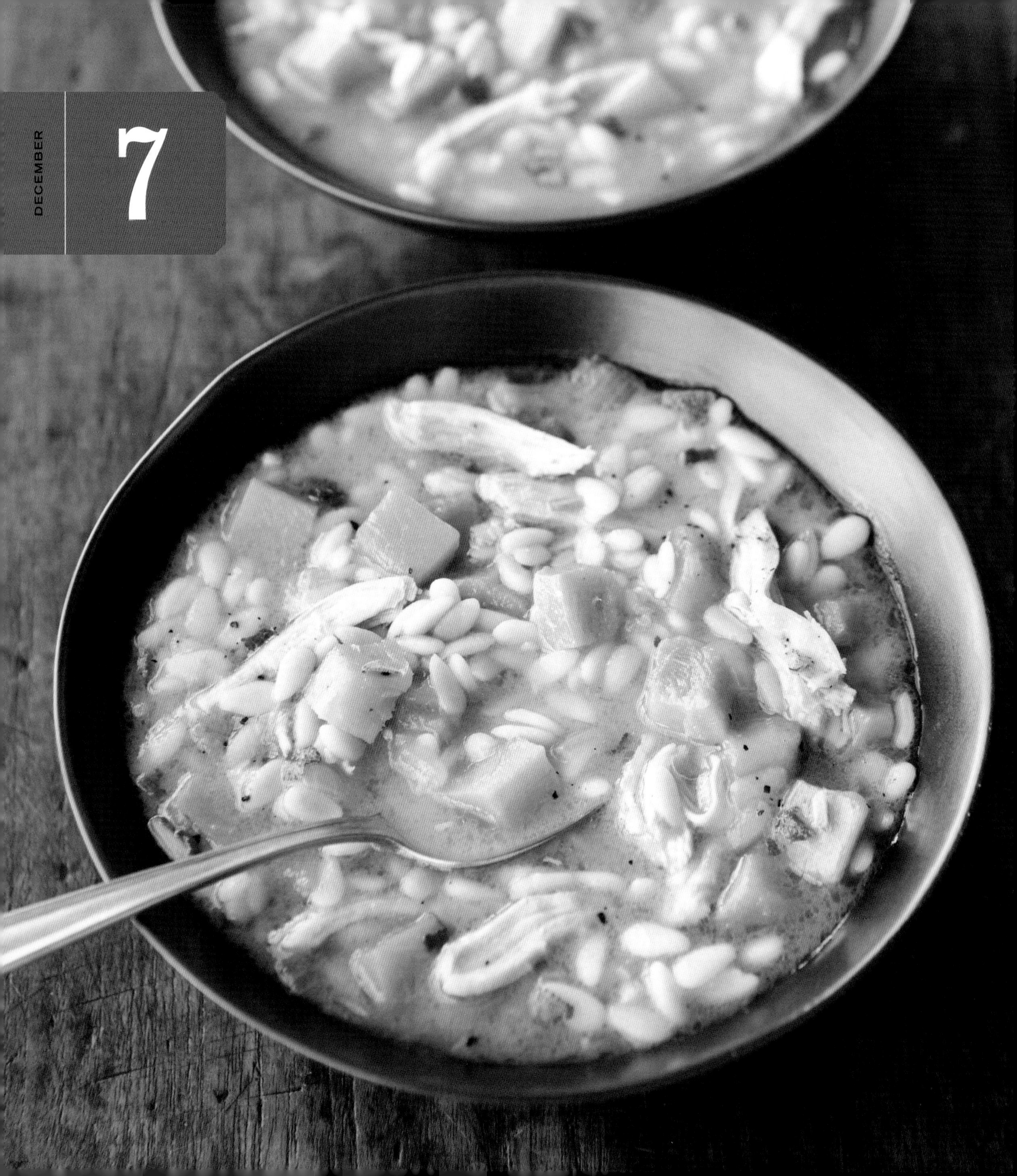

7

ORZO, DELICATA SQUASH & CHICKEN SOUP WITH SAGE

serves 4–6

4 delicata squash (2¾ lb/4 kg total), peeled, seeded, and cubed

3 Tbsp olive oil

Salt and freshly ground pepper

2 small skinless, boneless chicken breast halves (about ¾ lb/375 g total)

1 cup (7 oz/220 g) orzo

3 Tbsp unsalted butter

1 small yellow onion, chopped

3 cloves garlic, minced

5 sage leaves, torn into pieces

4 cups (32 fl oz/1 l) chicken broth

You can save time making this colorful and plentiful soup by using leftover rotisserie or roasted chicken. You can also substitute a different type of squash, or sweet potatoes. Make it meatless by omitting the chicken, substituting vegetable broth, and serving with shaved Parmesan.

Preheat the oven to 400°F (200°C) and line a baking sheet with parchment paper. Toss the squash with 2 Tbsp of the oil, season with salt and pepper, and spread on the prepared baking sheet. Place the chicken on another baking sheet, brush with the remaining 1 Tbsp oil, and season with salt and pepper. Place the squash on the top rack in the oven and the chicken on the lower rack. Roast until the chicken is cooked through and a thermometer inserted into the thickest part reaches 160°F (71°C), about 20 minutes. Remove the chicken from the oven and continue to roast the squash until it is tender and caramelized, about 10 minutes longer. When the chicken is cool enough to handle, shred it into bite-sized pieces.

Put 6 cups (48 fl oz/1.5 l) water in a saucepan over medium-high heat and bring to a boil. Add ½ tsp salt and the orzo and cook for 7 minutes. Drain the pasta and set aside.

In a large, heavy pot over medium-high heat, melt the butter. Add the onion, garlic, and sage and sauté until soft, about 5 minutes. Add the broth and bring to a boil. Add the orzo, shredded chicken, and squash and reduce the heat to low. Simmer for 15 minutes, then season to taste with salt and pepper and serve.

8

ROASTED SHALLOT & CRAB BISQUE

serves 6–8

1 lb (500 g) shallots, peeled

2 Tbsp olive oil

¾ cup (4 oz/125 g) canned diced tomatoes

Pinch of cayenne pepper

⅓ cup (2½ oz/75 g) white rice

4 cups (32 fl oz/1 l) crab, shellfish, or fish broth

½ cup (4 fl oz/125 ml) dry white wine

Shredded crabmeat from 1 lb (500 g) cooked king crab legs

⅓ cup (3 fl oz/80 ml) dry sherry

1 cup (8 fl oz/250 ml) half-and-half

1 Tbsp fresh lemon juice

Salt and ground white pepper

¼ cup (½ oz/15 g) minced chives

Mild-flavored shallots, sweetened with roasting, and shredded king crab meat star in this special seafood bisque worth adding to your holiday repertoire. Dry sherry, the iconic wine of Spain, provides an elegant underpinning for the briny-sweet flavors.

Preheat the oven to 400°F (200°C). In a bowl, toss the shallots with 1 Tbsp of the oil. Spread in a single layer on a rimmed baking sheet and roast in the oven for 20 minutes. Stir the shallots and continue roasting until browned and tender, about 20 minutes more.

In a large saucepan, warm the remaining 1 Tbsp oil over medium heat. Add two-thirds of the roasted shallots, the tomatoes with their juices, cayenne, and rice and stir to mix well. Add the crab broth and wine, raise the heat to high, and bring to a boil. Reduce the heat to low, cover, and simmer until the rice is completely tender, about 30 minutes. Remove from the heat and let cool slightly. Meanwhile, finely chop the remaining roasted shallots and set aside.

Working in batches, purée the soup in a blender. Pour into a clean pot. Add the chopped roasted shallots, crabmeat, sherry, half-and-half, lemon juice, 2¼ tsp salt, and pepper to taste. Place over medium-low heat and cook gently, stirring occasionally, until heated through, about 10 minutes. Taste and adjust the seasoning and serve, garnished with the chives.

9

SPAETZLE, ROAST CHICKEN & CHARD SOUP

serves 6

This hearty soup would seem right at home on a Sunday farmhouse supper table. Spaetzle, an egg pasta popular in Germany and Austria, comes in two shapes: button-like rounds and thin, short strands. Their cooking time differs, so follow the directions on the package. If you cannot find spaetzle, egg noodles or even orzo can be substituted.

¾ lb (375 g) skinless, boneless chicken breast halves

3 Tbsp olive oil

Salt and freshly ground pepper

6 oz (185 g) spaetzle

1 small yellow onion, chopped

2 cloves garlic, chopped

1 sweet potato (about ¾ lb/375 g), peeled and cut into ¾-inch (2-cm) cubes

1 can (14½ oz/455 g) whole plum tomatoes with juices

6 cups (48 fl oz/1.5 l) chicken broth

1 bunch chard (about ¾ lb/375 g), ribs removed, leaves chopped

½ cup (2 oz/60 g) grated Parmesan cheese

Preheat the oven to 375°F (190°C). Brush the chicken with 1 Tbsp of the oil and season with salt and pepper. Place in a small baking dish and roast until opaque throughout, about 25 minutes. When cool enough to handle, shred the chicken and set aside.

Bring a pot of salted water to a boil. Add the spaetzle and cook according to the package directions. Drain, rinse under cold water, and drain again. Set aside.

In a large, heavy pot, warm the remaining 2 Tbsp oil over medium-high heat. Add the onion and cook, stirring occasionally, until translucent, about 6 minutes. Add the garlic and sweet potato, season with salt and pepper, and cook, stirring occasionally, until the garlic is soft, about 2 minutes. Add the tomatoes with their juices and, using a wooden spoon, break up the tomatoes into smaller pieces. Add the broth, raise the heat to high, and bring to a boil. Reduce the heat to low and simmer until the sweet potato is fork-tender, about 15 minutes. Stir in the chicken, spaetzle, and chard and cook just until the chard wilts, about 2 minutes. Season with salt and pepper.

Serve, sprinkled generously with the cheese.

10

TURKEY STEW WITH FIGS & MADEIRA

serves 8

A boned, rolled turkey breast used in place of the bone-in breast simplifies the preparation. Serve with a soft bread, like challah, and a baby spinach salad dressed with mustard vinaigrette.

2 Tbsp canola oil

1 whole bone-in turkey breast, 3½–4 lb (1.5–2 kg)

¼ cup (2 oz/60 g) unsalted butter

2 large yellow onions, cut in half lengthwise and then crosswise into slices ½ inch (12 mm) thick

4 large carrots, peeled and cut into slices ½ inch (12 mm) thick

1 sweet potato, peeled and cut into ½-inch (12-mm) dice

1½ cups (8 oz/250 g) dried Calimyrna figs, stemmed and cut in half

3 cups (24 fl oz/750 ml) chicken broth

1 cup (8 fl oz/250 ml) Madeira wine

Salt and freshly ground pepper

In a large, heavy pot, warm the oil over medium-high heat. Add the turkey breast and brown on both sides, turning once, about 8 minutes.

Turn the turkey breastbone up and add the butter. When the butter melts, add the onions, carrots, sweet potato, and figs, stir to coat evenly with the butter, and cook until the vegetables begin to soften, about 8 minutes. Add the chicken broth and Madeira and bring to a simmer. Reduce the heat to medium-low, cover, and simmer gently for 2 hours.

Turn the turkey breast over, remove the bones, and continue to simmer gently, uncovered, until the turkey is tender and cooked through and the vegetables are soft, about 30 minutes.

Transfer the turkey breast to a cutting board and cut it across the grain into slices ½ inch (12 mm) thick. Cut the slices into bite-sized pieces, return to the pot, and stir to mix in with the vegetables. Heat to serving temperature, season with salt and pepper, and serve.

11

SWEET POTATO SOUP WITH CHEDDAR & CAVIAR CROUTONS

serves 8

8 baguette slices, ¼ inch (6 mm) thick

2 Tbsp olive oil

2 large sweet potatoes
(1½–2 lb/750 g–1 kg total)

4 cups (32 fl oz/1 l) chicken broth,
plus 2–4 cups (16–32 fl oz/250 ml–1 l)
more as needed

Salt and ground white pepper

¼ lb (125 g) white Cheddar cheese, shredded

2 oz (60 g) black caviar

This silky-sweet potato purée boasts unusual flavors and a striking presentation when topped with slices of baguette and bubbling oven-browned cheese. A final dollop of inky black caviar elevates it to the realm of swanky starters, fit for a special occasion.

Preheat the oven to 350°F (180°C).

Arrange the baguette slices in a single layer on a baking sheet and brush with 1½ Tbsp of the oil. Toast in the oven until lightly golden, about 15 minutes. Turn and toast until lightly golden on the second side, about 8 minutes. Set aside.

Rub the sweet potatoes with the remaining ½ Tbsp olive oil and place on a baking sheet. Bake until the skin is wrinkled and the flesh is easily pierced with a fork, 1–1½ hours. Remove from the oven. When the potatoes are cool enough to handle, cut in half lengthwise and scoop the flesh into a large, heavy pot. Add 4 cups (32 fl oz/250 ml) of the broth and whisk until smooth, adding more broth as needed to achieve a creamy but soupy consistency. Place over medium-high heat and bring to just below a boil, stirring often. Add ½ tsp pepper and salt to taste. Reduce the heat to low and simmer while you finish making the croutons.

Preheat the broiler. Sprinkle the toasted baguette slices with the cheese and arrange on a baking sheet. Broil just until the cheese melts, about 3 minutes.

To serve, ladle the soup into bowls. Spoon a dollop of caviar on top of each crouton and float a crouton in each bowl of soup.

12

ITALIAN-STYLE CLAM SOUP WITH PASTA

serves 6

Salt and freshly ground black pepper

¼ lb (125 g) small pasta shells

1 Tbsp extra-virgin olive oil

3 cups (24 fl oz/750 ml) fish broth

1 cup (8 fl oz/250 ml) dry white wine

2 cups (12 oz/375 g) canned diced tomatoes

4 cloves garlic, minced

6 flat-leaf parsley sprigs, tied together, plus 3 Tbsp finely chopped flat-leaf parsley

½ tsp chopped thyme

2 bay leaves

Cayenne pepper

4 lb (2 kg) clams, scrubbed

A light seafood supper can be a welcome break from richer holiday fare at this time of year. Serve with slices of toasted bread rubbed with cut garlic cloves and spread with aioli.

In a large pot, bring 3 quarts (3 l) water to a boil over high heat. Add 2 tsp salt and the pasta and cook until al dente, 12–15 minutes or according to package directions. Drain the pasta and toss it immediately with the olive oil. Set aside.

In a large pot, combine the broth, wine, 2 cups (16 fl oz/500 ml) water, the tomatoes with their juices, garlic, parsley sprigs, thyme, bay leaves, and cayenne to taste and bring to a boil over high heat. Reduce the heat to medium-low and simmer, covered, for 15 minutes. Remove and discard the parsley and bay leaves.

Add the clams to the pot, discarding any that do not close to the touch, and simmer, covered, shaking the pot occasionally, until the clams open, 3–5 minutes. Using a slotted spoon, remove the clams, discarding any unopened ones, and let them cool slightly. Remove the clams from the shells and discard the shells.

Return the clams to the pot. Add the pasta and chopped parsley and season with salt and pepper. Simmer until the pasta is heated through, about 1 minute, and serve.

13

CHICKEN & HOMINY SOUP WITH ANCHO CHILES

serves 6–8

Ancho chiles have very little heat, but they are rich with flavor—raisin, leather, tobacco, and even cocoa characterize their amazing complexity. Anchos give this hearty posole-inspired soup lusciousness and depth. Mild-tasting hominy balances the robust flavors, and cilantro and lime are sprightly finishing touches.

4 large ancho chiles, stemmed and seeded, flesh torn into pieces

1⅔ cups (13 fl oz/385 ml) boiling water

3 lb (1.5 kg) bone-in, skin-on chicken thighs

Salt and freshly ground pepper

2 tsp canola oil, or as needed

2 yellow onions, finely chopped

4 cloves garlic, minced

1 Tbsp ground cumin

1 Tbsp minced oregano

6 cups (48 fl oz/1.5 l) chicken broth

1 can (14½ oz/455 g) diced tomatoes

2 cans (29 oz/910 g each) hominy, drained

¼ cup (¼ oz/7 g) cilantro leaves

1 lime, cut into wedges

In a heatproof bowl, soak the chiles in the boiling water until softened, about 25 minutes. Transfer the chiles and their soaking liquid to a blender and purée. Strain though a fine-mesh sieve, pressing on the solids to extract as much liquid as possible. Discard the solids. Set the purée aside.

Season the chicken generously with salt and pepper. In a large, heavy pot, warm the oil over medium-high heat. In batches, place the chicken, skin side down, in the pot and cook until golden brown, about 5 minutes. Turn and cook until golden brown on the second side, about 5 minutes. Transfer to a large plate. Repeat to brown the remaining chicken, adding more oil to the pot if needed. When the chicken is cool enough to handle, remove the skin.

Pour off all but 1 Tbsp of fat from the pot and place over medium heat. Add about three-fourths of the chopped onions and sauté until softened, about 5 minutes. Stir in the garlic, cumin, and oregano and cook until fragrant, about 1 minute. Raise the heat to high, add the broth, bring to a simmer, and stir to scrape up any browned bits on the bottom of the pot. Add the chicken and any accumulated juices, the tomatoes with ⟶

their juices, and 1½ tsp salt and bring to a boil. Reduce the heat to low, cover partially, and simmer until the chicken is tender, about 40 minutes.

Transfer the chicken to a bowl. When cool enough to handle, shred the meat and discard the bones. Stir the shredded chicken, hominy, and chile purée into the pot. Simmer for about 15 minutes to blend the flavors. Season with salt and pepper, then stir in the cilantro. Serve, garnished with the remaining chopped onion and lime wedges.

14

KOREAN KIMCHI & TOFU SOUP

serves 4

You will need two traditional Korean ingredients for this homey recipe: kimchi, a ubiquitous fermented vegetable side dish, most commonly cabbage, and gochujang, a fiery chile paste used as both a table condiment and a kitchen seasoning. Both are sold in most grocery stores and many Asian markets. The best kimchi brands are stocked in the refrigerated section; choose the heat level— mild, medium, or spicy—according to your palate.

1 Tbsp vegetable or canola oil

½ yellow onion, chopped

2 tsp gochujang (see note)

1 jar (14 oz/440 g) mild kimchi, coarsely chopped, liquid reserved

2 cups (16 fl oz/500 ml) chicken or vegetable broth

1½ Tbsp low-sodium soy sauce

14 oz (440 g) silken tofu, drained and cut into 2-inch (5-cm) chunks

4 eggs

2 green onions, white and tender green parts, chopped

2 tsp sesame seeds, toasted

In a large, heavy pot, warm the oil over medium-high heat. Add the yellow onion and cook, stirring occasionally, until soft, about 6 minutes. Stir in the gochujang and then the kimchi, including all of the liquid from the jar. Add the broth and soy sauce and bring to a boil. Reduce the heat to medium-low, add the tofu, and simmer for 10 minutes.

Raise the heat to high and break the eggs into the soup, spreading them out so they will cook in a single layer. Cover and cook until the egg whites are set but the yolks are still runny, about 3 minutes. If you prefer the yolks set, spoon hot broth over them several times and they will cook all the way through.

Serve, including an egg in each bowl, and top with the green onions and sesame seeds.

DECEMBER 15

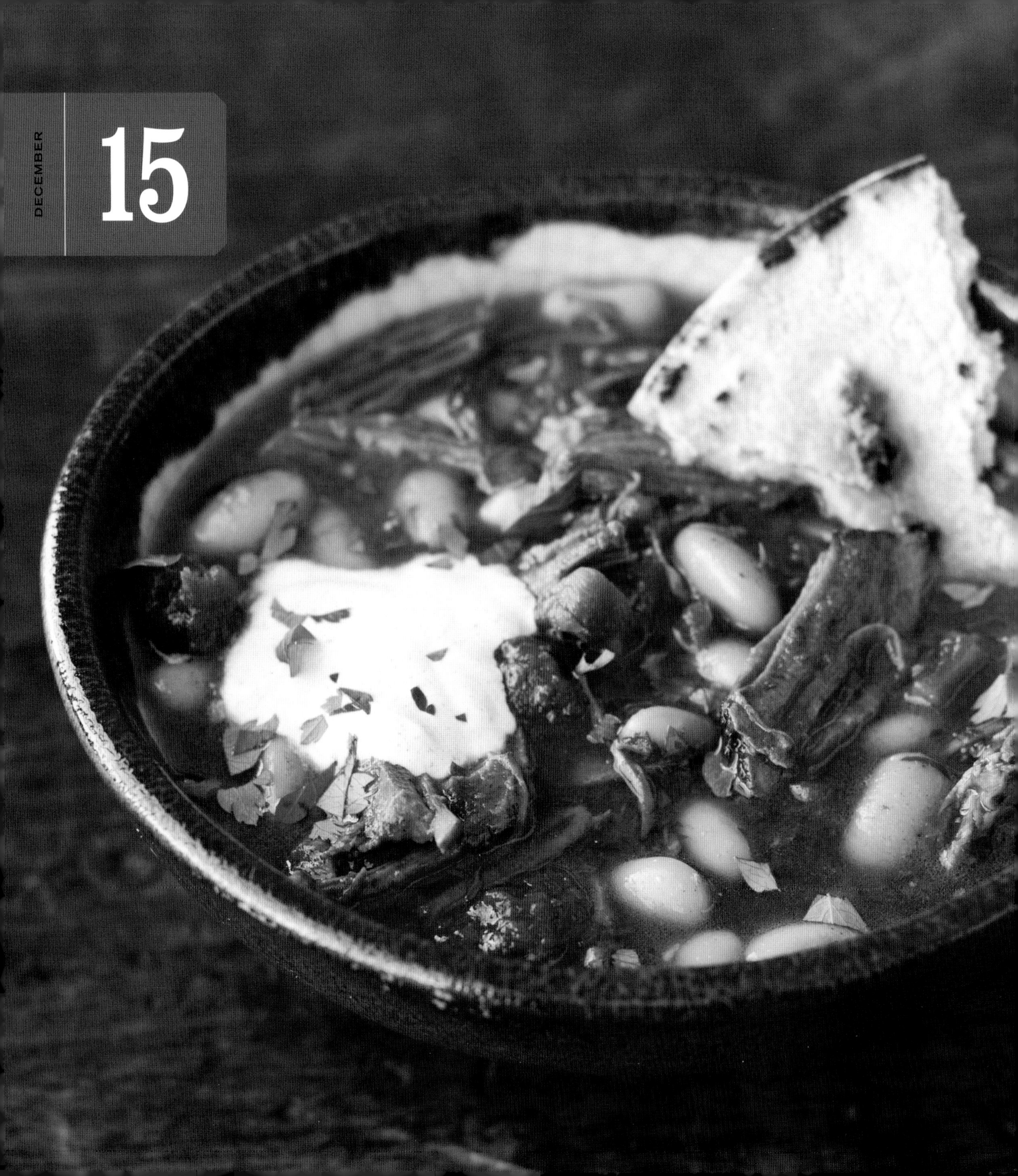

15

Short ribs braise slowly in the oven and come out caramelized and tender. This savory stew uses the shredded meat and the braising liquid. This is a great way to use leftover short rib meat (and if you don't have any leftover braising liquid, you can use beef broth).

SHORT RIB STEW WITH PAPRIKA SOUR CREAM

serves 4

3 lb (1.5 kg) short ribs, halved

Salt and freshly ground pepper

2 Tbsp olive oil

1 yellow onion, chopped

6 cloves garlic, minced

2 celery ribs, chopped

1 carrot, peeled and chopped

3 cups (24 fl oz/750 ml) dry red wine

2 bay leaves

4½ cups (36 fl oz/1.1 l) beef broth

1 can (15 oz/470 g) cannellini or other white beans, drained

1 can (14½ oz/455 g) diced tomatoes

¼ cup (⅓ oz/10 g) chopped flat-leaf parsley

FOR THE PAPRIKA SOUR CREAM

⅔ cup (5½ oz/170 g) sour cream

1 tsp fresh lemon juice

½ tsp smoked paprika

Salt

Season the short ribs with salt and pepper and refrigerate for at least 6 hours. Remove from the refrigerator, bring to room temperature, and season again with salt and pepper.

Preheat the oven to 350°F (180°C). In a large sauté pan, warm the oil over high heat until very hot. Sear the short ribs until they are browned on all sides, 6–8 minutes, then transfer to a large, heavy ovenproof pot.

Reduce the heat under the sauté pan to medium, add the onion, garlic, celery, and carrot, and sauté for 5 minutes. Add the wine and bay leaves, raise the heat to high, and boil until the liquid has been reduced by half, 10–12 minutes. Add the broth and bring to a boil. Pour the contents of the sauté pan into the pot. Cover tightly, transfer to the oven, and cook for 2½ hours.

Remove the short ribs from the pot and, when they are cool enough to handle, remove the meat from the bones and shred into bite-sized pieces. Strain the braising liquid and reserve 1¼ cups (10 fl oz/310 ml); discard the vegetables left in the sieve. »»

Put the shredded meat and the reserved braising liquid back into the pot and set over medium heat. Stir in the beans and the tomatoes with their juices and bring to a boil over medium-high heat. Stir in the parsley and season with salt and pepper.

To make the paprika sour cream, in a bowl, stir together the sour cream, lemon juice, paprika, and ¼ tsp salt. Serve the stew, topped with a generous dollop of the paprika sour cream.

16

Rutabagas, also known as swedes or yellow turnips, are often ignored because people just don't know what to do with them. They are sweet and very flavorful when roasted. Paired with carrots and allspice, they simmer into a delicious soup.

RUTABAGA & CARROT SOUP

serves 4–6

2 rutabagas (21 oz/655 g total), peeled and chopped

4 carrots, peeled and chopped

1 Tbsp olive oil

Salt and freshly ground pepper

2 Tbsp unsalted butter

1 yellow onion, chopped

2 cloves garlic, minced

½ tsp ground allspice

5 cups (40 fl oz/1.25 l) vegetable broth, plus more as needed

Preheat the oven to 400°F (200°C) and line a baking sheet with parchment paper. Toss the rutabagas and carrots with the oil and season with salt and pepper. Spread the vegetables on the prepared baking sheet and roast in the oven until tender, 20–25 minutes.

In a large, heavy pot, melt the butter over medium-high heat. Add the onion and garlic and sauté until the onion is translucent, about 5 minutes. Add the allspice, stir, and cook for 2 minutes. Add the broth and bring to a boil. Add the roasted rutabagas and carrots, reduce the heat to low, and simmer for 15 minutes. Remove from the heat and let cool slightly.

Working in batches, purée the soup in a blender. Return to the pot, add more broth if needed to achieve the desired consistency, season to taste with salt, and serve.

17

Oxtail is a highly flavorful, bony cut that must be slowly braised for a few hours to become tender. Look for a meaty oxtail, and if it is not already cut into pieces, ask the butcher to cut it into 2- to 3-inch (5- to 7.5-cm) pieces for you. Like many soups, braises, and stews, this dish tastes better after it has sat for a day or so, so prepare it on a lazy Sunday for a special weekday meal.

OXTAIL & ROOT VEGETABLE STEW WITH HORSERADISH CREMA

serves 4–6

3 lb (1.5 kg) oxtails, each cut into several pieces

Salt and freshly ground pepper

3 Tbsp olive oil

1 small yellow onion, chopped

4 cloves garlic, chopped

3 carrots, peeled and cut into ¾-inch (2-cm) pieces

2 parsnips, peeled and cut into ¾-inch (2-cm) pieces

2 rutabagas, peeled and cut into ¾-inch (2-cm) pieces

4 thyme sprigs

2 Tbsp all-purpose flour

1 cup (8 fl oz/250 ml) dry red wine

2 cups (16 fl oz/500 ml) beef broth

1 can (14½ oz/455 g) chopped tomatoes with juices

FOR THE HORSERADISH CREMA

¾ cup (6 oz/185 g) sour cream

1½ Tbsp prepared horseradish, or to taste

2 tsp Dijon mustard

1 Tbsp fresh lemon juice

Salt

Season the oxtails with salt and pepper. Let stand at room temperature for 30 minutes. Preheat the oven to 325°F (165°C).

In a large, ovenproof pot with a tight-fitting lid, warm 1 Tbsp of the oil over medium-high heat. Working in batches, add the oxtails and brown on all sides, about 6 minutes per batch. Transfer to a bowl and set aside.

In the same pot, warm the remaining 2 Tbsp oil over medium-high heat. Add the onion and cook, stirring occasionally, until soft, about 5 minutes. Add the garlic, carrots, parsnips, rutabagas, and thyme, and season generously with salt and pepper. Cook, stirring frequently, until the vegetables begin to soften, about 6 minutes. Stir in the flour and cook, stirring often, until it turns golden, about 3 minutes. Add the wine, broth, and tomatoes with their juices and bring to a boil. Add the oxtails along →→

with the accumulated juices. Cover, transfer to the oven, and cook until the meat is tender and falling off the bone, about 3 hours.

Remove the oxtails and, when cool enough to handle, pull the meat from the bones into large chunks. Stir the meat back into the stew. Remove and discard the thyme sprigs. Rewarm on the stove top over medium heat if needed. Season with salt and pepper.

To make the horseradish crema, in a small bowl, stir together the sour cream, horseradish, mustard, and lemon juice and season with salt.

Serve the stew, topped with a generous dollop of the horseradish crema.

18

In many parts of the world, soup is a breakfast food, and such is the case for Thailand's traditional khao tom moo, a rice soup inflected with tiny pork balls and garlic oil. It makes a wonderful, satisfying lunch or supper, too.

RICE SOUP WITH PORK DUMPLINGS

serves 6

6 cups (48 fl oz/1.5 l) chicken broth

1 Tbsp preserved radish or turnip, or tamarind paste (optional)

2 Tbsp Asian fish sauce, or to taste

Ground white pepper

¼ lb (125 g) ground pork shoulder

1½ cups (7½ oz/235 g) cooked long-grain white rice, preferably jasmine

3 Tbsp coarsely chopped cilantro

3 Tbsp chopped green onion, white and pale green parts

¼ cup (2 fl oz/60 ml) garlic oil

In a large saucepan, combine the broth, preserved radish, if using, fish sauce, and ⅛ tsp pepper. Bring to a boil over high heat, then reduce to medium heat. Adjust the heat to maintain a gentle simmer.

To make each dumpling, roll about 1 teaspoon pork into a tiny ball. Drop the balls, a few at a time, into the simmering broth and cook for 1 minute. Add the rice and simmer until the rice is soft and the soup is slightly thickened, about 5 minutes.

Serve, garnished with the cilantro, green onion, and garlic oil.

19

SHIITAKE BROTH WITH BUTTER-POACHED LOBSTER & CHIVES

serves 6

This is a very relaxed recipe when it comes to the ingredient list. It is absolutely fine to use frozen and thawed lobster tails. Be sure to keep the meat in the shells during poaching. This will ensure that they keep their shape, making for a better presentation when you slice them.

1 oz (30 g) dried shiitake mushrooms

2 Tbsp olive oil

1 small yellow onion, chopped

2 cloves garlic, minced

½ lb (250 g) fresh white mushrooms, diced

¼ cup (2 fl oz/60 ml) dry white wine

¼ cup (2 fl oz/60 ml) soy sauce

2 thyme sprigs

1 cup (8 oz/250 g) unsalted butter

2 lobster tails, in their shells

1 Tbsp chopped chives

Put the shiitakes in a small bowl, cover with very hot water, and soak for at least 30 minutes. Drain, reserving the soaking liquid. Remove the stems from the mushrooms and thinly slice. Strain the soaking liquid through a coffee filter and reserve ¾ cup (6 fl oz/180 ml).

In a large, heavy pot, warm the oil over medium-high heat. Add the onion, garlic, and white mushrooms and sauté for 5 minutes. Add the wine, soy sauce, thyme, the reserved mushroom soaking liquid, and 2 cups (16 fl oz/500 ml) water and bring to a boil. Reduce the heat to low and simmer for 1 hour. Strain the liquid, discarding the solids, and return the broth to the saucepan. Add the sliced shiitakes and keep warm over low heat.

To poach the lobster, in a very small saucepan, melt the butter slowly over medium-low heat, skimming off any foam that rises to the top. Add the lobster tails and poach, turning the tails once and frequently spooning the butter over the exposed parts, until they are cooked all the way through, 5–7 minutes. Transfer the lobster tails to a cutting board, remove the meat from the shells, and cut into ½-inch (12-mm) slices.

To serve, ladle the broth and mushrooms into shallow bowls. Place the lobster slices in the center of each bowl, garnish with the chives, and serve.

20

CHICKPEA SOUP

serves 4

Chickpeas, which are prized for their mild, nut-like flavor, are a popular ingredient in Mediterranean cooking, where they are used in soups, stews, and salads. Use your favorite pesto recipe for the garnish or, when basil is out of season, shop for a good-quality commercial brand, checking both the store shelves and the refrigerated case.

1 cup (6 oz/185 g) dried chickpeas, picked over and rinsed

⅓ cup (¾ oz/20 g) diced pancetta or bacon

1 yellow onion, chopped

1 clove garlic, minced

4 sage leaves, chopped

2 large tomatoes, peeled, seeded, and chopped

5 cups (40 fl oz/1.25 l) chicken broth

1 rosemary sprig

Salt and freshly ground pepper

Pesto for serving

Put the chickpeas in a bowl with cold water to cover and soak for at least 4 hours or up to overnight. Drain and place in a large saucepan. Add 6 cups (48 fl oz/1.5 l) water and bring to a gentle boil over medium-high heat. Adjust the heat to maintain a steady simmer, cover partially, and cook until the chickpeas are tender, about 1½ hours. Drain and set aside.

In a large, heavy pot, cook the pancetta over medium-low heat, stirring occasionally, until golden and crispy, 4–6 minutes. Add the onion and garlic and cook, stirring occasionally, until translucent, 4–6 minutes. Reduce the heat to low, add the sage and tomatoes, and cook, stirring occasionally, until the tomatoes are tender, 6–8 minutes. Add the chickpeas, broth, and rosemary sprig and cook, stirring occasionally, for 20 minutes. Remove and discard the rosemary sprig. Let cool slightly.

Working in batches, purée the soup in a food processor or blender. Return to the pot and season with salt and pepper. Serve, topped with a spoonful of pesto.

WEDDING SOUP

serves 6

3 qt (3 l) chicken broth

1 lb (500 g) dinosaur kale, escarole, or other sturdy greens, stems and ribs removed, leaves cut into bite-sized pieces

3 large carrots, peeled and chopped

1 celery rib, chopped

FOR THE MEATBALLS

1 lb (500 g) ground pork

2 eggs, lightly beaten

½ cup (2½ oz/75 g) minced yellow onion

½ cup (2 oz/60 g) fine dried bread crumbs

½ cup (2 oz/60 g) grated pecorino romano cheese

Salt and freshly ground pepper

3 Tbsp olive oil

Grated pecorino romano for garnish

Good enough to serve at any celebratory meal, this Italian soup traditionally included different cuts of pork and a large variety of vegetables, which were slowly simmered together until the ingredients were pronounced "married." Here is an updated and streamlined version.

In a large, heavy pot, bring the broth to a boil over high heat. Add the kale, carrots, and celery, reduce the heat to low, and simmer until the vegetables are tender, about 30 minutes.

Meanwhile, to make the meatballs, combine the pork, eggs, onion, bread crumbs, pecorino, 1 tsp salt, and several grindings of pepper in a large bowl and mix well. For each meatball, scoop up 1 teaspoon of the pork mixture, form into a meatball, and place on a plate.

In a large frying pan, warm the oil over medium-high heat. In batches, gently add the meatballs and brown on all sides, about 5 minutes per batch. Using a slotted spoon, carefully add them to the soup and simmer gently over low heat until the meatballs are cooked through, about 10 minutes. Season with salt and pepper and serve, garnished with pecorino.

CRAB RANGOONS IN CHILE-LIME BROTH

serves 4–6

2 cups (16 fl oz/500 ml) vegetable broth

1 Tbsp soy sauce

4 kaffir lime leaves, torn

½ tsp seeded and chopped red chile

FOR THE CRAB RANGOONS

¼ lb (125 g) fresh lump crabmeat, picked over for shell fragments

2 Tbsp cream cheese, at room temperature

1 tsp canola oil

1 tsp chopped chives, plus 1 Tbsp finely chopped chives

Salt and freshly ground pepper

24 wonton wrappers

Rangoons are usually deep-fried Asian dumplings. The ones here are not fried but simmered in broth and served as a soup. This soup is best eaten right away, as the rangoons tend to fall apart when reheated. Be careful not to overspice your broth; you can always add more chile and let it simmer longer.

Combine the broth, 2 cups (16 fl oz/500 ml) water, the soy sauce, lime leaves, and chopped chile in a large, heavy pot and put over medium-high heat. Bring to a boil, then reduce the heat to low and simmer for 5 minutes. Strain the broth, discard the solids, and return the broth to the pot. Set aside off the heat or keep warm over low heat.

To prepare the crab rangoons, in a small bowl, combine the crabmeat, cream cheese, oil, 1 tsp chives, ½ tsp salt, and ¼ tsp pepper. Place 1 tsp of the crab mixture in the middle of a wonton wrapper. Using your fingers, apply a small amount of water on all edges of the wrapper. Fold the wrapper diagonally, forcing out any air bubbles as you press to seal. Take the 2 points on the longest side of the triangle and fold so that the tips meet. Apply a small amount of water on one of the tips and press firmly to stick together. Repeat to use the remaining wrappers and filling.

Return the broth to a boil, reduce to a simmer, and carefully add the crab rangoons. Cook for 3 minutes to warm through, then serve, garnished with the finely chopped chives.

23

LEMONY BROCCOLI-TAHINI SOUP WITH SPICED PITA CHIPS

serves 4

2 Tbsp olive oil

2 leeks, white part only, chopped

2 cloves garlic, chopped

1 head broccoli, chopped into small florets

Salt and freshly ground pepper

3 cups (24 fl oz/750 ml) vegetable or chicken broth

¼ cup (2½ oz/75 g) tahini

2 Tbsp fresh lemon juice

FOR THE SPICED PITA CHIPS

3 Tbsp olive oil

¾ tsp ground cumin

½ tsp smoked paprika

Salt

3 pita rounds, each 4 inches (10 cm) in diameter, split and quartered

Although tahini, the iconic sesame seed paste found in kitchens in much of the Middle East and North Africa, is commonly used in spreads, dips, sauces, and desserts, here it adds its intense roasted sesame flavor to a simple broccoli soup. Because the oil in tahini naturally separates from the paste, always stir it well until blended before you measure and use it. The pita chips can be made a week in advance and stored in an airtight container at room temperature.

In a large, heavy pot, warm the oil over medium-high heat. Add the leeks and cook, stirring occasionally, until soft, about 5 minutes. Add the garlic and broccoli, season with salt and pepper, and cook, stirring occasionally, until the garlic is soft, about 2 minutes. Add the broth and bring to a boil. Reduce the heat to medium-low and cook until the broccoli is very tender, about 15 minutes. Let cool slightly.

Transfer the soup to a food processor or blender, add the tahini, and purée. Return to the pot and place over medium heat. Stir in the lemon juice and season with salt and pepper. Keep warm over low heat.

To make the spiced pita chips, preheat the oven to 350°F (180°C). In a small bowl, stir together the oil, cumin, paprika, and ½ tsp salt. Lay the pita quarters, cut side up, in a single layer on a baking sheet and brush with the oil. Bake until lightly golden and crisp, about 10 minutes.

Serve the soup and offer the pita chips on the side for dipping.

24

MUSHROOM SOUP EN CROÛTE

serves 6

3 Tbsp all-purpose flour, plus more for dusting

14 oz (440 g) frozen puff pastry, thawed

5 Tbsp (2½ oz/75 g) unsalted butter

1½ lb (750 g) cremini mushrooms, chopped

2 large shallots, minced

Salt and freshly ground pepper

2 cups (16 fl oz/500 ml) milk, warmed, plus more as needed

2 cups (16 fl oz/500 ml) chicken broth, warmed

1 egg, lightly beaten

Ready-to-use frozen puff pastry simplifies the preparation of this pastry-topped mushroom soup that makes an elegant first course. Brushing the pastry with an egg wash before slipping the soups into the oven yields a shiny, golden-brown crown. Pour a medium-bodied red wine to complement the earthy flavor.

Preheat the oven to 350°F (180°C). Line a baking sheet with parchment paper.

On a floured surface, roll out the puff pastry into a 15-by-10-inch (38-by-25-cm) rectangle about ⅛ inch (3 mm) thick. Cut into six 5-inch (13-cm) squares. Transfer to the prepared baking sheet. Refrigerate until ready to use.

In a large, heavy pot, melt 2 Tbsp of the butter over medium heat. Add the mushrooms and shallots and cook, stirring occasionally, for 1 minute. Reduce the heat to low, cover, and cook until the mushrooms are soft, 5–7 minutes. Uncover, raise the heat to medium-high, and cook, stirring, until the liquid evaporates, 3–5 minutes. Stir in 1 tsp salt and ⅛ tsp pepper. Transfer the mushrooms to a food processor or blender and pulse until finely chopped. Set aside.

In the same pot, melt the remaining 3 Tbsp butter over medium-low heat. Sprinkle in the flour and whisk until smooth. Slowly whisk in the milk until combined. Cook, stirring, until thickened, 8–10 minutes. While stirring, slowly add the broth and bring to a gentle simmer. Cook, stirring, until the mixture is opaque and beige in color, about 3 minutes longer. Stir in the mushrooms and season with salt and pepper. Thin with more milk, if needed. Ladle the soup into 6 ovenproof bowls and place on a baking sheet.

Brush the tops of the puff pastry squares with the beaten egg. Place 1 square on top of each bowl and press the edges to adhere. Bake until the pastry is puffed and golden, 15–20 minutes. Serve right away.

25

The intense flavor of this rich soup derives from a combination of shellfish and beef broths. Indulge in good lobster meat, and you won't need many other ingredients to let it shine. This is a luxurious treat for the season.

LOBSTER BISQUE

serves 4–6

2 Tbsp unsalted butter

¼ cup (1 oz/30 g) chopped shallots

½ cup (4 fl oz/125 ml) dry white wine

2 cups (16 fl oz/500 ml) shellfish broth

1 cup (8 fl oz/250 ml) beef broth

3 Tbsp long-grain white rice

1 Tbsp tomato paste

¾ lb (375 g) cooked lobster meat, picked over for shell fragments

1 cup (8 fl oz/250 ml) heavy cream

Salt

⅛ tsp cayenne pepper

In a large saucepan, melt the butter over medium-low heat. Add the shallots and sauté until softened, about 5 minutes. Raise the heat to medium, stir in the wine, and bring to a boil. Add the shellfish and beef broths, rice, and tomato paste and return to a boil. Reduce the heat to low, cover, and simmer until the rice is soft, 20–25 minutes. Add ½ lb (250 g) of the lobster meat to the saucepan, remove from the heat, and let cool slightly.

Working in batches, purée the soup in a blender. Return to the saucepan. Stir in the cream, ½ tsp salt, and the cayenne pepper and rewarm gently over medium-low heat. Serve, garnished with the reserved lobster meat.

26

Linguiça is a spicy Portuguese sausage that brings heat to this stew. Garnish with sour cream and serve with a cold lager.

LINGUIÇA & POTATO STEW WITH TWO PAPRIKAS

serves 4–6

½ lb (250 g) linguiça, cut into ¼-inch (6-mm) slices

2 Tbsp olive oil

1½ yellow onions, chopped

3 cloves garlic, minced

1 yellow bell pepper, seeded and diced

2 tsp smoked paprika

1 tsp sweet paprika

1 russet potato, peeled and diced

3 cups (24 fl oz/750 ml) chicken broth

1½ Tbsp tomato paste

1 Tbsp heavy cream

2 Tbsp chopped flat-leaf parsley

Salt

Warm a large, heavy pot over medium-high heat. Add the linguiça and brown on both sides, 5–7 minutes. Transfer to a bowl.

Warm the oil in the pot over medium-high heat. Add the onions, garlic, and bell pepper and sauté until the vegetables are softened, about 5 minutes. Add the smoked and sweet paprikas and cook for 1 minute. Add the potato, stir, and cook for 2 minutes. Add the broth and tomato paste and bring to a boil. Reduce the heat to low, add the linguiça, and simmer for about 30 minutes to blend the flavors. Stir in the cream and parsley, season with salt, and serve.

27
DECEMBER

The addition of snow peas, sesame oil, soy sauce, and ginger gives traditional chicken soup an Asian spin. With fresh veggies and precooked chicken, the recipe becomes dead simple—just add everything to the pot.

GINGER CHICKEN SOUP
serves 4–6

2 qt (2 l) chicken broth

2 cups (6 oz/185 g) thinly sliced cremini or stemmed shiitake mushrooms

½ cup (2½ oz/75 g) chopped snow peas

1 Tbsp peeled and minced fresh ginger

4 green onions, white and tender green parts, thinly sliced on the diagonal

2 Tbsp soy sauce

Salt and freshly ground pepper

1½ cups (9 oz/280 g) shredded cooked chicken

1 tsp Asian sesame oil

Pour the broth into a large, heavy pot and bring to a boil. Add the mushrooms, snow peas, ginger, green onions, soy sauce, 1 tsp salt, and the shredded chicken. Reduce the heat to low and simmer until heated through, about 5 minutes. Stir in the sesame oil and ⅛ tsp pepper. Taste and adjust the seasoning. Serve.

28
DECEMBER

When celery is sautéed with butter and other aromatics, its slightly tangy flavor is accentuated. For an even more pronounced flavor, swap in celery root for the celery and increase the amount of broth to achieve the desired consistency.

CURRIED CREAM OF CELERY SOUP
serves 4–6

2 Tbsp unsalted butter

1 yellow onion, chopped

1½ lb (750 g) celery, coarsely chopped

1 Tbsp curry powder

3 cups (24 fl oz/750 ml) vegetable broth

¼ cup (2 fl oz/60 ml) heavy cream

Salt and freshly ground pepper

In a large, heavy pot, melt the butter over medium-high heat. Add the onion and celery and sauté until the celery is very soft, about 10 minutes. Add the curry powder, stir, and cook for 1 minute. Add the broth and bring to a boil. Reduce the heat to low and simmer for 30 minutes. Remove from the heat and let cool slightly.

Working in batches, purée the soup in a blender. Return to the pot, stir in the cream, and bring just to a boil. Turn off the heat, season with salt and pepper, and serve.

29
DECEMBER

Andouille, a popular smoked sausage in both Creole and Cajun kitchens in Louisiana, is called for in this hearty soup brimming with chard and white beans, though here chicken andouille is preferred over the traditional pork sausage. Get out your sandwich press and accompany this big soup with a hot grilled turkey and cheese sandwich or other filling combination of your choice.

WHITE BEAN SOUP WITH SAUSAGE & CHARD
serves 6–8

¾ cup (5¼ oz/165 g) dried white beans, picked over and rinsed

1 cup (8 fl oz/250 ml) dry white wine

2 Tbsp olive oil

1½ lb (750 g) chicken andouille sausage

1 small yellow onion, diced

2 celery ribs, diced

1 carrot, peeled and diced

1 leek, white part only, diced

2 cloves garlic, minced

1 tsp minced thyme

6 cups (48 fl oz/1.5 l) chicken broth, warmed

1 cup (8 fl oz/250 ml) water, warmed

¼ lb (125 g) chard, ribs removed, leaves cut into ½-inch (12-mm) strips

Salt and freshly ground pepper

Grated Parmesan cheese for garnish (optional)

Garlic crostini for garnish (optional)

Put the beans in a bowl with cold water to cover and soak for at least 4 hours or up to overnight. Drain and place in a large saucepan. Add 3 cups (24 fl oz/750 ml) water and bring to a gentle boil over medium-high heat. Adjust the heat to maintain a simmer, cover partially, and cook until the beans are tender, 50–60 minutes. Drain and set aside.

In a small saucepan, boil the wine over medium heat until reduced to ½ cup (4 fl oz/125 ml), 7–10 minutes. Set aside.

In a large, heavy pot, warm the oil over medium heat. Add the sausage and cook until browned, about 5 minutes per side. Let cool, then cut into ½-inch (12-mm) slices.

In the same pot, cook the onion, celery, carrot, and leek over medium-low heat, stirring occasionally, until soft, about 10 minutes. Add the garlic and thyme and cook, stirring occasionally, for 2 minutes. Add the reduced wine, the broth, and water. Raise the heat to medium and simmer for 15–20 minutes. Add the sausage, beans, and chard and cook just until the chard wilts, 5–8 minutes. Season with salt and pepper.

Serve, garnished with cheese and crostini, if desired.

30

TURKEY MULLIGATAWNY

serves 4

3 Tbsp unsalted butter

½ boneless, skinless turkey breast
(about 1½ lb/750 g), cubed

1 yellow onion, finely chopped

3 celery ribs, finely chopped

2 carrots, peeled and finely chopped

1 clove garlic, minced

1 Tbsp Madras curry powder

4 cups (32 fl oz/1 l) chicken broth

½ cup (3½ oz/105 g) long-grain white rice

1 cup (8 oz/250 g) plain yogurt

Salt and freshly ground pepper

*Leftover turkey can
be put to good use
in this Anglo-Indian
soup. Curry powder
is responsible for
the vibrant yellow
color. Lentils may
replace the rice,
but will require
longer simmering.*

In a large, heavy pot, melt the butter over
medium heat. Add the turkey and sauté
until lightly browned, about 7 minutes.
Transfer to a plate. Add the onion, celery,
carrots, and garlic to the pot and sauté until
the onion is translucent, about 5 minutes.
Stir in the curry powder and cook, stirring,
for 2 minutes to blend the flavors.

Add the broth and turkey to the vegetables
and bring to a simmer over high heat. Reduce
the heat to medium, add the rice, and cook,
uncovered, until the rice is tender and the
turkey is cooked through, 15–20 minutes.
Stir in the yogurt and simmer for 10 minutes
to blend the flavors. Season with salt and
pepper and serve.

31

CHILLED BEET &
CUCUMBER SOUP

serves 8

2 lb (1 kg) beets (about 8 beets), trimmed

1 yellow onion, quartered

8 cups (2 qt/2 l) chicken broth

1 Tbsp sugar

2 English cucumbers, peeled, seeded,
and cut into thin strips, plus thinly sliced
cucumber rounds for serving

2 Tbsp fresh lemon juice

2 Tbsp rice wine vinegar

Salt and freshly ground pepper

¼ cup (⅓ oz/10 g) finely chopped dill

1 cup (8 oz/250 g) nonfat plain yogurt
or low-fat sour cream (optional)

*Eastern Europe has
given rise to many
versions of the
peasant soup of beets
known as borscht,
commonly served
with dark rye bread.
This vegetarian
version makes a cool,
festive, and bright
soup to cleanse the
palate and ring in
the new year. For a
party, garnish with
tangy yogurt, a few
feathers of dill, and
a dollop of caviar.*

In a large, heavy pot, combine the beets,
onion, broth, 1 cup (8 fl oz/250 ml) water,
and the sugar over medium-high heat.
Cover and bring to a boil. Reduce the
heat to low and simmer, covered, until
the beets are tender, 45–60 minutes.

Using a slotted spoon, transfer the beets
to a colander. Reserve the cooking liquid.
Peel the beets under cold running water.
Cut 3 of the beets in half. Cut the remaining
beets into strips 1 inch (2.5 cm) long and
¼ inch (6 mm) wide. Cover and refrigerate
the beet strips.

Strain the cooking liquid through a fine-
mesh sieve into a large bowl. Remove and
discard the onion. Purée the 6 beet halves
and 1 cup (8 fl oz/250 ml) of the strained
liquid in a food processor and add the purée
to the remaining strained liquid in the bowl.
Cover and refrigerate until well chilled, at
least 4 hours or overnight.

Add the beet strips, cucumber strips, lemon
juice, vinegar, ½ tsp salt, ¼ tsp pepper, and
half of the dill to the chilled beet mixture.
Stir to mix well.

Serve, garnished with the yogurt, if using,
the cucumber slices, and the remaining dill.

INDEX

weldonowen

1045 Sansome Street, Suite 100, San Francisco, CA 94111

www.weldonowen.com

Weldon Owen is a division of Bonnier Publishing USA

SOUP OF THE DAY

Conceived and produced by Weldon Owen, Inc.
In collaboration with Williams-Sonoma, Inc.
3250 Van Ness Avenue, San Francisco, CA 94109

A WELDON OWEN PRODUCTION

Printed and bound in China

First printed in 2016
10 9 8 7 6 5 4 3 2 1

Library of Congress Cataloging in Publication
data is available.

ISBN 13: 978-1-68188-139-3
ISBN 13: 1-68188-139-X

WELDON OWEN, INC.

President & Publisher Roger Shaw
SVP, Sales & Marketing Amy Kaneko
Finance & Operations Director Philip Paulick

Associate Publisher Amy Marr
Senior Editor Lisa Atwood
Associate Editor Emma Rudolph

Creative Director Kelly Booth
Associate Art Director Lisa Berman
Senior Production Designer Rachel Lopez Metzger

Production Director Chris Hemesath
Associate Production Director Michelle Duggan

Imaging Manager Don Hill

Photographer Erin Kunkel
Food Stylist Robyn Valarik, Lillian Kang
Prop Stylist Leigh Noe, Emma Star Jensen

ACKNOWLEDGMENTS

Weldon Owen wishes to thank the following people for their generous support in producing this book:
Donita Boles, David Bornfriend, Joe Budd, Sarah Putman Clegg, Alicia Deal, Ken DellaPenta, Judith Dunham,
David Evans, Gloria Geller, Alexa Hyman, Kim Laidlaw, Rachel Markowitz, Carolyn Miller, Julie Nelson,
Jennifer Newens, Elizabeth Parson, Hannah Rahill, Tracy White Taylor, Jason Wheeler, and Sharron Wood.